AN INTRODUCTION
TO INDIVIDUAL
APPRAISAL

AN INTRODUCTION TO INDIVIDUAL APPRAISAL

By

GEORGE P. ROBB, Ed.D.

Professor of Counselor Education
North Texas State University
Denton, Texas

and

ANN P. WILLIAMSON, Ph.D.

Coordinator of Graduate Affairs
Associate Professor of Education
North Texas State University
Denton, Texas

With a Foreword by

James J. Muro, Ed.D.

Dean of College of Education
North Texas State University
Denton, Texas

CHARLES C THOMAS • PUBLISHER
Springfield • Illinois • U.S.A.

Published and Distributed Throughout the World by
CHARLES C THOMAS • PUBLISHER
Bannerstone House
301-327 East Lawrence Avenue, Springfield, Illinois, U.S.A.

© *1981, by* CHARLES C THOMAS • PUBLISHER
ISBN 0-398-04473-2 (cloth)
0-398-04474-0 (paper)
Library of Congress Catalog Card Number: 80-27859

*With THOMAS BOOKS careful attention is given to all details of
manufacturing and design. It is the Publisher's desire to present books that are
satisfactory as to their physical qualities and artistic possibilities and
appropriate for their particular use. THOMAS BOOKS will be true to those
laws of quality that assure a good name and good will.*

Library of Congress Cataloging in Publication Data

Robb, George Paul, 1922-
   An introduction to individual appraisal.

   Bibliography: p.
   Includes index.
   1. Educational tests and measurements. 2. Psycho-
logical tests. I. Williamson, Ann P., joint author.
II. Title.
LB1131.R556   371.2'6   80-27859
ISBN 0-398-04473-2
ISBN 0-398-04474-0 (pbk.)

Printed in the United States of America
C-1

FOREWORD

THE TOPIC OF PUPIL APPRAISAL has long been a legitimate concern of counselors, psychologists, teachers, and school administrators. Recent federal legislation, such as Public Law 94-142, and media reports of parental disenchantment with students' academic progress have added additional and complex dimensions to the task of screening and evaluating children with a wide range of individual, personal, academic, and socioeconomic differences.

Few experienced educators will take issue with the fact that children learn at different rates, with different styles, and with varying degrees of motivation. Knowledge of such differences, however, has not produced comprehensive programs of assessment that provide reliable and valid data in a systematic and organized fashion. This problem stems, in part at least, from the lack of understanding about appraisal data among teachers and administrators and the professionals. This book by Professors George Robb and Ann Williamson of North Texas State University has been written to deal with that concern.

In a comprehensive and well-documented treatment of the major aspects of pupil appraisal, the authors lead the reader through a variety of topics ranging from basic statistics, measurement, and test data, to discussions of achievement, interest, mental ability, and social-emotional development. In addition the authors have developed detailed and readable chapters on learning disabilities, exceptional students, and minority students, all topics of vital concern to professionals in the 1980s.

This text, however, goes beyond a discussion limited to the gathering and understanding of appraisal data to include a presentation on the appropriate utilization of such information. In one sense, the history of appraisal is replete with incidents involving its misuse. When one must be concerned with a resource as valuable as our nation's children, the ethical considerations and the pragmatic application of the results of assessment and evaluation must rank as our foremost concern.

Although this book is entitled *An Introduction to Student Appraisal,* its scope is far more than introductory. It will be as equally appropriate for the casual reader as it is for the more serious student of the topic. Frequently posed questions — such as: Are we using the best available techniques to obtain information?, Is our staff qualified to use the data we now have?, and What restrictions should we place on the use of the information? — are extensively covered in this book.

There can be little doubt that the education profession has moved into an era of evaluation. Each of us involved in the appraisal of students and programs will be called upon in the decade ahead to provide rigorous procedures to assess the quality of our efforts. In this context, this book by Robb and Williamson should become an essential tool in professional and personal bookshelves. The authors have removed the mystery from appraisal and provided the reader with a meaningful and understandable love.

JAMES J. MURO, Ed.D.

PREFACE

T HIS BOOK was written to meet a very definite need — the need for a textbook that provides relevant appraisal information for school personnel, especially counselors, school psychologists, and teachers. Each chapter provides material that deals with important aspects of appraisal in a logical sequence. The main purpose of the book is to help school personnel utilize appraisal information for increased understanding of the individual student.

After a short introduction to the concept of appraisal in Chapter One, the authors present three chapters to provide a necessary foundation of elementary statistics, principles of measurement, and test-data interpretation techniques for understanding the concepts in subsequent chapters.

In Chapter Five there is a discussion of the nature and use of several worthwhile nontest appraisal techniques. While tests can be very useful for gathering appraisal data, they should not be considered to be sole means of collecting such data. Indeed, in some ways the nontest techniques surpass tests and inventories.

In the next four chapters, appraisal concepts are presented in the specific areas of achievement, interests, mental ability, aptitudes, and social-emotional development. Various instruments and techniques that are used to acquire data in the various appraisal areas are introduced and discussed briefly.

In Chapters Ten through Twelve, appraisal is discussed in relation to special populations of students, including those who have learning disabilities and those who belong to minority groups.

In Chapter Thirteen the reader will find cases that illustrate how appraisal information can be integrated to maximize the understanding of the individual student. This chapter is the culmination of the authors' efforts to enhance the reader's ability to utilize appraisal data efficiently and constructively.

The last chapter is presented to increase the reader's awareness of various aspects of ethics in the appraisal process. The chapter also provides useful guidelines for professionals who use appraisal instruments and data, so that the benefits of appraisal will be realized and the pitfalls avoided.

Two points should be emphasized here. The first is that in order to keep this introductory textbook at a manageable level, and cover the important aspects of student appraisal, we could not go as deeply into some content areas as we would have liked. Thus, the reader is expected to turn to advanced textbooks or college courses to acquire additional information. The second point is that although we have dealt with group data and norms, as well as individual cases, we firmly believe that appraisal efforts should focus on the *individual student*. We believe that each person is different from all others, and an appreciation of that uniqueness is necessary for maximum understanding of the individual. Furthermore, an individual lives in an environment that also is unique. Thus, school personnel should strive to understand the student in the student's world. That is the challenge as we see it, and we sincerely hope that those who accept it will find this book to be an asset.

We wish to acknowledge the valuable assistance received from Dr. Betty Mason, faculty member in the College of Education at North Texas State University and psychologist Dr. Arlene Koeppen, who served as consultants. We also acknowledge the excellent help of our typist, Sandy Blagg, for her typing and for her editorial assistance with the manuscript. Finally, we express our gratitude to the many test publishers who furnished us with graphic materials that add an important dimension to the book.

GEORGE P. ROBB
ANN WILLIAMSON

CONTENTS

AN INTRODUCTION
TO INDIVIDUAL
APPRAISAL

Chapter 1

INTRODUCTION

I F THE NATION'S leading educators and informed lay citizens were asked what the main purpose of education is today, responses would be varied. One could expect such statements as "To provide continuity for the culture," "To provide a foundation for civic responsibility," "To promote economic efficiency," "To develop adequate human relationships," or "To promote self-realization." These are diverse, general goals, but they all imply that education should bring about both personal and societal changes.

It is generally agreed that schools are built, organized, and maintained in order to provide children and youth with sound educational experiences. But, what is education? Seagoe (1970, p. 1) says that "Fundamentally, education is guided growth. In this sense it is inclusive, embracing all the activities of the child that mold behavior toward specific ends." Ideally, each student should receive an excellent education, and while the ideal may seem remote, educators can strive for at least an adequate education for every student.

The Education for All Handicapped Children Act of 1975 (Public Law 94-142) is based on the right of all American youngsters, with no exceptions, to an education. "The law's detailed blueprint was written to correct old and widespread injustices. Its primary goal is to give every child, including the most severely handicapped, the learning opportunities he needs to become as self-sufficient and productive as possible." (*Closer Look*, Project of BEH, p. 1.)

In order to maximize learning outcomes for every pupil, it is necessary to *understand* each pupil. Understanding involves knowing about such characteristics as abilities, interests, attitudes, problems, and aspirations. To facilitate the accomplishment of this task, schools generally maintain an appraisal program or service, although in some instances the program may be loosely organized or may not be readily identifiable.

As used in this book, appraisal is a process of collecting and analyzing data pertaining to an individual for the purpose of better understanding that individual and helping the person achieve self-understanding. The major functions of the service should be (1) the collection of data through the use of tests and nontest procedures; (2) the interpretation of collected data; and (3) the integration of appraisal data with other information to provide a meaningful picture of the student.

3

USES OF APPRAISAL INFORMATION

Specifically, how can appraisal data be used to enhance the education of students in school? In order to answer this question, it may be helpful to identify broad areas of use and to focus on the application of appraisal data in each area. Although they may not be entirely distinct and separate, the three categories of administration, instruction, and guidance are convenient for this purpose.

Administrative Use of Appraisal Information

Of what value is appraisal information to school administrators? Actually, several important aspects of administration can benefit from this kind of information.

One of the major responsibilities of a school principal is to maintain an adequate instructional program in the school. Standardized achievement tests can provide an objective basis for determining whether the pupils seem to be receiving adequate instruction, and therefore, reaching worthwhile educational goals. The superintendent of a school system can use test results to attempt to answer such questions as "Are the school system's curricula adequate for pupils of different ability and background?" "Are some areas in the curriculum in need of improvement?" "How do the schools in the system compare academically?" and "How do the schools compare with others throughout the state or nation?"

It must be emphasized that a school administrator should not use test results or other appraisal data as a basis for determining the competency of teachers, because student achievement is influenced by many factors, not just teacher effort and skill.

Comparisons of appraisal data for evaluative purposes often require the use of research procedures for meaningful results. Research methodology provides a scientific approach rather than a haphazard or casual approach in the acquisition and analysis of data relating to a school's academic status. Research would not have to be limited to an assessment of a school's present status, however, but could be applied to the evaluation of new programs, services, or procedures. Research that utilizes appraisal data can, for example, determine whether a new instructional approach is significantly more effective than a traditional approach. In this instance, test results and similar data can serve as outcome criteria for comparing the two approaches. A new approach to the teaching of mathematics would necessitate at least the careful analysis of measures of achievement in mathematics, such as grades and standardized test scores. Other appraisal data also might be studied in order to evaluate the new program.

An administrator may wish to use appraisal data for the purpose of maintaining or improving public relations and public support. The administrator could inform parents and other interested members of the community about the school's strengths, limitations, or progress as revealed by appraisal information. If kept informed about the school's programs, activities, and research efforts, it seems likely that the public will provide greater school support than if little or no information is provided.

Instructional Use of Appraisal Information

Jimmy, a sixth-grade pupil in South Elementary School, has just transferred from a school in another state and there are no test scores or other appraisal data available to his new teacher, Ms. Mary Richards. She has noticed that he has difficulty with his school work in general, but he has a special deficiency with respect to reading ability. She realizes that in order to give Jimmy the help he needs she will have to know more about him, so she arranges to have him tested by the school psychologist.

The familiar situation presented is hypothetical, but it has occurred many times and will continue to recur. The case is presented as an illustration of a need for appraisal data for instructional purposes. Specifically, the example calls attention to the fact that tests may provide objective measures of educational and psychological status for a student or a class. Test results help to determine where a pupil or a class stands at a particular time and also the level at which instruction should be aimed.

Craig (1966, p. 5) states that the teacher should ask two questions routinely: (1) What does a student need to know or be able to do before he can learn this new thing in the way I plan to teach it? (2) To what extent do my students possess the prerequisite knowledge and ability? Appraisal information can provide teachers with answers to these two questions and aid in individualizing teaching techniques.

At the start of the school year, teachers generally will look at the scholastic aptitude test scores of each student. This kind of information can be useful in planning activities, grouping students, and evaluating student academic growth during the year. To be useful, of course, a scholastic aptitude score would have to be a reasonably accurate indicator of learning potential for the individual student; for some students, such as those with a language handicap, typical scholastic aptitude tests may not be suitable.

Standardized achievement tests provide data that indicate a student's level of academic achievement or skills in one or more academic areas, such as reading, arithmetic, or science. Such information lets the teacher know where the student stands with respect to scholastic achievement. If the teacher is able to compare a student's present level of achievement with the achievement of others in the class, or other students on a regional or national basis, the teacher should be in a position to plan classroom activities that will be especially appropriate for that student. If the level of achievement appears to be much below the expected level based upon the student's scholastic aptitude score, the teacher can, and should, attempt to find the cause or causes for the discrepancy. A school counselor or psychologist should be able to serve as a consultant to the teacher for this kind of problem.

By examining group-average scores for achievement tests, the teacher also can obtain some information relative to the effectiveness of the instruction. Changes can be made in instructional approaches based upon achievement-test data if the data suggest the need for change. Of course, the nature of change, and the extent of it, often must involve a number of considerations specific to each situation.

Some types of achievement tests are referred to as diagnostic tests because they are designed to reveal student difficulties or weaknesses in certain areas, such as reading and arithmetic. With information that indicates a specific difficulty in arithmetic or reading, a teacher may be able to provide special remedial help that will correct or alleviate that difficulty.

Use of Appraisal Data for Guidance and Counseling

As Mark slowly walks into the counselor's office he looks tired and worried. "I've got a problem," he says to his counselor, Mr. Johnson. "Let's talk about it," says the counselor. Then Mark explains that he is trying to decide which vocation to choose. His parents have their own ideas about what he should do, but while he would like to please them, he wants to make his own decision. He really does not know what kind of future occupation he prefers or what occupations he should consider. In order to help Mark, Mr. Johnson may want to collect and evaluate appraisal data for Mark, and use that information in the counseling process.

The preceding example illustrates an instance in which appraisal information may be used to provide guidance for students. *Guidance* is a broad term that may be defined as the process of helping individuals understand themselves, set realistic life goals, and move toward increased self-actualization.

In individual counseling, a counselor may need information concerning student achievement, scholastic aptitude, special aptitudes, interests, personality traits, attitudes, or unique experiences. Such information can be useful to the counselor and student as they work through such problems as vocational choice, choice of college, poor achievement, financial difficulty, poor self-concept, and social inadequacies.

Sometimes counselors find it necessary or desirable to talk with parents about student difficulties, needs, progress, or future plans. Such parental counseling may involve the use of properly interpreted scores from tests and inventories or other assessment instruments or techniques.

Whether a counselor uses test results in counseling depends considerably upon that person's philosophy and approach. The "client-centered" counselor may prefer not to use tests at all, or only when the client suggests testing as a means of achieving increased understanding. In contrast, the "trait-factor" counselor considers testing to be essential and makes extensive use of tests and inventories.

Such authorities as Borden (1955), Boy and Pine (1963), and Rogers (1946) have criticized the use of test results in counseling. The reasons given by critics include doubt concerning the validity of the instruments; concern that the use of tests may foster dependence upon the counselor or test results; and belief that testing interferes with the counseling process, especially the counseling relationship.

In spite of the objections raised against the use of test results in counseling, tests and other appraisal devices are being used today on a large scale by counselors. The instruments are being used for the following purposes:

1. To provide data that can be used by the counselor to diagnose behavior. Many counselors feel that they can best help some counselees by collecting test data and then utilizing the data to diagnose certain aspects of the counselees' behavior. For example, a mental ability test might be used to assess an individual's level of general mental ability or specific intellectual factors, or a diagnostic test might be administered to identify specific student weaknesses in reading or arithmetic.
2. To provide data that can be used to *predict* future behavior or success. Perhaps a prediction of the outcome of a specific course of action is desired. For example, the counselee might ask, "What are my chances of success if I go to college?" Determining the probability of success in such an instance might be difficult, but the proper use of valid appraisal data should make the task easier.
3. To provide data that will facilitate *self-understanding*. Some counselees seek the services of a counselor because they want to know more about themselves — their needs, interests, aptitudes, personality traits, attitudes, etc. Tests and inventories are tools that may help the counselor provide some of the information desired by the counselee. In some instances, however, the need for such information becomes apparent following the initial interview with a client. Provided that useful information can be acquired and adequately interpreted, counselees may gain enough self-understanding to improve in such ways as greater achievement, better self-concept, reduced anxiety, and more positive attitudes.

Every counselor who uses test data should have a thorough understanding of the basic principles and concepts of tests and measurements. Counselors should be able to select tests that are sufficiently valid or useful for particular counseling situations, and they should be familiar with the strengths and weaknesses of the instruments that they use in counseling. In addition, counselors should have the ability to interpret test results for their counselees and for parents and school personnel. The process of interpreting test data may be either *statistical* or *clinical*.

When the statistical approach is used in test-data interpretation, the counselor relies upon statistical evidence of relationships between certain tests that serve as predictors and certain behavioral outcomes or characteristics that must be predicted or assessed. For example, a counselor may wish to determine the probability of success in college for a student who has made a particular score on a scholastic aptitude test. If the counselor knows the correlation between the test and college grades, as indicated by a correlation coefficient, he can make a prediction relative to the student's performance in college. In some cases a combination of predictors may be used. The counselor may also use an expectancy table for his prediction. Information concerning correlation techniques and expectancy tables will be provided in subsequent chapters in this book. It should be emphasized that the prediction of human behavior or performance is not a simple task.

The clinical approach is a more subjective and complex approach than the statistical approach. The clinician must depend heavily upon previous experience with similar cases, knowledge of human behavior, and the predictors used. Dunnette (1966, p. 172) states that nearly all studies comparing the two methods have shown that statistical prediction is as accurate or more accurate than clinical prediction.

If statistical prediction is as accurate as clinical prediction, when should the latter be used? Dunnette (1966) suggests two reasons for using clinical methods, the first being that the clinical approach may have to be used because no other basis for prediction exists. If this should be the case, counselors must take a careful look at the data that they have been able to collect and, using whatever evidence of validity they have, make the best inferences possible. Later, they should attempt to evaluate the predictions that were made. A second reason for using the clinical approach is that clinical methods may provide many useful elements of information concerning a counselee that will not be acquired through the statistical approach. That is, clinical prediction need not be as narrow or restricted as statistical predictions that are validated on specific data, such as test scores.

It seems reasonable to assume that the counselor who uses both the statistical and clinical approach effectively in assessing and predicting behavior will be better prepared to help clients than the one who relies on just one approach.

THE TESTING PROGRAM

While the testing program of a school will not provide all of the appraisal information needed by school personnel, it will probably provide a very high percentage of it. The success of the program will depend to a great extent upon whether the program has certain essential characteristics.

The testing program should be *continuous, comprehensive,* and *flexible.* To say that it should be continuous is to say that necessary testing should be done each year and should be done for each group for which test results are required. That is, the testing should be done on a steady, planned basis rather than sporadically when someone feels like doing it. A comprehensive program covers all grades in the school and utilizes a variety of types of tests: achievement, aptitude, diagnostic, etc. A flexible program is one that can be altered when change seems advisable or necessary. This means that a testing sequence might be changed, that older tests might be replaced by newer ones, that some testing might be discontinued, that some additional testing might be initiated, or that a procedure for reporting results might be changed.

The testing program should be designed specifically for each individual school as variations are to be expected from school to school in terms of school size, school budget, characteristics of the school population and community, needs of students and faculty, state laws, etc. Generally speaking, schools will schedule achievement tests every year, scholastic aptitude tests about every third year, and other tests as needed.

The testing program should be an integral part of the whole educational program. That is, it should not be an isolated or independent program that is unrelated to the curriculum or the educational goals of a school. When the testing program is well integrated with the total school program, the students and school personnel should be able to benefit to such an extent that the time and expense of testing can be justified.

REFERENCES

Arbuckle, Dugald S.: *Counseling: Philosophy, Theory and Practice.* Boston, Allyn and Bacon, 1965.

Barnette, W. L.: *Readings in Psychological Tests and Measurements.* Homeswood, Illinois, The Dorsey Press, 1968.

Borden, Edward S.: *Psychological Testing.* New York, Appleton-Century-Crofts, Inc., 1955.

Boy, Angelo V. and Pine, Gerald J.: *Client-Centered Counseling in the Secondary School.* Boston, Houghton Mifflin Company, 1963.

Craig, Robert C.: *The Psychology of Learning in the Classroom.* New York, The Macmillan Company, 1966.

Department of Health, Education and Welfare, Office of Education; Bureau of

Education for the Handicapped: *Report From Closer Look:* Washington, D.C., U.S. Government Printing Office, 1976-1977.

Dunnette, Marvin D.: *Personnel Selection and Placement.* New York, Wadsworth Publishing Company, Inc., 1966.

Meehl, P. E.: *Clinical Versus Statistical Prediction.* Minneapolis, Minnesota, University of Minnesota Press, 1954.

Muro, James and Dinkmeyer, Don: *Counseling in the Elementary and Middle Schools,* Dubuque, Iowa, Wm. C. Brown Company, 1977.

Ohlsen, Merle M.: *Guidance Services in the Modern School,* 2nd ed. New York, Harcourt Brace Jovanovich, Inc., 1974.

Rogers, Carl R.: Psychometric tests and client-centered counseling. *Educational and Psychological Measurement, 6:*139-144, 1946.

Seagoe, May V.: *The Learning Process and School Practice.* Scranton, Pa., Chandler Publishing Company, 1970.

Shertzer, Bruce and Stone, Shelley C.: *Fundamentals of Guidance,* 3rd ed. Boston, Houghton-Mifflin Company, 1976.

Sproles, H. A., Panther, E. E., and Lanier, J. E.: PL 49-142 and its impact on the counselor's role. *Personnel and Guidance Journal, 57:*210-212, 1978.

Chapter 2

STATISTICS FOR APPRAISAL

R AW APPRAISAL data, such as the scores obtained from tests and inventories, generally must be treated statistically to make them meaningful. Raw scores that have been acquired through testing can be converted by statistical procedures into such meaningful measures as percentile ranks and standard scores. These *derived* scores are presented along with the raw scores in tables in the manuals that test publishers provide for test users.

In order to be able to make good use of the derived scores that are provided in the test manuals, the reader must have some knowledge of the statistical concepts and procedures that were used to obtain the derived scores. This statistical knowledge also can be quite helpful when one reads professional articles or research reports that involve measurement.

In presenting a discussion of those basic statistical concepts and procedures that are especially important in relation to measurement and the use of appraisal data, a logical first topic is the organization of data.

ORGANIZATION OF DATA

When several test scores (or similar data) have been acquired for a group of individuals, the scores generally must be organized in such a way as to facilitate the processing and use of them. One commonly used arrangement of scores is the *frequency distribution,* which shows the scores obtained and the frequency of the scores. Consider the following hypothetical set of scores:

56, 42, 56, 33, 45, 58, 61, 79, 48, 55, 57, 57, 56, 51, 38, 77, 64, 53, 66, 73, 50, 47, 62, 56, 67, 54, 41, 72, 54, 56, 44, 65, 57, 39, 69, 60, 61, 58, 53, 46, 65, 52, 49, 63, 72, 66, 42, 44, 55, 52, 53, 57, 46, 55, 55, 59, 63, 54, 54, 61, 50, 50, 58, 59, 52.

As the scores appear above, a person would have a difficult time deriving much useful information from them. If the scores are arranged as in Table I, to make a frequency distribution, a step has been taken toward a better understanding of the data. Table I is an example of a *simple frequency distribution.* The column headed by Score (X) shows the raw score values obtained for the group. The raw score generally is the number of correct responses that a person made for a given test. It is obvious that the scores were arranged from high to low,

11

An Introduction to Individual Appraisal

TABLE I

FREQUENCY DISTRIBUTION FOR SIXTY-FIVE SCORES

Score (X)	Frequency (f)	Score (X)	Frequency (f)
79	1	55	4
77	1	54	4
73	1	53	3
72	2	52	3
69	1	51	1
67	1	50	3
66	2	49	1
65	2	48	1
64	1	47	1
63	2	46	2
62	1	45	1
61	3	44	2
60	1	42	2
59	2	41	1
58	3	39	1
57	4	38	1
56	5	33	1

and that the frequency column shows the number of times that each score appeared in the total distribution.

Sometimes the organization of data requires the grouping of scores into *classes,* or *class intervals.* Table II shows a *grouped frequency distribution* based on the scores shown in Table I. The size of each class interval in Table II is five score points. In other words, each interval spans five possible score values. The highest ranked class is 75-79, and it includes the possible scores of 75, 76, 77, 78, 79. The next class (70-74) may have the scores of 70, 71, 72, 73, and 74. Thus each class or class interval has a class size of *five* in this particular grouped frequency distribution.

TABLE II

GROUPED FREQUENCY DISTRIBUTION FOR SIXTY-FIVE SCORES

Class Interval	f
75-79	2
70-74	3
65-69	6
60-64	8
55-59	18
50-54	14
45-49	6
40-44	5
35-39	2
30-34	1

The interval size for this distribution was found by dividing the range of scores for the distribution by 10 (in order to get an approximation of the desired interval size) and then rounding the resulting figure. The *range* of scores is the difference between the highest and lowest scores in the distribution, or in this instance the range is 79 minus 33, which equals 46. Forty-six divided by 10 is 4.6, and, when rounded, the value becomes 5, the desired class interval size. Dividing the range by 10 yielded ten groups. In order to obtain more groups, one could have divided the range by a larger number, say 12 or 15; then the interval size would have been smaller. It is advisable to use an odd number for the class interval size because an odd number provides a whole number for a midpoint of the class interval. For example, the midpoint of the class 30-34 is 32.

At this point it is appropriate to explain that single scores as well as class intervals have *limits*, and that the *apparent limits* are not the same as the *real limits*. For instance, a single score of 40 has real limits of 39.5 and 40.5. The class interval of 40-44 has apparent limits of 40 and 44 but real limits of 39.5 and 44.5. The real limits, then, extend five-tenths of a point below the lower apparent limit and five-tenths of a point above the upper apparent limit. Real limits are used because (at least theoretically) fractional score values can occur in a distribution.

GRAPHICAL REPRESENTATION OF DATA

In order to attain a better understanding of grouped test data it may be necessary to construct graphs. The *frequency polygon, histogram,* and *ogive* are the three graphs that most often are used to display score distributions. Figure 1 shows a *frequency polygon* that was constructed from the grouped frequency distribution in Table II.

The horizontal axis of the graph in Figure 1 shows the midpoints of the class intervals, while the vertical axis shows the frequency of scores for each class interval. In order to determine how many scores fall in the class interval whose midpoint is 52, one would locate the dot over 52 and read across to the frequency axis. In this case, the frequency would be 14, so there would be 14 scores in that class (50-54). The frequency polygon was made by marking off the score values and frequencies on the two axes and then placing dots directly over the midpoints of the class intervals to show the correct frequency for each class interval. The *histogram* shown in Figure 2 was constructed in a manner similar to that for the frequency polygon. For the histogram, however, columns are centered over the midpoints of the class intervals to show the correct frequencies for the classes.

Whether a person should use a frequency polygon or a histogram to show data graphically depends upon the kind of data to be displayed and the purpose of the display. When two *distributions* are to be shown in a single graph, however, the frequency polygon is the better graph to

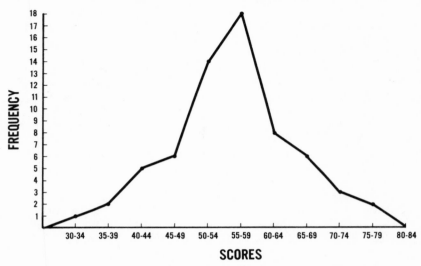

Figure 1. Frequency polygon for a distribution of 65 scores.

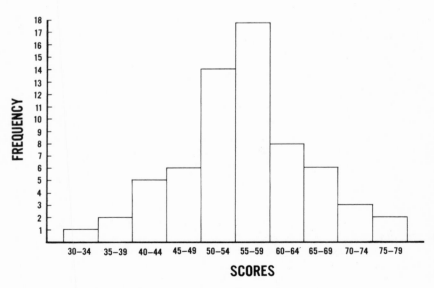

Figure 2. Histogram for a distribution of 65 scores.

TABLE III
CUMULATIVE FREQUENCIES AND CUMULATIVE PERCENTS FOR A
GROUPED FREQUENCY DISTRIBUTION

Class Interval	f	Cumulative f	Cumulative Percent
75-79	2	65	100
70-74	3	63	97
65-69	6	60	92
60-64	8	54	83
55-59	18	46	71
50-54	14	28	44
45-49	6	14	22
40-44	5	8	12
35-39	2	3	4.5
30-34	1	1	1.5

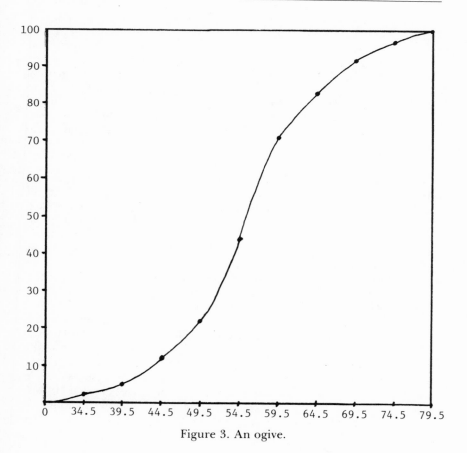

Figure 3. An ogive.

use because it will not obscure data as much as the histogram with its columns that might overlap.

Table III is a cumulative frequency and percent table that is useful in the construction of an ogive (or cumulative frequency percentage curve). In addition to the grouped frequency distribution, Table III presents cumulative frequencies and cumulative percents for the score distribution. The cumulative frequencies in this table were found by starting with the frequency of the lowest class (n = 1) and adding to that frequency the next higher class frequency (n = 2) to get 3, and so on, to the top of the grouped frequency distribution. In order to get the values in the cumulative percent column, the cumulative frequencies are divided by the total number of scores, or in this case, by 65. Thus, for the class interval 35-39, which has a cumulative frequency of 3, the cumulative percent is 3/65, which equals .045, or 4.5 percent.

The ogive shown in Figure 3 was constructed from the data in Table III. The points plotted in the graph indicate the cumulative percent of scores for each class interval. Thus, this graph is useful when a person wants to determine what percent of scores is found below a particular score value. For example, to find what percent of the scores appears below a score of 59, one should locate this score along the horizontal axis of the graph, then read upward to the curve and straight across to the vertical axis and find the cumulative percent value of 71. There-fore, 71 percent of the scores in this *distribution* are lower than a score of 59. This is a way to find percentile ranks, a topic that will be taken up later.

POPULATIONS AND SAMPLES

The term *population* may be defined as a set of measures (such as scores or other values) that might be obtained for each of a set of entities or individuals. For example, an achievement test score for each senior in a certain high school would constitute a population of mea-sures (the test scores). A population may be very small or extremely large, and it may be finite or infinite. A *sample* is a subset of measures drawn from the population. The sample size may be as small as one or as large as the population. Usually the sample is just a fraction of the size of a population. Samples are used instead of populations when it is not possible to secure the whole population or when it would not be practical to do so.

Samples can be drawn from a parent population in several different ways. Usually, however, researchers try to work with samples that are representative of the populations from which they are taken. A *random sample* is one that has been drawn in such a way that every measure or individual in the population has had the same chance of being included in the sample. A random sample could be selected by pulling names or numbers out of a container in a random fashion, but generally a table of random numbers is used to acquire this kind of sample.

DESCRIPTIVE STATISTICS

In educational and psychological measurement, certain terminology is widely used to describe various aspects of samples and populations. Such terms as mean, variance, and standard deviation are used in referring to the characteristics of distribution of data. When the characteristics relate to samples, they appropriately are termed *statistics*, but when they refer to populations they are *parameters*. Symbols are used to represent the characteristics of distributions of data. The following symbols are commonly seen in statistics books and in articles involving tests and measurements:

Characteristic	Statistic	Parameter
Mean	$\overline{X}$	μ
Variance	s^2	σ^2
Standard Deviation	s	σ

When the values of parameters and statistics have been calculated for a distribution, the values are very useful for describing the distribution and for understanding it. For example, a measure of central tendency for a distribution of scores will indicate where the scores are most concentrated in the distribution.

Measures of Central Tendency

The three most common measures of central tendency in educational and psychological measurement are the *mode*, the *arithmetic mean*, and the *median*. The mode is the simplest of these three measures in the sense that it can be found merely by inspection. The mode is the most common or frequent value in a distribution of values. Consider the following distribution of scores: 31, 27, 35, 21, 20, 20, 20, 18, 17, 15, 10, 9. The most frequent score is 20, so this is the mode. Because the mode lacks stability (may vary considerably from sample to sample), it is not considered to be as useful as the other two measures of central tendency. Another shortcoming of the mode is that in some distributions there may be two or more modes. A distribution having two modes is said to be *bimodal*.

The *arithmetic mean* or simply the *mean* is often referred to as the "average" value in a distribution of values. It is found by the formula:

$$\overline{X} = \frac{\Sigma X}{N}$$

where

$\overline{X}$ = mean value of the distribution
Σ = sum of the scores of the distribution
N = number of scores in the distribution

The mean, therefore, is just the total of the values (scores) in a distribution divided by the total number of values. For a test, the mean score would equal the sum of the scores divided by the total number of scores in the distribution of scores obtained from the test. Consider the scores previously used to illustrate the mode: 31, 27, 25, 21, 20, 20, 20, 18, 17, 15, 10, 9. The sum of the scores (ΣX) is 233, and $N = 12$, so the mean ($\overline{X}$) = 233/12 = 19.42.

The mean generally is considered to be the most useful measure of central tendency, but for some distributions it is less appropriate than the *median*. Specifically, extreme scores in a distribution have a strong effect on the mean of a distribution, and if a few extreme scores occur at either the high or low end of a distribution, the mean will be "pulled" in the direction of the extreme scores. The *median* is less affected by extreme scores than the mean. The median is the 50th percentile, or the value that divides a distribution into halves on the basis of frequency. That is to say, there are as many scores above the median as below it in a distribution of scores. The term *percentile* may be defined as the point below which a certain percent of the values in a distribution fall. In a distribution of scores, the 30th percentile is a point below which 30 percent of the scores fall.

Computing Percentiles and Percentile Ranks

To find the median or any other percentile, one can use the following formula:

$$\text{Percentile} = \text{LRL of class} + i \left(\frac{n\text{th case} - \text{cum. } f \text{ below}}{f \text{ of class}} \right)$$

where

$$\begin{aligned}
\text{LRL} &= \text{lower real limit} \\
i &= \text{class-interval size} \\
n &= \text{number of cases or scores being considered} \\
\text{cum. } f \text{ below} &= \text{total number of scores below the interval in which the } n\text{th case is found} \\
f \text{ of class} &= \text{frequency of the interval in which the } n\text{th case is found}
\end{aligned}$$

In order to illustrate the computation of a percentile through the use of the formula, the distribution of Table IV will be introduced. By simply counting scores upward from the lower end of the distribution in Table IV until 25 scores are reached (or half of the 50 scores) one can find the median or 50th percentile. The value in question, of course, is midway between score value 35 and score value 36. Thus, the median is 35.5. The formula will give the same result:

$$\begin{aligned}
\text{50th percentile} &= 34.5 + 1 \left(\frac{25 - 20}{5} \right) \\
&= 34.5 + 1 \left(\frac{5}{5} \right) \\
&= 34.5 + 1 \, (1) \\
&= 35.5
\end{aligned}$$

TABLE IV
UNGROUPED DISTRIBUTION OF 50 SCORES

Score (X)	Frequency (f)	Score (X)	Frequency (f)
56	1	35	5
52	1	34	3
50	2	33	3
49	1	32	1
45	2	31	2
44	2	30	2
43	1	29	1
42	2	28	1
41	2	27	1
40	3	25	2
39	1	21	1
38	1	17	1
37	2	12	1
36	4	10	1

Suppose that the problem was to find the 25th percentile, or the first quartile (Q_1). The computation would be as follows:

$$25\text{th percentile} = 30.5 + 1\left(\frac{12.5 - 11}{2}\right)$$
$$= 30.5 + .75$$
$$= 31.25$$

Thus, below a score of 31.25 there are 25 percent of the scores in this distribution. The reader should note that the value of i is 1 (one) when the scores are not grouped into class intervals.

Test scores often are converted from raw scores to percentile ranks so that the scores are more meaningful or easier to interpret. The term *percentile rank* refers to the position of a score or other value in a distribution of values in terms of the percent below the score in question. For example, a percentile rank of 40 means that below the given raw score there were 40 percent of the score in the distribution.

$$PR = 100\ \frac{\left(\dfrac{\text{Raw score} - \text{LRL of class}}{i}\right) \times (f\text{ of class}) + \text{cum. } f\text{ below}}{N}$$

PROBLEM: What is the percentile rank of a raw score of 50 in the distribution in Table IV?

$$\text{LRL of class } 50 = 49.5$$
$$i = 1$$
$$f\text{ of class} = 2$$
$$\text{cum. } f\text{ below} = 46$$
$$N = 50$$

$$PR = 100 \frac{\left(\frac{50 - 49.5}{1}\right) \times 2 + 46}{50}$$

$$= 100 \frac{\left(\frac{.5}{1}\right)(2) + 46}{50}$$

$$= 100 \frac{(1) + 46}{50}$$

$$= 100 \frac{47}{50}$$

$$= \frac{4700}{50}$$

$$= 94$$

Thus, 94 percent of the scores fall below the score of 50 in this distribution, and the raw score of 50 has a percentile rank of 94.

The formulas presented in this chapter for finding percentiles and percentile ranks may be used for grouped frequency distributions as well as ungrouped distributions (as shown in the examples). As stated previously, for ungrouped data the value of i is 1, but for grouped data, i would equal the size of the class interval.

Variability

Another characteristic of a distribution of scores that is useful in the interpretation of test scores and similar appraisal data is *variability*, which may be defined as the spread or dispersion of scores in a distribution of scores. Two sets of data may have the same mean but very different dispersions of the data. For example, consider the following sets of scores:

    Set A: 42, 42, 42, 42, 42, 42, 42, 42, 42, 42, 42, 42
    Set B: 34, 36, 37, 38, 39, 40, 42, 43, 45, 47, 49, 54
    Set C: 20, 30, 36, 40, 41, 42, 43, 44, 46, 48, 54, 60

Each set of scores has the same mean of 42, but the scores of Set A show no deviation from the mean. Set B has score differences, so there is some variability. Set C shows much more dispersion or scatter than Set B, so it has greater variability than B.

One measure of variability that is quickly obtained for a distribution of scores is the *range*. The range is found simply by subtracting the lowest score from the highest score in a distribution. Because the range is based upon only two scores that may vary greatly from sample to sample, it lacks stability, and it is not a very widely used measure of variability.

Another measure of variability is the *semi-interquartile range*. This statistic (Q) is found by dividing the interquartile range ($Q_3 - Q_1$) by 2:

$$Q = \frac{Q_3 - Q_1}{2}$$

where

Q_3 = 3rd quartile or 75th percentile
Q_1 = 1st quartile or 25th percentile

Like the range, the semi-interquartile range is not very stable, and it does not reveal much about the scatter of most of the scores in the distribution. Therefore, its use as a measure of variability is very limited.

The statistics that are most commonly used as measures of variability are the *variance* and *standard deviation*. The advantages of these statistics over the other variability statistics are that both are relatively stable, both are based upon all of the scores of the distribution rather than a couple of scores, and both are useful in computing other necessary statistics. Because the variance is the simpler statistic, and the standard deviation is derived from the variance, the variance will be considered first.

The variance is defined as the mean of the squares of the deviations of values from the mean. The basic formula used to compute the variance is written as follows:

$$s^2 = \frac{\Sigma x^2}{N - 1}$$

where

s^2 = variance
Σx^2 = sum of squared deviations
N = number of scores or values in the distribution

The following example illustrates the computation of the variance and standard deviation:

Score (X)	$(X - \bar{X})$ or x	x^2
33	13	169
30	10	100
25	5	25
22	2	4
20	0	0
20	0	0
20	0	0
16	-4	16
12	-8	64
12	-8	64
10	-10	100
$\Sigma X = 220$		$\Sigma x^2 = 542$

$$\text{Mean} = (\overline{X}) = \frac{\Sigma X}{N} = \frac{220}{11} = 20$$

$$\text{Variance} = s^2 = \frac{\Sigma x^2}{N-1} = \frac{542}{10} = 54.20$$

$$\text{Standard deviation} = s = \sqrt{\frac{\Sigma x^2}{N-1}} = \sqrt{54.20} = 7.36$$

It will be noted in the example shown above that the standard deviation is found by computing the square root of the variance. Thus, the square root of the variance with a value of 54.20 is 7.36, or the standard deviation.

A raw-score formula also can be used to find the variance and standard deviation. This formula has the advantage of not requiring the computation of deviations. The "raw-score" formulas for variance and standard deviation are written:

$$s^2 = \frac{N \Sigma X^2 - (\Sigma X)^2}{N(N-1)}$$

$$s = \sqrt{\frac{N \Sigma X^2 - (\Sigma X)^2}{N(N-1)}}$$

where

$$
\begin{aligned}
s^2 &= \text{variance} \\
s &= \text{standard deviation} \\
X &= \text{raw score} \\
\Sigma X^2 &= \text{sum of squared raw scores} \\
(\Sigma X)^2 &= \text{square of sum of raw scores} \\
N &= \text{total number of scores}
\end{aligned}
$$

To illustrate the use of the raw-score formulas the same data will be used as was used for the previous illustration.

Score (X)	X^2
33	1089
30	900
25	625
22	484
20	400
20	400
20	400
16	256
12	144
12	144
10	100
$\Sigma X = 220$	$\Sigma X^2 = 4942$

$$s^2 = \frac{N\Sigma X^2 - (\Sigma X)^2}{N(N-1)}$$

$$= \frac{11(4942) - (220)^2}{11(10)}$$

$$= \frac{54{,}362 - 48{,}400}{110}$$

$$= 54.20$$

$$s = \sqrt{54.20} = 7.36$$

The "raw-score" formula is especially appropriate for finding a standard deviation when an electronic calculator is available. With the squaring of raw scores, the products and totals can become quite large, but the calculator can reduce the amount of work and the possibility of error considerably.

Some textbooks show the formula for standard deviation written with N in the denominator instead of $N - 1$. This is appropriate for large samples:

$$s = \sqrt{\frac{\Sigma x^2}{N}} \qquad \text{(deviation formula)}$$

$$s = \sqrt{\frac{\Sigma X^2}{N} - \left(\frac{\Sigma X}{N}\right)^2} \qquad \text{(raw score formula)}$$

Standard Scores

An ordinary raw score, such as the number of correct answers on a test, does not convey much meaning. Derived scores (such as percentile ranks) can be quite meaningful, and thus the effort that goes into their calculation can easily be justified. Standard scores, such as the z-score, are derived scores that have received extensive use in the field of measurement.

The z-score is computed by means of the following formula:

$$z = \frac{X - \bar{X}}{s} \text{ or } \frac{x}{s}$$

where

z = standard score
X = raw score in a distribution
$\bar{X}$ = mean score of the distribution
x = deviation of a raw score from the mean
s = standard deviation of the distribution

Using the score distribution presented earlier, an example of the computation of z-scores follows:

Raw Score (X)	Deviation (x)	x/s	z-score
33	13	13/7.36	1.77
30	10	10/7.36	1.36
25	5	5/7.36	.68
22	2	2/7.37	.27
20	0	0/7.36	.00
20	0	0/7.36	.00
20	0	0/7.36	.00
16	− 4	− 4/7.36	− .54
12	− 8	− 8/7.36	− 1.09
12	− 8	− 8/7.36	− 1.09
10	− 10	− 10/7.36	− 1.36

In calculating the z-scores that correspond to raw scores in a given distribution, the following steps are taken:

1. Compute the mean of the distribution.
2. Compute the standard deviation of the distribution.
3. Compute the deviation of each raw score from the mean.
4. Divide each deviation by the standard deviation.

The mean of this distribution is 20 and the standard deviation is 7.36, so these values can be substituted in the formula to get the z-score for each raw score in the distribution. For example, a raw score of 33 equals a z-score of 1.77:

$$z = \frac{X - \bar{X}}{s}$$
$$= \frac{33 - 20}{7.36}$$
$$= \frac{13}{7.36}$$
$$= 1.77$$

A raw score of 33, then, is 1.77 standard deviations above the mean of 20. Consider another example, in which the raw score is 10:

$$z = \frac{10 - 20}{7.36} = \frac{- 10}{2.36} = - 1.36$$

The z-score of − 1.36 indicates that the raw score of 10 was approximately one and one-third standard deviations *below* the mean.

There are two somewhat bothersome features of z-scores: these derived scores can be quite small, and they can be negative (requiring use of a minus sign). These two disadvantages can be overcome by converting z-scores to Z-scores. The Z-score formula is written:

$$Z = 10 \left(\frac{X - \bar{X}}{s} \right) + 50$$
$$= 10z + 50$$

An example will perhaps clarify the use of the formula to compute a Z-score. Suppose that a person wished to compute a Z-score for a raw score of 33. It has already been determined that the z-score equivalent of 33 is 1.77, and thus that value can be substituted as follows:

$$
\begin{aligned}
Z &= 10z + 50 \\
&= 10\ (1.77) + 50 \\
&= 17.7 + 50 \\
&= 67.7 \text{ or } 68
\end{aligned}
$$

For a raw score of 10, the Z-score calculation is:

$$
\begin{aligned}
Z &= 10z + 50 \\
&= 10\ (-1.36) + 50 \\
&= -13.6 + 50 \\
&= 36.4 \text{ or } 36
\end{aligned}
$$

From the calculation of a Z-score for a raw score of 10, it can be seen that even though the z-score was negative, the Z-score was not. Also, a larger score value was obtained with the Z-score formula. While the z-score distribution has a mean of 0 and a standard deviation of 1, the Z-score has a mean of 50 and standard deviation of 10. Thus, a z-score value of 2.5 is two and one-half standard deviations above the mean, and that is the same relative position as for a Z-score of 75. A z-score of −1.5 is one and one-half standard deviations below the mean, as is a Z-score of 35.

Both z-score and Z-score distributions retain the shape of the original raw-score distribution; usually the original distribution is not "normal" (a normal distribution is bell-shaped and symmetrical). In order to create a normal distribution of standard scores from a nonnormal distribution, a normalizing procedure must be used. The procedure involves the following steps:

1. Each raw score is converted to a percentile rank.
2. A normal-curve table is used to obtain the z-scores that correspond to the percentile ranks.
3. The Z-score formula is used to compute the normalized standard scores from the z-scores.

Instead of Z, the symbol for the normalized standard score becomes T. Thus, $T = 10z + 50$. T-scores are widely used in the field of measurement because they are easily interpreted.

Normal Curve

The normal curve, or normal frequency distribution curve, is an extremely useful concept in appraisal because it can be used to facilitate the interpretation of appraisal data, such as test scores. The normal curve, which is bell-shaped and symmetrical, is based on a mathematical formula, so it has certain fixed characteristics.

It has been known for quite some time that many human characteristics (physical, mental, and psychological) tend to be "normally" distributed. That is, a large distribution of human measurements (such as reading-ability scores) generally will approximate a normal curve if plotted on a graph. Figure 4 shows a normal curve.

The normal curve has a mean of zero and a standard deviation of one. The horizontal axis or baseline shows standard-deviation units, while the vertical axis shows the frequencies for different points along the baseline. Thus, as the curve rises, the frequency increases. The curve reaches the highest point at the mean, so the greatest frequency of scores or other measurements is at the mean of the distribution. The lowest frequencies are found at the extreme ends of the curve.

The percents shown in the different sections of the curve in Figure 4 indicate the percent of total area that each section of the curve contains as well as the frequency of values (i.e., scores) between different points along the curve. For example, Figure 4 shows 34.13 percent area between the mean and $+1\sigma$. This means that the proportion of total area found under this one section of the curve is .3413. It also means that, in a normal distribution, 34.13 percent of all the cases in the distribution have values between the mean value and plus one standard deviation. Likewise, between $+1\sigma$ and $+2\sigma$ there will be 13.59 percent of all the cases in the distribution. Because the curve is symmetrical, the percents shown on the left half of the curve are the same as those shown on the right half. Between values of -1σ and $+1\sigma$ in a normal distribution there will be 68.26 percent of all the cases (i.e. scores) in the distribution. Approximately 95 percent of the values range from -2σ to $+2\sigma$. Because z-scores have a standard deviation of one, we can also say that approximately 95 percent of the cases in the normal distribu-

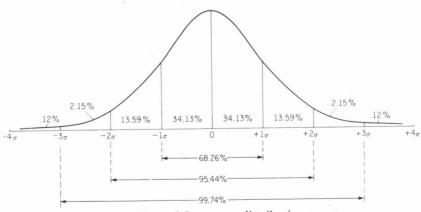

Figure 4. Normal frequency distribution curve.

tion have z-score values between $z = -2.00$ and $z = +2.00$, where the mean of $z = 0$. It must be emphasized that the percents shown in Figure 4 do not apply to non-normal distributions.

A normal-curve table is shown in the Appendix. From this table a person can read z-scores and their corresponding proportions of area under the normal curve. Because the area proportions correspond to frequency proportions, one can also determine percentile ranks based upon z-scores. Suppose, for example, that the problem is to find the percentile rank for a raw score that has a z-score value of 1.83. First one should locate 1.83 in the column headed by z and then read across to the column headed by area. The value found in the table is .4664. Because all of the figures found in the Appendix are for the proportion of total area under the curve between the mean and various z-scores, and because the z-score of 1.83 is positive (lies to the right of the mean) it is necessary to add .50 to .4664. The reason for adding .50, of course, is to add the percent for the lower half of the curve to the table value and thus get the total percent below a z of 1.83. The sum of .4664 and .50 is .9664 or 96.64 percent, so the percentile rank for a z-score of 1.83 is 96.64 or 97 (rounded). Thus, approximately 97 percent of the values in a normal distribution are found below a z-score of 1.83 (or below a point that is 1.83 standard deviations above the mean).

In order to obtain a z-score for a given percentile rank, one would first locate the percentile rank in the normal-curve table and then read the corresponding z-score. For example, suppose that one wanted to find a z-score for a percentile rank of 33. A percentile rank of 33 means that 33 percent of the total distribution frequency is below this point. Because the table figures are for areas *from the mean*, it is necessary to subtract .33 from .50 and obtain the difference, which is .17, or .1700. The next step is to locate .1700 and read to the left in the table. The correct z-score is $-.44$, because the 33rd percentile is *below* the mean.

An example may serve to illustrate one of the ways in which the normal-curve concept can be applied in a specific situation. *The Wechsler Intelligence Scale for Children — Revised* (WISC-R) yields intelligence quotients (IQs) that are normally distributed in large populations. The mean IQ is considered to be 100 points and the standard deviation is 15 points. If the average or "normal" range of intelligence is 90 to 110, what percent of the children tested will be expected to have IQs in the normal range? The first step in the solution of this problem is to compute the z-scores for 90 and 110:

$$z = \frac{90 - 100}{15} \qquad\qquad z = \frac{110 - 100}{15}$$

$$= -\frac{10}{15} \qquad\qquad\qquad = \frac{10}{15}$$

$$= -.67 \qquad\qquad\qquad\quad = .67$$

Next one should compute the percent of scores found between the mean and each z-score. The table shows that the area under the curve that is between the mean and z of .67 is .2486. Because the area of concern lies on both sides of the mean, it is necessary to double .2486, and this yields .4972, or 49.72 percent. Thus, 49.72 percent of the children can be expected to have measured IQs that fall in the 90 to 100 range. Approximately one-half of the children can be expected to have "normal" intelligence, as determined by the WISC-R.

Skewness

Many sample distributions of test scores can be expected to depart from the normal curve, especially if they are small. Some nonnormal distributions are *skewed*. A skewed distribution of scores typically has a few extreme scores on one end and a preponderance of scores near the other end. Examples of positive and negative skewness are shown in Figures 5 and 6.

The *positively* skewed distribution shown in Figure 5 has just a few extreme scores at the right-hand side of the curve, or the positive side. The "tail" of the curve is at the right, so the curve is positively skewed or skewed to the right. The *negatively* skewed curve in Figure 6 has its "tail" on the negative side, the left-hand side, so the curve is skewed to the left. One can expect positive skewness to occur when a test is too difficult for a group and negative skewness to occur when a test is too easy for a group.

In a normal distribution, the mean, mode, and median are the same value. In a skewed distribution, however, the mean and median will differ from the mode, and the mean will be found closer to the "tail" of the curve than will the other two measures.

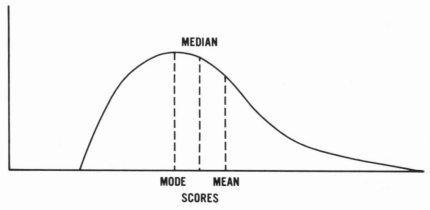

Figure 5. A positively skewed distribution.

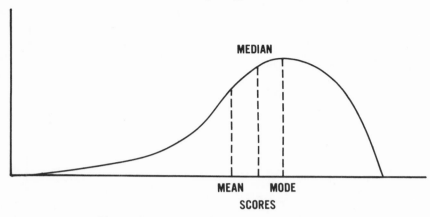

Figure 6. A negatively skewed distribution.

Correlation

The previous discussions in this chapter have dealt with the characteristics of a single set of data, such as a single distribution of test scores. Sometimes it is necessary to know the relationship between two sets of data, such as two distributions of scores. It might be important to know, for example, the extent to which the results of a scholastic aptitude test correlate with the results of a scholastic achievement test. That is to say, a person might want to know the extent to which the scores of the two tests increase and decrease together, or are *correlated.* This knowledge could be useful in a number of ways; for example, in predicting a score for one test on the basis of the score from some other test.

For the most part, the data used for appraisal purposes will show a "linear" (straight-line) relationship when two sets of data are compared. For example, when the two sets of data are plotted on a scattergram, the coordinates on the graph will tend to show a straight-line pattern. A "line of best fit" could be drawn on the pattern, and it would be a straight line. This will be made clearer by an example. Consider the two sets of values in Table V.

Figure 7 shows the two sets of scores plotted on a scattergram. The Test-X scores are plotted on the horizontal axis and the Test-Y Scores are plotted on the vertical axis. The scattergram shows a positive linear relationship in which the scores tend to rise and fall together. That is, the pattern is elliptical and as the Test-X scores get larger, the Test-Y scores also tend to get larger. Conversely, as the Test-X scores decrease, there is a tendency for the Test-Y scores to decrease also.

If the correlation had been perfect for the two sets of data, all of the plotted coordinates in Figure 7 would have been on a straight line. The top student on Test X would have also been highest on Test Y, and the

TABLE V
SCORES FROM TEST X AND TEST Y FOR SIXTEEN SUBJECTS

Subject	Test X Score	Test Y Score
001	50	53
002	47	46
003	43	49
004	40	48
005	39	45
006	36	41
007	36	40
008	36	38
009	35	37
010	33	35
011	30	35
012	30	36
013	29	35
014	28	34
015	26	30
016	22	25

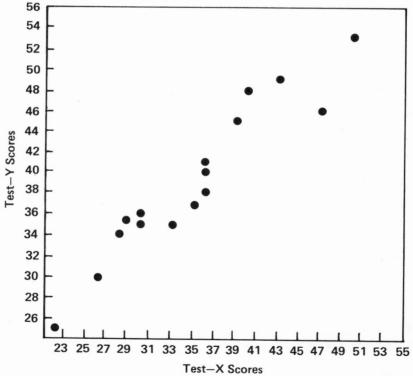

Figure 7. Scattergram showing relationship between scores for test X and test Y.

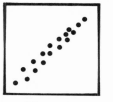  

Figure 8   Figure 9   Figure 10

Figure 8. Scattergram depicting a positive correlation.

Figure 9. Scattergram depicting a negative correlation.

Figure 10. Scattergram depicting zero correlation.

second highest on Test X would have been second ranked on Test Y, the third highest student would have ranked third on both tests, etc.

The scattergram in Figure 8 resembles the scattergram shown in Figure 7.

The pattern for a positive correlation extends from the low left portion of the scattergram to the high right portion. The pattern in Figure 10 shows no correlation, while the pattern in Figure 9 is for a *negative* correlation. A negative correlation occurs when the high scores for Test X are accompanied by low scores for Test Y. In other words, the ranking of subjects on one measure tends to be the reverse of ranking on the other.

One can get a general idea of the nature of the relationship for two variables by the inspection of the data or by looking at a scattergram, but for a precise measure of correlation it is advisable to use a correlation formula and obtain a correlation coefficient. The Pearson product-moment correlation coefficient is widely used to obtain an accurate estimate of the amount of correlation between two sets of data. The Pearson formula can be shown in different variations, but the commonly used "raw-score" formula will be used to illustrate the computation of a correlation coefficient.

Computation of a Correlation Coefficient

The raw-score formula for calculating a Pearson product-moment correlation coefficient is written as follows:

$$r = \frac{N\Sigma XY - \Sigma X\Sigma Y}{\sqrt{[N\Sigma X^2 - (\Sigma X)^2][N\Sigma Y^2 - (\Sigma Y)^2]}}$$

where

r = Pearson product-moment correlation coefficient
N = number of pairs of scores
ΣXY = sum of the products obtained by multiplying each X-score by each corresponding Y-score
ΣX = sum of the X-scores
ΣY = sum of the Y-scores
ΣX^2 = sum of the squared X-scores

ΣY^2 = sum of the squared Y-scores
(ΣX^2) = square of the sum of the X-scores
(ΣY^2) = square of the sum of the Y-scores

The computation of the Pearson r, based upon the data in Table V, follows:

X	Y	X^2	Y^2	XY
50	53	2500	2809	2650
47	46	2209	2116	2162
43	49	1849	2401	2107
40	48	1600	2304	1920
39	45	1521	2025	1755
36	41	1296	1681	1476
36	40	1296	1600	1440
36	38	1296	1444	1368
35	37	1225	1369	1295
33	35	1089	1225	1155
30	35	900	1225	1050
30	36	900	1296	1080
29	33	841	1089	957
28	34	784	1156	952
26	30	676	900	780
22	25	484	625	550
$\Sigma X = 560$	$\Sigma Y = 625$	$\Sigma X^2 = 20{,}466$	$\Sigma Y^2 = 25{,}265$	$\Sigma XY = 22{,}697$

$$r = \frac{(16 \times 22{,}697) - (560 \times 625)}{\sqrt{[16 \times 20{,}466 - (560)^2][16 \times 25{,}265 - (625)^2]}}$$

$$= \frac{13{,}152}{\sqrt{13{,}856 \times 13{,}615}}$$

$$= \frac{13{,}152}{\sqrt{188{,}649{,}440}}$$

$$= \frac{13{,}152}{13{,}734.97}$$

$$= .957 \text{ or } .96$$

Interpretation of a Pearson Coefficient

In the interpretation of a correlation coefficient one must consider both the size of the statistic and its sign (+ or −). The size of a correlation coefficient indicates the *amount* of relationship between two variables, which may be referred to as *X* and *Y*. The maximum size of a correlation coefficient is ±1.00. For perfect positive correlation the coefficient is +1.00, and for perfect negative correlation it is −1.00. The sign + or − (that precedes the coefficient) indicates whether the variables tend to rise and fall together (positive correlation) or whether there is an inverse relationship (negative correlation) in which one variable increases while the other decreases. Generally speaking, correlation coefficients as large as .80 or higher indicate very high correlation, while correlation coefficients below .20 indicate very little correlation.

Correlation coefficients should not be considered to be the equivalents of percents in the usual sense. That is, a coefficient of .50 does not mean 50 percent of something. We can, however, square the coefficient and obtain the value of r^2, which is referred to as the coefficient of determination, d. The square of .50, of course, is .25. When d equals .25 we can say that 25 percent of the variations (score differences) in variable X are attributable to variations in variable Y and vice versa. The coefficient does not, however, tell us whether Y causes X or whether Y is the result of X. It only tells us that the two variables are correlated. If r = .80, we know that d = .64, and that 64 percent of the variability of either X or Y may be attributed to the variability of the other. The reader will readily see that as we approach 1.00, or perfect correlation, the value of d also approaches 1.00 at an increasingly greater rate. If we want to predict one variable from another, it helps considerably to have a high correlation, either positive or negative.

It should be stated that while the foregoing discussion dealt with the most common kind of correlation coefficient, the Pearson r, there are also other important measures of correlation. The partial correlation coefficient, the biserial coefficient, the point-biserial coefficient, the tetrachoric coefficient, and the multiple correlation coefficient all have special uses in measurement. These statistics are discussed in various statistics and psychometrics textbooks.

Equation of a Regression Line

The Pearson r can be applied in the prediction of one variable from another. With perfect linear correlation, a straight line can be drawn that will pass through all the plotted points on a scattergram. When the correlation is *less than perfect,* however, one can develop a "line of best fit" for the plotted points. This is a *regression line* based upon a formula. By means of a formula, approximations of values can be predicted for one variable on the basis of knowledge of the other variable.

The equation for predicting the Y variable from the X variable is:

$$Y' = r\frac{s_y}{s_x}(X - \overline{X}) + \overline{Y}$$

The equation for predicting X from Y is:

$$X' = r\frac{s_x}{s_y}(Y - \overline{Y}) + \overline{X}$$

In the foregoing equations, Y' is the predicted Y value and X' is the predicted X value. An example will show how a regression equation may be used for prediction.

Suppose that the correlation coefficient for the relationship between Test-X scores and Test-Y scores is .78. Also assume that $s_x = 4.2$, $s_y = 8.4$, $\overline{X} = 63$, and $\overline{Y} = 55$.

$$Y' = .78 \left(\frac{8.4}{4.2}\right)(X - 63) + 55$$

$$= 1.56 \, (X - 63) + 55$$
$$= 1.56 \, X - 98.28 + 55$$
$$= 1.56 \, X - 43.28$$

Now suppose that one wanted to predict the Test Y score for a person who had a Text X score of 50. The computation would be:

$$Y' = 1.56 \, (X) - 43.28$$
$$= 1.56 \, (50) - 43.28$$
$$= 78 - 43.28$$
$$= 34.72 \text{ or } 35$$

Thus, an individual who earned a score of 50 on Text X would be predicted to earn a score of 35 on Test Y. Predictions of scores in this manner will involve a degree of error, but the predictions generally will be much better than mere guesswork.

INFERENTIAL STATISTICS

How much confidence can I place in the descriptive statistics that I am using? This question, which should be asked by a person using appraisal data, may be partially answered through the application of *inferential* or sampling statistics. Such statistics serve to indicate the probability that an obtained statistic is a close approximation of the parameter for the population from which the sample was drawn. Any statement of probability regarding the statistics is based upon the important assumption of randomness for the sample. For the sake of brevity, the mathematical and theoretical bases for sampling statistics will not be covered in this book. In the section that follows, certain *standard errors* (which are inferential statistics) are discussed.

Standard Errors

The arithmetic mean, standard deviation, correlation coefficient, and other statistics have *standard errors*. Each standard error serves as an estimate of the standard deviation of a distribution of like statistics. The standard error indicates how much variation one should expect if one were to compute the same statistic, such as the mean or standard deviation, for several samples like the sample in question. These standard errors decrease in size as the number of scores in the sample increases and the variability of the scores decreases. In using test results there is an advantage to having the smallest possible standard error, because the smaller the value, the greater the confidence that may be placed in the statistic. Three commonly used standard errors will be discussed in the section that follows.

Standard Error of Measurement

The statistic that is known as the *standard error measurement* is widely used in testing, particularly in the interpretation of test results. This standard error involves a measure of reliability and, in fact, is used to gauge the reliability of a test score. The formula used to compute the standard error or measurement follows:

$$SE_m = s \sqrt{1 - r_{xx}}$$

where

SE_m = standard error of measurement
s = standard deviation for a distribution of scores for the test
r_{xx} = reliability coefficient for the test

The standard deviation and the reliability coefficient are values based upon a large sample of test scores obtained through previous administrations of the instrument in question. The example that follows will show how the standard error of measurement can be determined for a test and then utilized.

Suppost that a test is reported to have a standard deviation of 11 and a reliability coefficient of .91. With this information one can use the formula and compute the standard error of measurement:

$$SE_m = 11 \sqrt{1 - .91} = 11 \sqrt{.09} = 11 \times .3 = 3.3 \text{ or } 3.$$

Now suppose that Sarah Sullivan earned a score of 68 on the test. The standard error of measurement can be applied to this *obtained* score to find a good approximation of Sarah's *true* score for the test. To attempt to locate the *true* score one can add to, and subtract from, the obtained score the standard error of measurement that was just computed. This procedure gives an interval of 68 ± 3, or 65-71. Now it may be said that Sarah's true score probably lies somewhere between 65 and 71. These last statements may require some clarification. When an individual takes a test on a given day, many factors influence the score: the nature of the test, the person's attitude, emotional state, environmental conditions, the examiner, etc. Thus, if the examinee were to take the test a number of times, it should be expected that the test scores would vary. For Sarah, the obtained score of 68 probably differs from her true score, but the extent of the difference is not known. The *true* score is the score that she should have made on the test. The best that one can do to determine her true score, unless she is tested repeatedly, is to apply the standard error of measurement and state that her true score probably lies within the range of 65 to 71. This, therefore, is the confidence interval. Because test scores are not exact and precise, it makes sense to use confidence intervals or bands that are based upon the standard error of measurement when test results are interpreted.

Standard Error of a Product-Moment Correlation Coefficient

The symbol S_r is used to represent another type of standard error, namely, the *standard error of a product-moment correlation coefficient*. This statistic is useful for estimating the amount of variation expected in correlation coefficients for samples of various sizes. When N exceeds 30, or r exceeds .50, the following formula will suffice for the computation of S_r:

$$S_r = \frac{1}{\sqrt{N-1}}$$

where

S_r = standard error of a product-moment correlation coefficient
N = number of pairs of score in the sample

When the correlation coefficient is for a small sample, it is advisable to use the appropriate table in a statistics textbook. S_r helps a person answer the question of statistical significance for an obtained Pearson correlation coefficient: How certain can we be that an obtained correlation represents a true correlation between pairs of test scores, and that the obtained correlation did not occur by chance? If a person had obtained an r of .42 for 65 pairs of scores, what would the S_r value be, and would it indicate a high level of statistical significance for the correlation coefficient?

$$S_r = \frac{1}{\sqrt{65-1}} = \frac{1}{\sqrt{64}} = \frac{1}{8} = .125 \text{ or } .13$$

With S_r equal to .13, it is reasonable to say that approximately 68 percent of the correlation coefficients one might obtain through sampling should have values ranging between $+.13$ and $-.13$. Likewise, it can be said that only 32 percent of the coefficients would be expected to exceed the limits of $+.13$ and $-.13$ by chance. If the S_r value is doubled $(2S_r)$, to obtain $+.26$ and $-.26$, one should expect approximately 95 percent of the chance coefficients to fall within the interval bounded by $+.26$ and $-.26$. The coefficient of .42 clearly exceeds the range of $\pm.26$, the 95 percent confidence interval, so one can feel quite confident that there is a positive correlation between the two variables that were compared. A statistical table showing the values of r at the .05 level of significance will indicate nearly the same value (.26) as the formula, when there are $N - 2$ degrees of freedom $(65 - 2)$, or 63 df. The table values should be considered to be the more precise values. Tables that show the required values of r for certain levels of significance are found in many statistics books.

Standard Error of Estimate

At times a test user may wish to use a statistic that provides information concerning the accuracy of estimates. The appropriate statistic in this instance is the *standard error of estimate*. The formula used to obtain it follows:

$$SE_{xy} = s_y \sqrt{1 - r_{xy}^2}$$

where

s_y = standard deviation of variable y
r_{xy} = correlation coefficient between variables x and y

The application of the statistic SE_{xy} can be illustrated very simply with an example. Assume that a correlation of .60 was found between Test X scores and Test Y scores, and that the standard deviation of Test Y was known to be 6.7. The computation of SE_{xy} is as follows:

$$SE_{xy} = 6.7 \sqrt{1 - .60^2} = 6.7 \sqrt{.64} = 6.7 \times .8 = 5.36$$

With SE_{xy} equal to 5.36, it may be expected that approximately 68 percent of the "errors" made in predicting Test Y scores from Test X scores will be within 5.36 points of the predicted score. Also, one should expect that 95 percent of the prediction errors would be within 10.72 of the predicted score. The predicted scores would probably be made on the basis of a regression equation (explained earlier in the chapter).

For extensive treatment of the statistical concepts and formulas presented in this chapter, the reader is referred to textbooks on statistics or psychometrics, such as those listed in the references.

REFERENCES

Downie, N. M. and Starry, Allen: *Descriptive and Inferential Statistics.* New York, Harper and Row, 1977.

Ferguson, George A.: *Statistical Analysis in Psychology and Education*, 4th ed. New York, McGraw-Hill, 1976.

Guilford, J. J. and Fauchter, Benjamin: *Fundamental Statistics in Psychology and Education.* McGraw-Hill, New York, 1978.

Nunnally, J. C.: *Introduction to Psychological Measurement.* New York, McGraw-Hill, 1970.

————: *Psychometric Theory.* New York, McGraw-Hill, 1967.

Roscoe, J. T.: *Fundamental Research Statistics*, 2nd ed. New York, Holt, Rinehart, and Winston, 1975.

Runyon, R. P. and Haber, Audrey: *Fundamentals of Behavioral Statistics Reading.* Massachusetts, Addison-Wesley, 1971.

Silverman, E. N. and Brody, Linda: *Statistics, A Common Sense Approach.* Prindle, Weber and Schmidt, Boston, 1973.

Turney, B. L. and Robb, G. P.: *Statistical Methods for Behavioral Science.* Harper and Row, New York, 1973.

Chapter 3

PRINCIPLES OF MEASUREMENT

THE MEASUREMENTS obtained from tests and inventories (or similar devices) are obtained indirectly rather than directly, for it is not possible at this time to make direct measurements of such traits as aptitudes, interests, attitudes, or achievement. The best one can do presently is to infer that an individual who is tested possesses a certain amount of the trait, quality, or behavior that the instrument is supposed to measure. Thus, when a person administers an achievement test, a sample performance is obtained with the hope that it accurately indicates the examinee's level of achievement. Whether the sample is truly representative depends upon many factors, such as previous experiences, motivation, attitudes, and certain test properties, such as validity, reliability, and usability.

VALIDITY

The term *validity* may be defined as the extent to which a test (or other similar device) measures what it is supposed to measure. For instance, if a particular test has been constructed for the purpose of measuring mental ability, the test is said to be valid if it accomplishes this purpose. Validity, however, is a matter of degree. A test is not generally valid or invalid, but relatively valid or invalid, and validity depends not only upon the nature of the instrument but also upon how it is used. For instance, an interest inventory may have sufficient validity to measure areas of interest but may have practically no validity for predicting *achievement* in any area of work or study.

The concept of validity as it applies to tests is rather broad and may be treated in different ways and with different terminology. In this chapter, however, the generally accepted terms of content validity, criterion-related validity, and construct validity will be explained.

Content Validity

Tests that measure level of achievement or that measure social behaviors should possess a high degree of *content validity*. These tests should provide an adequate sampling of the tasks, processes, skills, or conditions that relate closely to the definition of the test. For an academic achievement test, the skills, abilities, or understandings that are sampled by the test items should be the same as those that the school's faculty members expect the students to acquire. If the test has many items that do not relate to the academic objectives of the school, it will not possess a high degree of content validity, and it will lack validity for use in that school. One simple way to obtain evidence of content validity for a test is to have a competent evaluator read each item and respond to it. This person should be able to identify those items that are not valid with respect to content.

Criterion-Related Validity

The term *criterion-related validity* refers to the degree to which the scores of a test relate to some other measure, the criterion, which is regarded as valid. Ideally, the criterion should provide a direct measure of the particular ability or characteristic in question (spatial aptitude, for example). A correlation coefficient generally is the statistic used to show the degree of relationship between the results of a test and the criterion. A high positive correlation coefficient for the relationship between the test and criterion is regarded as evidence of criterion-related validity. We often find that an established mental-ability test has been used as the criterion for a new intelligence test, and we often find that grade-point average has been used as the criterion for new achievement tests.

The test whose validity is being assessed by means of the criterion procedure may be evaluated either for its *concurrent* validity or for its *predictive* validity. If the scores of the test are correlated with data obtained at approximately the same time, the correlation coefficient is a measure of current validity. An example of this would be the correlation of the scores of a certain *group* mental-ability test with the scores of a certain *individual* mental scale. If the correlation turns out to be high, and the individual scale is considered valid, then the group test can be said to have *concurrent* validity. The importance of this finding would be that the group test could be used instead of the individual test, with an appreciable saving of time. Suppose that the group mental-ability test was administered to high school seniors and the results were correlated with college grades obtained later. If the resulting coefficient were high, there would be evidence of *predictive* validity, for then the mental-ability test scores could be used to predict future success in college.

Construct Validity

This kind of validity is defined as the extent to which a test measures some relatively abstract quality or "construct." Aptitude tests, mental-ability tests, and personality tests are expected to have construct validity.

In order for a test to have a high degree of construct validity, the scores yielded by the test must agree to a great extent with certain concepts that are fundamental to the underlying theory upon which the test is based. Performance on the test should agree with the theoretical construct or trait that the test is supposed to measure. Examples of constructs are anxiety, self-concept, dogmatism, verbal reasoning, and clerical aptitude.

To determine the construct validity of a test, a researcher must really test the theory underlying the test, or specifically, the theory used in the development of the instrument. Essentially, the researcher formulates a hypothesis about performance on the test, gathers data to test the hypothesis, and finally draws an inference from the findings concerning the adequacy of the theory for explaining the data collected. If the researcher finds that the data collected cannot be explained satisfactorily by the theory, it is necessary to revise the interpretation of the test results, discard the theory, revise the theory, or revise the test.

One method used to investigate the construct validity of a test is to correlate the scores from the test with the scores of other tests. If the test has a high degree of construct validity, it will correlate highly with similar tests (convergent validity) but will show low correlation with dissimilar tests (discriminant validity). The test should, in other words, be more closely related to other measures of the same psychological dimension than to measures of supposedly independent dimensions. Thus, through correlation studies, a researcher can determine whether a test shows either convergent validity or discriminant validity or both. For example, a personality inventory's scores would not be expected to show a high degree of correlation with the scores of a test of general mental ability.

Factor analysis is another method that often is used to study the construct validity of a test. Factor analysis is a rather complex operation that involves the use of correlation coefficients to identify psychological factors or traits. Because it is beyond the scope of this book it will not be discussed here, but the reader is referred to advanced statistics or psychometrics books for information on this topic.

It should be emphasized that the validity of a test is a function of the use made of the test as well as the test itself. As stated earlier, an interest inventory may be valid for showing a student's preferences for activities or kinds of work, but it will seriously lack validity for predicting achievement in school courses or occupations.

RELIABILITY

Test validity is dependent to a great extent upon *test reliability*. If validity is thought of as appropriateness, then reliability refers to accuracy. If a test is highly reliable, it is consistent, for it gives similar results each time that it is used with a specific individual or group. If the test is not reliable, or gives quite different results each time it is administered, it is not dependable, and it cannot be highly valid. High reliability, however, does not *insure* validity. For example, a certain "mechanical aptitude" test might give very consistent results, but it might be measuring interest rather than mechanical aptitude, and thus would not be a valid test.

Methods of Determining Test Reliability

Comparison of test results over time yields information concerning the stability of the scores of a test. It generally is desirable to know the extent to which a test's scores will remain constant if the test is repeated after an interval of time. The less the scores fluctuate from time to time, the more reliable the test, and therefore the more certain we can be of its results.

The *test-retest method* is often used to obtain a correlation coefficient that indicates the stability of a test over a period of time. This method requires the administration of a test to a group of subjects, recording their scores, administering the test at a later date, again recording the scores, and then correlating the two sets of scores. The correlation coefficient for the two sets of scores is referred to as the *coefficient of reliability*. If the subjects who take the test rank similarly both times, the reliability coefficient will be high, perhaps approaching 1.00. Of course, if the ranks change much from test to retest, the reliability coefficient will be low. Because of "practice effect," this method may produce higher scores on the second test than on the first. If all subjects increase their scores the same amount, the coefficient will not be affected, but if some raise their scores more than others, the coefficient will be lowered.

The time interval between the test and retest is an important factor that can influence the reliability coefficient. If the first test administration is followed immediately by the second test administration, the subjects may remember their responses and answer questions in the same way the second time, and this will produce a spuriously high reliability coefficient. If the retest is delayed too long, changes in the subjects' lives or additional learning may result in a decreased coefficient of reliability.

The nature of the test activity may also affect the rest-retest reliability coefficient. Any activities that result in unequal gains by subjects upon repetition of the test will tend to produce a depressed correlation coefficient.

The *equivalant-forms method* can be used to obtain a reliability coefficient and avoid some of the shortcomings of the test-retest procedure. When two very similar (alternate) forms of a test are available, both forms can be administered to a group of subjects and the two sets of scores can be correlated to produce a reliability coefficient. The alternate-forms method has a twofold value: it indicates stability of the test and also the equivalency of the forms. A high correlation coefficient between the forms indicates that the forms are very comparable. Thus, the two forms of the test should yield similar results and should be interchangeable.

A major problem relative to obtaining alternate-forms reliability is that it is necessary to take into consideration the number of items, difficulty of the items, and the content of the items. Differential practice effect (some subjects gaining more than others on the second form) also is a problem with regard to this method, for it can lower the reliability coefficient if it occurs.

The *split halves method* of determining a test's reliability provides an estimate of *internal consistency*. When a test is supposed to measure some generalized homogeneous trait, such as reading ability, its items ought to differentiate in the same way with respect to examinee performance on the test. If the test items do not function in a similar way in this kind of a test, the test will lack internal consistency, and the test will in a sense not be as reliable as it should be.

Estimates of internal consistency usually are obtained through the use of split-halves method or the use of a Kuder-Richardson formula. The split-halves procedure consists of dividing the test into two comparable halves (usually by considering the odd-numbered items to be one test and even-numbered items to be another test) and correlating the scores made by a group of subjects on the two halves. Actually, the whole test is given to a group of individuals, then the test is divided, and the two sets of scores are correlated. This procedure provides a measure of equivalence between the two halves, and in addition it provides a measure of sampling adequacy. Because the splitting of the test shortens the test, and because reliability tends to be affected by the length of the test (a short test is less reliable than a long test), the reliability coefficient obtained by the split-half method should be corrected for the test's full length. The usual way to make this correction is to employ the Spearman-Brown formula, which in this instance is written:

$$r_{tt} = \frac{2r'_{tt}}{1 + r'_{tt}}$$

where

r_{tt} = estimated reliability coefficient for the full-length test
r'_{tt} = coefficient obtained between the two halves

For example, suppose that a test yielded a reliability coefficient of .90 when the split halves method was used. What would the full-length test reliability coefficient be expected to be?

$$r_{tt} = \frac{2\,(.90)}{1 + (1)\,(.90)} = \frac{1.80}{1.90} = .95$$

A weakness of the Spearman-Brown formula is that it is based upon the assumption that the variabilities of the scores of the halves are equal, when in actuality, this may not be the case. Guttman (1945) has provided a formula that takes into consideration the variabilities of the scores of the test halves:

$$r_{tt} = 2\left(1 - \frac{\sigma_a^2 + \sigma_b^2}{\sigma_t^2}\right)$$

where

$\qquad r_{tt}$ = estimated reliability coefficient of the total test
$\qquad \sigma_t^2$ = square of the standard deviation of the total test
$\sigma_a^2 + \sigma_b^2$ = squares of the standard deviations of the half tests

Assume that one has the following data and wishes to use the Guttman formula to estimate full-test reliability: $\sigma_t^2 = 100$; $\sigma_a^2 = 35$; $\sigma_b^2 = 25$. What is the estimated reliability coefficient of the total test?

$$r_{tt} = 2\left(1 - \frac{35 + 25}{100}\right) = 2\left(1 - \frac{60}{100}\right) = 2(.40) = .80$$

A major difficulty that occurs in using the split-halves method for determining test reliability is the problem of dividing the test so that the halves are comparable. If the test items are arranged in order of difficulty, from the easiest item to the most difficult, it usually is possible to split the test into odd-numbered and even-numbered items. Then, the odd-numbered items constitute one test and the even-numbered items constitute the other one. The split-halves coefficient is not appropriate for tests in which speed is an important factor.

As previously stated, a measure of internal consistency can be obtained through the use of Kuder-Richardson formulas. The commonly used formulas are KR 20 and KR 21. These formulas were constructed as a means of solving the problem of obtaining different split-halves reliability estimates when a test is highly heterogeneous or has parts that differ greatly from one another, for example, vocabulary, arithmetic, perceptual speed. The Kuder-Richardson formulas provide measures of consistency between items, and these represent the average coefficients obtained by dividing a test in various ways. The formulas should be used only when the test items are similar in level of difficulty and intercorrelation. The two formulas, KR 20 and KR 21 are written as follows:

KR 20: $\qquad\qquad r_{tt} = \left(\frac{n}{n-1}\right) \frac{\sigma_t^2 - \Sigma pq}{\sigma_t^2}$

KR 21: $\qquad\qquad r_{tt} = \left(\frac{n}{n-1}\right) \frac{\sigma_t^2 - n\bar{p}\bar{q}}{\sigma_t^2}$

where
$\qquad n$ = number of test items
$\qquad p$ = proportion passing an item
$\qquad q$ = $1 - p$
$\qquad \bar{p}$ = average proportion passing an item
$\qquad \bar{q}$ = average proportion failing an item
$\qquad \sigma_t^2$ = squared standard deviation of the test

Usually formula KR 20 provides a close approximation of an equivalent-forms reliability coefficient. Formula KR 21 is somewhat less accurate, but it is easy to use and will provide a quick estimate of the coefficient of equivalence if the test is scored by the "number right" formula (Cronbach, 1960, p. 141).

Because the prerequisites of equal levels of difficulty and similar intercorrelation of items are seldom completely attained in tests, it may generally be assumed that the Kuder-Richardson formulas will provide reliability coefficients that are too low. This may not be the case, however, if speed is an important factor with respect to performance of the test. Wesman and Kernan (1952) found that the Kuder-Richardson formulas may produce spuriously high reliability coefficients if used with speed tests.

Factors That Influence Reliability

Certain factors can exert a considerable amount of influence on test reliability. For convenience of discussion, such factors may be classified as either test factors or situational factors.

Test Factors

The principal factors within the test itself that affect reliability are test-item ambiguity, length of the test, and the level of difficulty of the test.

Generally speaking, a test item should be worded so clearly that its meaning is understood in the same way by each reader. That is to say, the item should not be vague or unclear. When an item is ambiguous, the responses to it will be less consistent than they should be, so the reliability of the item is decreased. Obviously, if a test has several ambiguous items, the reliability of the whole test is certain to be adversely affected to a high degree. A thorough item analysis is an effective way to locate ambiguous items in a test. An item analysis is a systematic process for evaluating an item with respect to its ability to discriminate and its difficulty (see Chapter 6).

Another test factor that affects reliability is the length of the test, because the length is a reflection of how adequately the test samples the particular behavior that the test measures. The longer a test is, the more likely that it will sample the trait in question adequately, and therefore the more likely that it will provide consistent scores. Because tests that are very long may fatigue the examinees who take them, test authors strive to construct tests that are long enough to provide a high degree of reliability but short enough to avoid fatigue or boredom. The examiner who uses only parts of tests or subtests for diagnostic purposes should realize that a portion of the test will generally be less reliable than the entire instrument will be. When subtest reliability data are not available, extreme caution should be used in the interpretation of the *subtest* results.

Level of difficulty of a test is a third test factor that influences reliability. If a test is constructed for the purpose of evaluating individuals who have a wide range of ability or age, the reliability may vary at the different levels of ability or age. The test may be so difficult for the least able or the youngest examinees that their scores will be influenced considerably because of only one item that was passed or failed. If the examiner finds that the test manual gives only one reliability coefficient that is based upon some diverse group, evidence should be sought that the test is equally reliable for other groups of specific ability or age levels.

Situational Factors

Test reliability can be affected by conditions that are not inherent in the test but prevail at the time that the instrument is administered. For example, a person may take a test when sick, and therefore not perform well because of that handicap. If that subject were to take the test a week later, when feeling well, the test score most likely would be higher. Similarly, a student may have a particularly bad case of test anxiety during the test and consequently have a depressed test score. At another time, with less anxiety, the person may perform better on the test. Similar instances can be cited relative to motivation for a test, ability to follow directions at the time the test is administered, attitude toward the examiner, etc. The fluctuations in performance tend to lower test reliability coefficients.

The examples first given are all instances of examinee-incurred variables that may influence examinee performance. Examiner-scorer influences may also have an adverse effect upon test reliability. Specifically, if the examiner fails to follow the test-administration directions, gives extra help to students taking the test, or allows too much or too little time, the test reliability can be seriously altered. That is to say, such examiner behaviors tend to exert a varying influence on the test scores and consequently contribute to the error variance of the test. For some tests, the scoring is somewhat subjective, so the manner in which the *scorer performs* can affect error variance and reduce reliability.

Such environmental conditions as lighting, ventilation, noise level, writing surface, distractions, and seating arrangement can have an adverse effect upon the reliability of tests. An extremely hot or cold room may prevent some examinees from performing near their best level, as may noises, poor light, or cramped seating. Also, when students must sit too close together, cheating may occur and this factor can seriously alter test results.

Use of Reliability Information

The reliability coefficients that one generally finds in a test manual have been obtained through the administration of the test to a selected group. The reported reliability, therefore, is not inherent in the test to the extent that it remains constant, but in reality it is an estimate of reliability that was computed at a particular time for a certain group. The test user must decide whether the instrument will be just as reliable for the individuals who are to be tested. If the persons who are to be tested are comparable in every important way to the group upon which test reliability is established, the test user may assume that the reported reliability will be dependable. Of course, this assumption is difficult to make, because the necessary data seldom are available for establishing the comparability of the groups. The problem can best be dealt with by establishing the reliability of the test in question for the local population with whom it will be used.

Another problem that relates to the use of reliability data appears when the test user attempts to determine reliability for a particular *individual*. Even when the reliability of a test has been determined locally, the reliability coefficient is a group statistic, and a given individual's test performances may be more or less consistent than that of the group as a whole. However, while it is not possible to make a foolproof assessment of a subject's particular test score, one can look at the available evidence that may aid in making an estimation of reliability. For example, one might look at the results of previous testing for the individual to see whether that person's performances tend to be consistent or erratic. Also, observation of the individual's testing behavior may be considered in relation to consistency of performance. Finally, if the test results are discussed with the individual shortly after testing, the subject may provide some clues that relate to reliability, such as attitude toward the test or emotional state during testing.

The test user should remember that reliability should be considered in relation to the purpose of testing. If long range predictions are to be made, the stability of the test over a period of time is important. However, if the test user is attempting to evaluate a person's performance within a group, within-group reliability deserves special attention.

OBJECTIVITY

As used in this section, the term *objectivity* refers to the scoring of a test. A highly objective test can be scored by any competent person and the same result obtained. That is, the opinions, beliefs, values, biases, etc., of the scorer play no part in the establishment of the test score for the examinee. On the other hand, a highly *subjective* test can lead to a wide range of scores for a person because the scoring does not restrict the scorer much (if at all) in terms of deciding which responses are acceptable or not acceptable, or deciding the *degree* of acceptability of responses. A multiple-choice test is an example of an objective test, and an essay-type test is an example of a subjective test. Standardized tests almost always are of the objective type, and the reason for this is apparent — objective scoring increases the validity and reliability of the test. Test standardization will be discussed later.

Most standardized group tests have a very high degree of objectivity because the instructions are clearly stated, the items are clear and specific, the possible answers are precisely stated, and the test may be scored by means of a key or by machine. Standardized *individual* tests, such as the Wechsler scales, are administered to one subject at a time and they tend to have somewhat less objectivity than group tests. The administrator of the individual test is expected to follow the directions for administration closely but is given some latitude in scoring the responses for some of the test items.

The subjective nature of the scoring of some individual test items necessitates special preparation of examiners in a course that provides close observation of the student who is learning how to administer individual tests or scales. Carelessness, lack of knowledge concerning the instrument, or lack of skill may seriously and adversely affect the results for individual tests.

Adequate training is absolutely essential as a means of minimizing the subjectivity of individual instruments, but even when the examiner is well trained a small degree of subjectivity may be present during a test administration. Masling (1959) found that when test subjects (who were accomplices) acted in a friendly manner toward the examiner, there was a tendency for the scoring of responses to become more generous and the number of reinforcing responses to be increased. "Cold" behavior from the subject tended to result in less leniency and fewer reinforcing responses. Sattler and Theye (1967) found that the performances of groups such as the elderly, mentally deficient, or disturbed are more likely to be affected by deviations from the standardized testing procedures than are performances of normal persons. These researchers also reported that the performances of children are more likely to be affected than the performances of older examinees when there are departures from the standardized testing procedures.

STANDARDIZATION

In order for a test to be standardized, it must be administered with a standard set of directions under uniform conditions to a sample of examinees representative of the group for whom the test is intended to be used. This systematic procedure is used in order to obtain a set of raw scores from the standardization sample. The raw scores must then be converted to the desired derived scores, such as percentile ranks, stanines, or standard scores. The standardization group is referred to as the *norm group*. The derived scores for the norm group may be used as a frame of reference for interpreting raw scores made by examinees in the future.

NORMS AND NORM GROUPS

When an individual's test score is compared with the comparison group, it is possible to determine whether that person's performance on the test is fairly typical, somewhat above or below average, very high or very low. The average score for the norm group is the *norm*. Norm tables, which show raw scores and their corresponding percentile ranks, standard scores, IQs, or stanines provide a convenient way to determine how the examinee's score compares with the norm group's scores. Norm tables may show data for scores that were collected on a nationwide basis to provide *national* norms, or they may show data collected from a single school or from a single school district or from a single firm's job applicants to provide *local* norms.

The norms provided in test manuals generally are presented as national norms. When the test in question is administered to a random sample of the entire population of subjects, such as all sixth grade students in the country (target population), and the resulting scores are used in the norm table, the term national norm is appropriate. When, however, the sample of subjects who were tested does not represent all sections of the country, the use of the term national norm is questionable, for the results may be biased in favor of (or against) certain individuals who were not represented in the "national sample."

Random selection of the sample to be tested from the target population will ensure representativeness, but such a procedure can be very time-consuming and expensive. The most frequently used procedure for obtaining the national norm group is the stratified random sample procedure, which requires that the target population be divided into relevant subgroups, so that these groups will be represented in the same proportion as their numbers in the target population. The individuals who comprise the subgroup should be selected by means of a random sampling procedure.

The sample from which the norms are derived for a particular test should be described explicitly in the test manual. When scores for the subgroups differ greatly, it is advantageous to have separate norms reported for the subgroups.

When the national norms provided in test manuals are not appropriate, the test user may wish to make use of local norms. In education, local norms may apply to a classroom, school, or a school district, whereas in industry they may apply to a shop, plan, or company. A counselor in a high school who uses a particular scholastic aptitude test may be more interested in local norms pertaining to a particular college attended by most of the high school's graduating seniors than in national norms for that test. Most counselors probably prefer to have both national and local norms.

Those who use test data should keep in mind that norms are not standards or goals. A test merely provides a sample of data from a sample of individuals who took the test. Norms merely show how a certain group of examinees have performed in the past when administered a particular test. When someone remarks, "The norms are too high" or "The norms are too low" there is an implication that the norms are being thought of as standards. Norms should not be considered to be standards of performance because standards are levels of attainment that are specifically set for an individual school or school district, firm, or agency. If the attainment in question is achievement of some kind, the standard should be established first and then testing should be done to determine how well the standard is being met. Any comparison with a norm group, then, should be for the purpose of interpreting data rather than for drawing a conclusion that a standard has or has not been met. If, for example, the standard for reading proficiency in the fourth grade states, in effect, that each student should have a reading proficiency that is at or above the student's level of scholastic aptitude, the determination of whether the standard was reached could be made on the basis of valid measures of reading proficiency and scholastic aptitude.

TEST ADMINISTRATION AND SCORING

Even when the most valid, reliable, and usable test is selected, there is the possibility that the results will be invalid because of careless administration or scoring. This applies to both group and individual tests of all types. Careful planning prior to testing should serve to minimize testing problems and errors. This planning should involve securing a suitable room for testing, deciding how many students should be tested at one time and when they should be tested, and deciding how the scoring should be done.

For group testing, the room ought to have sufficient space to provide each student with ample writing space. If the chairs or desks are close together, every other one should be used. Sufficient space between examinees should make them more comfortable and reduce the possibility of cheating or talking during testing. The room should be well lighted, well ventilated, and free from distractions. A notice posted on the door of the testing room, stating that testing is in progress, should prevent persons entering the room during the testing period. All test materials should be prepared well in advance of testing, so that the test administrator is not "caught short" when the testing is about to begin. Tests, answer sheets, pencils, and scratch paper should be counted and arranged in the sequence needed for testing. The timer should be available and functioning well. Scoring should be done carefully, and the answer sheets should be double-checked for accuracy. Answer sheets should be examined for stray marks or incorrect marking.

Tests publishers often provide an elaborate scoring service that can provide a wealth of useful test data. If a school can afford the use of such a service, and if the service is dependable as well as reasonably speedy, the commercial scoring service is generally recommended over the hand-scoring procedures. One should be alert for errors even when a commercial scoring system is used, and if the results seem to be questionable an investigation is in order.

Here are some suggestions for the proper *group administration* of tests and inventories:

1. Have the writing surfaces cleared prior to passing out materials.
2. Have "left-handed" chairs for the left-handed examinees.
3. Have a few extra copies of the test booklet available during testing.
4. Have examinees seated in every other seat.
5. Hang a "Test In Progress" sign outside the door of the testing room.
6. Read the directions for the test very clearly.
7. Try to make certain that the examinees understand the directions.
8. Once the test has started, move quietly around the room to see that the examinees are proceeding correctly.
9. When the test is in progress, respond to any individual examinee's questions concerning procedures but do not help examinees with answers to the questions.
10. Adhere very strictly to the designated time limits for the test.
11. Be aware of any cheating or attempts to cheat and write notes of any unusual or unacceptable behavior. Include the notes in a report covering the test administration.
12. After the completion of the test, collect all material systematically and account for all test booklets and other materials.

The administration of an *individual* test or scale, such as the *Wechsler Intelligence Scale for Children — Revised* (WISC-R) is quite different from the administration of a group instrument, because an individual test is given to only one person at a time. The testing room used for individual testing generally is relatively small, for there are just two people involved, and the nature of the test activity generally is different from that for group testing. A group instrument can be given to one person at a time also, but this is rarely done because obviously it is much more economical to test several persons at the same time with the group instrument.

Every individual test has certain specific directions for administration, stated in the test manual, and these must be adhered to very strictly to make the test results as valid as possible. Still, there are some general suggestions that can be made for administrators of individual tests:

1. Use a suitable room for the individual testing. This means one that is well lighted, well ventilated, and free from distractions.
2. Make certain that all of the needed test materials are in the kit before starting the test. This inspection should also include a determination of the *condition* of the materials to see whether they are in good physical shape for testing.
3. Establish rapport with the examinee as soon as possible. A friendly smile and greeting should help put the person at ease before testing starts. A bit of "small talk" on an appropriate topic may help also. If rapport cannot be established, the testing should be postponed.
4. Try to ascertain whether the examinee knows the purpose of the test. Children especially should have a simple explanation of the reason for the test. With *very young* children, the examiner might say something like "Jimmy, I'd like to play some games with you."
5. Use the examinee's name occasionally during testing. This helps maintain rapport and makes the testing experience seem less formal.
6. Use comments like "Fine, you're doing well, Molly," or "That seemed a little difficult, didn't it?" when such comments are appropriate, in order to foster examinee effort. The examiner must be careful, however, to avoid reinforcing correct responses positively and incorrect responses negatively or with silence. The main idea is to encourage the examinee to keep trying through the testing session.
7. Ideally, the examiner is able to give all the directions for administering the items exactly as they are stated in the manual without having to read them, so that full attention can be given to the examinee. In actual practice, the examiner generally knows the wording in the manual well enough to be able to adhere closely to the directions by merely glancing at the manual occasionally. A departure from the standardized directions may alter the examinee's responses to an unknown degree.
8. Observe the examinee very carefully. Observation should start when the subject enters the room and should continue until the time when the subject leaves. Examinee appearance, attitude, remarks, fatigue, reaction to frustration, and handicaps should be observed and recorded in testing notes.
9. When fatigue or boredom is evident in a young child, the examiner should take a short break in the session. Just walking around the room may be beneficial to the child.
10. Because some of the *scoring* takes place during the administration of the individual test, the examiner should be familiar with the instrument's scoring procedures. Obviously, careless or faulty scoring can produce erroneous results.

REFERENCES

Anatasi, Anne: *Psychological Testing,* 4th ed. New York, Macmillan, 1976.

Buros, Oscar K., ed.: *The Seventh Mental Measurements Yearbook.* 2 Vols. Highland Park, N.J., Gryphon Press, 1972.

Cronbach, L. J.: *Essentials of Psychological Testing,* 3rd ed. New York, Harper and Row Publishers, 1960.

———— and Meehl, P. E.: Construct validity in psychological tests. *Psychological Bulletin, 52:*281-303, 1955.

Ebel, R. L.: *Essentials of Educational Measurement,* 2nd ed. Englewood Cliffs, N.J., Prentice-Hall, 1972.

Guttman, L.: A basis for analyzing test-retest reliability. *Psychometrics, 10:*255-282, 1945.

Masling, Joseph: The effects of warm and cold interaction of the administration and scoring of an intelligence test. *Journal of Consulting Psychology, 23:*336-341, 1959.

Mehrens, W. A. and Lehman, I. J.: *Measurement and Evaluation in Education and Psychology,* 2nd ed. New York, Holt, Rinehart, and Winston, 1978.

Noll, V. H., Scannell, D. P., and Craig, R. C.: *Introduction to Educational Measurement,* 4th ed. Boston, Houghton Mifflin, 1979.

Nunnally, J. C., Jr.: *Introduction to Psychological Measurement.* New York, McGraw-Hill, 1970.

Payne, D. A.: *The Assessment of Learning: Cognitive and Affective.* Lexington, Massachusetts, D. C. Heath, 1974.

Sattler, J. M. and Theye, J.: Procedural, situational, and interpersonal variables in individual intelligence testing. *Psychological Bulletin, 68:*347-360, 1967.

Thorndike, R. L. and Hagen, Elizabeth. *Measurement and Evaluation in Psychology and Education,* 4th ed. New York, John Wiley and Sons, 1977.

Wesman, A. G. and Kernan, J. P.: An experimental comparison of test-retest and internal consistency estimater of reliability with speeded tests. *Journal of Educational Psychology, 53:*292-298, 1952.

Chapter 4

INTERPRETATION OF TEST DATA

"**W**HAT DO THESE test results mean?" This is the very difficult question that someone must ultimately try to answer through the interpretation of test data. The process of test data interpretation is the means by which one can make test data meaningful; or in other words, it is the process of making sense out of raw scores or derived scores.

Mastery of basic statistical concepts and the major principles of measurement should provide a test user with a good foundation for effective test-data interpretation. For greater expertise in this important area, however, one must have additional knowledge and skill related to the use of interpretation aids and techniques.

Test-data interpretation helps provide answers to questions about individuals, such as "Why is Billy making poor progress in his school work?" "Why does Mary seem to be socially isolated?" "What kinds of occupations should Carol consider?" "Is Judy likely to succeed in college?" These questions are complex and generally cannot be answered solely on the basis of test data, but such data can facilitate the answer-finding process.

The process of test-data interpretation involves knowledge of the instruments from which the scores were obtained, understanding of the fundamentals of measurement, and reasoning with pertinent available data. A test generally provides a sampling of some ability, trait, or condition of a person, so sound reasoning with the data obtained should lead to useful inferences about the person to be helped, and the inferences should lead to working hypotheses. Such hypotheses should be intelligent, tentative statements about the individual. Suppose, for example, the question to be answered is "Why is Billy having difficulty in learning?" The analysis of test data might lead to the hypothesis that Billy has minimal brain dysfunction. This hypothesis, which would be confirmed or rejected at some future time, would be based upon an analysis of test scores and other pertinent information, such as Billy's medical record, home environment data, social history, educational history, teacher observations, etc. Of course, the answer to some other question, such as "Is Judy capable of doing college work?," may require considerably less appraisal data.

In Chapter 2 several statistical procedures for converting relatively meaningless raw scores into meaningful derived scores were discussed. These derived scores will be reintroduced in order to focus on their use in test-data interpretation.

DERIVED SCORES

Percentile ranks, standard scores, intelligence quotients, stanines, and grade equivalents are the derived scores that most often are used in the interpretation of test data. Each type of score has its particular advantages and limitations, so the applicability of each will vary according to the characteristics of the client and the requirements of the situation.

Percentile Ranks

The derived score that is reported most often in test records and test manuals is the percentile rank. Its popularity probably stems from its simplicity: it is rather easily explained to students, teachers, parents, and others, and it is easy to calculate (especially when a calculator or computer is available). As explained in Chapter 2, the percentile rank of a score indicates the percent of cases or scores in a distribution that fall below that specific score. For example, suppose that Penny Parker had a raw score of 59 on a test, and that the raw score was found to have a percentile rank of 63. This result should be interpreted to mean that 63 percent of the persons in the group that Penny is being compared with scored lower than Penny did. One could also say that if one hundred persons took the test, sixty-three would be expected to score lower than Penny.

There are two major disadvantages in the use of percentile ranks. One is that although test scores generally are distributed normally, percentile ranks have a rectangular distribution. The consequence of this fact is that relatively small differences in raw scores near the *mean* of a distribution produce large percentile-rank differences, and relatively large raw-score differences at the *ends* or *extremes* of a distribution produce small percentile-rank differences. The person who interprets test data in the form of percentile ranks must try to avoid the pitfall of misinterpreting large percentile-rank differences that are at or near the middle of a distribution where a relatively small difference in performance can produce a relatively large percentile-rank difference.

Another limitation of percentile ranks is that, because the units are unequal, the ranks cannot be added, subtracted, multiplied or divided. Thus, they cannot be averaged. In order to find one individual's average percentile rank on several tests, it is necessary to convert the percentile ranks to z-scores using a normal-curve table, then average the z-scores, and finally convert the mean z-score to a percentile rank, using the normal-curve table. The use of this method, however, assumes that there is a normal distribution for each test and that the same normative group is used for each test.

When using percentile ranks, it is important to make certain that the client understands that a percentile rank does not refer to the percent of questions answered correctly, but rather to the percent of examinees whose performance the client has surpassed. The test interpreter also should try to define clearly the group with whom the client is being compared.

Standard Scores

The computation of z-scores, Z-scores, and T-scores was discussed in Chapter 2. The formula for calculating a z-score is $z = (X - \bar{X})/s$, while the Z-score formula is $Z = 10[(X - \bar{X})/s] + 50$. The formula for calculating a T-score is the same as the Z-score formula, and it can be written as $T = 10z + 50$. The symbol T should be used instead of Z when the distribution of raw scores is normal, or when the raw-score distribution is normalized. The normalizing procedure was explained in Chapter 2. The z-score distribution has a mean value of zero and a standard deviation value of one (1.00). The Z-score and T-score distributions have a mean of 50 and a standard deviation of 10. A few tests have standard scores with means other than 50 and standard deviations other than 10.

Standard scores make raw-score data meaningful because the standard score describes an examinee's performance on a test as the distance of the raw score from the mean score in terms of the standard-deviation unit. Thus, a z-score of 1.00, based upon raw-score data, indicates that the examinee scored one deviation above the mean, and a z-score of -1.00 indicates that the examinee scored one standard deviation below the mean. Likewise, a Z-score or T-score of 60 indicates a performance that is a standard deviation above the mean, because these standard scores have a mean value of 50 and a standard deviation of 10. If Willie Wilson's T-score for a test is reported to be 65, we interpret his performance as one and one-half standard deviations *above* the mean (15/10 = 1.5). Likewise, if Hardley Able has a T-score of 30, he has scored two standard deviations *below* the mean.

When standard scores are reported in test records or test manuals, they nearly always are reported at T-scores. These scores are not as easily explained to students, teachers, parents, or the lay public as percentile ranks, but nevertheless they are useful to the skilled test user, and they are especially advantageous because T-scores can easily be related to a normal distribution or to a normal-curve chart or table.

Stanines

The stanine ("standard-nine") scale is a standard-score scale with score values ranging from 1 to 9. This scale was devised for use by the United States Army Air Corps during World War II in connection with training programs. Since that time the scale has been used extensively by many institutions and test publishers. The stanine score may be computed by using the formula: Stanine $= 5 + 2z$. The mean of a stanine distribution is 5 and the standard deviation is approximately 2.

For a normal distribution, the percentage of cases assigned to each stanine value (1 to 9) are as shown:

Stanine	1	2	3	4	5	6	7	8	9
Percent	4%	7%	12%	17%	20%	17%	12%	7%	4%

Stanines computed for a nonnormal distribution of data, of course, will not be distributed in this normal fashion.

Stanines are advantageous when one merely wants to group scores in nine categories and then label them, such as very low (Stanine 1), below average (Stanines 2, 3), average (Stanines 4, 5, 6), above average (Stanines 7, 8), and very high (Stanine 9). Such a procedure tends to reduce the possibility of treating scores as more precise measures than they really are. One could argue, though, that the stanines based upon broad bands of scores really are not precise enough for test-data interpretation, and certainly this would be true in some instances.

Intelligence Quotients

Tests of mental ability generally yield intelligence quotients, commonly referred to as IQs. In contrast to the original Binet scales, which provided an IQ based upon a mental-age score, most of today's mental-ability tests are point scales that provide an intelligence quotient based upon the distribution of point scores. The Binet scale IQ was based upon the formula (MA/CA)100, so the resulting IQ value was a *ratio* IQ. For instance, if a ten-year-old subject earned a mental age of 8, the obtained IQ would be 80. Because the *Stanford-Binet Intelligence Scale,* a revision of the original Binet Scales, was found to yield different IQ distributions at different age levels, a deviation IQ formula was developed. The formula may be written:

$$DIQ = (IQ_x - IQ_m) K + 100$$

where

DIQ = Deviation IQ

IQ_x = $\dfrac{MA}{CA} \times 100$

IQ_m = 1937 scale mean IQ for age being considered

K = $\dfrac{16}{SD}$ (this is a constant in which SD is the standard deviation of the age considered)

It is seldom necessary to use the formula in order to obtain deviation IQs because they are provided in the Stanford-Binet manual. The deviation IQ is considered to be a better measure than the ratio IQ because the DIQ has been adjusted for the variability of the scores from age to age. Thus, a DIQ of 88 for a six-year-old child is interpreted in the same way as a DIQ of 88 for a nine-year-old child. The Wechsler scales and other mental-ability tests also provide deviation IQs.

The term intelligence quotient appeared in the literature in 1912 when Stern and Kuhlmann recommended it as a measure of brightness. Terman, however, was the psychologist who actually put the concept to practical use. "The simplicity of the measure, the ease with which it could be computed, together with the fact that it supplemented but did not displace the mental-age concept which proved so valuable, as an aid to understanding the mental capacities of children, appealed at once to those who had been groping for a quantitative measure that would have equivalent meaning for all" (Goodenough, 1949, p. 63). The term IQ became popular as an indicator of the *rate* of mental growth, for it seemed to indicate how mentally mature the subject was for his or her age. Thus, the child with a measured IQ of 120 was believed to be developing mentally more rapidly than the child whose obtained IQ was 110.

The popularity of the concept has diminished considerably since its inception, because the IQ has been found wanting in certain ways. For instance, the measure is not as constant as was first assumed. The growth rates of children often fluctuate from year to year, and sometimes to a considerable degree. That is why it is inaccurate to say, "Her IQ is 125," as though the figure is fixed and precise. Also, different tests will yield different IQs for the same individual, and one generally will not know which IQ score to accept as the most valid measure. The term IQ has become "value laden," and its use probably should be discontinued. It is discussed in this book to help the reader develop an awareness of the shortcomings and misconceptions associated with it.

Grade-Equivalent Score

Test data may be expressed as *grade-equivalent* scores or *grade-placement* scores. This type of derived score is commonly used for reporting the results of standardized achievement tests. The grade-equivalent scores for a particular test may be determined by means of the following procedure:

1. Test several pupils at several grade levels through the administration of the test.
2. Calculate the average score for each grade-placement group.
3. Plot these averages on a graph and connect the points plotted with as straight a line as possible.
4. Extend the line at both extremes in order to provide for scores above and below the averages computed (this is called *extrapolation*).
5. Use the graph to determine the grade-equivalent score for each raw score and print these grade equivalents in a table.

Grade-equivalent scores generally are given in tenths of a school year. Thus, 4.5 refers to the fifth month of grade four, and 6.2 means the second month of the sixth grade. Consider the following example.

Suppose that Wilma Williams, a sixth-grade student in the fifth month of school (6.5) has the following grade-equivalent scores: Reading 7.2; Mathematics 6.1; and Language 6.5. Her achievement score for reading is similar to that of the average student in the second month of the seventh grade. In mathematics she performed like the "typical" student in the first month of the sixth grade, and in language like the typical student in the fifth month of grade 6. Now, at first glance it would appear that she is achieving well in reading, satisfactorily in the language area, and poorly in mathematics. Such an assumption could be in serious error, however, because unless we know the standard deviations of the test-score distributions, we cannot make accurate comparisons of the grade equivalents. A grade-equivalent score of 7.2 for reading could place a student at the 65th percentile, while an apparently lower grade-equivalent score of 6.1 in mathematics could place the student at the 70th percentile, which really is a higher rank. Thus, a lower score on one test may indicate a better performance than a higher score on another test. Score variability, indicated by standard deviations, should be checked in the test manuals when one is using grade-equivalent scores. Of course, the standard deviations vary for the tests within a battery distributed by a particular test publisher, and they also vary for similar tests produced by different test publishers. The different publishers have used somewhat different norm groups, the test items are somewhat different, and the test formats are different, so we should expect differences in test results, including different mean scores and standard deviations for score distributions. Perhaps the uncertainty about what a grade-equivalent or grade-placement score really means is sufficient reason to abandon the use of such scores.

STANDARD ERROR OF MEASUREMENT

The computation of this very useful statistical measure was discussed in Chapter 2, but its application in test-data interpretation deserves further elaboration. The term suggests that measurement is subject to error, and this indeed is the case where tests are concerned. We know that every test score has an element of error that stems from such sources as the behavior of the examinee who took the test, testing conditions, the instrument, examiner, etc. When we look at a subject's test score we never know what portion of the score is the true score (the score that the examinee should have made) and what portion is error score. Although error score nearly always contributes only a very small fraction of the obtained score when compared with the true score, the conscientious, thorough test user generally wants to know the standard error of the test in question.

Suppose, for instance, that Tommy Thompson earned a score of 44 on a test. If he were tested again, would he get the same score on the test? Probably not, although that is possible. If he were given the same test several times, one would expect that the scores would vary. Calculation of the mean of the several scores would yield a figure that was rather close to the "true" score for Tommy. Instead of testing Tommy repeatedly, which would be very time-consuming and impractical, one could apply the standard error of measurement to the obtained score and find a confidence interval within which the "true" score is likely to fall. If the standard error for the test that Tommy took were 4 points, one would simply add four points to, and subtract four points from, the obtained score in order to build a confidence interval. The confidence interval in this instance is 40-48. It is reasonable to assume that Tommy's "true" score *probably* lies within the range of 40 to 48. If Tommy were tested repeatedly with the comparable forms of the same test, most of his scores would range between 40 and 48, but some would fall outside the range. One should not state a probability figure (such as 68 percent of the scores will lie within the confidence interval) because the standard error of measurement is applied to the "true" score, and one never knows the "true" score. It is appropriate, however, to say merely that the "true" score *probably* lies within the confidence interval.

The confidence interval (or confidence band) is useful in the interpretation of test scores and in another important way; specifically, in the interpretation of differences between scores. Many tests yield multiple scores, such as the several subtest scores for an aptitude test battery. When there are two or more scores reported, a question arises concerning the significance of differences between the scores. In Figure 11, for example, do the percentile bands (shaded areas) indicate a real difference between the verbal portion of the test and the quantitative part?

The percentile bands in Figure 11 indicate the standard errors of measurement for the three parts of the test (SCAT). Each percentile band covers a distance of one standard error of measurement on either side of the obtained score. These bands also can be considered to be the confidence intervals. Because the bands overlap, one is not justified in assuming that there is a real difference in the person's performance on the verbal and quantitative portions of the test. That is, measurement error could account for the apparent score differences.

CRITERION-REFERENCED AND NORM-REFERENCED MEASUREMENTS

For many years, the standardized tests that were used in the schools provided only *norm-referenced* measurements. This means that the scores earned by the examinees were evaluated in terms of the norms for a comparison group. Although most tests in use today are norm-referenced, some test publishers are providing *criterion-referenced* measurements for their *achievement* tests. The two kinds of measure-

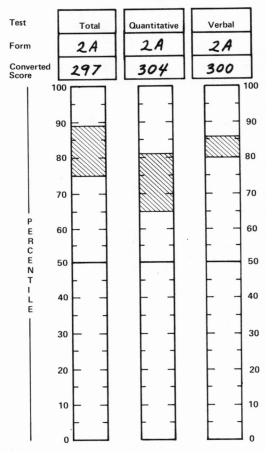

SCAT STUDENT PROFILE
School and College Ability Tests

Figure 11. SCAT student profile. (From SCAT Manual. Reproduced by permission of the copyright owner, Educational Testing Service, Princeton, N.J.)

ments have certain advantages and disadvantages, which will be examined. First, an explanation of the criterion-referenced measure seems to be in order.

While the norm-referenced test will provide a single score as an indicator of achievement in some area, the criterion-referenced test will provide as many scores as there are objectives to be achieved. For example, the *SRA Assessment Survey* (Achievement Series) provides test results for several skill categories (criteria of achievement) for several broad achievement areas. Under the achievement area of Science the skill categories are: Living Things, Matter and Energy, Earth and Space, Experimentation, Charts and Tables, and Reading. A ratio of the number of correctly answered items to the total number of items for each category is reported. This particular instrument provides norm-referenced data as well as criterion-referenced results, as do certain other achievement test batteries.

The norm-referenced test, because of its more extensive sampling of achievement, probably yields a more reliable measure of a pupil's *general* level of achievement in a subject of study, while the criterion-referenced test provides more reliable indications of whether *certain objectives* have been reached. Proponents of *norm-referenced* tests firmly believe that the norm-referenced test, which has been familiar to test users for quite a long time, still serves a useful function, even though in recent years criterion-referenced measurement has received a lot of attention and strong support. As Ebel (1978, p. 4) states:

> If the substance of learning is an infinity of particulars, too numerous to be specified separately, too inter-dependent to be studied or mastered separately; if the goal of learning lies beyond acquisition to understanding; and if understanding results from coming to know the multitude of relationships among the particulars, then a test that probes for these relationships at as many different points and from as many different points as possible is the kind of test that ought to be used. Such a test is now commonly referred to as a norm-referenced test.

W. James Popham (1978), a well-known advocate of *criterion-referenced* tests, has criticized norm-referenced tests with respect to their construction and with respect to their use in schools. He acknowledges that criterion-referenced tests are still in their "infancy" and that there are relatively few now available that are of high quality, but he suggests that more adequate tests of this type can be constructed. According to Popham, criterion-referenced tests will correct three "key deficits" of norm-referenced tests: First, criterion-referenced tests will reduce the discrepancy between what is taught and what is tested; second, criterion-referenced tests will provide more adequate instructional targets by providing more precise descriptions of what is being measured and a greater number of items per measured behavior; third, criterion-referenced tests will retain valid items that are lost through the item-analysis procedure used for norm-referenced test development.

It seems likely that future achievement tests will be both norm-referenced and criterion-referenced. Both types offer advantages to teachers, counselors, and others who use achievement-test results.

TEST INTERPRETATION AIDS

The task of explaining what test scores mean is by no means an easy one, and it behooves the test interpreter to use methods and techniques that clarify verbal statements that are made to the client. Expectancy tables, profiles, and the normal-curve chart can serve as aids in test-interpretation session.

Expectancy Tables

Suppose that students want to know their chances for succeeding in particular courses, or suppose that a personnel officer wants to determine the probability that a job applicant will succeed in a particular job. Questions like these can be partially answered through the use of a chart that may be referred to as an *expectancy table*. Expectancy tables also are known as experience tables or probability tables, for they tell us about the past performance of a group of subjects when their test scores are related to a criterion. Consider the example shown in Figure 12.

The expectancy table shown in Stage 3 at the bottom of Figure 12 shows the relationships between the scholastic aptitude test scores and the criterion scores (grade-point averages) for a hypothetical group of subjects. The chart at the top of Figure 12 (Stage 1) indicates how tally marks were used to indicate how each subject scored with respect to the two variables in question (test score and g.p.a.). For example, the chart indicates that four persons had scores in the range of 71-80. One of these had a g.p.a. in the range of 3.01-3.50, and three had g.p.a. values between 3.51 and 4.00. After the tallies are made, the frequencies in each cell are determined (Stage 2). Finally, the frequencies are converted to percents (Stage 3). Thus, in the score range of 71-80, one person out of four had a g.p.a. between 3.01 and 3.50. The ratio of one-fourth or .25 is equivalent to 25 percent. Likewise, three subjects who scored in the 71-80 range on the test had grade-point averages in the 3.51-4.00 range, so the ratio is three-fourths or .75, which equals 75 percent. Based upon the data shown, it can be said that the probability is 75 percent that a student who scores in the 71-80 range on the scholastic aptitude test will have a g.p.a. somewhere between 3.51 and 4.00. Also, the table shows that there is a 60 percent probability of having a g.p.a. in the range of 1.01-1.50 for the person who has a test score in the 11-20 range.

The expectancy table shown in Figure 13 is based upon *American College Test* (ACT) scores and grade-point averages for a group of 605 college students at a university. The table would be quite useful to a high school or college counselor. For example, a counselor could show a prospective college student how students with a particular ACT score tended to achieve in the past at that university, with respect to grades received.

GRADE-POINT AVERAGE

	SCORE	1.01-1.50	1.51-2.00	2.01-2.50	2.51-3.00	3.01-3.50	3.51-4.00
	71-80					/	///
	61-70				++++	////	///
	51-60			++++	++++ ++++ //	++++ ++++ //	////
	41-50		++++ ////	++++ ++++ ++++ ++++ //	++++ ++++ /	++++ ++++ /	//
Stage 1.							
	31-40		++++ ++++ ++++	++++ ++++ ++++ ++++	++++ ++++	++++	
	21-30	++++	++++ ++++ ++++ ///	++++ ////	////		
	11-20	++++ /	//	//			

SCORE	f	1.01-1.50	1.51-2.00	2.01-2.50	2.51-3.00	3.01-3.50	3.51-4.00
71-80	4					1	3
61-70	12				5	4	3
51-60	33			5	12	12	4
41-50	55		9	22	11	11	2
31-40	50		15	20	10	5	
21-30	36	5	18	9	4		
11-20	10	6	2	2			

Stage 2. (row label at 41-50)

SCORE	1.01-1.50	1.51-2.00	2.01-2.50	2.51-3.00	3.01-3.50	3.51-4.00
71-80					25	75
61-70				42	33	25
51-60			15	36	36	13
41-50		16	40	20	20	4
31-40		30	40	20	10	
21-30	14	50	25	11		
11-20	60	20	20			

Stage 3. (row label at 51-60)

Figure 12. Three stages in the construction of an expectancy table.

In Figure 14, there is a double-entry expectancy table based upon *Academic Promise Test* (APT) scores and grades in science. The table is referred to as a double-entry table because two predictors are used, rather than one. In Figure 14 the predictors are APT-Numerical score and APT Language-Usage score. The scores may be combined to predict grades in science. For example, eleven of the thirty-one students who earned a grade of A in science scored at least 40 on the APT-N test and at least 30 on the APT-LU test. Of the sixty-three

**Expectancy Tables for Total Success Group, Semester 8
(Graduation on Time)**

| | GPA Frequencies | | | | | GPA Percentages[a] | | | |
Group	0.0-1.0	1.1-2.0	2.1-3.0	3.1-4.0	ACT Scores	0.0-1.0	1.1-2.0	2.1-3.0	3.1-4.0
Composite									
139	0	0	52	87	25-36	0	0.00	37.41	62.59
285	0	2	177	106	19-24	0	0.70	62.11	37.19
168	0	1	145	22	13-18	0	0.60	86.31	13.09
13	0	0	12	1	1-12	0	0.00	92.31	7.69
605	0	3	386	216		0.00	0.50	63.80	35.70
Males									
74	0	0	31	43	25-36	0	0.00	41.89	58.11
102	0	1	66	35	19-24	0	0.98	64.71	34.31
53	0	1	45	7	13-18	0	1.89	84.90	13.21
6	0	0	5	1	1-12	0	0.00	83.33	16.67
235	0	2	147	86		0.00	0.85	62.55	36.60
Females									
65	0	0	21	44	25-36	0	0.00	32.31	67.69
183	0	1	111	71	19-24	0	0.55	60.65	38.80
115	0	0	100	15	13-18	0	0.00	86.96	13.04
7	0	0	7	0	1-12	0	0.00	100.00	0.00
370	0	1	239	130		0.00	0.27	74.59	35.14

[a]All rows = 100%.

Figure 13. An expectancy table based upon ACT scores and grade-point averages. (From: Robert W. Rowan, "The Predictive Value of the ACT at Murray State University Over a Four-Year College Program." *Measurement and Evaluation in Guidance,* 11 (3), October, 1978, p. 148. Copyright 1978 American Personnel and Guidance Association. Reprinted with permission.

students who scored 19 or below on both tests, only one earned an A, two earned Bs, 22 had Cs, 19 had Ds, and 19 had Es in science. The combination of APT-N and APT-LU scores provides a good basis for predicting grades in science for the students represented in the table.

Expectancy tables are useful because they are easy to construct, simple to understand, and useful in revealing the relationships between predictor variables and a certain criterion. Thus, they can be used effectively to interpret data for students, teachers, parents, supervisors, applicants for positions, etc. There are limitations, however, to the use of expectancy tables. One shortcoming is that a considerable amount of time may be needed to collect the necessary data. A second limitation is that a particular table is valid only for the group for whom the data were collected, so generalization of the results to other groups must be made with extreme caution. Another limitation is that a particular individual may not perform in the manner that the table indi-

Relationship between APT-N and APT-LU Scores, and Grades in Science
Seventh Grade Students (N = 294)

Numerical Score	Language Usage Score 19 & below	20-29	30-39	40 & above	Row Total
40 & above	A B C D E	A B C 2 D E	A 6 B 6 C 1 D E	A 5 B 2 C 1 D E	A 11 B 8 C 4 D E
30-39	A 1 B C 2 D E 1	A 1 B 7 C 8 D E	A 4 B 12 C 12 D E	A 5 B 10 C 3 D E	A 11 B 29 C 25 D E 1
20-29	A 2 B 3 C 9 D 8 E 3	A 3 B 7 C 25 D 6 E 7	A B 6 C 17 D 1 E	A 1 B 8 C 2 D E	A 6 B 24 C 53 D 15 E 10
19 & below	A 1 B 2 C 22 D 19 E 19	A 1 B 2 C 18 D 6 E 4	A 1 B C 1 D E 1	A B C D E	A 3 B 4 C 41 D 25 E 24
Column Total (by grade)	A 4 B 5 C 33 D 27 E 23	A 5 B 16 C 53 D 12 E 11	A 11 B 24 C 31 D 1 E 1	A 11 B 20 C 6 D E	**Grand Total** A 31 B 65 C 123 D 40 E 35

Figure 14. Double-entry expectancy table based upon two different test scores and grades in science. (From: *Test Service Bulletin No. 56.* Used with permission of The Psychological Corporation.)

cates. Error in measurement and variability of human performance can lead to results that a given expectancy table does not indicate. That is, the table is seldom reliable for all of the individuals with whom it is intended to be used. The user of the table should be alert for the exceptions to the rule.

Test Profile

The test profile, which may be called a psychograph, is a graphic representation of the results of a number of tests. The results may apply to one individual or for a whole group, and they are expressed in comparable terms, such as percentile ranks or standard scores. Generally speaking, a profile has several derived scores reported for one individual, and the scores are for the subtests of a test battery.

Test profiles have some important advantages. First, they provide a convenient means of presenting related test data to the examinee who took the tests or to the professional who is interested in the data. That is to say, related data are presented together on a single sheet that may be handled and examined with comparative ease. Second, the use of a profile greatly enhances the explanation of the meaning of related data. The test results can be seen in relation to a mean score and in relation to the other scores that make up the profile. Finally, the profile shows the strengths and weaknesses of examinees, and this may be important with respect to their gaining self-understanding, for they can see that their traits or abilities vary — that their test performances will vary from test to test, and that they are not simply average, gifted, or dull individuals. Of course, a few examinees will score high or low on all the tests included in the profile.

In using profiles, we must always be aware of the limitations of the tests and be alert for the possibility that the profile is not accurate. If the data are faulty, for any reason, the profile will simply present an inaccurate picture of the examinee.

It would be impractical or impossible to present illustrations of all possible profile sheets that are currently in use. Instead a few commonly used profile sheets will be discussed to introduce this kind of test-interpretation aid. In subsequent chapters other profiles will be discussed.

The profile in Figure 15 has straight lines connecting the points that indicate the score on each of the aptitudes measured by the instrument. Such a profile is simple and easy to read. The interpretation of the scores is enhanced when the profile is used to interpret the data for a person whose knowledge of tests and measurements is very limited.

The profile in Figure 16 has bars or columns to show the score recorded for the various subtests that make up the *Academic Promise Test*

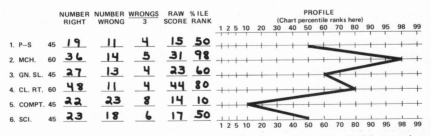

Figure 15. A sample profile of *Aptitude Tests for Occupations*. (Used with permission of Bobbs-Merrill Company, Inc.)

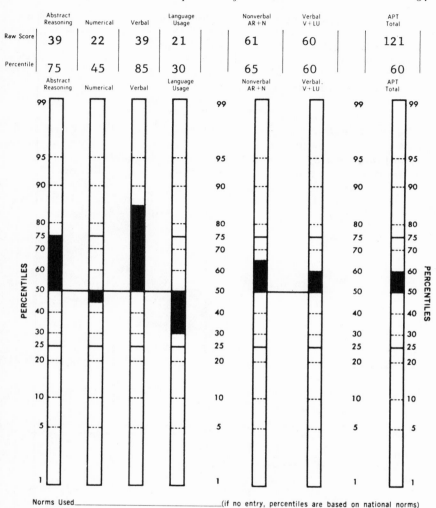

Figure 16. A sample profile of *Academic Promise Tests*. (Reproduced by permission of The Psychological Corporation.)

battery. The score for the combinations of AR + N and V + LU are shown as well as the APT total score. The APT Student Report Form that includes the profile of scores has some excellent features, such as the purposes of the test, the meanings of the terms used for the abilities (abstract reasoning, numerical, verbal, and language usage), and an explanation of the process of deciding whether subtest scores are significantly different.

The two different profiles just presented are only meant to serve as an introduction of an important device for aiding in the complex process of test-data interpretation. In subsequent chapters other profiles will be introduced and discussed. It goes without saying that a profile has little value for the unsophisticated student or client unless there is an adequate interpretation of the data displayed in the profile.

Normal-Curve Chart

The normal-curve chart shown in Figure 17 is useful in the interpretation of test results when one can assume that there is a normal distribution of scores for the same group of individuals. For tests that are standardized, and have been administered to hundreds or thousands of persons, a normal distribution of the scores is generally assumed. The normal-curve chart is useful to the test user, because it permits moving vertically to transform one kind of score to another.

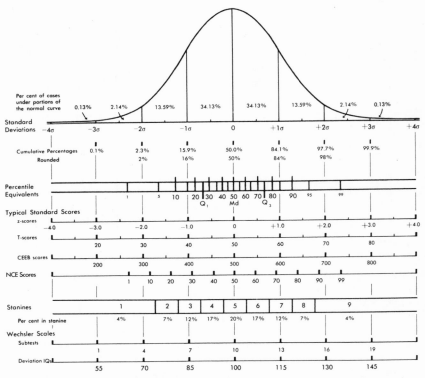

Figure 17. A normal-curve chart. (Reproduced by permission of The Psychological Corporation.)

Let us assume that Sandy Shore had a CEEB score of 700. On the chart in Figure 17, this score is the equivalent of a stanine score of 9, a *T*-score of 70, a *z*-score of 2.00, and a percentile rank of 98. We can also say that Sandy had a score that was two standard deviations above the mean. We could not say with certainty what her Wechsler Scale score or AGCT score would be because those are tests that are different from the CEEB test, and have different norm groups.

The normal-curve chart is useful to the knowledgeable test user, but generally would not be helpful to a student, parent, or client in a counseling situation because of a lack of understanding of the concepts involved.

SUGGESTIONS FOR CONDUCTING A TEST-INTERPRETATION INTERVIEW

The interpretation of test data in an interview with an examinee is of the utmost importance because of the possible consequences of the experience. A well-conducted interview can lead to such positive outcomes as increased self-understanding, enhancement of the decision-making process, and personal growth; however, a poor interview can have negative consequences. The possible negative outcomes include confusion, misconceptions, unrealistic vocational choices, and diminished self-esteem. The following rules are offered as a means of maximizing the value of a test-interpretation interview.

1. Review the test and test data in order to be familiar with them before discussing them with the examinee or client.
2. Try to put the examinee or client at ease before beginning the discussion of the test data.
3. Try to determine what the examinee expects to learn from the data.
4. Try to make certain that the client knows what each test is supposed to measure.
5. Use terms and expressions that are likely to be understood by the individual.
6. Use graphic aids, such as profile sheets, expectancy tables, or other charts to facilitate the explanation of test results.
7. Be mindful of the fact that validity is a function of the use made of the test as well as of the test itself.
8. Be aware of all relevant variables related to the test data, and be mindful of the fact that test scores are only segments of a large and complex picture.
9. Encourage the interviewee to express attitudes, feelings, concerns, and perceptions relative to the test results.
10. Value the examinee more than the test results.
11. Be realistic in the use of test and inventories.

12. Treat test results as confidential information, and try to make certain that examinees do not have to reveal their scores to others.

REFERENCES

Aiken, Lewis R.: *Psychological Testing and Assessment,* 3rd. Boston, Allyn and Bacon, 1976.

Andrulis, Richard A. and Bajtelsmith, John: *Adult Assessment: A Source of Tests and Measures of Human Behavior.* Springfield, Illinois, Charles C Thomas, 1977.

Brown, Joe and Kiltveit, Thomas: Individual assessment: a systematic approach. *Personnel and Guidance Journal, 55:*271-276, January, 1977.

Cunningham, William: How to explain tests scores to parents. *School Management, 12:*86-87, 1968.

DeBlassie, Richard R.: Test anxiety: Education's hang-up. *The Clearing House, 46:*526-530, 1972.

Ebel, Robert L.: The case for norm-referenced measurements. *Educational Researcher, 7:*3-5, 1978.

Forsyth, Laurie B.: After testing is over. *The Guidance Clinic, 8:*809, 1976.

Goodenough, F. L.: *Mental Testing: Its History, Principles and Applications.* New York, Holt, 1949.

Lister, James L. and McKenzie, Donald H.: A framework for the improvement of test interpretation in counseling. *Personnel and Guidance Journal, 45*(1):61-65, 1966.

Lyman, Howard B.: *Test Scores and What They Mean,* 3rd ed. Englewood Cliffs, New Jersey, Prentice-Hall, 1978.

Massad, Carolyn E.: Interpreting and using test norms. *The Reading Teacher, 27:*286-292.

Noeth, Richard J.: Converting student data to counseling information. *Measurement and Evaluation in Guidance, 9:*60-69, 1976.

Popham, W. James: The case for criterion-referenced measurements. *Educational Researcher, 7:*6-10, 1978.

Predizer, Dale J. and Fought, Louise: Local test validation and use of results. *Measurement and Evaluation in Guidance, 5:*366-372.

Robb, G. P., Bernardoni, L. C., and Johnson, R. W.: *Assessment of Individual Mental Ability.* New York, Harper and Row, 1972.

Rost, Paul: Useful interpretations of standardized tests. *The Clearing House, 47:*319-320, 1973.

Rowan, Robert W.: The predictive validity of the ACT at Murray State University over a four-year college program. *Measurement and Evaluation in Guidance, 11*(3):143-149, 1978.

Seashore, H. G. (Ed.): Expectancy tables — a way of interpreting test validity. *The Psychological Corporation Test Service Bulletin, 38:*11-15, 1949.

———— (Ed.): How accurate is a test score? *The Psychological Corporation Test Service Bulletin, 50:*1-3, 1956.

———— (Ed.): Norms must be relevant. *The Psychological Corporation Test Service Bulletin, 39:*16-19, 1950.

Snyder, Frank W. (Ed.): *Parent's Guide to Understanding Tests.* CTB/McGraw-Hill, New York, 1976.

Thompson, Albert P.: Client misconceptions in vocational counseling. *Personnel and Guidance Journal, 50:*30-33, 1976.

Wesman, A. G.: Double entry expectancy tables — a way of interpreting test validity. *The Psychological Corporation Test Service Bulletin, 56:*1-12, 1966.

Chapter 5

NONTEST APPRAISAL METHODS AND TECHNIQUES

C ERTAIN HUMAN TRAITS and aspects of behavior can be assessed better with nontest techniques or procedures than they can with tests and inventories. The nontest techniques generally are nonstandardized, so their validity and reliability tend to be somewhat difficult to evaluate. Even so, some counselors and teachers who eschew testing are willing to use nontest procedures for appraisal purposes. Obviously, the two sources of appraisal data can be complementary.

Several nontest procedures will be discussed in this chapter. Those that have been included were selected because they are relatively easy to construct and use, and because they have relatively high potential for yielding useful appraisal data. The order of presentation has no particular relevance.

OBSERVATIONAL PROCEDURES

Direct systematic observation of an individual's behavior can be an excellent procedure for collecting appraisal data, provided that the observer is alert, perceives accurately, and reports objectively on the observation made. Mental alertness is necessary in order to catch the most significant aspects of behavior. Accurate perception is necessary because an observer's emotions, biases, motives, and values can operate to distort perceptions of people and events observed. Objective reporting is necessary in order to provide a valid record of the observation for those who must make use of the data acquired.

The recording of an observation is quite important, for an accurate record generally must be available for future use. A videotape recording may be made if equipment and facilities are available, and the tape can be studied later to obtain specific information. When such recording is not feasible or possible, an observer can take notes or use a prepared checklist. The checklist (or an outline if one is used) should be well designed, with special attention given to the kinds of behavior or characteristics to be observed. In some instances the observer actually can be seen by the person being observed and may even be a participant in an activity with the observed individual. In such a situation, the note taking may have to wait until after the observation period is terminated.

Preparation for a formal observation includes deciding what kind of behavior to look for, determining where and when that behavior can best be observed and under what conditions, and determining whether a series of observations should be made. Generally it is advisable for the observer to observe a single subject at a time and concentrate on a single behavior, but there are some instances in which a whole group should be observed and perhaps more than one behavior assessed. It is recommended that there be frequent observations of an individual spread out over a period of a few weeks and at different times of the day, if possible, in order to provide a good sample of the behavior.

Even when a formal observation is made and reported by a competent observer, there are some limitations for this appraisal technique. One shortcoming is that when individuals know they are being observed they may not display their typical behavior. That is, they may intentionally try to create a favorable or unfavorable impression on the observer. Observations are relatively time-consuming, and they will not always yield the data hoped for, so these are possible drawbacks for the technique. Finally, when it is necessary to observe without the subject's knowing about the observation, special equipment and facilities (such as one-way vision glass, a special recording system, and a camera) may be needed, and these may not be available.

Anecdotal Record

As the name implies, the anecdotal record is a report made of an informal, or unplanned, observation. A teacher, for example, may observe an incident that occurred in a classroom, in a school corridor, or on a playground and write a report describing the event. This kind of report, which may be as brief as a single sentence, or as long as a few paragraphs, is referred to as an *anecdotal record*. An example is provided in Figure 18.

Notice that the anecdotal record form has space allotted for the date of the incident, place where it occurred, description of the instrument, and comments. A well-written anecdotal report may provide useful information related to an individual's personal characteristics or behavior. The well-written report need not be lengthy, but it must meet certain criteria:

1. The date of occurrence of the incident should be shown, and the report should be written as soon as possible after the behavior occurred. The date is important in judging the relevance of the information and in establishing the sequence of time when several reports have been written for the individual.
2. The place where the incident took place should be noted. Shouting at a party is likely to have a different meaning than shouting in class.
3. The anecdotal record should be selective. That is, only relevant details that seem to have significance should be recorded. Trivial or irrelevant events or details should not be included in the report.
4. The anecdotal record should be specific rather than general. A

ANECDOTAL RECORD

Student_____Barbara Johnson_____   Class_Tenth-grade English_

Date	Place	Incident	Comments
5-9-79	Classroom	Barbara, who always seems to be very cheerful and enthusiastic in class, seemed to be very quiet and sorrowful today. After class I asked her whether anything was wrong, and she said "no" in an almost inaudible voice.	I feel certain that something significant has happened in Barbara's life to cause her to have this sudden and extreme change of mood. I will check again in a day or two.

Observer_____Paula Sullivan_____

Figure 18. An anecdotal record form.

statement such as "seems to be interested in group activities" is too general to be useful to a teacher or counselor.

5. The description of the incident should be as accurate, complete, and factual as possible. The reporting should be objective, with any interpretation of what occurred or why it occurred, written separately as a comment. The "mixed" anecdotal report is undesirable because it forces the reader to attempt to distill the factual account from the total report, and this may be an impossible task in some instances.

While the anecdotal record has such important values as providing useful information concerning students, providing samples of relevant behavior, and encouraging school personnel to focus on individual behavior rather than group behavior, the device also has some limitations that should be noted:

1. Anecdotal reporting requires a definite skill that some school personnel do not possess, so some of the records will be incomplete, inaccurate, or misleading.
2. Even when well written, the anecdotal record provides a rather limited sample of behavior.
3. Unless there are safeguards, a majority of the records may be negative, and useful positive incidents will not be reported. Furthermore, the negative statements may be remembered long after they are no longer valid.
4. There is risk involved in reporting an incident out of the setting which it occurred and reporting it in isolation.

5. The writing of good anecdotal records requires an investment of time that school personnel may not have or be willing to make, thus the use of the device may be severely curtailed.

Caution must be used to make certain that the writing of anecdotal reports does not violate school policy or state and federal laws. The Family Educational Rights and Privacy Act of 1974, designed to protect the privacy of students, permits students and parents access to students records. Therefore, it would be wise for school personnel to refrain from writing reports that could be interpreted as defamatory or detrimental to the welfare of the student. If a school's policy prohibits the placement of negative reports in the student's cumulative record, the value of anecdotal records will be diminished somewhat. There still may be, however, enough value in positive or neutral reports to make them useful.

Rating Scales

As is the case with anecdotal records, rating scales provide a record of one or more observations of an individual's behavior. A rating scale requires essentially that the rater evaluate a person with respect to certain traits or characteristics.

Rating scales can vary considerably in terms of appearance and structure, but in general they consist of a set of descriptive words, phrases, or statements to be checked by a rater who can make judgments about the person to be rated. Sometimes the scales require that persons rate themselves on the dimensions in question, and then of course they are self-rating appraisal tools.

Three common types of rating scales are the graphic scale, descriptive scale, and numerical scale. The basic *graphic* rating provides a continuum for each characteristic or behavior to be considered.

The *descriptive scale,* which is very similar to the graphic scale, contains descriptive words or phrases that indicate the extent to which the person rated possesses the characteristics in question. The example in Figure 19A illustrates such a scale.

Either of the two types of scales can be altered to make a *numerical* scale. All that would be required would be to add the numerals 1, 2, 3, 4, and 5 to the top of the scale in order to obtain a quantified rating for each trait and/or the whole scale. For instance, one could modify the Behavior Rating Scale as shown in Figure 19B.

Because sometimes it is difficult to find a published rating scale that fits a particular population or situation well, it may become necessary to construct one. By using the following rules, one can minimize construction and rating errors and thus improve the quality and validity of a rating scale:

1. Provide clear directions for use by raters.
2. Provide ample space between the items.

BEHAVIOR RATING SCALE

Directions: Place an X in the box to indicate the general frequency of occurrence of each behavior stated below.

Behavior	Rating				
	Never	Seldom	Sometimes	Usually	Always
1. Accepts constructive criticism					
2. Shows concern for others					
3. Follows instructions					
4. Expresses creative ideas					
5. Gets along with others					
6. Shares ideas with others					
7. Appears cheerful and optimistic					
8. Expresses own opinions					
9. Seeks approval of others					
10. Exhibits calm, relaxed behavior					

Figure 19. Example of a descriptive rating scale.

3. Provide only enough items to obtain the data needed.
4. Define traits or characteristics included in the scale.
5. When phrases are used, underline the key words.
6. Only include traits or behavior that are readily observed.
7. In descriptive scales that call for graduation or degree levels, define the levels clearly.

Behavior	Rating				
	Never 1	Seldom 2	Sometimes 3	Usually 4	Always 5
1. Accepts constructive criticism					
2. Shows concern for others					

Figure 19B. Modified description rating scale.

8. When a rating line is used, have the neutral or average point at the center of the line.
9. If possible, avoid the use of phrases that are so extreme raters will seldom mark them.
10. Have space on the scale designated for the name of the person to be rated, the date of the rating, and the signature of the rater.

Rating scales can furnish a rather quick means of providing appraisal data, provided the rater is familiar with the behavior of the person being rated and provided the rater perceives others accurately. There are certain errors that occur with such frequency that the results of rating scales should be considered cautiously. These common errors are referred to as halo effect, personal bias, generosity error, error of central tendency, and logical error.

Halo effect refers to the rating error that is made when a rater tends to rate a subject as being high on several different traits because of a general impression formed of that person. For example, if rater Jones values conformity highly, any highly conforming person is likely to be rated high on all the traits of the scale by Jones. The reverse of this condition, the "olah" effect, occurs when the rater lets a negative impression concerning a trait affect all ratings for the individual being rated.

Personal bias is a common error that occurs because the rater is prejudiced with respect to a certain group of persons. The bias, which may be racial, political, religious, etc., can result in unduly high or low ratings for a rated person who belongs to the particular group if the rater is biased and allows the bias to prevail. For instance, a rater who is biased against blacks will tend to rate blacks unjustifiably low on many or all of the characteristics listed on the scale.

Generosity error refers to the tendency of some raters to rate every individual as average or above on all traits. It might be referred to as leniency error because the rater seems reluctant to give low ratings even when they are justified.

Error of central tendency occurs when raters mark the subject as average on all characteristics included in the scale. This often occurs when the rater does not know the person well enough to make good judgments about the traits or behavior to be considered, and thus decides to minimize errors by marking down the middle of the scale. Thus, although Mike Danner is a very sociable person, the rater does not really remember Mike well, so the rater may guess at the middle of the scale rather than the low end, and hope to avoid a very large error.

Logical error occurs when the rater does not understand the meaning of one or more of the terms used in the scale, and therefore rates the person erroneously. If a word such as *initiative* is not understood by the rater, an error in judging the person on that trait can easily occur. Like the other errors just discussed, it occurs so often that it is labeled as a *common error.*

METHODS OF QUESTIONING

Sometimes all that one needs to do to get appraisal information is simply ask questions. The questions may relate to many different areas of inquiry, such as attitudes, opinions, experiences, behaviors, goals, etc. Although there are other questioning devices that may serve a useful purpose in appraisal, the three most commonly used ones are the *survey interview,* the *questionnaire,* and the *checklist.*

Survey Interview

This type of interview, which may be called a fact-finding interview, should not be confused with the counseling or therapeutic interview. The counseling interview is not conducted to acquire data (although there may be some information received) but rather to bring about change in client attitudes or behavior.

The survey interview may be either *structured* or *unstructured.* If it is structured, each person who is interviewed is asked the same questions in the same order and same manner. Some structured interviews require that the answers fit a standard scoring system to facilitate data processing. The unstructured interview permits a more flexible approach in questioning, because there are no restrictions placed upon questions asked or the responses given. Thus, the interviewer is free to vary the questions or to follow responses with additional related questions. While the structured interview has the possible advantages of greater control and simplified data processing, the unstructured interview has the possible advantages of questioning in depth and following up important cues.

In preparing a survey the interviewer should decide what data are needed, what type of interview seems to be most advantageous (structured or unstructured), and how the responses to the questions will be recorded and processed.

Having prepared an interview format, the interviewer should give careful consideration to the interviewing *process*. First and foremost, a positive relationship between interviewer and client is important. Good rapport enables the client to feel at ease and free to answer questions freely. Rapport can be enhanced by greeting the client in a friendly manner, offering a comfortable chair, and initiating a pleasant conversation. A smiling, relaxed interviewer will model relaxed behavior for a client, and thus facilitate the interview process.

Response elicitation is the second phase of the interview process. In this part of the interview, the questions are asked and responses are recorded (either by writing down the responses or making a recording of the interview). Attention to the following rules will promote the collection of usable interview data:

1. Make sure that the client understands the question.
2. Repeat a question if it seems necessary to do so.
3. Avoid suggesting answers to the questions.
4. Listen carefully to the client's responses.
5. When the client answers the questions, observe facial expressions, gestures, tone of voice, posture, and other nonverbal expressions.
6. Be alert for responses that seem to be vague or evasive.
7. Keep the interview moving, but allow sufficient time for responses.
8. If a controversial topic emerges, maintain a neutral position during the interview.
9. Tactfully bring the interviewee back to the question if the individual strays from it.
10. In an unstructured interview, ask additional questions to clarify responses, to follow-up cues, and to obtain additional data.

The use of a tape recorder provides the interviewer with an accurate record of the interview, provided that the apparatus is functioning properly. If the subject should object to having a recording made, or if for some other reason one cannot use a tape recorder, it becomes necessary to take good notes that include responses to questions and perhaps other information, such as client behavior during the interview. Even when a tape recording is made, a few notes probably should be taken. Another suggestion that has merit is to compare the client's responses with similar data from other sources as a means of checking on the accuracy and veracity of responses, if such other data can be obtained.

Questionnaire

Because of its adaptiveness, flexibility, and relative simplicity, the questionnaire has been used extensively for a long period of time as a tool for collecting information of various kinds. This is not to say, however, that anyone can put together a set of questions quickly and have a good data-collecting instrument.

As the name implies, the questionnaire is a set of questions or statements to which a person is asked to respond. The questions or statements may ask for attitudes, facts, opinions, or other data. The questionnaire may be designed for administration to a single person or a large group of subjects, and it may be administered by mail, for convenience.

Very few questionnaires will fit more than a single purpose or population of subjects, and thus a questionnaire often must be specifically designed to fit the needs of a particular situation. A questionnaire should be designed with an attractive format in order to gain acceptance. Attractiveness can be enhanced by selecting a title that is clear, as concise as possible, and descriptive of the project for which it is to be used (such as a follow-up study). The questions or statements should be well typed or printed, well spaced, and easy to read. Similar questions should be grouped together, if possible.

Questionnaire items generally may be classified as open-form or closed-form items. The *open-form* (or open-end) item is a "free response" question or statement, because following the item there is space provided for the respondent to write in an answer. An example follows:

What are your education/occupation plans after graduation?

_____

_____

The *closed-form* item is rigidly structured, or restricted, because the respondent's answer to an item is limited to certain choices or options, such as "yes" or "no." Variations may include underlining a selected word or phrase, checking a response from a list of responses, or ranking choices. An example follows:

How often have you sought the help of a school counselor during the past year? —— Often (at least 10 times); —— Occasionally (fewer than 10 times); —— Never.

The closed form item has the advantage of facilitating the tabulation and processing of data and improving the reliability of the data collected, but this item type has certain limitations:

1. The respondent is not permitted to explain why certain responses are given.
2. In scope and depth the responses are restricted, and therefore so is the use of the item for measuring attitudes or feelings.
3. At times the available responses provided in the questionnaire are not appropriate for the respondent.

The usability, validity, and reliability of a questionnaire can be enhanced through adherence to certain criteria for construction of the instrument. These criteria follow:

1. Each item used should be relevant.
2. Each item should be grammatically correct.
3. Each item should be written as clearly and succinctly as possible.
4. Key words in the items should be underlined for emphasis.
5. When choices are provided, they should be relatively easy to make.
6. Qualitative words (such as "good" or "bad" or "few" or "many") should be avoided, if possible.
7. Items should be stated in such a way that biased responses are minimized.
8. Only enough items should be used to collect the data desired; the questionnaire should be as short as possible.
9. Open-form items generally should be stated in a manner that will elicit depth of response.
10. Items should be stated in such a way that they are not likely to be objectionable to respondents.

Having decided what format and item type to use for the questionnaire, one can proceed with the writing of a sufficient number of suitable items. Generally speaking, it is advisable to produce a first draft of the instrument, have it examined and critiqued by another qualified person, and then perhaps try out a second draft on a few suitable subjects. The try-out can be useful in making the final questionnaire.

For individual appraisal purposes, it is necessary to have a place on the questionnaire where the name of the respondent can be written — to identify the sources of the data when necessary. For *group* appraisal it often is not necessary to ask for names, and this practice may yield more complete data because some respondents will respond more freely when they need not identify themselves. When names are required, the respondents should be informed that the results will be held in strict confidence, and this pledge should be honored strictly.

Cover and Follow-up Letters

When a questionnaire is mailed to a respondent it should be accompanied by a cover letter that includes an explanation of the purpose of the questionnaire and a request that the instrument be completed and returned to the sender. A self-addressed return envelope will generally facilitate the return of questionnaires. If the questionnaire is sponsored by a school or agency, that information should be provided in the cover letter.

A follow-up letter generally should be sent to those persons who fail to return a questionnaire, if they can be identified through a record-keeping process. Along with the follow-up letter, a second copy of the questionnaire may be sent to anyone who failed to respond, just to replace one that may have been lost or misplaced. Also, a telephone call may be made to request the return of a questionnaire.

There are some shortcomings of questionnaires that should be kept in mind by those who use them. For instance, one can not know the extent to which each respondent has answered accurately or truthfully. Also, some responses may be incomplete or some questionnaires may be only partially completed. Faulty memory or distorted perceptions may reduce the validity of responses. If the forms are mailed, the percent of return may be small, and the sample may be biased. These shortcomings may not always be present when a questionnaire is used, but if they are, the data collected may be of doubtful value.

Checklist

A special structured form of questionnaire is the *checklist*. This instrument consists of a set of words, phrases, or sentences to be checked by a respondent. Generally speaking, checklists are designed to acquire data pertaining to preferences, attitudes, behaviors, etc. Checklists are relatively easy to construct and administer.

Some *published* checklists are available for appraisal purposes, among these being the *Money Problem Check List, Billett-Starr Youth Problems Inventory,* and *SRA Youth Inventory.* These three instruments are designed to help counselors, teachers, psychologists, and others identify the problems of individuals or groups. Manuals are available to aid in the administration and scoring of the checklists and in the interpretation of results. The *Walker Problem Behavior Identification Checklist* is another example of a published checklist, and it is designed to collect data pertaining to the nature of children's behavioral problems.

The strengths and weaknesses of the checklist are very similar to those for a closed-form questionnaire. As with other forms of questionnaires, the amount of valid, reliable data collected can vary greatly.

AUTOBIOGRAPHY

The autobiography simply is a written account of an individual's life history. The story may be told in a relatively lengthy fashion or it may be brief; it may be relatively complete or incomplete; and it may be highly accurate or inaccurate. Consider what an eighth-grade student once wrote for one of her teachers:

> When I was in sixth grade, I was a typical sixth grader. I had straight, sensible hair, straight, sensible clothes for my straight, sensible figure and received high grades in school. My teachers loved me, my parents loved me, my parents' friends loved me. I am now in eighth grade. I have indecent, ratted hair, indecent clothes at an indecent length, wear too much makeup, and am lucky if I'll be in ninth grade next year. My teachers hate me, my parents hate me, my parents' friends hate me, and sometimes I hate myself.

This is not a typical autobiography because it is much too short to tell much about the individual's life history. It deals briefly with a very limited aspect of a girl's life — her feelings about herself. Yet, even such a partial autobiography can reveal an "inside" portion of her life that might otherwise go undetected, provided that the student is honest and not trying to deceive, impress, or shock the teacher.

Autobiographies may be classified in different ways. For example, an autobiography may be structured or unstructured. If it is of the *unstructured* type, the person is merely asked to "write the story of your life." No outline is given or suggested, and the author of the autobiography must decide what to write about. When the structured type of autobiography is used, the writer follows a suggested outline, such as the one in Figure 20.

The outline in Figure 20 is only an example of how an autobiography might be structured. The exact nature of the outline or instructions given to the writer of the autobiography should be based upon the needs of the situation, the age of the writer, the purposes of the autobiography, and other relevant factors.

Structuring an autobiography provides some assurance that the writers will discuss specific aspects of their lives, and structuring seems to make the task easier for those who have difficulty expressing themselves in writing. On the other hand, the unstructured autobiography

MY LIFE

Family
> My parents
> My brothers and sisters
> Activities of my family

Friends
> The special qualities or characteristics of my friends
> Activities with my friends

School history
> My attitude toward school
> My feeling about teachers
> My feeling about subjects studied
> My academic record in school

Health
> My present health status
> My past illnesses
> My previous accidents or injuries

Hobbies and Interests
> Things that I like to do
> Things that I would like to be able to do
> Things that I do especially well

Plans for the Future
> My educational goals
> My vocational goals
> Other future goals

Figure 20. Outline for an autobiography.

may facilitate the discussion of important matters that are not specifically called for in the outline.

Autobiographies may also be categorized as *topical* and *comprehensive*. The topical type is limited to one aspect of the person's life, such as the family. The comprehensive type covers a wide range of interrelated life experiences over a relatively long period of time. The topical type has the possible advantage of getting detailed information on a specific aspect of the person's life because the writer is encouraged to focus on one specified area. The disadvantage, however, is that many other important areas probably will not be covered, and the interrelationships of the many facets of the person's life may be missing. While the comprehensive type is generally preferred, the topical autobiography should be considered for special purposes or situations.

Having a person write a partial or relatively complete life history report has certain advantages. This experience may help the writer clarify feelings, attitudes, and goals. For instance, the experience may afford students with a good opportunity to think about themselves systematically, and thus gain some personal insights. Writing about oneself can be *supportive*, for the individual may be able to perceive some important positive behaviors or qualities and may perceive that someone cares. The task of writing the document may be *cathartic* if the individual is able to release some pent-up emotions during or after the writing. Because this experience of writing about one's self can elicit emotions or concerns, *counseling* should be available to those who write autobiographies. That is to say, the person whose feelings have been aroused should have the opportunity to talk with a trained professional who can help that person deal with those feelings and related concerns.

Autobiographies need not be limited to use in schools, but when they are used in schools, certain suggestions are in order. One is that the autobiography should be used as an appraisal device and should not be graded as an English theme would be. If the paper is considered to be a course requirement, and graded as such, much of the appraisal value is likely to be lost. Another suggestion is that autobiographies should not be written every semester or every year. If the writing is too frequent, students will lose interest in the activity, and it will become a meaningless experience. It is suggested that students be told about the activity, and then a few days should be allowed for them to think about what they will write. Then a class period can be used for the actual writing. Finally, the students should always be informed about the purpose of the autobiography. They should know who will read the papers and why the request is being made. This gives them the opportunity to disclose whatever they choose to disclose, and it affords them the right to know how the information will be used.

What should one look for when reading and analyzing an autobiography? First, the general appearance and impression of the paper may yield some useful information. A lengthy paper *could* indicate writing ability, a high level of motivation for writing, or a subconscious desire to seek help. Conversely, a short paper might indicate poor motivation for writing, difficulty with writing, or reluctance to self-disclose. A carelessly written or messy paper might indicate indifference toward the assignment or a general tendency toward slovenliness. Whether the person usually performs in such a manner would have to be determined through examining other samples of written work.

In reading the autobiography one should also consider carefully the content of the paper. What has the subject written about, and what has been omitted? Are emotionally charged words, such as love or hate, used frequently? What general mood is conveyed? Are there apparent errors or discrepancies in the paper?

The answers to the questions posed above may give the reader a much better understanding of the subject than would be possible without the autobiography. Essentially, the paper can give the reader a view of the "inside" portion of a person that is not readily perceived by others. Autobiographies, however, have some serious limitations. Their value depends upon the willingness of the person to write honestly about personal matters, the ability to express thoughts in writing, and the level of self-understanding. Thus, the validity of an autobiography is difficult to assess. Knowledge of the author of the paper, in some instances, can be used to verify the accuracy of the content.

SOCIOMETRIC TECHNIQUES

The term sociometry refers to the measurement of the social relationships that prevail among a group of individuals. Social relationships may have an important bearing upon the way individuals function in such settings as school, home, or work. Generally speaking, people need a certain amount of social acceptance and social status in order to be able to lead reasonably happy and successful lives. When social needs are not met, various aspects of living are likely to be affected adversely.

While one could assess social interaction by means of observation, a more systematic approach is to make use of one of the sociometric techniques. The sociometric techniques permit graphic and quantitative representations of social interaction in a group to which a particular individual belongs. One commonly used sociometric tool is the sociogram.

Sociogram

A sociogram is simply a diagram that shows lines of social interaction for a particular group of people. By examining a sociogram for a group, one can acquire knowledge of individual social preferences, group leadership, and the degree of group integration.

To construct a basic sociogram, one normally begins with a sociometric question, or criterion, such as "With whom would you prefer to work on a small-group science project? Each member of a group is asked to write down the names of the preferred persons on a sheet of paper and sign the sheet. These sheets are then collected from the group members. If a special form is used for this purpose, it might be constructed as shown in Figure 21.

Directions:
In order to improve my understanding of you, and to be able to work with you more effectively, I need some sociometric information. This simply means that I wish to know which people you would prefer to be with in a specified situation. The responses you make will not be revealed to the other students.

Question:
With which three persons in this class would you most like to work on a social studies project? List the names of your first, second, and third choices.

1. _____

2. _____

3. _____

_____
Your Name

Figure 21. A sociometric question form.

At the time that this procedure is carried out, an effort should be made to ensure that the group members understand what they are being asked to do and the reason for the request. Furthermore, they should be told that the information obtained will be kept confidential to the extent that their choices will not be revealed to other group members. The sociometric question may be written to ask for the names of group members that the person does *not* want to be with. For example, "Which person (or persons) do you prefer *not* to have on your committee?" There is a serious limitation involved in asking the negative question: it may suggest that people should reject other people.

Certain basic assumptions should be kept in mind when a sociogram is made. One assumption is that the criterion is specific to a particular purpose and group. A question such as "which two persons would you prefer to have sit next to you?" might yield different results than a question like "whom would you like to work with on a social-studies project?" This is especially true if a mark or grade is involved in the latter situation. The first question (the "psyche" criterion) is more personal than the second (the "socio" criterion). Another assumption is that a particular sociogram is specific with respect to time. A week or two later one might obtain somewhat different results with the same question and group, although the results would not be expected to be greatly different.

The next step in the construction of a sociogram is to record the choices made by the group, showing who chose whom with respect to first, second, and third positions. The sociometric question does not have to suggest three choices, however. Other options are a single-choice question, a two-choice question, or even a no-limit question that permits listing any number of group members. The number of choices will depend upon the specific use that is to be made of the data and the purpose of the sociogram. The three-choice item is useful when groups are to be formed (such as committees), for it lends flexibility of placement that a two-choice item does not permit; and yet the three-choice item places a limit on the number of choices, which may be desirable or necessary.

In order to show the tabulation of responses, a sociometric data sheet may be constructed from the responses on the forms collected from the group members. Such a sheet appears in Table VI. This form shows the name and assigned number of each group member, the three choices made, times chosen, and total choices received. The first person listed is Doris, who selected number 3 (Sue) as her first choice, number 7 (Karla) as second choice, and number 14 (Steve) as third choice. These results are found under the heading of *Members' Choices*. The *Times Chosen* column indicates that Doris herself was not given a first choice, but did receive one second and one third choice for a total of two choices. The total of 2 is recorded in the *Total Choices* column.

The *Total Choices* column indicates that five different members received at least five choices. Because they received a relatively high

TABLE VI

SOCIOMETRIC DATA FOR A HYPOTHETICAL HIGH SCHOOL CLASS

Group Members	Members' Choices			Times Chosen			Total Choices
	1st	2nd	3rd	1st	2nd	3rd	
1. Doris	3	7	14	0	1	1	2
2. Jay	14	4	1	2	2	1	5
3. Sue	4	7	12	4	0	1	5
4. Bill	7	10	11	3	2	0	5
5. Joe	2	8	14	0	0	0	0
6. Linda	9	12	13	2	1	0	3
7. Karla	4	1	3	1	2	0	3
8. Bruce	2	4	13	0	2	0	2
9. Jill	6	12	13	1	1	1	3
10. Glenn	3	11	2	0	1	0	1
11. Jim	4	2	14	0	1	1	2
12. Sally	6	9	13	1	2	2	5
13. Cindy	12	6	9	0	0	5	5
14. Steve	3	2	12	1	0	3	4
15. Lois	3	8	13	0	0	0	0

number of choices, they may be referred to as *stars*. Joe and Lois were not selected by any group member, so they are termed *isolates*. Any group member who is seldom chosen, such as Glenn, may be classified as a *neglectee*. When group members are asked to indicate a person or persons they prefer *not* to be with, any person so designated is labeled a *rejectee*.

The sociometric data in Table VI were used to make the sociogram in Figure 22. The steps followed in the construction procedure are as follows:

1. Position the names (or numbers) of the *stars* at or near the center of the sociogram. Usually squares are used to designate males and circles are used for females, but triangles or other forms may be used to represent the sexes.
2. Position the names of the members who received the next highest number of choices near the center of the sociogram.
3. Position the neglectees and isolates in the outermost area of the sociogram.
4. Draw lines between the circles and squares to indicate the choices made, with arrowheads indicating the direction of choice. A solid

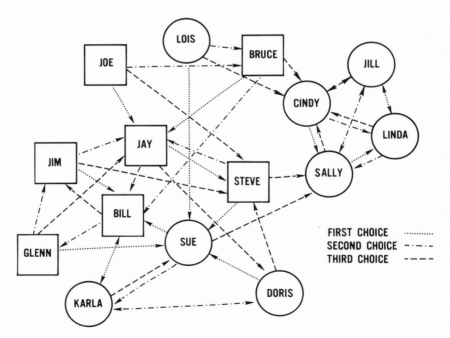

Figure 22. A sociogram for a hypothetical high-school class.

line may be used to indicate a first choice, a wavy line a second choice, and a broken line a third choice. Colors may also be used to indicate the different choices. When the same choice is mutual, as when Bill selected Karla as a first choice and Karla chose Bill as a first choice, a single line with an arrowhead at each end should be used to minimize the number of lines. The greater the number of lines, the more difficult it is to read the sociogram. An attempt should be made to position the squares and the circles in such a pattern that the number of crossing lines is minimized, for the fewer the crossed lines, the easier it is to read the sociogram.

The sociogram in Figure 22 represents the basic form of sociometric diagrams. Another form is the *target sociogram,* which consists of concentric circles that indicate the number of times each group member was chosen (See Figure 23). The stars are placed in the center ring of the target, the members who are often chosen but are not quite stars are in the next ring or two, and the neglectees and isolates are in the remaining rings. Arrows may be used to show the choices made by group members.

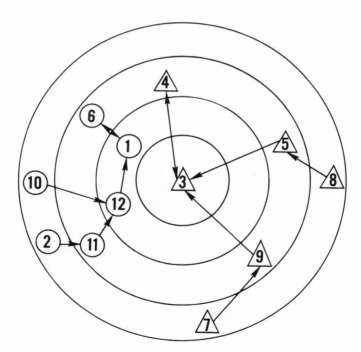

Figure 23. Target sociogram for a hypothetical sixth-grade class.

Whether the basic sociogram or a variation of it, such as the target sociogram, should be constructed is merely a matter of preference of the person who wishes to use a sociogram. Any well constructed sociogram should provide a meaningful picture of the social interaction within a particular group.

Interpretation of a Sociogram

The proper construction of a sociogram consumes a lot of time and requires much work, and the time and effort should culminate in an accurate interpretation of the sociometric data. One should begin by looking for the major outline or characteristic shape of the diagram. Long lines or chains of interaction with considerable overlap of choice and many reciprocal choices will indicate a well-integrated social structure for the group, suggesting good leadership, communication, and group spirit. Divisions in a group, termed cleavages or cliques, indicate poor social structure. A *cleavage* is a splitting of the group on the basis of sex, race, socioeconomic status, or some other factor. At the elementary school level it is not surprising to see a cleavage related to sex, with boys choosing boys and girls choosing girls. The lines of interaction may indicate that a *clique* is present. A *clique* is a small group of persons, perhaps three or four, who tend to choose only themselves. Cliques may be indicative of antagonisms, disagreements, lack of cooperation, or indifference with respect to other group members. In some cases group members may be "forced" into the formation of such a special group and in other cases not. Nevertheless, the presence of one or more cliques reduces the overall group interaction and reduces the opportunity for the exchange of ideas or expression of feelings, and thus tends to be an inhibiting factor where social development is concerned. The analysis also involves locating the stars, neglectees, and isolates in the group.

In looking at the sociogram in Figure 22, one can easily see that there is a clique in the group, there are several stars, two isolates, and only one neglectee. Cindy, Sally, Linda, and Jill form a very noticeable clique. None of these four girls chose anyone outside their own group. However, both Cindy and Sally were chosen by two other people outside their clique; Sally and Cindy were chosen five times altogether. Sue, Bill, and Jay do not belong to any clique, and each was also chosen five times. They appear to be stars in the class. There are two isolates, Joe and Lois, who were not chosen by anyone. Glenn is a neglectee, chosen only once. There are several reciprocal choices. Outside the clique, there are several fairly long chains of interaction in which one person chooses another, who selects another, etc. This seems to suggest group integration and cohesiveness (except for the clique, the two isolates, and one neglectee).

For a thorough interpretation of sociometric data it is advisable to utilize as much information about the group members as possible. If the group is a class in school, the teacher or counselor who is using the data should try to gather data concerning where the students live, what their home situations are like, their family socioeconomic status, their cultural backgrounds, and their handicaps or talents if any. A sociogram alone will not indicate why some individuals are neglectees, isolates, or rejectees, but additional data may shed light on this question.

Sociometric Matrix

Much useful sociometric data can be obtained from a sociometric matrix without going through the elaborate process of constructing a sociogram. Table VII provides an example of a matrix based upon the data in Table VI. Table VII indicates the three choices made by each group member, but does not show which choice was first, second, or third. Generally speaking, it is not possible to determine whether the first choice is more important than the third, etc., so no weights are attached to the choices, and the choices are regarded as equal in value. The matrix shows for example, that Doris chose Sue, Karla, and Steve, but the order of choice (first, second, and third) is not evident in the matrix.

When the column tallies are added, the total choices can be determined. Thus, Doris was chosen twice, Jay five times, Sue five times, etc. The matrix indicates that the two isolates, Joe and Lois received no choices from other group members. Stars, neglectees, and isolates can be determined quickly from the matrix, and one can also discover which members chose other members, but the picture of social integration is not so clear and interesting as it would be with a sociogram.

Sociometric Indexes

For research purposes a whole set of sociometric indexes can be calculated. The *choice status index* indicates numerically the extent to which a person was chosen by group members. The formula for computing the index may be written as follows:

$$CS_j = \frac{\Sigma c_j}{N - 1}$$

where

CS_j = the choice status of the individual j
Σc_j = the sum of the choices in subject column
N = the number of individuals in the group ($N - 1$ is used because the individuals do not choose themselves)

Table VIII shows choice-status index values for the data in Table VII. Note that the table has the times chosen and index value for each group member. For example, Doris was chosen twice, so her choice-

TABLE VII

SOCIOMETRIC MATRIX FOR A FIFTEEN-MEMBER GROUP

Student (i)		Student (j)														
		1	2	3	4	5	6	7	8	9	10	11	12	13	14	15
1.	Doris	0	0	1	0	0	0	1	0	0	0	0	0	0	1	0
2.	Jay	1	0	0	1	0	0	0	0	0	0	0	0	0	1	0
3.	Sue	0	0	0	1	0	0	1	0	0	0	0	1	0	0	0
4.	Bill	0	0	0	0	0	0	1	0	0	1	1	0	0	0	0
5.	Joe	0	1	0	0	0	0	0	1	0	0	0	0	0	1	0
6.	Linda	1	0	0	0	0	0	0	0	1	0	0	1	1	0	0
7.	Karla	0	0	1	1	0	0	0	0	0	0	0	0	0	0	0
8.	Bruce	0	1	0	1	0	0	0	0	0	0	0	0	1	0	0
9.	Jill	0	1	0	1	0	1	0	0	0	0	0	1	1	0	0
10.	Glenn	0	1	1	0	0	0	0	0	0	0	1	0	0	0	0
11.	Jim	0	0	0	0	0	0	0	0	1	0	0	0	0	1	0
12.	Sally	0	0	0	0	0	1	0	0	1	0	0	0	1	0	0
13.	Cindy	0	1	1	0	0	1	0	0	0	0	0	1	0	0	0
14.	Steve	0	0	1	0	0	0	0	1	0	0	0	1	0	0	0
15.	Lois	0	0	0	0	0	0	0	0	0	0	0	0	1	0	0
	Totals	2	5	5	5	0	3	3	2	3	1	2	5	5	4	0

TABLE VIII

CHOICE-STATUS INDEX VALUES FOR A FIFTEEN-MEMBER GROUP

Student	Times Chosen	Index
1. Doris	2	.14
2. Jay	5	.36
3. Sue	5	.36
4. Bill	5	.36
5. Joe	0	.00
6. Linda	3	.21
7. Karla	3	.21
8. Bruce	2	.14
9. Jill	3	.21
10. Glenn	1	.07
11. Jim	2	.14
12. Sally	5	.36
13. Cindy	5	.36
14. Steve	4	.29
15. Lois	0	.00

status is equal to 2/14 or .14. For Jay, the choice status index value is 5/14, which equals .36. A teacher, counselor, or psychologist might find such scores useful in a systematic study of the amount of change in social interaction that occurs for individuals over a period of time. Comparison between *different* groups, however, generally cannot be made on the basis of such scores unless the groups are nearly equal in size.

Another sociometric index, the *social-expansiveness index*, provides a measure of the overall extent to which group members tend to choose others. The formula for the social-expansiveness index may be written as follows:

$$E = \frac{\Sigma c_{ij}}{N}$$

where

E = expansiveness
Σc_{ij} = the sum of all choices made by all group members
N = the number of individuals in the group

In order to obtain this index value for a group it is necessary to phrase the sociometric question in such a way as to permit the group members to choose as many other persons in the group as they wish. The question might be stated as follows: "Which individuals in this group would you invite to a social activity? List as many names as you wish."

Guess Who Technique

The *Guess Who Technique* is a sociometric procedure that was developed by Hartshorne, May, and Maller. The technique involves the use of a set of statements concerning the characteristics or behaviors of group members, and/or classmates. The statements may be positive or negative, and they may be written to elicit a specific kind of information about the members of a group. An example follows:

> Instructions: Please match the students in your class with the statements listed below. You may use your own name if you wish, and you may list more than one person for each statement.
>
> 1. This person is very friendly: _____
> 2. This person likes to talk a lot: _____
> 3. This person is unpopular — has very few friends: _____
> 4. This person is well liked — has lots of friends: _____
> 5. This person likes to have his/her own way: _____
> 6. This person often breaks the rules: _____
> 7. This person seems to care about others: _____
> 8. This person often tries to be helpful: _____
> 9. This person listens to what others have to say: _____
> 10. This person often does things without regard for the welfare of others: _____

The respondent is not asked to sign the form or reveal authorship in some other way, for this almost certainly would affect the responses. A greater number of accurate responses probably will be given if there is no means of identifying the person who completed the form.

A "guess who" form may be scored by computing the total number of times an individual has been listed for each statement. If half the statements in the form are positive and half are negative, the total negative listings for a person can be subtracted from the total positive listings to give the sociometric score. A negative score could result if the individual had more negative nominations than positive ones. Much can be learned, of course, from noting which positive and negative statements were assigned to a person frequently. Thus, Jean Jackson may be perceived as being very friendly by many peers, if a high percentage of classmates so indicated, but she might also be perceived as being opportunistic. Data from the "guess who" form, coupled with data from a sociogram, can amount to a rich source of useful information pertaining to the social status and development of an individual.

Application of Sociometric Data

Of what value are the results obtained from sociometric techniques? Actually, several practical applications of such data can be suggested, beginning with the selection of individuals for small-group activities. In theory and practice, sociometrically formed groups tend to function more effectively than those constructed in a random fashion or on some other basis.

In order to form groups on the basis of sociometric data, one would need to know the sociometric choices made by the group members. This information could come from the sociometric data sheet. With the data at hand the following procedure may be followed:

1. Decide how large each group should be. Generally speaking, from five to eight members should be in a group.
2. Begin with the isolates and give them their first choices, but avoid having two isolates in the same group. If there are no isolates, proceed with the neglectees. If two neglectees have made a mutual first, second, or third choice, place them in the same group, if possible.
3. Continue the process of moving from the individuals who received the fewest choices to those who received the most choices as the groups are formed. Try to satisfy the chooser's reciprocated choice first and then the highest level of unreciprocated choices next. As this is done, the stars receive the least amount of consideration simply because they are the least in need of social development.
4. After these steps are taken, and the groups are tentatively formed, check to see that these conditions are met:
   a. All members of a group should have at least one person of their choice in the group. A three-choice question makes this condition easier to meet than the two-choice question.
   b. Cliques should be partially broken up, if possible. A four-person clique can be split by placing two persons in one group and the other two in another. If there are three in the clique, one's best judgment should be used to determine whether to place the three in different groups, or place all three in the same group. The latter alternative generally is the less desirable alternative unless the three are in a large group of perhaps seven or eight members where they cannot dominate the group.
   c. Cleavages should be diminished, if possible, and one should avoid placement of a member of a subgroup alone in a group.
   d. A rejectee (if such choices were indicated) should not be placed with the person who made the rejection.
   e. There should be as many mutual choices in each group as possible.

Employing the data shown in Table VI, three groups (of five members each) could be formed as follows:

Group I	*Group II*	*Group III*
Joe	Lois	Glenn
Jay	Sue	Jim
Steve	Sally	Bill
Linda	Cindy	Karla
Jill	Bruce	Doris

It should be emphasized that there is no single correct configuration for the groups that might be formed with the available sociometric data. Rather, one should strive to use the criteria listed above, and consider any relevant factors that may suggest a deviation from the criteria. In short, one should use the criteria and common sense in constructing groups.

Groups formed sociometrically should be allowed to engage in the activity that is stated or implied in the sociometric question. If the sociometric question asks, "With whom would you like to work on a science project?" the teacher should use the information for the implied purpose. Without the "follow through," future attempts to use a sociometric questionnaire may not be successful.

In addition to improving the construction of subgroups, there are other important outcomes that may result from the use of sociometry. One of these is to help teachers and counselors understand the social needs of individual students in order to help them develop socially, emotionally, and academically. Sociometric data can also be used to improve the social climate of a school class or similar group. A sociometric data sheet and sociogram can help identify the isolates, neglectees, rejectees, stars, cliques, and cleavages. With this information, a teacher can construct better subgroups and thereby gradually help the least-chosen students improve their social status. Additionally, cliques and cleavages may be diminished or eliminated, and leadership may be developed. Consequently, class spirit and achievement should improve.

In order for sociometric data to be useful, however, the data must be sufficiently valid, and validity is subject to these conditions:

1. The group members must know each other sufficiently well to make meaningful choices.
2. The group members must have real preferences or dislikes.
3. The group members must have rapport with the teacher or other person who administers the sociometric questionnaire.
4. The group members must believe that their choices will be used for the stated purpose.
5. The criterion must be considered to be specific and the data used accordingly.

Sociometry has certain limitations that should be kept in mind. One limitation is that sociometric data show relationships, but not the *intensity* of the relationships. Caution must be used in trying to judge how strong a preference or dislike is between two group members. Another limitation is that sociometric data do not explain *why* some individuals are chosen and some are not. Choices may be related to many factors, including the personal qualities of individuals (friendliness, thoughtfulness, etc.), the mutual assistance that may be rendered, and the commonality of interests, ideas, attitudes, or values.

Q-SORT TECHNIQUE

William Stephenson (1953) is given credit for developing the Q-Sort procedure, an interesting technique that may be used to assess various dimensions of personality. The technique involves the use of a set of phrases or statements related to the specific aspect of personality that must be assessed.

In the construction of a particular Q-Sort, several statements are written and then typed or printed on separate cards. Generally speaking, as few as 50 or as many as 200 such cards are made, and each statement is written in such a way that it represents a degree of expression of the trait or characteristic in question (such as self-esteem).

The administration of the Q-Sort simply requires directing the subject to sort the deck of cards into a number of piles or stacks so that the statements that are most descriptive of the subject are placed on the first pile, and those that are least descriptive are placed on the last pile. The number of cards and stacks, and the rules for sorting, may be varied to fit a particular trait or situation. The following is an example of a distribution of 100 cards in nine stacks.

	Most descriptive							*Least descriptive*	
Stack	1	2	3	4	5	6	7	8	9
Number of cards	4	7	12	17	20	17	12	7	4

Standard decks of cards are available and may be used for assessment of certain aspects of personality (Block, 1962).

The Q-Sort data obtained from a subject may be evaluated in a number of different ways. The simplest evaluation is a mere inspection of the way that the subject arranged the cards, noting which statements were placed in the different stacks, and especially noting which statements appear to be least descriptive and most descriptive. Another procedure for evaluating the results is to locate the median position of the trait being assessed (locate the point below and above which half the statements were placed) and consider the statements at that point to be characteristic of that person. One also may correlate the results with other criteria. For example, Jerry's "ideal self sort" might be compared with his "real self sort"; or Nancy's perception of her own behavior might be compared with a teacher's perception of Nancy's behavior (Kroth, 1973). Still another example of the use of the procedure would be to assess some personality change, such as for assertiveness, from the beginning to the termination of counseling.

The Q-Sort provides for ipsative measurements rather than normative measurements. That is, the data reveal something about the sorter's self-perception but not how the sorter's perception compares with that of other persons in a norm group. However, the *Child Development Center Q-Sort,* by Schachter (Stoelting Company) can be used to correlate the personality profile of a real child (or adolescent) with the "ideal" profile of a child of the same age and sex.

While this technique is relatively flexible, and thus can be applied to many different aspects of behavior or personality, it is rather time-consuming and its validity is highly dependent upon the accuracy of the sorter's perceptions. Bias or indifference in sorting the statements may render the results of the procedure useless or misleading. Provided these limitations are kept in mind, the technique can be a useful appraisal device.

SENTENCE COMPLETION

The sentence-completion technique is a projective device that may be used to elicit verbal responses that reflect needs, concerns, attitudes, or certain other aspects of behavior. Typically the instrument consists of a set of partial sentences that the respondent is expected to complete with a word or a phrase. For example:

1. I feel _____
2. Most men are _____
3. Each day seems _____
4. I remember _____
5. My mother is _____

The instructions generally read "Complete these sentences to express your real feelings. Try to complete each one and try to make complete sentences."

The incomplete sentences, of course, can be completed in various ways, and this flexibility permits a person to respond in a unique way that may reflect an important facet of thought, feeling, value, or attitude. Flexibility also is apparent in the adaptations that can be made in the structuring of a sentence completion form. For example, all of the items can be restricted to self-concept or perhaps future goals or plans. McKinney (1967), for instance, sees the device as a useful means of assessing student self-actualization.

An example of a sentence completion form follows. The reader may wish to note the nature of the responses and try to make a tentative evaluation of them.

Name Amanda A. Grade 4th Date 3/2/78

1. Today I feel _____ dizzy _____.
2. When I have to read _____ I read _____.
3. I get angry when _____ I get mad _____.
4. To be grown up _____ I have to grow _____.
5. My idea of a good time is _____ when I read stories _____.
6. I wish my parents _____ loved each other _____.
7. I can't understand why _____ I have so many classes _____.
8. School is _____ fun and work _____.
9. I feel bad when _____ I do something bad _____.

10. I wish teachers ___were like Mrs. Johnson and more of them___.
11. I wish my mother _____would remarry my daddy_____.
12. I think that books _____are fun_____.
13. People think I _____talk too much_____.
14. I like to read about _____people_____.
15. On weekends I _____play_____.
16. I'd rather read _____than eat_____.
17. I think homework is _____lots of fun_____.
18. I hope I never will _____fail in school_____.
19. I wish people would not _____say I talk too much_____.
20. I am afraid _____I will fail_____.
21. Comic books _____are second grade books_____.
22. When I take my report card home ___I feel good and bad___.
23. I am at my best when _____work comes_____.
24. Most brothers and sisters _____are mean and nice_____.
25. I don't know how _____hard sixth grade is_____.
26. I feel proud when _____I go to class_____.
27. The future looks _____great_____.
28. I wish my father _____loved my mother_____.
29. I like to read when _____I go to class_____.
30. I would like to be _____a good girl_____.
31. I often worry about _____my report card_____.
32. I wish I could _____have lots of friends_____.
33. Reading science _____is fun_____.
34. I look forward to _____never failing_____.
35. I wish _____I was a good girl_____.
36. My only regret _____is talking too much_____.

When we look over the responses that Amanda wrote, we can see she shows much concern about her school record and the possibility of failing. She is disturbed about the separation of her parents. Judging from her concern about talking too much, failing, and wanting to be a good girl, one can hypothesize that her self-concept is not as positive as it should be. Perhaps, also, she is a lonely child because she states that she wishes she could have lots of friends. Just by completing the form, Amanda has told us something about her feelings and concerns.

Standardized forms, such as the *Rotter Incomplete Sentence Blank*, published by the Psychological Corporation, and the *Rohde Sentence Completion Test* (Rohde, 1957) are available for use by teachers, counselors, psychologists, and others who wish to make use of this relatively simple technique but do not wish to develop one. With the aid of the manual for the standardized instrument and forms for the interpretation and scoring of responses, one can make a rather detailed analysis of the completed standardized sentence completion form.

CASE STUDY

The most comprehensive of the nontest techniques for appraisal is the *case study*. It may be defined as an intensive investigation of various aspects of the life of an individual, generally for the purpose of determining the underlying causes of present behavior. It differs from an autobiography because it is not a self-report, and it is likely to follow a highly structured and detailed format. Tests, inventories, interviews, rating scales, and other devices may be used to gather the necessary information for the case study. Sometimes a case study is referred to as a case history or life history.

The case study may cover the entire life of an individual or merely a selected segment of that person's life. Whether it deals with a few important factors or many of them depends mainly upon the purpose of the study and the availability of data pertaining to the individual being studied.

While there is no specific procedure that must be followed in conducting and reporting a case study, the following guidelines for collecting data are recommended:

1. All relevant data concerning the person should be considered.
2. Longitudinal data should be used rather than cross-sectional data to attempt to show physical and behavioral changes over a period of time.
3. The culture in which the subject was reared should be studied carefully.
4. Conceptualization of the person should be continuous, and as each bit of information is collected it should be incorporated in the study.
5. All collected data should be carefully considered and evaluated in terms of accuracy and authenticity.

Although the case study can be initiated, developed, and written up without an outline or set of guidelines, an outline can facilitate the organization of the study. An example of a case study outline is given in Figure 24.

The outline in Figure 24 shows that certain areas are key areas of investigation (such as problem, family, etc.), but it also indicates that there are sections in the case study for the analysis of data, recommendations, and follow-up.

After the data are collected, someone must integrate and synthesize the various data into a meaningful whole. The good case study is more than just a collection of facts. It is a kind of sketch of the subject that shows the continuum of the person's development. While that sketch does not reveal all there is to know about the subject, it should show the interrelationships among important factors that influence growth and development, it should indicate the subject's current status, and it should suggest the outlook for the future.

The analysis of the case study can vary, from a rather unsophisti-

CASE STUDY OUTLINE

1. IDENTIFYING DATA. Name, address, age, date and place of birth, race, and school grade.

2. PROBLEM (if study is made because subject seems in need of special assistance). Nature, onset, seriousness, frequency, and duration (chronological order). Feelings and attitude of subject toward problem. Opinions and attitudes of parents, teachers, counselors, and others, such as school nurse and doctor.

3. FAMILY. Name, age, sex, and educational attainment of family members living in home or closely associated with subject. Other persons, such as boarders, living in home but not of immediate family. Residential history of family (rural, small town, urban). Immigrant background if pertinent. Occupations of wage earners. Special health problems of any member. Religious affiliation(s). Apparent socioeconomic status. Special culture patterns. Nature of home life and quality of interpersonal relations. Subject's adjustment and special role in family. Attitudes of other members toward subject. Method and amount of parental control.

4. PHYSICAL HEALTH DATA. Serious illnesses or diseases. Findings of medical examination(s). Growth characteristics, nutrition, and general health. Attitude of subject toward own health and appearance.

5. OBJECTIVE TEST DATA AND INTERPRETATION.

6. EDUCATIONAL HISTORY AND ACHIEVEMENT. Progress in past. Present status not only in terms of marks but also in terms of other criteria such as creative expression, good work habits, etc. Attitude toward school. Special abilities and disabilities. Strong likes and dislikes with regard to school courses and activities. Educational plans and ambitions. Behavioral problems, if any. Attitudes of teachers toward subject.

7. SOCIAL DEVELOPMENT. Sociability and adaptability. Companions and close associates. Rivalries. Group affiliations. Nature and extent of participation in groups. Acceptance by others. Status in various groups. Relations to neighbors and other adults in community. Social competence and confidence. Recreational interests. Special interests and accomplishments. Significant experiences. Civic participation in and out of school. Asocial tendencies. Court record if any.

8. EMOTIONAL DEVELOPMENT. General mental health. Predominant moods. Sense of self-confidence. Attitude toward self. Significant limitations. Symptoms of conflicts, such as tics, stutterings, tantrums, truancy, lying, stealing, etc.

9. WORK EXPERIENCE. Place and dates (from _____ to _____) of employment. Nature of work done. Attitude toward work.

10. VOCATIONAL PLANS.

11. GENERAL APPRAISAL, INTERPRETATION, AND HYPOTHESES. The generalizations and conclusions should be developed from data. The writer takes care not to generalize from too few instances or from atypical instances. Hypotheses are considered tentative. The writer points to contraindications as well as calls attention to confirmatory data. Writer studies to see all parts of the picture and their interrelations in order to analyze the complex pattern of the whole and perceive the underlying meanings and implications.

12. RECOMMENDATIONS. Following the case study there should be treatment and follow-up. In the case of students, treatment is probably more often developmental and preventive rather than, or as well as, corrective.

13. FOLLOW-UP REPORT(S). As long as the student is in school, the investigator periodically brings the study up to date by reporting additional information on the subject's development and the outcomes of efforts in his behalf. If the student is referred to someone for special assistance, reports from that person are incorporated in the report or appended to it.

Figure 24. A case-study outline.

cated general perusal of the data followed by a summary of the content to a very detailed and formalized system for dealing with constructs, such as one developed by Bucklew (1960). It is likely that the more detailed the analysis procedure, the less likely that it will be used by busy counselors, teachers, or psychologists.

The well-developed case study can be extremely useful as a technique for acquiring a better understanding of the "whole" person, thereby enhancing efforts to help that person. The major limitations for the technique are that the data collected are not always current and accurate, and that a complete case study requires a relatively great amount of time and effort.

REFERENCES

Block, J.: *The Q-Sort Method in Personality Assessment and Psychiatric Research.* Springfield, Illinois, Thomas, 1961.

Bonney, M. E.: Sociometric study of agreement between teacher judgments and student choices. *Sociometry, 10:*133-146, 1947.

Bucklew, J.: *Paradigms for Psychopathology: A Contribution to Case History Analysis.* Philadelphia, J. B. Lippincott, 1960.

Davis, Everett E.: An analysis of autobiographical statements of adolescents. *Measurement and Evaluation of Guidance, 6(2):*117-121, 1973.

Doby, John, Ed.: *An Introduction to Social Research,* 2nd ed. New York, Appleton-Century-Crofts, 1967.

Gardner, E. F. and Thompson, G. G.: Measuring and interpreting social relations. *Test Service Notebook No. 22.* Harcourt, Brace, and World, Tarrytown, New York, 1959.

Gronlund, N. E.: *Sociometry in the Classroom.* New York, Harper and Row, 1959.

Herbert, J. and Attridge, C.: A guide for developers and users of observation systems and manuals. *American Educational Research Journal, 12:*1-20, 1975.

Jennings, H. J.: *Sociometry and Group Relations.* American Council on Education, Washington, 1965.

Kroth, Roger: The behavioral q-sort as a diagnostic tool. *Academic Therapy, 8(3):*317-330, 1973.

McKinney, Fred: The sentence completion blank in assessing student self-actualization. *The Personnel and Guidance Journal, 45(7):*709, 1967.

Mueller, Richard, Schmieding, O. A., and Shutz, J. L.: Four approaches to writing autobiographies. *School Counselor, 2(3):*160-164, 1964.

Rohde, Amanda R.: *The Sentence Completion Method.* New York, Ronald Press, 1957.

Smith, Donald E., Cary, Julie, and Smith, Julie: Q-Sort: Understanding personal assessment. *TPGA Journal, 7(1):*39-47, 1979.

Stephenson, William: *The Study of Behavior: Q-Technique and Its Methodology.* Chicago, University of Chicago Press, 1953.

Chapter 6

APPRAISAL OF ACHIEVEMENT

F OR AS LONG as instruction has existed, school personnel have attempted to assess the outcome of that instruction. Parents, administrators, counselors, school psychologists, teachers, and even students themselves are desirous to know the progress being made as a result of the teaching and learning that has taken place.

Obvious measures of achievement include standardized achievement tests and batteries of tests, which yield data useful for making comparisons of student progress at the individual grade level, school level, district level, and state and national levels. Test batteries of this nature are often administered by counselors and/or school psychologists, who in turn interpret the results for other school personnel, parents, and students.

Besides the standardized measures of achievement, there are many other forms of assessment of instruction and/or achievement. Chapter tests, unit tests, and final examinations are all an attempt on the part of the instructor to assess achievement. The English teacher gives a spelling test; the home economics instructor examines a seam binding; the physical education teacher measures growth in physical coordination on the parallel bars. All are engaging in the same activity — assessing achievement. Some are academic tasks; some are nonacademic. Yet, all are attempting to measure growth or attainment of proficiency in a given area. This chapter covers both standardized and teacher-made tests as forms of assessment.

HISTORY OF ACHIEVEMENT TESTS

Teachers of earlier centuries measured their students' achievement through questioning and evaluating the verbal response of the pupils. While Socrates' method lacked the sophistication of today's achievement tests, he certainly engaged in testing situations that allowed him to assess to an extent his pupils' growth in desired areas. Intuitively, he and his contemporaries were able to discern, through oral expression and recitation, the level of achievement of their pupils and how they compared in growth to others of similar age, ability, and experience. In later years, this practice continued as students recited formally before boards of education.

In contrast to this subjective type of achievement evaluation, today's instructors spend over one hundred million dollars a year in assessing growth or achievement. What caused this great change in achievement testing? Compulsory education was among the early and most powerful forces in the shift. With overflowing classrooms, teachers no longer had the luxury of the oral method of appraisal of students. Also, with a multitude of students, it became advantageous to have a more objective way of comparing students to their peers for measurement purposes. A more time-efficient and objective method was called into practice — the paper-and-pencil test.

In the United States, Dr. Horace Mann was among the first to substitute, in 1845, a uniform written examination for the oral examination before the boards of education. He rationalized that these written tests would provide greater objectivity, equalize testing conditions for all students, and provide a broader range for sampling student achievement. He was influential in beginning a shift away from oral examinations as the sole criterion for determining achievement.

However, the first objective achievement test in the United States is usually credited to Dr. J. M. Rice who developed a fifty-word spelling test in 1897. Traveling around the country, he administered the spelling test to a total population of 16,000 pupils. He compiled his data into norms, thus establishing the idea that a test could be an objective tool used to evaluate educational procedures and to assess pupil knowledge. Interestingly, he found little correlation between the ability to spell and the time spent in spelling instruction. While best remembered for his spelling test, he also authored achievement tests in the areas of arithmetic and language arts.

In 1900, college entrance examinations or "college boards" as they are often called, were begun, still widely used today in the selection of students for admission to colleges and universities. Following Rice's direction, a number of test authors emerged. Stone produced an arithmetic reasoning test in 1908, Courtis developed an arithmetic computation test in 1909, and Ayres published a handwriting scale in 1911. E. L. Thorndike wrote the first textbook in educational measurement and influenced many students who later made great contributions to the field of achievement testing.

Thorndike's influence caused a revolution in testing in the 1920s and 1930s. It was during these decades that content and methods of instruction began to be scientifically based on objective data. The modern testing movement, along with research bureaus, research journals, texts, and standardized tests, had begun.

In 1923, the *Stanford Achievement Test,* the first standardized survey test battery, was published. It represented a team effort of scholars from several universities, including Teachers' College, Columbia, Minnesota, Ohio State, Michigan, Harvard, Peabody, Chicago, and Stanford. The *Stanford Achievement Test* was designed for elementary school pupils. The *Iowa High School Content Examination,* the first achievement survey battery for high school pupils, was published two years later in 1925.

Today, educational testing is a big business. Along with the highly scientific, valid, and reliable tests are the single-subject-matter tests, test batteries, diagnostic and prognostic tests produced by amateurs. These tests lie side by side in the market place. It becomes incumbent upon the educator to ferret out the quality instruments for measuring instruction and assessing pupil growth.

USES OF ACHIEVEMENT TESTS

A story recently made the rounds that a popular reading readiness test had finally sold many more copies than there were actual first graders in the United States. While there may be some doubt as to the veracity of that story, the fact is that achievement tests are popular with parents, school personnel, and school boards and are continuing to gain in popularity in this age of educational accountability. For what specific purposes are they being used? Several are listed below.

1. Achievement tests are used to determine the progress of individual pupils in a variety of content areas. Comparisons may be made of a student's scores from September to May and to determine the individual's growth rate. This information is often helpful to the teacher, diagnostician, or parent in determining areas in which a child may be failing to make appropriate progress. One weakness of the achievement test might be pointed out at this time. While the test may be accurate in pin-pointing an area of weakness, specific causes for the pupils' failure to make adequate progress are much more difficult to determine. An astute teacher or counselor can use the information to formulate some hypotheses from which to begin instruction.

2. Achievement tests are used to determine the level of performance of local pupils as compared with others of like age and grade placement nationally. This is the kind of information that is reported to local boards of education to allow them to determine whether their school population is typical in progress. Caution should be used in utilizing data in this manner. Many times, local populations are atypical. There may be logical explanations as to why the local group is performing significantly above or below the national norms.

3. Achievement tests are used to determine the effectiveness of instruction. Strengths and weaknesses of the curriculum may be manifested in the results of the achievement tests. Few teachers, however, are willing to have their instruction measured in terms of a single achievement test. Too many other types of variables enter into the instructional situation. In studying achievement test data over a period of years, it would be possible to detect a curricular weakness in a particular school system and to take measures to shore up instructional strategies in that skills area.

4. Achievement and aptitude data may be compared to determine if individuals are learning at their predicted level and rate. Through the years, expectancy formulas have been devised to determine the level at which a given pupil may be expected to learn. Through these studies have come terms such as *underachiever* and *overachiever*. Underachiever refers to the students whose achievement test data are considerably lower than their aptitude test data. Overachiever refers to pupils whose achievement test data surpass their aptitude test data. While most educators accept the term underachiever, many reject the idea of overachievement. How, they ask, can students achieve higher than their aptitude to achieve? If this happens, perhaps the aptitude test score is inaccurate. At any rate, it is somewhat dangerous to put a ceiling on the level of expectation of any pupil. Expectancy formulas, if used, should be used with extreme caution and understanding.

5. Achievement tests can aid the teacher in grouping, tentatively at least, for instruction. For example, pupils who scored poorly in arithmetic reasoning may be grouped together for maximum instructional benefits. These scores may be used as a screening device for more thorough diagnostic testing.

6. Achievement tests may be used to aid the classroom teacher, administrator, or school counselor in providing vocational and educational guidance. While the data may be limited, they provide a baseline from which the advisor may begin in determining an individual's strengths and weaknesses.

7. Achievement tests may be used to aid school personnel in screening for special programs such as remedial reading, resource room help, Title I programs, and training programs for specific vocations. If the achievement test data should be used in this manner, other data sources should support the decision, and the achievement test data should demonstrate high predictive validity.

NONSTANDARDIZED MEASURES OF ACHIEVEMENT

As was earlier stated, as long as instructors have taught, measures of achievement have been employed. Long before the modern testing movement, teachers were attempting to measure changes in pupil behavior and performance. Today, even with the high degree of measurement sophistication, informal classroom measures of achievement yield highly valuable information about the learner and the learning process.

While all school personnel will employ nonstandardized measures of achievement, the classroom teacher is likely to rely heavily on information gained from measures other than standardized achievement tests. Nontest appraisal methods and techniques are discussed in detail in the previous chapter of this book. In assessing achievement, the classroom teacher and other school personnel will use observational procedures, the anecdotal record, rating scales, interviews, questionnaires, and checklists, as well as other informal devices.

Nontest appraisal methods and techniques of assessing achievement will yield more subjective results than more formal methods of evaluation. Yet, there are times when the informal methods have advantages over formal testing devices. A distinct advantage of observation and other forms of nontest appraisal is their use in nonacademic areas. Affective growth in the areas of motivation, enthusiasm, cooperation, and resourcefulness may be assessed through these methods.

Another advantage of nontest assessment in evaluating achievement is that it allows school personnel to determine the extent to which students are making application of new knowledge and skills. School personnel can observe the process through which pupils move in order to solve problems.

Teacher-Made Tests

Besides nontest appraisal methods and techniques, school personnel rely heavily on teacher-made tests to aid in the appraisal of pupil achievement. Classroom teachers, in particular, must appraise the quality of work done both in school and in out-of-class assignments. This is ordinarily done through teacher-made tests. Teacher-made tests have several advantages over standardized tests: (1) They are keyed to individual units of study and to specific classroom situations. Thus, they are reflective of current educational objectives of the local school; (2) Compared to standardized measures of achievement, teacher-made tests are inexpensive to produce; (3) Individual students can learn from marked errors. Teachers can give immediate feedback and help the students note errors as they occur.

Teacher-made tests are used for a variety of purposes. First, they may be diagnostic and prescriptive in nature. The teacher can quickly determine, through testing, the level of instruction best suited to both the large group and to individuals. The tests are particularly helpful in planning individualized instruction. Second, tests can stimulate students for additional study. Frequent testing causes students to stay current in their preparation. Third, tests enable the teacher to compare and contrast specific abilities of students in the class. They are helpful, along with other information, in determining marks of individuals and in forming groups or instruction.

Teacher-made tests, in order to be effective for each of the above uses as well as others, must be carefully planned and constructed. Selection of the appropriate test format should be determined by the objectives to be measured. Short-answer or objective-test formats lend themselves well to measuring knowledge and skills. Extended test formats, such as essay exams, lend themselves to measuring problem-solving abilities, application, and appreciation. Objective tests are more difficult to construct than essay types. However, the objective tests are by far the easier to grade and more time-efficient in evaluating student responses than the essay type.

Test Objectives

The teacher-made test should evaluate all important instructional outcomes, and thus it should have an appropriate variety of items to accomplish this task. If a test has an excessive number of simple recall items, it is certain that some essential outcomes are not being assessed adequately. The simple recall items that ask only for correct names, dates, and places, etc., are easy to write, but they are of limited value because they do not require understanding, reasoning, application of knowledge, evaluative judgments, or other important abilities. Ebel (1965, p. 68) states that most of the questions in good classroom tests can be classified according to the following categories (the examples are provided by the authors):

UNDERSTANDING OF TERMINOLOGY

A. As used in sociology, the word culture refers to:
   1. formal education
   2. art and music
   3. the standard of living of a society
   4. the total way of life of a group of people

UNDERSTANDING OF FACT AND PRINCIPLE

B. Radar is effective in tracking aircraft because very high frequency radio waves
   1. travel faster than light
   2. give off light energy when they strike an object
   3. are reflected from things more dense than air
   4. can penetrate any substance, no matter how dense

ABILITY TO EXPLAIN OR ILLUSTRATE

C. Of the following, which is the best way to determine whether a solution is basic or acidic?
   1. Taste it
   2. Heat it with a Bunsen burner
   3. Feel some of it between the fingers
   4. Use a piece of litmus paper

ABILITY TO CALCULATE

D. During a sale, a $40 table radio was reduced 20 percent. What was the sale price?
   1. $8.00

2. $20.00
3. $32.00
4. $38.00

ABILITY TO PREDICT

E. What probably would happen if salt water were used to water a garden?
1. The plants would die.
2. The plants would grow very large.
3. The fruit or vegetables would taste salty.
4. The plants would mature especially early.

ABILITY TO RECOMMEND APPROPRIATE ACTION

F. Which of the following generally would be most beneficial in correcting anemia?
1. Adding iron to the diet
2. Adding vitamin C to the diet
3. Getting a greater amount of rest
4. Reducing the amount of carbohydrates in the diet

ABILITY TO MAKE AN EVALUATIVE JUDGMENT

G. Which completion item is best constructed?
1. Columbus discovered America in _____.
2. The Louisiana Purchase was completed in the year _____.
3. _____ wrote "Call of the Wild."
4. "Clearly" is a part of speech called an _____.

Common Types of Objective Tests

The most frequently used objective forms of teacher-made tests are (1) true-false, (2) matching, (3) completion, and (4) multiple choice.

TRUE-FALSE TESTS. The true-false test is thought by most teachers to be relatively easy to construct. However, the most common violation of item construction is ambiguity. The item writer should be sure that the item as written can be classified without question as either true or false. The following rules should assist item writers in constructing true-false statements:

1. Avoid the use of all-inclusive terms such as *never, always, all.* Students will use these cues to answer correctly items for which they may have no prior knowledge.
2. Avoid the use of negative statements and double negatives as students usually require more time to answer these. Also, the semantic and syntactic difficulty causes confusion unrelated to the actual content intent of the question.
3. Attempt to limit the true-false items to a single idea. The reading

difficulty becomes a factor when multiple, complex ideas are presented.
4. Avoid a pattern of responses, consistently overloading a test with a majority of false items or a majority of true items.
5. Avoid using words or phrases that can be interpreted in a number of ways.

Examples of poor and acceptable true-false items follow:

Poor: Silas Marner, throughout the novel, is always portrayed as a victim of injustice. (The word *always* will signal to the student that this is a false statement.)

Better: Silas Marner is consistently portrayed by the author as a victim of injustice.

Poor: Silas was not changed significantly by his love for Eppie. (The negative phrase adds confusion to the statement.)

Better: Silas Marner's love for Eppie brought about significant changes in his character.

Poor: Dunsey Cass is a thorn in Godfrey's flesh, thus having a strange hold over Godfrey, turning him into a reckless, dissipated idler. (This statement is too complex, with multiple ideas presented.)

Better: Godfrey was negatively influenced by Dunsey Cass.

Poor: Nancy Lammeter was the apple of her sister's eye. (This item contains a metaphor that may be confusing to the student and interpreted in a number of ways.)

Better: Nancy Lammeter has admiration for her sister.

MATCHING TESTS. The matching test item is good for measuring literal comprehension or factual recall. Items consist of two sets of words or phrases to be matched according to test directions. The following rules should assist item writers in constructing matching items:

1. All items within the set should refer to the same class or group — for example, states, authors, books, forms of government.
2. Keep the set of items relatively short, but allow extra choices to avoid the process of elimination.
3. Use headings for each column that accurately describe the items.
4. All items on a matching test should be kept on a single page. The student should not be expected to go back and forth from page to page.
5. Items must be stated with as much precision and clarity as possible to avoid confusion and misinterpretation.
6. Arrange options and items alphabetically or numerically so that students do not have to waste time in searching for the correct response.
7. Provide complete directions on *how* students are to respond. If students are not provided with clear instructions, they could miss every item on this section of the test.

Examples of poor and acceptable matching items follow:

POOR:

	Column I		*Column II*
a.	Constance Rourke	1.	"The Douglas Tragedy"
b.	J. Frank Dobie	2.	"Mustangs"
c.	short story	3.	Clarence Day
d.	ballads and tales	4.	"The White Tiger"
e.	"Life With Father"	5.	Helen Keller

(This is a poor example of matching for several reasons. First, there are no headings that accurately describe the items in each. Second, the items do not refer to a single class or group. Authors, genres, and titles are mixed. Third, there are no directions to assist the student in the matching exercise. Last, the items have no particular arrangement such as alphabetical order.)

Better: Directions: The first column consists of poets who wrote lyric poems in the second column. Place the letter of the poem in the second column with the poet in the first column who composed it. Poems may be used only once or not at all.

	Poets		*Lyric Poems*
___1.	Pardraic Colum	A.	"Trade Winds"
___2.	Allan Cunningham	B.	"Travel"
___3.	Joyce Kilmer	C.	"The Ticket Agent"
___4.	Edna St. Vincent Millay	D.	"A Wet and Flowing Sea"
___5.	John Masefield	E.	"Roofs"
___6.	Edmund Leamy	F.	"An Old Woman of the Roads"
		G.	"Ode to a Grecian Urn"

COMPLETION TESTS. Completion is probably the oldest form of the objective test. Bringing closure to a sentence, often called *cloze,* is an effective way of testing comprehension of subject matter content. This test form does not allow as much guessing as do the true-false, matching, and multiple-choice items. Again, there is a danger of ambiguity. A student teacher recently included this item on a test: "Aaron Burr was shot in ___." Did the teacher expect the response to be a year, a place, a body part?

The following rules may assist the item writer in constructing completion tests:

1. Items should be written so that the required response is a significant specific word or phrase.
2. The blanks should be conveniently arranged for scoring and should be the same length so as not to give graphic clues.
3. Use only one blank per item.
4. The blanks should occur toward the end of a sentence rather than at the beginning to prevent students' from having to reread items.
5. Avoid specific determiners such as *a* or *an.*

Examples of poor and acceptable completion items follow:

Poor: Abraham Lincoln was born in _____. (The reader is not given a specifically desired response. The item is ambiguous. Students might respond with a place, a date, or even a phrase describing conditions of his birth.)

Better: Abraham Lincoln was born in the year _____.

Poor: "The Monkey's Paw," a _____, was written by _____ who was born in _____. (Completion items should be limited to one blank per sentence.)

Better: "The Monkey's Paw" was written by _____, born in 1863.

Poor: _____ wrote "The Oregon Trail." (The blank should not appear at the beginning of the sentence.)

Better: "The Oregon Trail" was written by _____, a poet well known for his lyric poetry.

Poor: When two angles have a sum total of 120°, the triangle is called an _____ triangle. (The determiner *an* may give the answer away.)

Better: When two angles have a sum total of 120°, the triangle is called (a, an) _____ triangle.

Multiple-Choice Tests. Multiple-choice items allow more variety in measurement than other types of objective tests. Higher levels of comprehension than just the factual recall can be assessed. The multiple-choice is perhaps the most difficult of all the objective forms to construct. The item usually consists of the problem, or the stem, and the choices. Among the choices are the correct answer, and one or more distractors or foils.

The following rules may prove helpful in constructing multiple-choice items:

1. Include as many words as possible in the stem so that they are not repeated in the choices.
2. Keep the options short and approximately the same length.
3. Avoid negatives when possible.
4. Keep the syntactical structure consistent.
5. Be sure there is only one correct answer or clearly best answer.

Poor: "Julius Caesar"

____1. was written by William Shakespeare.
____2. is a long narrative poem.
____3. has modern implications in that propaganda is used as a method for controlling people's minds and can be paralleled in other civilizations' disappearing democracy.
____4. was written over five hundred years ago.

(This item is poorly written and violates several of the rules set forth for good multiple-choice items: Very little information is given in the stem;

option number three is disproportionate in length to the others; and there are more than one clearly correct answers. The syntactic structure is not consistent among the choices.)

Better: "Julius Caesar," written three hundred years ago by William Shakespeare, may be classified in literary genre as:

_____1. a narrative poem
_____2. a full-length play
_____3. a novel
_____4. a lyric poem

In summary, when constructing objective test items, there are some general principles to keep in mind. First, consider the reading level of the test. Be sure the vocabulary level and the concept complexity are appropriate for the group being tested. Second, try to make each item independent so that students are not doubly jeopardized when they miss an item. Third, avoid testing on trivia and trick questions. The more capable students are often handicapped to a greater extent than the less able by trick questions because their logic is interrupted. Last and foremost, avoid ambiguity. This is probably the test constructor's greatest fault. One *Peanuts* cartoon showed Peppermint Patty taking a test. The one question asked was, "Discuss World War II. You may use the back of your paper if necessary." Peppermint Patty's dilemma is, unfortunately, not that rare in today's classrooms.

Item Analysis

Teachers who develop their own achievement tests can improve the quality of their tests by doing an item analysis on each test after it has been used at least once. The purpose of the item analysis is to discover which items are functioning well and which have serious weaknesses. After an item analysis is performed, the teacher has empirical data to use in eliminating poor items or revising them for future use. The item analysis should include a determination of the level of difficulty of the item and a determination of the degree to which the item discriminates between the high-scoring and low-scoring students. That is, a good item will be answered correctly more often by the students who earn a high score on the *whole* test than by students who earn a low score on the whole test. In addition, for a multiple-choice test, the analysis should show how each option of the item is functioning (the correct answer and all of the incorrect options for the item). While test publishers use elaborate procedures for item analyses, the teacher generally must rely upon a relatively simple process. The following section explains one simple method that a teacher might use.

Before the item analysis is begun each test item should be typed (double-spaced) on a separate card, perhaps a 5 by 7 card. The back of the card can be used to record data. The cards can be stored conveniently in a card file and retrieved when needed.

In order to determine the relative *difficulty* of an item, one might simply determine what proportion of the students who were given the test passed the item, and what proportion failed it. For example, in a group of 100 students, if 75 students passed Item No. 37, while 25 students failed it, the passing proportion is 75/100 or 75. This would be a relatively easy item as compared with one for which the passing proportion is, for example, 40/100 or 40. The teacher generally should place the easiest items at the beginning of the test in order to let the student build some confidence and momentum early in the testing period. The difficulty factor, say .40, could be recorded on the back of the item card.

As previously stated, the item analysis should include an examination of the item in order to evaluate its performance in the test as a whole. One question to be answered is, does the item tend to differentiate between the strong and weak student? Another question is, can the quality of the item be improved by minor changes, or should the item be discarded? Using the common multiple-choice item as a model, the following procedure is recommended for this aspect of the item analysis.

Figure 25 shows an example of an item typed on the front side of an item card. Figure 26 shows the back side of the item card as it might appear after the item has been used and the responses to the possible answers (options) have been tallied.

Item No. *12*

A molecule of H_2SO_4 contains how many atoms?

    a. One
    b. Two
    c. Three
    d. Six
    e. Seven

Figure 25. Example of the front side of an item card.

Item No. *12*

Group	A	B	C	D	E*
High	0	3	1	1	20
Low	3	6	3	9	4

*correct answer

Figure 26. Example of the back side of an item card.

While one could use the response data from all the students who took the test, a better procedure is to use only the data for top and bottom third or fourth of the group who took the test, according to total scores. The rationale for this alternative is that it is better to use the extreme cases, such as the top quarter and bottom quarter of the group, to designate strong and weak performance on the test than just the top and bottom halves of the whole group. That is, performance by the top fourth of the class is clearly high and performance by the lowest fourth is clearly low, but this is not necessarily true for the top and bottom halves, because the scores near the mean are not clearly high or low. The example in Figure 26 shows how the top and bottom fourths of a group of students might have performed on a test. It can be seen that three students of the low group (lowest fourth) chose option A, but none of the high group did. Six lows and three highs chose option B. Three lows and one high chose C, while nine lows and one high chose D. Finally, 20 of the high group chose the correct answer (E), but only four students in the low group did so. This item discriminates well between the high-scoring and low-scoring students. All of the distractors (incorrect options) are working in favor of the high group, and the high group clearly knew the answer (except for a few students).

Figures 27 and 28 show a somewhat different picture. Of course, the item is different from that in Figure 25, but so is the distribution of responses.

The response pattern indicates two serious flaws in the item, No. 16.

Item No. *16*

White blood cells are most likely to increase in number when a person

    a. exercises vigorously
    b. is in need of sleep
    c. acquires an infection
    d. begins a high-calorie diet
    e. eats foods that are rich in iron

Figure 27. Second example of the front side of an item card.

Item No. *16*

Group	A	B	C*	D	E
High	2	0	15	2	6
Low	5	0	15	4	1

*correct answer

Figure 28. Second example of the back side of an item card.

First, as many of the low-scoring students as high-scoring students chose the correct option (C), and second, no students chose option B. The person who wrote the item should scrutinize it and then alter it for a better performance in the next test. Perhaps a better distractor can be written for option B to make it an attractive distractor or foil for the low group. The other options also could be examined to determine whether they can be improved (including the answer). Sometimes the stem of an item, rather than the options, needs improvement.

After an item analysis is made, the best items can be retained in their original form, some items can be revised and used again, and some can be discarded. Gradually a teacher can build a sound test. The item cards can be kept in a card file for future use, and if many good items are written, they can be selected through a random procedure to make alternate test forms. This, of course, takes a lot of time and effort. True-false, matching, and completion items also may be subjected to an item analysis, but the procedure just explained must be altered appropriately.

Essay Tests

The essay examination has major advantages over the objective test forms. The teacher is better able to assess the higher levels of comprehension — inference, evaluative thinking, synthesis, application, and problem-solving abilities. The student has the advantage of not only engaging in these thought processes but in organizing and presenting thoughts in an orderly systematic fashion. Thus, the student is provided the opportunity of becoming proficient in a much needed skill — written expression. Even in the preparation for an essay examination, the student is involved in outlining, organizing, and summarizing important thinking and study skills.

Major disadvantages of the essay examination are the difficulty of grading in terms of time and objectivity, the advantage verbal students have over the more nonverbal ones, and the inability to make interclass comparisons because of the unreliability of the evaluation.

The following suggestions are presented as guides for improving essay examinations, both in constructing and evaluating them.

1. Give pupils much practice in writing answers to essay questions in nonpressure situations before the actual examination.
2. Decide what mental processes are to be tapped before starting to write the question.
3. Avoid ambiguity. Clearly define for the student the expected task and how it should be accomplished.
4. On controversial issues, ask pupils for substantiation or documentation and presentation of evidence.
5. Adapt the length and complexity to the ability level of the students to be tested.

6. Allow the students a choice of answering three of four questions, or five of seven, for example, to allow them present quality responses. This helps avoid the encouragement of students' verbalization on content with which they are unfamiliar.
7. Try to evaluate the responses without being influenced by prior knowledge of students' abilities.
8. The following guide words may prove to be helpful in constructing essay examinations. The key is in the careful selection of the verb, in contrast to the overuse of *discuss, explain,* and *describe* — all rather ambiguous terms. The student needs to be taught to look for a specific focus and to write to that focus. Also, it will be beneficial to teachers in evaluating if they have specified the information for which they are asking. Examples of specific verbs follow:

compare	justify
contrast	list
criticize	outline
define	prove
diagram	relate
enumerate	review
evaluate	summarize
illustrate	trace
interpret	

When teachers and students become more exact in constructing and interpreting essay questions, the essay examination will become less subjective as an evaluative tool and will yield more accurate information for determining student marks and class groupings. Most important, examinations can provide rich learning experiences for the students as papers are critiqued and corrected.

Teacher-made tests include true-false, matching, completion, multiple choice, and essay. The choice of test items should depend on the objective to be measured. However, it is important to provide a balance throughout the school term in order to give students opportunities to demonstrate their various kinds of skills and abilities and to provide practice for them in a variety of test-taking skills. This practice will prove invaluable as students progress through their school career.

STANDARDIZED MEASURES OF ACHIEVEMENT

Upon examining a standardized achievement test, one will note that the items are not unlike the items on teacher-made tests, previously discussed in this chapter. Standardized tests measure many of the same areas of knowledge. What, then, are standardized tests and why are they so widely used?

A standardized test is commonly defined as a test designed to provide a systematic sample of individual performance, administered according to prescribed directions, scored in conformance with definite rules, and interpreted in reference to certain normative information. Some would further restrict the usage of the term "standardized" to those tests for which the items have been chosen on the basis of experimental evaluation, and for which data on reliability and validity are provided. Others would add "commercially published" and/or "for general use." Norms or averages for different age or grade levels have been predetermined.

Types of Standardized Achievement Tests

There are more standardized achievement tests constructed, sold, and administered than any other type of tests. Standardized achievement tests can be divided into three classifications — survey, diagnostic, and readiness or prognostic.

Survey Tests

Survey tests assess pupil growth either in a single subject area or a group of subject matter areas. The survey tests are available from primary to adult level, though the majority are used in the elementary schools. The survey test yields information that allows a teacher to determine a pupil's relative standing in a subject matter area as compared to a uniform normative sample.

Single survey tests, such as the well-known *Gates-MacGinitie Reading Test,* permit a thorough evaluation of a student's performance in a specific content area. They typically yield only one to three overall scores and reveal no information as to possible causative factors for low achievement. Therefore, they cannot be used for diagnostic purposes. They do yield valuable information, however, in determining present level of performance and growth when used as a pre- and postassessment.

Survey test batteries are the most comprehensive way of assessing general achievement. Survey test batteries yield valuable information in determining pupils' relative achievement in the basic skills and the various subject areas. Individual performance in different content areas may be compared directly since the various tests in the battery are standardized in the same population. Survey test batteries usually yield individual profiles that aid in assisting the teacher or curricular decision-maker in determining specific strengths and weaknesses. The *Iowa Tests of Basic Skills* is an example of a survey test battery. Representative of most test batteries, it yields scores in five areas of basic skills — vocabulary, reading comprehension, language skills, work-study skills, and arithmetic skills.

An obvious advantage of the test battery over the single content test is that it yields a variety of scores for comparative purposes. A disadvantage is that each of the tests in a survey battery contains a more limited sample of the performance in a single content area.

Diagnostic Tests

Survey tests enable school personnel to do some initial screening of pupils who score well below other students of like age and grade placement. They are not, however, diagnostic in nature, nor do they suggest areas of possible remediation. For this purpose, a teacher would need to select a *diagnostic* achievement test designed to enable teachers and counselors to determine pupils' performance and yield information on the causes of difficulty in skills areas such as reading, arithmetic, and language.

Unlike general survey tests, which usually yield from one to three scores, the diagnostic test yields scores on each of several skills. These tests are considerably longer than survey tests, containing more items in each area of the specific skill being measured. For this reason, they usually take longer to administer, may require special equipment, and are more complicated to administer. Interpretation is usually more complex.

While the *Gates-MacGinitie Reading Test* is an example of a *survey* test in reading yielding three scores (vocabulary, comprehension, and rate), the *Gates-McKillop Diagnostic Reading Test* is an excellent example of the *diagnostic* reading test. It yields many scores in such areas of reading as syllabication, auditory blending, oral reading, and use of context in word analysis. Most diagnostic tests are in the area of reading, but more and more are emerging in areas of mathematics, spelling, and language usage. A diagnostic test should be used when it is desirable to have a detailed analysis of a pupil's disability in a specific area and to determine possible causes for that disability. Results of diagnostic tests should guide the teacher or counselor directly into instructional strategies for remediation.

Readiness or Prognostic Tests

Readiness or prognostic tests are administered to predict how well the pupil may be expected to achieve in specific school subjects. Reading readiness tests are a prime example of prognostic tests. Such tests yield data used to make decisions about time of entrance into first grade or whether particular students are ready to profit from instruction in reading.

At the secondary level, prognostic tests in areas such as algebra, geometry, and foreign languages have been developed to predict students' probable success in learning the skills involved in those areas. Readiness or prognostic tests are like aptitude tests in that they predict future achievement in a specific area.

Achievement Test Batteries

More standardized achievement test batteries are available at the elementary school level than at the secondary school level. Among the most commonly used achievement test batteries are the *California*

Achievement Test, Metropolitan Achievement Test, Stanford Achievement Test, and *Iowa Tests of Basic Skills*. All of these tests include subtests in the areas of reading comprehension, vocabulary, fundamentals of arithmetic, arithmetic reasoning, language, and spelling. Science and social studies may be an added measure in the upper grades. Some of the features of each of these achievement batteries will be discussed briefly. For more complete information readers should write to the publishers for specimen sets of the batteries, including the manuals.

The *California Achievement Test,* Forms C and D, copyrighted in 1977 and 1978, is a battery of achievement tests that provides information for use in making education decisions leading to the improvement of instruction in the basic skills. Both norm-referenced and criterion-referenced information is included. The tests purport to measure knowledge and understanding in reading, language, spelling, and reference skills from kindergarten level through grade 12. The *California Achievement Test* does not include measures of science and social studies. A helpful resource included in the test is a class management guide, which helps the teacher make optimum use of the obtained test results for improving instruction. The *California Achievement Test* is a useful instrument for schools seeking a general achievement test (K to 12) in the areas of reading, arithmetic, and language. It is published by California Test Bureau/McGraw-Hill.

The *Metropolitan Achievement Test,* copyrighted in 1970, is published by Harcourt Brace Jovanovich, Inc. The battery is normed for a K.6 to 9.5 population. The test measures skills in language, reading, and arithmetic, and at the upper levels, the mastery of study skills, science, and social studies content. The content of the tests leans toward a more traditional curriculum, with much emphasis on factual recall. Scores are reported in standard scores, grade equivalents, percentile ranks, and stanines.

The *Stanford Achievement Test* was revised in 1973 and is published by Harcourt Brace Jovanovich, Inc. It measures knowledge and skills in the areas of reading, language arts, and arithmetic, and, for grades four and above, science and social studies. Two forms each are available at eight levels, spanning from grades 1.5 through 13 (college). The tests were standardized on a national population, stratified according to geographical area, family income, type of school, and education level of family. The content is based on an analysis of widely used textbooks and general curriculum is fairly traditional.

The *Iowa Tests of Basic Skills,* developed by A. N. Hieronymous and E. F. Lindquist, and published by Houghton Mifflin, are designed to assess the basic educational skills that are essential for academic achievement. The five major skill areas of the ITBS are Vocabulary, Reading, Language Skills (Spelling, Capitalization, Punctuation, and Usage), Work-Study Skills (Map Reading, Reading Graphs and Tables,

Knowledge and Use of Reference Materials), and Mathematics Skills (Mathematics Concepts, Mathematics Problem Solving). The ITBS is available for several grade levels ranging from 1.7 to 9. Scores are reported in the form of age equivalents, grade equivalents, percentile ranks, standard scores and stanines.

Validity and Reliability

In the technical reports and test manuals provided by the publishers of the standardized achievement tests, one can generally find a copious amount of data concerning the tests' reliability. The reliability coefficients are reported for subtests and for the total batteries. The reliability coefficients may range from as low as the .40s to the upper .90s, but they tend to be in the upper .80s and lower .90s (rather respectable figures). The coefficients of reliability for the total batteries (composite scores) tend to be higher than the subtest coefficients, which is to be expected because the subtests are much shorter than the total batteries.

Validity data generally are less prominent than reliability data in the manuals and technical reports. As the test authors often state, *content* validity for an achievement test cannot be determined statistically. Each school should compare the test being considered with the school's curriculum content and then decide whether the test is sufficiently valid.

The technical manuals often contain some criterion-related validity data to show how the test results are correlated with such achievement criteria as grade-point average (school or college), scores on other achievement tests, or scores on mental-ability tests. The correlations between a particular achievement battery's composite score and the composite score for some other achievement battery tend to range from approximately .70 to approximately .90. The achievement-test composite score correlates less well with grades in school or college than with composite scores for other achievement tests, with most of the reported reliability coefficients being in the .50s and .60s. The correlations between achievement-test composite scores and mental-ability test scores appear to range from about .30 to about .70, and this is about what should be expected. Mental-ability is related to achievement but is not the only important factor that affects achievement.

The test user is urged to examine the evidence of validity and reliability for all tests that are being used or being considered. While the technical reports are major sources for this information, relevant articles in professional journals should be utilized too.

REFERENCES

Ahmann, J. Stanley and Glock, Marvin D.: *Evaluating Pupil Growth,* 4th ed. Boston, Allyn and Bacon, Inc. 1967.

Aiken, Lewis R.: *Psychological Testing and Assessment,* 3rd ed. Boston, Allyn and Bacon, Inc., 1979.

Chase, Clinton I.: *Measurement for Education Evaluation.* Reading, Massachusetts, Addison-Wesley Publishing Company, 1974.

Durost, Walter, et al.: *Manual of Directions for the Metropolitan Achievement Tests.* New York, Harcourt, Brace and World, Inc., 1964.

Ebel, R. L.: *Measuring Educational Achievement.* Englewood Cliffs, N.J., Prentice-Hall, 1965.

Educational Testing Service: *Making the Classroom Test: A Guide for Teachers.* Princeton, N.J., Educational Testing Service, 1973.

Green, John A.: *Introduction to Measurement and Evaluation.* New York, Dodd, Mead, and Company, 1970.

Kelley, Truman, et al.: *Stanford Achievement Test Technical Supplement.* New York, Harcourt, Brace and World, Inc., 1966.

Kibler, R. J., et al.: *Objectives for Instruction and Evaluation.* Boston, Allyn and Bacon, 1974.

Lien, Arnold J.: *Measurement and Evaluation of Learning,* 2nd ed. Dubuque, Iowa, Wm. C. Brown Company Publishers, 1971.

Lindquist, E. F. and Hieronymous: *Manual for Administrators, Supervisors, and Counselors for the Iowa Tests of Basic Skills.* New York, Houghton-Mifflin Company, 1964.

Smith, Fred M. and Adams, Sam: *Educational Measurement for the Classroom Teacher.* New York, Harper and Row, Publishers, 1966.

Thorndike, Robert L. and Hagen, Elizabeth: *Measurement and Evaluation in Psychology and Education.* New York, John Wiley and Sons, Inc., 1969.

Tiegs, E. W. and Clark, W. W.: *Test Coordinator's Handbook for the California Achievement Tests.* Monterey, California, CTB/McGraw-Hill, 1970.

Webb, L. W. and Shotwell, Anna Mark: *Testing in the Elementary School.* New York, Farrar and Rinehart, Inc., 1939.

Chapter 7

APPRAISAL OF INTERESTS

THE APPRAISAL of a student's interests necessitates discovering the preferences or dislikes that the person has with regard to activities, tasks, school courses, jobs, or occupations. How does one go about assessing a person's interests? In answering this question, it may be helpful to examine the four kinds of interests given by Super and Crites (1962, pp. 337-380); namely, expressed interests, manifest interests, tested interests, and inventoried interests.

Expressed interests are those that are verbally stated by a person. If Peggy is asked in what kinds of work she is most interested, her reply may include a list of occupations, such as nursing, social work, teaching, law, etc. The difficulty with such a method of determining interests is that expressed interests fluctuate greatly, and too often they may be related to such factors as peer influence or glamorized stereotypes of the day. As the person gets older, attains greater maturity, and gains new experiences, expressed interests may change considerably.

Manifest interests are determined by noting which activities or occupations the individual participates in. If Jamie plays tennis and golf, works in a sporting goods store on Saturdays, serves as treasurer of the junior class, and takes all the mathematics and business classes he can take, there is some solid evidence that he is interested in sports and business activities. Still, sometimes students participate in activities for reasons other than strong interest; for example, to be with friends or to please parents.

Tested interests are those that are inferred from the results of standardized tests, such as achievement tests. If Ruth scores well on tests that measure achievement in English usage and reading comprehension, one could assume that she has a strong literary interest. Such an assumption may be unsound, however, because achievement is likely to be more closely related to ability than to interest.

Inventoried interests are determined by presenting a person a list of activities (or occupations) and requesting that the individual indicate which activities are preferred over the others. The sampling of interests in this way is likely to be more dependable than the other methods because the subject who responds to an interest inventory has many different activities to consider (including some that might not ordinarily come to mind), and the responses are arranged to fit a meaningful classification scheme. This systematic approach should make interest assessment more valid. This is not to say that interest

123

inventories are infallible, for they are not, and their limitations will be discussed later in this chapter.

INTEREST INVENTORIES

The history of the development of interest inventories probably goes back to 1907 when psychologist G. Stanley Hall developed a questionnaire for measuring children's recreational interests. Another notable year was 1919 because it was then that a graduate seminar on interests was held at the Cargenie Institute of Technology. The seminar was conducted in order to construct test items that could be used to discriminate interests according to occupations. This seminar led to further efforts aimed at measuring interests, the most notable one being the construction of the *Strong Vocational Interest Blank* (SVIB), by E. K. Strong. The development of the SVIB was innovative in two respects: (1) the inventory's items required that the subject indicate activities that were liked and disliked and (2) the responses were criterion keyed, or keyed for different occupations.

In 1939 a different style of interest inventory appeared on the scene, the Kuder Preference Record, by G. F. Kuder. Kuder's inventory differed greatly from Strong's with respect to keying because Kuder used homogeneous keying. This means that the Kuder items were selected in such a way that they were analogous in content and were significantly correlated to indicate a certain area of interest.

Other early inventories were the *Lee-Thorpe Occupational Interest Inventory* (OII), which appeared in 1943, and the *Guilford Interest Inventory*, of 1948. The OII was unique because a logical approach to validity was used, which means that items were selected for content rather than on the basis of empirical data. The Guilford inventory was different because of two features: (1) the use of factor analysis in the development of the interest scales and (2) the provision of separate scores for avocational and vocational interests.

Several other interest inventories have been constructed since these earlier ones, but attention will be given to just a few of the widely used inventories that may be employed in school settings.

The Kuder Inventories

The *Kuder General Interest Survey* (G. F. Kuder) is published by Science Research Associates, Inc. It is a downward extension of Forms B and C, which were developed earlier. It is discussed first in this chapter because it is used with younger subjects. The *Survey* (Kuder, 1971, p. 3) "was developed in response to a need for such an instrument for use with younger people, particularly at the junior high level." The *Survey*, according to the manual, has a sixth-grade vocabulary level and an improved scale for detecting carelessness, lack of understanding, or faking (intentionally giving inaccurate responses).

The normative data for the *Survey* were developed in the spring of 1963, when the survey was administered to a stratified sample of boys and girls in grades 6 through 12 in public schools in the United States (Kuder, 1964, p. 17).

The manual (pp. 23-35) shows numerous test-retest and K-R 20 reliability coefficients that are mainly in the .70s and .80s, with higher correlations for the 9-12 grade group than for the 6-8 grade group, indicating higher reliability for the older or more mature students. The results of several studies in which Kuder inventory were found to be positively related to job satisfaction appear to provide some evidence of criterion-related validity.

The *Kuder Survey*, or Form E, uses a forced-choice triad format, which means that activities are grouped in units of three and the subject is asked to respond by checking the most preferred and least preferred of the three activities. For example:

a. Read a book to yourself.
b. Read a book to someone else.
c. Have someone read a book to you.

Kuder chose the forced-choice triad because he felt that research indicated that it is relatively free of the response bias that may occur in other kinds of items, such as those that allow the subject to indicate simply "like" or "dislike" or "agree." That is to say, some people tend to respond *yes* or *no* in a biased manner when given freedom to do so. For instance, Paula may respond "like" for everything she does not strongly dislike, and Betty may mark "dislike" for all activities for which she does not have a strong preference. Paula shows a tendency toward "aye saying," and Betty shows a tendency toward "nay saying."

In addition to having a forced-choice format, Kuder E also is partially *ipsative* (Kuder, 1971). The term *ipsative measurement* refers to the condition in which each variable in a set of scales is compared with all of the other variables in the scale. This means that the score on each scale is relative to the subject's other scores, and the choice of a given variable necessitates rejection of the variable with which it is being compared. Thus, the number of times that one variable is chosen over others becomes the score for the scale to which it relates. With this ipsative structure, the total of the scales is the same for all subjects, and no individual can obtain all maximum or all minimum scores. Form E (Kuder, 1971, p. 4) "is ipsative in the limited sense that some triads are scored differentially on more than one scale. Activities in a given area are compared with a wide range of other activities, not all of which are scored for other areas."

The interest scales of Kuder E are Outdoor, Mechanical, Computational, Scientific, Persuasive, Artistic, Literary, Musical, Social Service, and Clerical. The raw scores of these scales are converted to percentile ranks. A percentile rank of 25 or under is supposed to indicate low interest, and a percentile rank at or above 75 is believed to be indicative of high interest. A verification (V) score is also reported to provide an estimate of the accuracy of the subject's responses.

The *Kuder Preference Record-Vocational Form C* (1960) measures interest in the same broad areas as the *General Interest Survey:*

> *Outdoor:* Preference for work or activity that keeps one outside most of the time — usually work dealing with plants and other growing things, animals, fish, and birds. Examples: foresters, naturalists, fishermen, telephone linemen, and farmers.
>
> *Mechanical:* Preference for working with machines and tools. Examples: aviator, toolmaker, machinist, plumber, automobile repairman, and engineer.
>
> *Computational:* Preference for working with numbers and an interest in math courses in school. Examples: bookkeeper, accountant, bank teller, and engineer.
>
> *Scientific:* Preference for work involving discovery or understanding of nature and the solution of problems, particularly with regard to the physical world. Examples: physician, chemist, engineer, laboratory technician, meteorologist, dietitian, and aviator.
>
> *Persuasive:* Preference for work that involves meeting and dealing with people, in convincing others of the justice of a cause or a point of view, or in promoting projects or things to sell. Examples: salesman, personnel manager, and buyer.
>
> *Artistic:* Preference for doing creative work with the hands — usually work involving design, color, and materials. Examples: artist, sculptor, dress designer, architect, hairdresser, and interior decorator.
>
> *Literary:* Preference for reading and writing. Examples: novelist, English teacher, poet, editor, news reporter, and librarian.
>
> *Musical:* Preference for musical activities. Examples: musician, music teacher, and music critic.
>
> *Social Service:* Preference for activities that involve helping people. Examples: nurse, Boy Scout or Girl Scout leader, counselor, tutor, personnel worker, social worker, hospital attendant, and religious worker.
>
> *Clerical:* Preference for work that involves specific tasks requiring precision and accuracy. Examples: bookkeeper, accountant, file clerk, salesclerk, statistician, teacher of commercial subjects, and traffic manager.

Form C consists of 168 items that are arranged in triads (as in Form E) and it utilizes the forced-choice method. The inventory may be hand scored or machine scored. Scale scores at or above the 75th percentile are supposed to indicate very strong interest, while scale scores below 25 are supposed to show low interest.

The Form C manual (Kuder, 1960) provides a list of occupations that may be suggested for a high score in a broad vocational area as well as a list of occupations for combinations of scores. For example:

MUSICAL

Professional
    Musician; Teacher of Music
    Composer
    Arranger
Semiprofessional
    Dancer; Chorus Girl

LITERARY-MUSICAL

Professional
    Actor; actress
    Author; editor, reporter
    Music Teacher
Semiprofessional
    Broadcasting Worker
    Music Commentator

Kuder-Richardson reliability coefficients are reported in the .80s and .90s. Validity information is scant.

Three other Kuder inventories are available: *Personal Preference Survey* (Form A), *Preference Record-Occupational* (Form D), and *Occupational Interest Survey* (Form DD).

Form A has 168 items and is designed for use with high school students and adults. It has five personal interest scales: Group Activity (participation in group activities), Stable Situations (being in familiar and stable situations), Dealing with Ideas, Avoiding Conflict, and Directing (or influencing) others. K-R reliability coefficients are reported to range from .76 to .89 for different samples of subjects who were administered Form A. The manual has data related to interest scores and job satisfaction as evidence for validity of the instrument.

Form D is a 100-item inventory that may be used for high school students and adults. The items for Form DD are the same as those in Form D. With Form DD, Kuder introduced a new scoring concept, which resulted in improved discrimination between occupational groups (Kuder, 1971). Form DD may be used with high school subjects, college students, and adults. There are 77 occupational scales and 29 college-major scales for men, 57 occupational scales and 27 college-major scales for women, and 8 experimental scales. A subject's score for a scale is a modified biserial correlation coefficient between the subject's interest responses and those of the criterion group. For these scales (and DD), the reported reliability coefficients tend to be centered near .90 for different samples. Evidence of validity is presented mainly through the use of errors-of-classification studies.

Strong-Campbell Interest Inventory

The *Strong-Campbell Interest Inventory* (SCII) (Campbell, 1977) was first published in 1974 by the Stanford University Press. The SCII was developed by combining the men's and women's *Strong Vocational Interest Blanks*, eliminating items with sexual bias, eliminating references to gender, and adding new scales. Another major change was the utilization of J. L. Holland's theoretical system of classifying occupations into six themes: Realistic, Investigative, Artistic, Social, Enterprising, and Conventional.

The SCII is suitable for use with high school students and adults. The SCII is oriented toward the professional, semiprofessional, and managerial occupations that college students are likely to enter.

The SCII contains 325 items that are grouped as follows:

Part   I Occupations (131 occupational titles)
       II School Subjects (36 school subjects)
     III Activities (51 general occupational activities)
    IV Amusements (39 spare-time activities)
     V Types of People (24 types of people)
    VI Preferences Between Two Activities (30 pairs of contrasting activities)
   VII Your Characteristics (14 personal characteristics)

SCII Scales

The SCII profile in Figure 29 provides data for Administrative Indexes, General Occupational Themes, Basic Interest Scales, Occupational Scales, and Special Scales.

In examining and interpreting the results shown in the profile, one should start with the Administrative Indexes. The indexes serve as indicators of response sets or carelessness in responding. If the total number of responses differs greatly from 325 or if the number of infrequent responses is as large as 32, the profile probably is not valid. In this case, the answer sheet should be examined and perhaps rescored. Another alternative, of course, is retesting of the subject. Because the Administrative Indexes are satisfactory in the profile (Fig. 29), one can proceed to the *General Occupational Themes*. The Themes are based upon Holland's (1973) classification system for occupations, and they provide rather broad classes of interest: *R*ealistic (outdoor, technical, mechanical interests); *I*nvestigative (scientific, inquiring, analytical interests); *A*rtistic (dramatic, musical, self-expressive interests); *S*ocial (helping, guiding, group-oriented interests); *E*nterprising (entrepreneurial, persuasive, political interests); *C*onventional (methodical, organized, clerical interests). The scores shown for the Themes are standard scores that are designated very low, moderately low, average, moderately high, and very high. In the profile (Fig. 29) the subject's Social Theme score of 57 is moderately high, the Enterprising Theme score is very low, the Conventional Theme score is moderately low, and the other three scores are average.

Turning to the Basic Interest Scales section of the profile, one can see that there are twenty-three scales that are grouped according to the six themes. These scales were constructed by grouping together those items that are highly correlated with each other. The raw scores are converted to standard scores, and these are then classified qualitatively as being very low, low, average, high, and very high. In the profile, the subject's scores are very high for agriculture, military activity, public speaking, and law/politics, but very low for business management.

There are 124 Occupational Scales, and they were constructed by comparing SCII item responses of people in specific occupational groups with responses of people in general. T-scores are shown in the profile and these are classified as very dissimilar, dissimilar, average, similar, and very similar. The profile indicates "very dissimilar" scores for Instrument Assembly, Physicist, Interior Decorator, Buyer, Business Education Teacher, Accountant, and Secretary. "Very similar" scores are not indicated, but there are "similar" scores for Physical Education Teacher, Physical Therapist, College Professor, Director of Christian Education, Secondary Social Science Teacher, and Lawyer.

There are two Special Scales in the profile: Academic Orientation (AOR) and Introversion-Extroversion (IE). The AOR scale is a "rough index of the degree of comfort a person feels, or might feel, in an academic environment, especially a high quality liberal arts-and-science university environment" (Campbell, 1977, p. 90). A score above 50 may be considered to be high and a score below 30 may be considered low. The IE scale measures sociability to some extent. The person who scores high (60 or above) is not likely to be talkative and the one who scores low, say below 40, is likely to be very comfortable in a social situation and will talk freely. Considering the profile scores, one would expect the subject to be academically oriented and sociable.

A very general and brief interpretation of the profile would suggest that the subject has a preference for social activities, and is a sociable, academically oriented person. Such occupations as teaching, physical therapy, law, or religious work are suggested for further exploration with regard to vocational choice. Clerical work, business occupations, and occupations in service appear to be discrepant with inventoried interests, and this suggests that such occupations should not be considered seriously by the person, unless other important data indicate that

GENERAL OCCUPATION THEMES

THEME	SCORE	RESULTS
REALISTIC	43	AVERAGE SCORE
INVESTIGATIVE	53	AVERAGE SCORE
ARTISTIC	52	AVERAGE SCORE
SOCIAL	57	MOD-HIGH SCORE
ENTERPRISING	36	VERY LOW SCORE
CONVENTIONAL	44	MOD. LOW SCORE

ADMINISTRATIVE INDEXES

TOTAL RESPONSES 325
INFREQUENT RESPONSES 2

	RESPONSE %		
	LP	IP	DP
OCCUPATIONS	40	8	52
SCHOOL SUBJECTS	69	3	28
ACTIVITIES	41	2	57
AMUSEMENTS	59	8	33
TYPES OF PEOPLE	75	0	25
PREFERENCES	53	0	47
CHARACTERISTICS	64	0	36

SPECIAL SCALES

ACADEMIC ORIENTATION 55
INTROVERSION-EXTROVERSION 37

BASIC INTEREST SCALES

THEME	SCALE	SCORE
R	AGRICULTURE	68
	NATURE	49
	ADVENTURE	63
	MILITARY ACTIVITY	76
	MECHANICAL	38
I	SCIENCE	57
	MATHEMATICS	39
	MEDICAL SCIENCE	54
	MEDICAL SERVICE	57
A	MUSIC/DRAMATICS	54
	ART	43
	WRITING	55
S	TEACHING	62
	SOCIAL SERVICE	61
	ATHLETICS	63
	DOMESTIC ARTS	51
	RELIGIOUS ACTIVITY	64
E	PUBLIC SPEAKING	67
	LAW/POLITICS	66
	MERCHANDISING	40
	SALES	41
	BUSINESS MGMT.	35
C	OFFICE PRACTICES	41

(Scale markers: VERY LOW, LOW, AVERAGE, HIGH, VERY HIGH — 30, 40, 50, 60, 70)

OCCUPATIONAL SCALES

CODE	SCALE	SEX	SCORE
RC	FARMER	M	18
RC	INSTRUM. ASSEMBL.	F	14
RCE	VOC. AGRIC. TCHR.	M	20
REC	DIETITIAN	M	31
RES	POLICE OFFICER	M	36
RSE	HWY. PATROL OFF.	M	24
RE	ARMY OFFICER	F	44
RS	PHYS.-ED. TEACHER	F	49
R	SKILLED CRAFTS	M	6
RI	FORESTER	M	25
RI	RAD. TECH.(X-RAY)	F	36
RI	MERCH. MGR. OFF.	M	28
RI	NAVY OFFICER	M	18
RI	NURSE, REGISTERED	M	46
RI	VETERINARIAN	M	29
RIC	CARTOGRAPHER	M	20
RIC	ARMY OFFICER	M	38
RIE	AIR FORCE OFFICER	M	26
RIA	OCCUP. THERAPIST	F	33

CODE	SCALE	SEX	SCORE
AE	INT. DECORATOR	M	27
AE	ADVERTISING EXEC.	M	43
A	LANGUAGE TEACHER	F	31
A	LIBRARIAN	F	24
A	LIBRARIAN	M	18
A	REPORTER	M	42
A	REPORTER	F	53
AS	ENGLISH TEACHER	F	42
AS	ENGLISH TEACHER	M	55
SI	NURSE, REGISTERED	F	40
SIR	PHYS. THERAPIST	F	39
SRC	NURSE, LIC. PRACT	M	36
S	SOCIAL WORKER	F	37
S	SOCIAL WORKER	M	33
S	PRIEST	M	49
S	DIR., CHRISTIAN E	F	46
SE	YWCA STAFF	F	41
SIE	MINISTER	M	46

(Scale markers: VERY DISSIMILAR, DISSIMILAR, AVE, SIM., VERY SIM. — 15, 25, 45, 55)

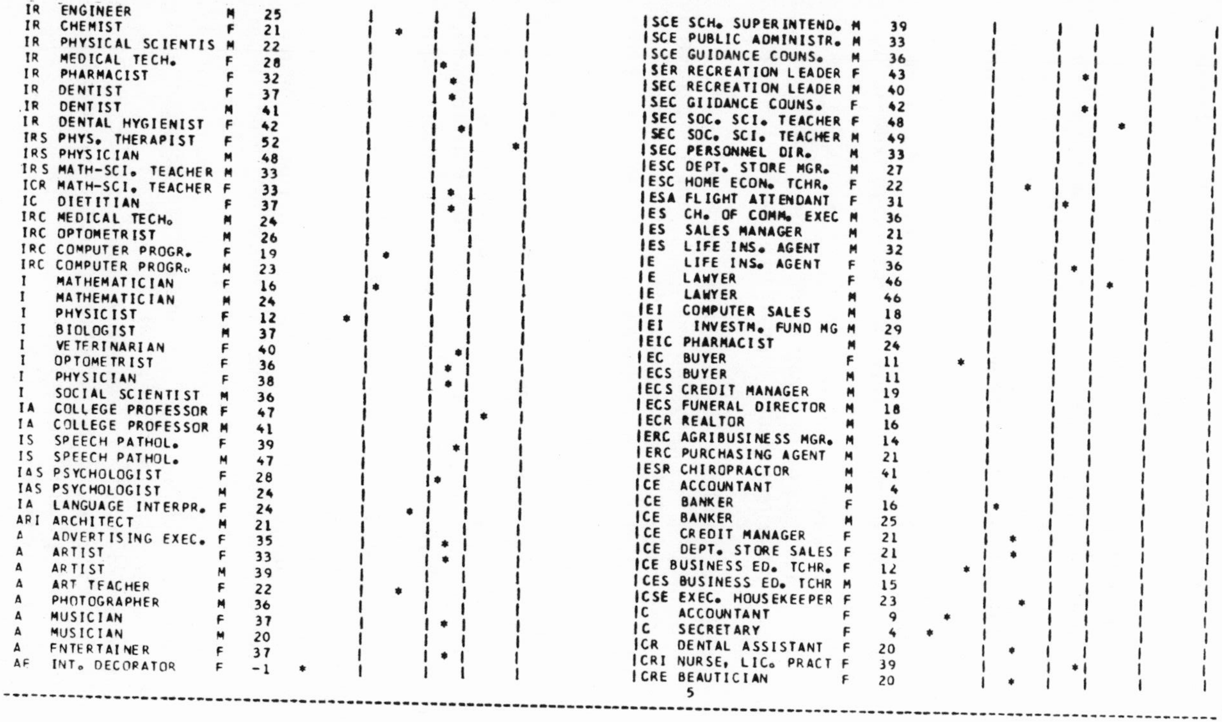

Figure 29. SCII profile. (Copyright 1974 by the Board of Trustees of Leland Stanford Junior University. Reprinted by permission.)

they should be considered. It is strongly advised that for a thorough interpretation, one should follow suggested guidelines in the manual closely.

Reliability and Validity of the SCII

The manual contains a considerable amount of information pertaining to the reliability and validity of the SCII. Median test-retest coefficients of reliability of .90, .88, and .85 are reported for three samples tested and retested over periods of two weeks, thirty days, and three years, respectively.

Data concerning concurrent and predictive validity are presented in the manual. The amount of overlap between criterion and reference samples is one kind of concurrent validity information provided. The reported overlap for the Occupational Scales is judged to be relatively small, and therefore indicative of concurrent validity. Another kind of concurrent validity information is mean-score comparison on the Occupational Scales. This criterion also appears to indicate validity for the SCII.

The case for predictive validity is based mainly upon the research of E. K. Strong with the *Strong Vocational Interest Blanks,* but some recent studies are cited in the manual. These studies relate to the tendencies of subjects with high or low interests in occupations to remain in or drop out of occupations. The evidence for predictive validity is difficult to obtain and what has been provided seems meager.

Ohio Vocational Interest Survey

The *Ohio Vocational Interest Survey* (OVIS) was developed by A. G. D'Costa and associates and is published by Harcourt Brace Jovanovich, Inc. The inventory was designed to assist students in grades eight through twelve with their educational and vocational plans (D'Costa, et al., 1972). It was standardized on a national sample of more than 45,000 students in school systems.

The OVIS consists of three parts: (1) an information questionnaire, (2) a local survey information section, and (3) an interest inventory. The inventory consists of 280 items, based upon the *Dictionary of Occupational Titles.* The items are grouped into clusters of five to six items. The inventory has 24 broad interest areas or scales. Of the 24 scales, 19 are common to males and females, and five are differentiated by sex. The 24 scales are listed in Figure 30.

For each item of the inventory the examinee indicates the degree of interest in the activity (such as model clothes for a department store) by marking one of the five possible answers:

I would *like* this activity very much. (L)

I would *like* this activity. (l)

I am *neutral.* I would neither like nor dislike this activity. (n)

OIS PROFILE CHART

Date of Testing

Grade 9   Age 1 4   yrs. 7   mos.   Sex M

NAT   Reference Group 9TH GRADE MALE

Scale Number	Scale Name	Scale Score	%ile Rank	Stanine Profile									Scale Clarity Index
				Low			Average			High			
				1	2	3	4	5	6	7	8	9	
13	NUMERICAL	49	96									9	H
2	MACHINE WORK	45	93								8		F
11	TRAINING	44	96									9	H
16	APPLIED TECH	42	75						6				H
7	CRAFTS	41	88							7			F
14	APPRAISAL	36	70						6				F
20	SALES REPRESENT	36	82							7			F
18	MANAGEMENT	35	62						6				F
22	ENTERTAINMENT	34	82							7			H
6	INSPECT-TESTING	33	89								8		F
23	TEACH-COUN-SOC W	33	64						6				F
17	PROMOTION-COMMU	32	59					5					F
21	MUSIC	30	56					5					I
15	AGRICULTURE	29	54.					5					F
8	CUSTOMER SERVICE	27	56					5					F
5	CLERICAL WORK	26	68						6				I
24	MEDICAL	26	63						6				F
10	SKILLED PER SERV	25	70						6				I
4	CARE PEOPLE-ANIM	24	49					5					I
9	NURSING	24	57					5					H
3	PERSONAL SERVICE	23	64						6				H
19	ARTISTIC	23	27				4						F
1	MANUAL	22	57					5					H
12	LITERARY	*											

Figure 30. OVIS profile chart. (Used with permission of Harcourt Brace Jovanovich, Inc.)

I would *dislike* this activity. (d)

I would *dislike* this activity very much. (D)

Scores for the scales are expressed in percentile ranks and stanines (see Fig. 30). Scale Clarity Indexes are used to indicate how consistent the subject was in responding: H (highly consistent), F (fairly consistent), or I (inconsistent). Several of the scales are for occupations other than professional occupations, and this would be advantageous for some students who are not college bound. The profile chart in Figure 30 shows high interests for numerical work, machine work, training, crafts, sales representative, entertainment, and inspecting and testing.

Reliability and Validity of OVIS

The authors of OVIS report internal consistency reliability estimates ranging from .80 to .94 for two large samples of students (eighth and tenth grade) from the national standardization population. Test-retest reliability coefficients ranging from .72 to .90 are reported for two other large samples of eighth and tenth grade students in Arkansas and Wisconsin schools. The test-retest interval was two weeks.

Evidence of validity for the OVIS, which appears to be a well-constructed instrument, is not as abundant as one would like for it to be. A claim for validity is made on the basis of the careful selection of the items, and the intercorrelation of the items. Evidence of concurrent and predictive validity appears to be lacking. It would be good to know that students who express strong interests in occupations tend to enter them or that those who dislike certain occupations tend not to enter them.

Minnesota Vocational Interest Inventory

The *Minnesota Vocational Interest Inventory*, by K. E. Clark and D. P. Campbell (1961), is published by The Psychological Corporation. The MVII was developed through the research of K. E. Clark during and after World War II. Clark's research involved Navy men and civilians. The inventory is an empirically keyed inventory that is designed to measure interests in *nonprofessional* occupations.

The MVII has 158 forced-choice triads of statements that describe tasks or activities involved in a variety of trades or nonprofessional occupations. Examinees must indicate their preference for the tasks by choosing one activity "liked most" and one "disliked most," while leaving the third unmarked. For example:

L D Study carpentry
L D Study first aid
L D Study welding

Scores are obtained for twenty-one Occupations Scales and nine Area Scales. Scores for the Occupations Scales indicate the extent of similarity that there is between the examinee's inventoried interests and those of men in general employed in the following occupations:

1. baker
2. food service manager
3. milk wagon driver
4. retail sales clerk
5. stock clerk
6. printer
7. tabulating machine operator
8. warehouseman
9. hospital attendant
10. pressman
11. carpenter
12. painter
13. plasterer
14. industrial education teacher
15. truck driver
16. truck mechanic
17. sheet metal worker
18. plumber
19. machinist
20. electrician
21. radio-tv repairman

Scores from the Area Scales indicate likes and dislikes for certain types of work activities that are common to several occupations. The raw scores are converted to standard scores.

Reliability and Validity of the MVII

The MVII manual provides test-retest reliability coefficients (30-day interval) ranging from .62 to .80, with most of the coefficients being in the .80s.

Validity data are scant for the MVII. The manual cites "percentage of overlap" between each criterion group and the Tradesmen-in-General group. The median overlap reported is 40 percent. A few predictive validity studies are reported. The correlations between interest scores for the MVII and such criteria as achievement and job satisfaction tend to be positive but low. This points up the fact that interest inventories lack validity as predictors of *success* and should not be used for such a purpose.

Other Interest Inventories

Many other interest inventories are available for use with school-age subjects. Among these are the *California Occupational Preference Survey* (Educational and Industrial Testing Service), the *Gordon Occupational Check List* (The Psychological Corporation), and the *Jackson Vocational Interest Survey* (Research Psychologists Press).

Use of Interest Inventories

Of what value are the data that one may obtain from interest inventories? The practical application of such information in schools can be placed mainly under the headings of instructional purposes and guidance purposes, although some overlap of function will occur.

Instructional Purposes

Teachers at both elementary and secondary school levels can make effective use of interest data in their classes. For example, interest may serve to indicate topics of study. If a teacher is assigning projects for students, and Connie is strongly interested in science, a science project would seem to be in order for her. If Tony is in a remedial reading class, his teacher may wish to make use of his interest profile to help him select books to read. One would expect him to make more progress with material that interests him than with other reading matter.

The teacher of an occupations class may wish to use student interest profiles to stimulate the students to think about what they may want to do for their life's work. Interest data can also be used to narrow down occupations for further study.

Guidance Purposes

There are two major guidance activities that can involve the use of interest-inventory results. One of these activities is helping students choose academic courses or programs. Certainly interests should not constitute the *sole* criterion for choosing courses, but they may provide a starting point. Aptitudes, academic record, and values are other factors that generally should be considered in connection with such decision making. The second guidance activity that can involve interests is *counseling*.

Individual counseling, especially when the problem of the student involves vocational planning, may necessitate the use of interest data. Walter may be certain that he wants to go to college or trade school, but he does not know how to go about making a sound vocational choice. The counselor may wish to approach the problem by identifying student preferences in order to narrow the field of investigation. As was mentioned previously, other pertinent variables also would be brought to bear on the problem.

Sometimes students have made their educational or vocational choice but are seeking a counselor's help in evaluating the choice. They want assurance that the choice is a good one. If the choice seems to be out of line with inventoried and expressed interests, the counselor may want to spend some time in discussing the basis for the choice. Perhaps the interest profile can be used to call attention to other occupations for which the student may be suited in terms of aptitudes and abilities.

Limitations of Interest Inventories

As is true of other paper-and-pencil appraisal instruments, interest inventories have certain distinct limitations. One serious shortcoming is that they can be "faked" by examinees who do not want to reveal their real interests. For example, Sammy, who wishes to appear to be interested in science to please his father, may deliberately choose science activities over those related to art and music where his strong interests lie. One way to check on "faking" is to compare the inventory scores with other evidence of interests, such as manifest interest.

Another important limitation is that the inventories sometimes require the subject to make choices among activities or occupations about which the subject has too little knowledge to make meaningful choices. How can a student choose among such occupations as machinist, architect, and chemist if the student does not have a good understanding of what people do in these occupations?

Finally, interest is not highly correlated with academic or vocational success, and yet interest scores may be erroneously considered to be useful prediction of achievement. This really is more of a criticism of the person who misinterprets interest scores than a criticism of the inventories.

If used cautiously, interest inventories can be helpful in teaching, guidance, and counseling, but if used carelessly they may do more harm than good.

REFERENCES

Campbell, D. P.: *Manual for the Strong-Campbell Interest Inventory.* Stanford, California, Stanford University Press, 1977.

Clark, K. E. and Campbell, D. P.: *Minnesota Vocational Interest Inventory Manual.* New York, The Psychological Corporation, 1961.

D'Costa, A. G., et al.: *Ohio Vocational Interest Survey Manual.* New York, Harcourt Brace Jovanovich, 1972.

Kuder, Frederic G.: *General Interest Survey Manual.* Chicago, Science Research Associates, Inc., 1971.

———: *Kuder Preference Record Manual.* Chicago, Science Research Associates, Inc., 1971.

———: *Occupational Interest Survey Manual.* Chicago, Science Research Associates, Inc., 1971.

Super, D. E. and Crites, J. O.: *Appraising Vocational Fitness.* New York, Harper and Row, 1962.

Zytowski, Donald G.: *Contemporary Approaches to Interest Measurement.* Minneapolis, University of Minnesota Press, 1973.

Chapter 8

APPRAISAL OF MENTAL ABILITY
AND APTITUDES

MENTAL ABILITY, or intelligence, is an extremely important characteristic because it influences so many aspects of human behavior. This can be realized quickly if one only tries to think of any
human behavior in which intelligence does not play a part.

What do we mean when we use such terms as intelligence or mental
ability or when we say that a person is smart, gifted, bright, dull, etc.?
The definitions are numerous and they vary greatly. Some are succinct,
and some are extremely lengthy, but the concept is an extremely
complex one. As a starting point for the discussion of the appraisal of
mental ability, several formal definitions of intelligence will be considered.

DEFINITIONS OF INTELLIGENCE

Alfred Binet, whom many consider to be the originator of modern
intelligence testing, apparently did not formulate a specific definition
of intelligence. Nevertheless, he believed that in order to behave intel-
ligently, one would have to be able to reason, make judgments, and
comprehend. The intelligence test that Binet and Simon constructed in
1905 reflected the emphasis on these abilities.

Terman (1921, p. 128) defined intelligence as the ability to carry on
abstract thinking, which may be defined as the ability to use symbols
and concepts in dealing with unfamiliar situations or problems. Verbal
and mathematical symbols and abstract concepts are used in tests that
are supposed to tap this type of mental ability. Terman's test items tend
to reflect the emphasis on abstract thinking.

Thorndike (1927) referred to intelligence as the power of good
responses from the point of view of truth or fact. He and his co-workers
considered intelligence to be the ability to perform intellectual tasks,
and they believed that the ability could be measured through the use of
a series of "tasks," referred to as CAVD. The first letter, C, represents a
task that requires supplying words to make a statement true and
sensible. The letter A represents the solving of arithmetic problems.
The letter V stands for the ability to understand words, and D to
understand connected discourse, as in paragraph reading. It is apparent that the CAVD tests measured academic achievement, and thus
may have been achievement tests rather than intelligence tests in the
strict sense.

138

Stoddard (1943, p. 4) defines intelligence as "the ability to undertake activities that are characterized by (1) difficulty, (2) complexity, (3) abstractness, (4) economy, (5) adaptiveness to a goal, (6) social value, and (7) the emergency of originals, and to maintain such activities under conditions that demand a concentration of energy and a resistance to emotional forces." It is interesting to note that Stoddard's definition includes such nonintellective factors as social value and motivation. This lengthy, comprehensive definition may be too cumbersome to be of practical value.

Fromm and Hartman (1955) look at intelligence from a gestalt point of view and see it as a function of the total personality of a person. Intelligence, they maintain, is interrelated with emotions, physical health, and life experience. Thus, intelligence testing must involve a thorough assessment of the subject's personality. This position appears to have merit, but lacks practicality, for the time and effort required for such assessment would seriously limit intelligence testing.

Wechsler (1958, p. 7) defines intelligence as "the aggregate or global capacity of the individual to act purposefully, to think rationally, and to deal effectively with his environment." His position is that intelligence is not simply the sum of mental abilities or components that can be measured because (1) intelligent behavior also includes the way in which the components are combined, (2) such psychological factors as needs and drives are involved, and (3) a high degree of one aptitude or ability contributes little to the effectiveness of behavior as a whole. He maintains that various elements of intelligence must be measured in order to obtain a measure of general mental ability — a global mental capacity.

Wesman (1968, p. 267) considers intelligence to be "a summation of learning experiences." This definition implies that mental ability tests measure the product of a person's many life experiences rather than an innate entity. The definition avoids the difficulty of having to explain differences in aptitude, achievement, and intelligence tests because all these are considered to be tests of what a person has learned, and the labels merely indicate the purposes of the different types of tests.

Fischer (1969, p. 669) has still another definition of intelligence: "Effectiveness, relative to age peers, of the individual's approaches to situations in which competence is highly regarded by the culture." Fischer's definition emphasizes the individual's effectiveness rather than potential or aptitude. The age-peer comparison suggests that effectiveness may change with age. Fischer maintains that present intelligence tests reflect the abilities that culture has come to value.

Definitions of intelligence have been difficult to formulate because the concept of intelligence is so complex and so difficult to understand. In fact, the question "What is intelligence?" still remains to be answered. Definitions can serve useful purposes, however. One purpose has just been implied: because there are definitions that vary greatly, it should be apparent to test users that caution must be used in making assumptions about intelligence tests. Second, definitions call attention to the fact that a given test may only be measuring intelligence as defined by the author of the test. In a sense, then, the definition may suggest what a test does and does *not* measure. Knowing the strengths and limitations of the test should help one to use the results cautiously and well.

THEORIES OF INTELLIGENCE

What is the underlying "structure" of intelligence or general intellectual ability? This question has been answered "in theory" differently by several different psychologists. A few of the prominent theories or models of intelligence will be discussed briefly in order to help the reader gain some understanding of the complexity of the concept.

Thorndike's Multifactor Theory

Thorndike (1927) conceptualized intelligence as a collection of minute, specific elements. These "abilities," he theorized, can function together during intelligent behavior. Thus, he assumed that intellectual activities are the combined effect of large numbers of very small but independent factors (abilities). Different mental activities produce correlations of performance, he reasoned, because they have some factors in common. A complex mental activity, such as verbal comprehension, according to the theory, would have several factors or abilities functioning at the same time.

Spearman's Two-Factor Theory

Charles Spearman (1927), a British psychologist, made use of factor analysis in order to formulate his theory of intelligence, the two-factor theory. He correlated the results obtained from several tests in a battery of tests and concluded that an individual's performance on a given test or task depends upon a broad, general mental ability (g) and also upon one or more specific abilities (s). The "g" factor is believed to be common to all intellectual activities and the "s" factor is considered to be specific to a particular activity. For example, writing a poem would require "g" and at least one specific factor.

Spearman theorized that "g" is responsible for the correlations found among many tests that are measuring the same factor to a degree. Spearman felt that "g" represents insight into relationships, while specific factors, like rote memory, do not. Spearman believed that the ideal test of intellectual ability should have high loading on the "g" factor.

Spearman's theory has been criticized for being too simple and for not providing for group factors. While Spearman and his co-workers have conceded that group factors may exist, they regard them as rare and insignificant.

Thurstone's Group-Factor Theory

Thurstone (1938) also used factor analysis to formulate a theory of intelligence. Thurston did not accept the assumption of a simple common or general factor, but he maintained that test correlations indicate that several group factors make up intelligence. In his major factor analysis study, published in 1938, he administered a battery of 56 tests to 218 college students, and seven factors were identified. The seven factors were S = spatial ability, P = perceptual speed, N = numerical ability, V = verbal meaning, M = memory, W = word fluency, and R = inductive reasoning. Thurstone assumed that these were primary mental abilities and that intellectual performance was based upon a combination of these factors. There is no evidence that strongly supports the claim that abilities are "primary," either neurologically or psychologically speaking. At first, Thurstone insisted that no general factor existed, but later he found that his "primary" factors were correlated. He then explained this fact by identifying a second-order general factor. Thus, in a sense, he at least acknowledged the possibility that a general factor of intelligence exists.

Vernon's Hierarchical Theory

Vernon (1951) proposed a hierarchical theory of intelligence that utilizes the results of factor-analysis studies in yet a different way. His model, illustrated in the diagram in Figure 31, provides for the existence of a general factor, plus major and minor group factors and finally several specific factors. Vernon based his model on the results of test data obtained from British Army and Navy recruits.

In Vernon's model, the general factor is the most important factor in

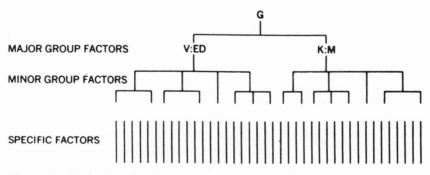

G

MAJOR GROUP FACTORS   V:ED   K:M

MINOR GROUP FACTORS

SPECIFIC FACTORS

Figure 31. Hierarchy of abilities. (Modified from Philip E. Vernon: *The Structure of Human Abilities*, 1951, p. 22. Courtesy of Methuen and Co., Ltd.)

the structure of intellect. The major group factors, V:ed (verbal-education) and K:m (spatial-mechanical) break down to minor factors, and these in turn to even more limited specific or special factors.

According to Vernon (1960), intelligence corresponds to the general level of complexity of a person's "schemata" that have been accumulated and developed during a lifetime. One's innate ability limits the ability to build up schemata, but the more one acquires, the greater the tendency to develop schemata that are even more complex and flexible. As the schemata are developed, the later ones will be of a higher order and will be weighted more heavily with the general factor, while the earlier ones will be more specific. Vernon's theory also holds that, if the environment is stimulating, a person's schemata will increase in flexibility and complexity. Vernon also has expressed the belief that the "g" factor is not constant throughout one's life and that it varies widely in children. According to the theory, adults become very specialized, and thus "g" is not a good measure of their intellectual abilities later in life.

Butcher (1972, p. 50) sees two major advantages of this theory over other theories of intelligence:

> It accounts for the proliferation of apparently conflicting findings and the multiplicity of ability factors that have been described and labelled. Much of the apparent confusion has been caused by the comparison of factors operating at different levels in the hierarchy, and this in turn is largely due to the initial selection of tests and people. To this extent, the criticism of factorial methods, "that you only get out of a factor analysis what you put in" is correct. The second major advantage is that one is thus enabled to recognize that different kinds of factors, and the tests based on them, serve very different purposes in assessment and prediction.

Piaget's Theory

Jean Piaget, a Swiss biologist and epistemologist, developed a theory of intelligence in which mental ability is considered to be an extension of certain basic biological characteristics. His more recent studies (1963) have been on children's thinking and the development of intelligence. He defines intelligence as the coordination of operations that are reversible actions.

Piaget (1950) theorizes that *organization* and *adaptation* are two important aspects of intellectual functioning. Organization may be thought of as the system underlying a person's behavior oriented toward maintaining a state of equilibrium. Adaptation may be defined as the system of utilizing change in order to interact successfully with the environment. Adaptation can be subdivided into the two complementary functions called *assimilation* and *accommodation*. A person assimilates new events into existing structures and accommodates for new cognitive experiences. As the individual strives to maintain equilibrium, cognitive structural units (schemata) are developed. As the schemata develop, they form interlocking systems, or classes of similar action sequences. The mental structures are elaborated and refined through experience.

Piaget's model of intelligence categorizes intelligent behavior according to *content, structure,* and *function.* Content refers to raw, uninterpreted behavior of the individual (observable behavior), structure represents the cognitive structures that are developed as one gets older and function involves broad characteristics of intelligent behavior at all ages. According to Piaget, moral and cognitive development occur in stages. His greatest impact on psychology and curriculum has been due to this aspect of his theory. The stages of cognitive development are as follows:

Sensori-motor stage (age 0-2 years). In this stage, intelligent action is not expressed in language. The most important development at this stage is the schema of the permanent object.

Pre-operational stage (age 2-7 years). The pre-operational child does not think logically. During this stage the child does not understand problems associated with conversion or invariants. For example, he does not understand that the amount of water poured from one size container to another size container does not change while it is being poured.

Concrete Operations (ages 7-12 years). The child in concrete operations thinks logically and can reverse his actions. At the beginning of this stage he cannot understand volume and weight nor deal with parts and whole at the same time. The child needs concrete experiences and materials to manipulate during this period of development.

Formal Operations (ages 12-___). This stage is also called propositional operations and continues throughout adolescent development. The adolescent begins to think abstractly.

Piaget's ideas have been subjected to much research in recent years, but probably much more research is needed in order to validate his theory. His work has been of value in stressing importance of *process* as an important aspect of intelligence.

Cattell's Theory: Fluid and Crystallized Intelligence

R. B. Cattell (1963) theorizes that mental ability is comprised of *fluid intelligence* (g_f) and *crystallized intelligence* (g_c). Fluid intelligence is said to be more dependent on heredity than crystallized intelligence and is used in the performance of tasks requiring adaptation to new situations. Crystallized intelligence is more dependent upon environment and is specific to certain situations, such as learning in school. Fluid ability seems to reach a peak at around fifteen years of age, but crystallized ability seems to develop until perhaps age 30 in most individuals.

Guilford's Structure-of-Intellect Model

J. P. Guilford (1967) has developed a three-dimensional model of intelligence (Fig. 32) that utilizes three major categories: *contents, products,* and *operations.*

Content refers to the kind of material that a mental task or operation involves. The four kinds of content are figural, symbolic, semantic, and behavioral. *Figural* content is the term that applies to information in concrete form as perceived in the form of images. *Symbolic* information pertains to information in the forms of signs, such as letters or numerals. *Semantic* information refers to the meanings of words, as in verbal thinking or communication, but semantic information sometimes is not verbalized. *Behavioral* information is essentially nonverbal, involving human interaction such as attitudes, desires, or perceptions of people.

Products are the forms in which information occurs, and may be units, classes, relations, systems, transformations, and implications. *Units* are things separated out from the whole, such as figure on ground, and generally are represented by nouns. *Classes* are groups of units placed together by common properties. *Relations* are connections

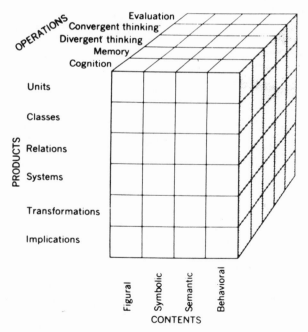

Figure 32. Structure-of-intellect model. (From *The Nature of Human Intelligence* by Guilford. Copyright © 1967 McGraw-Hill Book Company. Used with permission of McGraw-Hill Book Co.)

or bridges between things. *Systems* are organizations of interacting parts. An example would be a program or an equation. *Transformations* are revisions or modifications in information. *Implications* are made when one proceeds mentally from information given to something expected, anticipated, or predicted on the basis of the information.

Operations are the intellectual processes involved in the use of information that a person can discriminate. The categories of operations are cognition, memory, divergent production, convergent production, and evaluation. *Cognition* refers to awareness, discovery, or recognition of information, or some kind of comprehension. *Memory* is the storage of information in such a way that it can be available for later use. *Divergent thinking or production* pertains to the generation of information from given information with emphasis upon variety of output. *Convergent thinking or production* refers to the generation of information with an attempt to achieve a better or unique outcome or solution. *Evaluation* means judging the worth of information on the basis of specified criteria.

Wesman's Amorphous Model

Wesman (1968) theorizes that one's intellect is comprised of small bits of information or skill that may be in the form of either content or process. According to Wesman, these "modules" are multidimensional, but not all have the same number of dimensions. Each module is subject to change through learning experiences. Each learning experience may create new modules or change existing ones. Furthermore, the modules are not considered to be independent. Thus, according to this theory, intelligence is a complex unstructured or amorphous mass having many dimensions and interrelationships. Wesman contends that mental ability can only be measured fully by sampling from every aspect of one's learning experiences.

Sternberg's Model

Sternberg (1979) has proposed still another theory of intelligence. His theory organizes mental abilities into four levels — composite tasks, subtasks, information-processing components, and information-processing metacomponents. Sternberg posits that composite tasks can be decomposed into subtasks, and subtasks into components (Fig. 33).

The *composite* task, or full task as a person perceives it, is the first level of the theory. The selection of tasks for a mental-ability test is difficult, and Sternberg favors the use of four criteria: quantifiability (must be measurable), reliability, construct validity, and empirical validity. An example of a component task in a test is the following completion item: Romans in the Coliseum were bees in the _____. In this item the examinee would have to choose an answer from such options as (a) bonnet or (b) hive.

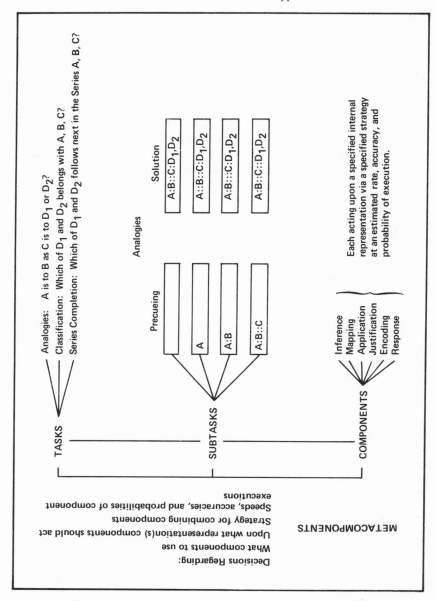

Figure 33. Outline of a theory of mental abilities, with examples at right of figure. (Copyright 1979 by the American Psychological Association. Reprinted by permission.)

Composite tasks can be subdivided into *subtasks* (second level of the theory) in different ways; for example, into the two groups referred to as induction tasks and deduction tasks. An example of an induction task in a test is the following analogy item: Lawyer : Client : Doctor :: (1) medicine, (b) patient. An example of a deduction item is the question: John is taller than Pete; who is tallest? John, Pete.

Information-processing components make up the third level of mental ability. A component is defined as an "elementary information process that operates on internal representations of objects or symbols." There are three kinds of components: general, class, and specific. General components are required for performance on all tasks within a given universe of tasks, class (or group) components are needed for performance of classes of tasks within the task universe, and specific components are needed for performance of single specific tasks in the task universe. In the Sternberg model, the tasks that are used to measure mental abilities can be arranged in a hierarchical manner. Successive vertical levels of the hierarchy differ in task complexity, and the higher the level the greater the complexity.

Information-processing metacomponents make the fourth level of mental abilities, and this level determines what happens at the component level. Metacomponents are the processes by which a person determines which components, representations, and strategies should be applied to a particular problem.

This theory is similar in some respects to the Vernon and Guilford theories but appears to be conceptually closer to Spearman's two-factor theory. Sternberg (1979) reports that he has empirical data which suggest that the general (g) factor comprises the components and metacomponents of mental abilities.

USE OF THEORIES OF INTELLIGENCE

The foregoing section provides only brief summarizations of several models of intelligence that have been proposed by psychologists who sought to understand and explain intellectual performance. The word *brief* must be stressed because whole volumes have been written about some of these theories. The fact that years of study and research have been devoted to this problem may prompt one to ask why theories or models of intelligence should be developed. What purposes can they serve beyond just satisfying someone's "urge to know?"

One major value derived from a study of the models of intelligence is that they accentuate that the structure of intellect can be conceptualized in different ways, and therefore it is not fully understood. This should prompt us to be cautious in our use of the term intelligence and our use of test results. Another value is that the models help test makers in their construction of tests of mental ability. If, for example, the model stresses certain group factors, test items can be written in order to measure those factors. Thus, while tests may have been used to build and verify a theory of intelligence, other tests may be constructed to measure the factors identified through factor analysis or other statistical procedures.

EFFECTS OF ENVIRONMENT AND HEREDITY ON INTELLIGENCE

Early in the history of intelligence testing it was assumed that intellectual ability was inherited and that it remained constant throughout one's life. Since that time many researchers have concluded that environment also affects intelligence, at least the scores earned on mental-ability tests. The question concerning the degree of effect of environment on test scores is an important one because if they knew how much effect environment has, school personnel could plan more effectively for the intellectual development of students.

Several studies relating to the heredity-environment issue, e.g. Speer (1940), Wellman (1940), Goldfarb (1943), Yarrow (1961), Erlenmeyer-Kimling and Jarvik (1963), Skeels (1965), Jensen (1969), and Scarr and Weinberg (1977), have been reported with such varied results that the proportional effects of the two factors are still unknown. As Wintsch (1979, p. 12) says: "Attempts to unravel genetic from environmental influences have met with little success: they often generated heated controversies that only confuse the issue."

Because research has not yet revealed the exact extent of influence on intellectual performance that comes from either environment or heredity (and perhaps the answer to this question never will be known), it seems sensible to assume that both are important and to take this into account when using data from mental-ability tests.

OTHER FACTORS RELATED TO MENTAL ABILITY

In addition to heredity and environment, what other factors may play a part in intellectual development and performance? A few of the many variables that have been studied seem worthy of mention.

Biological and Physiological Factors

While it is obvious that the brain is the organ that serves as the center for intellectual activity, it is not yet clear just how the various regions of the brain function with respect to intelligence. Certainly intelligence is not centered in one small region of the brain. Research findings indicate that the prefrontal lobes appear to be important, but so do other areas, as is apparent from the effects of injuries to the brain. When there is damage to the left temporal lobe of the brain (in the *dominant* cerebral hemisphere for most people) verbal-symbolic performance is adversely altered more than perceptual-spatial performance. When the right temporal lobe is injured, however, perceptual-spatial abilities are adversely affected to a greater extent than verbal-symbolic abilities. Research results also reveal that the effects of brain damage tend to be greater in children than in adults. As Rappaport (1979) points out, however, opinions are divided on the matter of how the halves of the brain function, and caution should be used in drawing conclusions from the available studies. More research on hemispheric specialization seems to be necessary before certain important questions can be answered, such as "What is the relationship between dyslexia and hemispheric specialization?"

It has been known for many years that the hormone thyroxin has an effect on intellectual development. When this chemical compound is seriously deficient in infants, the condition known as *cretinism* occurs. If the infant is administered thyroxin soon enough after birth, the condition may be prevented or at least alleviated; but, if this corrective action is not taken, the child will grow up as a mentally deficient individual. Other hormones have been linked tentatively with mental ability, but much more research must be done in order to achieve definitive results.

Nutrition definitely has been linked with the development of intellectual ability. While it is very doubtful that any diet can boost intelligence-test scores of normal persons, there is very solid evidence that *malnutrition* can prevent mental development in children, just as it can slow physical growth and development. The genetic disorder phenylketonuria (PKU) is a case in point. If an infant has not inherited a gene that is responsible for the enzyme that brings about the oxidizing of phenylalanine, this chemical compound will accumulate in the blood and prevent the normal development of mental ability. This prevention of the disorder can be accomplished by placing the affected child on a phenylalanine-free diet when the child is still very young.

Sex appears to be a variable that is related to mental ability even though males and females apparently do not differ as far as general intelligence is concerned. The few differences that may occur between the sexes seem to involve special aptitudes or abilities. Wechsler (1958) found that males tend to be superior in terms of mechanical aptitude, spatial aptitude, and problem solving, while females tend to excel males in terms of vocabulary, verbal fluency, and rote memory. Witelson (1976), basing her conclusions on a study of a small group of boys and girls, believes that the same area of the brain may have different cognitive functions in girls and boys at the same age, and this may account for differences in performance on mental-ability tests. It has also been hypothesized that adult attitudes and behavior related to child rearing may produce the differences in test performance. Perhaps boys are expected to perform better at problem solving, and girls better at language usage, so parents and other adults unknowingly reinforce certain behaviors related to the expected performances.

Susie may get attention for her good spelling, but not for building a miniature bridge. Sammy, however, gets praise when he solves his arithmetic problems without help, but not when he tries to write a poem. The answer to the question of sex differences in mental-abilities is not at all clear at this time.

Racial and Cultural Differences

Racial and cultural differences pertaining to intelligence test scores have been reported and studied for several years. In the early history of intelligence testing it seemed sufficient to administer the tests to various racial or cultural groups, and then simply conclude that a group tended to score below the mean for the standardization group. In time, concerned researchers questioned the results of such studies, because the tests had not been standardized on the divergent populations with different cultures. These researchers pointed out that culture affects behavior and therefore may influence test scores.

An attempt was made to solve the validity problem stemming from differences in culture by constructing culture-free or culture-fair tests. These tests generally were made up of nonverbal items in order to get away from language difficulties. Very often various geometric figures or designs were used. The approach has been criticized because it was found that the tests (1) measure only a limited area of intelligent behavior, (2) are not really culturally "fair" to more than a very few cultures, and (3) generally have no practical use because the results fail to predict performance well. The problems associated with the construction of valid and useful culture-fair tests are truly great. The problems involve difficulty in obtaining representative samples of various populations and difficulty in controlling for such variables as educational background, socioeconomic status, and test-taking motivation.

Studies indicate that Orientals tend to earn scores that are similar to those of white Americans, but black Americans, Mexican-Americans, and American Indians tend to score lower than whites. Most of the racial-differences studies have compared the scores of blacks and whites. Some researchers (Shuey, 1966; Jensen, 1969, 1979; Eysenck, 1971; and others) have concluded that the differences in test performance of blacks and whites have a genetic basis, but others (including Lee, 1951; Klineberg, 1963; Kagan, 1969) have attributed the differences to differences in cultural background. Samuda (1975) has summarized the literature pertaining to this problem and has concluded that there is a slight difference in mean test performance in favor of whites, but there is a large amount of overlap in scores for the two groups, with many blacks scoring above the mean score for whites and many whites scoring below the mean score of blacks. See Chapter 12 for appraisal techniques related to minority groups.

INDIVIDUAL TESTS OF MENTAL ABILITY

In 1905 Alfred Binet and his co-worker Theodore Simon produced an intelligence scale that was to become the forerunner of the modern day individual test of mental ability. These French psychologists reasoned that the intelligence of a child could be inferred from behavior exhibited if the subject was required to perform a variety of mental tasks, such as naming objects shown in pictures, repeating digits, drawing geometric figures, and stating the similarities of common objects. Binet and Simon revised their scale and published the revision in 1908. Their revised scale was longer and had the items grouped according to age levels.

In 1916, three Americans, H. H. Goddard, Frederic Kuhlmann, and Lewis Terman adapted the Binet-Simon scale for use with American subjects. At Stanford University, Terman standardized his version of the scale on a sample of 1000 children and 400 adults. Terman selected items from the Binet-Simon scale and added new ones. The items were carefully selected on the basis of content, and on the basis of the percent of subjects who could pass the items at each age level.

The 1916 scale yielded a mental age, which was calculated from the number of tests passed at each age level, and this MA was used to compute a ratio IQ:

$$IQ = \frac{MA}{CA} \times 100$$

This concept (IQ) was discussed in Chapter 4.

The 1937 Stanford-Binet Scale

Terman and Maud Merrill (1960) revised the 1916 scale in order to make two forms, L and M, to extend the scale downward and upward, and to improve standardization at the lower and higher levels. The scale was improved by providing subtests at ages eleven and thirteen where none existed previously, and by providing groups of test items at half-year levels from ages two to five. The use of half-year groups provided greater testing accuracy at ages where mental growth is rapid. Further improvement was made by improving the directions for administering and scoring the subtests, and this change improved the scale's reliability.

The scale was standardized on over 3000 American-born subjects who came from homes that appeared to be representative of the general population. The standardization sample included subjects from eleven states that represented different parts of the nation.

One advantage of having two forms for the scale was that retesting could be done quickly while avoiding practice effect. Another advantage was that the two comparable forms of the scale provided the opportunity to determine the scale's reliability through the alternate-forms procedure.

The 1960 Stanford-Binet Scale

The *Stanford-Binet Intelligence Scale* was revised in 1960 by Terman and Merrill, who selected the best test items from forms L and M and combined them to produce Form L-M. Terman and Merrill (1960) believed that the single revised form offered certain advantages: (1) avoiding the duplication of subtests in order to have a sufficient number of good items at each level; (2) providing enough satisfactory items to have an alternate subtest at each level; and (3) permitting the selection of only the finest items from Form L and Form M for inclusion in Form L-M. Terman and Merrill (1960) chose their items on the basis of the results of tests administered to nearly 5000 subjects who ranged in age from 2.25 to 18 years of age. The subjects had been administered both 1937 forms during the period from 1950 to 1954.

Although the individuals in the main sample did not comprise a truly representative sample of American students, Terman and Merrill attempted to avoid the effects of selective factors. They also included in their assessment group two stratified samples of California students. These groups were stratified on the basis of father's occupation and student's grade placement. The test results from the new samples permitted Terman and Merrill to assess possible changes in item difficulty and possible differences in examinee performance related to regional or socioeconomic differences.

The 1960 scale provides deviation intelligence quotients or DIQs (discussed in Chapter 4). Deviation IQs are advantageous because they may be interpreted in the same way regardless of the chronological age of the examinee. The 1960 scale (Terman and Merrill, 1972) now has a new set of norms (1972) based upon a stratified sample of children ranging from 2 to 18 years of age. The scale's test-retest reliability is reported to be over .90. Validity coefficients based upon comparison of IQs with school marks and standardized achievement test results generally range between .40 and .80, centering around .60.

Content of the 1960 Scale

The 1960 scale contains both performance items (those that generally require the ability to manipulate objects or do nonverbal tasks) and verbal items. These two item types are mixed throughout the scale, but an increasing percentage of verbal items is found as the scale proceeds from age 2 to the highest level (SA III). An example of a performance item is Block Building at Year II, and an example of a verbal item is Verbal Absurdities at Year XI.

Administration and Scoring of the 1960 Scale

Figure 34 shows the test materials that are contained in the Form L-M testing kit. There are several small objects, such as autos, doll, flag, blocks, beads, and scissors. There are two booklets containing printed

Figure 34. Stanford-Binet Intelligence Scale. (Copyright © 1978 by Houghton Mifflin Company. Reprinted by permission of Houghton Mifflin Company. All rights reserved.)

cards and materials, and there is a test manual. Of course, the small objects are used only at the lower age levels.

The test manual's main purposes are to provide directions for administering and scoring the items and to provide the IQ tables. For proper administration of the scale, the examiner must follow the directions closely and record the subject's responses accurately in the *test booklet*. Notations concerning the subject's behavior also should be made in the booklet and, of course, in the test report if one is written.

The 1960 scale has the subtests arranged from chronological age 2 (II) to Superior Adult III. From level II to level V the items are grouped by half-year levels: II, II-6, III, III-6, IV, IV-6, V. Beyond level V and up to level XIV the levels are on a yearly basis, but beyond XIV they go to AA (Average Adult), SAI (Superior Adult), SAII (Superior Adult II), and SAIII (Superior Adult III). Each level has six items (or subtests) except AA, which has eight.

In addition to the regular subtests, at each level there is an additional, or alternate item. The alternate is used only when there is a need for it, such as when the examiner spoils the item by improper directions. The alternate subtests are rarely used.

Administration of the scale usually is begun at, or slightly below, the subject's estimated mental-age level. If very little is known about the examinee, the chronological age can provide a reasonable estimate of mental age. If the chronological age is 12, one might start with items at level XII. If the examinee is known to be bright, a higher level is recommended, and if the subject is known to be dull, it would be wise to start at a lower level. Wells and Pedrini (1967) suggest starting by administering the Picture Vocabulary or Verbal Vocabulary first in order to get an estimate of the examinee's general performance. The reason for this practice is twofold: (1) the vocabulary subtests appear at different levels, so would be used eventually, and (2) vocabulary performance correlates positively and well with full-scale performance for most examinees.

When the Stanford-Binet is administered, the examiner must determine as soon as possible the subject's *basal age*. The basal age is the highest level at which all of the items of the level have been passed. If the examiner starts at a certain level and all the subtests are passed, the examiner proceeds to the next level. If one or more items are failed, the examiner must drop back to a lower level to find the basal age and then proceed upward again. Finally, the level at which *all* of the items are failed is the *ceiling* age. Testing is discontinued when the ceiling age is reached. When the basal age is used, the assumption is made that the subject can pass all of the tests at lower levels; when the ceiling age is used, the assumption is made that the examinee would fail all of the higher-level items. These are sound assumptions, but occasionally they may not hold for a particular subject.

Typically, the Stanford-Binet is scored as the examiner administers the instrument. The directions for an item are given by the examiner, who waits for the subject's response, records it in the booklet, and marks the response as passed or failed (with a + or a − or some other symbols). The subject's mental age is determined by adding months of credit earned to the basal age. From level II to level V, each subtest passed is worth one month credit toward the mental age score. Between levels VI and AA, each passed test receives two months credit. At level SAI each test is worth four months of credit, and at levels SAII and SAIII, each item passed receives five and six months of credit respectively. An example of a calculated mental age follows in Table IX.

The preceding section gives very limited coverage of the *Stanford-Binet Intelligence Scale*. For more detailed information, it is suggested that the reader turn to the 1960 manual and several of the references at the end of this chapter. Certainly one who must use the results of the scale should have thorough knowledge of it. In order to administer and score the scale properly, and in order to interpret results of the scale, a person should have the necessary training and experience.

The Wechsler Scales

Psychologist David Wechsler is the author of a series of scales that are designed to measure general mental ability. These instruments have become increasingly popular and have replaced the Stanford-Binet scale to a large extent. One reason for the Wechsler scales' popularity is that, in addition to a full-scale IQ, the scales provide separate perform-

TABLE IX
MENTAL AGE AND INTELLIGENCE QUOTIENTS BASED ON THE
STANFORD-BINET INTELLIGENCE SCALE

Year	No. of Items Passed	No. of Months of Credit for Each Item Passed	Total Credit
VIII (Basal Age)	6	2	8 yrs., 0 mos.
IX	4	2	8 mos.
X	3	2	6 mos.
XI (Ceiling Age)	0	2	0 mos.
			8 yrs., 14 mos.
			(9 yrs., 2 mos.)
CA = 10-3	MA = 9-2	Ratio IQ = 89	DIQ = 88

ance and verbal IQs, and a scaled score for each subtest. Many test users believe that they get more information from the Wechsler scales than from the Stanford-Binet, which continues to be a useful individual scale for measuring general mental ability, especially with children.

Wechsler's first scale, the *Wechsler Bellevue Scale,* was published in 1939. This scale was completely revised and restandardized and was published as the Wechsler Adult Intelligence Scale in 1955 (Fig. 35).

The Wechsler Adult Intelligence Scale (WAIS)

The WAIS was designed to measure the intelligence of adults whose ages range from 16 to 75 years. The principal standardization sample was comprised of 850 females and 850 males whose ages ranged from 16 to 64 years, but a sample of 475 subjects was utilized in order to develop norms for persons who are older than 64. The subjects used for the standardization or norm group were considered to be representative of the American adult population (Wechsler, 1955). The standardization subjects were proportioned according to the 1950 United States census with respect to such factors as race, geographic area, level of education, occupation, and rural versus urban residence.

Content and Functions of the WAIS

The WAIS has six subtests that comprise the Verbal Scale and five that make up the Performance Scale. The Verbal Scale subtests are Information, Comprehension, Arithmetic, Similarities, Digit Span, and Vocabulary. The Performance Scale subtests are Digit Symbol, Picture Completion, Block Design, Picture Arrangement, and Object Assembly.

In Table X are presented several different functions of the subtests of the WAIS, and factors that tend to influence results, as discussed by

Figure 35. The *Wechsler Adult Intelligence Scale.* (Reproduced by permission of the Psychological Corporation.)

Freeman (1962), Wechsler (1955), Kitzinger and Blumberg (1951), Rappaport et al. (1945), Zimmerman (1973) and other researchers. Whether these are the only functions measured by the subtests is impossible to determine, so caution should be used in making definitive judgments about performance on the various subtests.

Administration and Scoring of the WAIS

Administration of the WAIS and other Wechsler scales requires the same thoroughness that the proper administration of the Stanford-Binet requires. The directions for administering the subtests should be adhered to closely, attention should be paid to the behavior of the examinee, notes should be taken when necessary, and responses recorded accurately. The performance subtests are timed, so the examiner should be adept at using a stop watch. Because timing procedures make some subjects anxious, the examiner should use common sense in the use of the watch, perhaps even keeping the watch out of sight of the examinee. Another important aspect of administration that must be stressed is familiarity with the WAIS Manual in order to be able to

TABLE X
FUNCTIONS OF THE WAIS SUBTESTS

Subtest	Functions	Influencing Factors
Information	Association and organization of experience	Cultural background Education
	Old learning and memory	Interests
Comprehension	Concept formation	Emotional status
	Organization and application of knowledge	Moral code Social and cultural
	Reasoning with abstractions	background
	Social judgment	
Arithmetic	Alertness and concentration	Education
	Arithmetic skills	Occupational experiences
	Logical reasoning and abstraction	
Similarities	Analysis of relationships	Cultural background
	Logical abstract thinking	and opportunities
	Verbal concept formation	
Vocabulary	Concept formation	Cultural background
	Language development	and opportunities
	Range of ideas, interests, experiences	Education
Digit Span	Attention and concentration	Attention span
	Auditory imagery	Level of anxiety
	Retentiveness	
Picture Completion	Concentration and appraisal of relationships	Cultural experiences Visual acuity
	Visual alertness and memory	
	Visual imagery and perception	
Picture Arrangement	Ability to comprehend a whole situation	Cultural background Visual acuity
	Ability to pick out essential cues	
	Anticipation and planning	
Block Design	Ability to perceive form	Psychomotor speed
	Analysis and synthesis	Visual acuity (color)
	Visual-motor integration	
Object Assembly	Recognition of patterns	Psychomotor speed
	Visual-motor integration	and precision
	Visual perception and synthesis	
Digit Symbol	Rote recall	Psychomotor speed
	Speed and accuracy in learning and writing symbols	
	Visual imagery	

Adapted from Robb et al., 1972, p. 127. Courtesy of Harper and Row.

Figure 36. Administration of the *Wechsler Adult Intelligence Scale.* (Reproduced by permission of The Psychological Corporation.)

conduct the proper administration and scoring of the items and tests (see Fig. 36).

The scoring for the WAIS starts with the evaluation of the individual responses to items. Each response should be considered carefully and scored according to the guidelines in the manual. A few errors can make a big difference in a subtest score or IQ score. The scoring of items should be done as the test proceeds, but careful rescoring is recommended after the completion of the testing.

After the scale has been administered, each subtest has a raw score that must be converted to a scaled score through the use of a table. The scaled scores for the Verbal Scale are added and this total score is used to obtain the Verbal IQ in the appropriate table in the manual. This procedure is repeated for the Performance Scale to obtain the Performance Scale IQ. A Full Scale IQ is determined by adding the sum of the scaled scores for the Verbal Scale to the sum of the scaled scores for the Performance Scale and taking this total to the appropriate table in the manual. Thus, one can obtain three different intelligence quotients from an administration of the WAIS: Verbal IQ, Performance IQ, and Full Scale IQ.

For those test users who wish to use the subtest results for diagnostic purposes, the scaled scores may be useful. The mean of the scaled scores of the subtests is always 10, and the standard deviation is 3 for all age levels. Thus, a scaled score of 13 would be a standard deviation above the mean, while a scaled score of 7 would be a standard deviation below the mean.

The mean IQ for the three scales (V, P, and FS) is 100, and the standard deviation is 15. Therefore, an IQ score of 85 on any of the scales would be a standard deviation below the mean, and an IQ of 115 would be a standard deviation above the mean.

The other Wechsler scales (WISC and WPPSI) have the same scoring system as the WAIS. They have scaled scores and IQs with the same means and standard deviations.

Wechsler Intelligence Scale for Children (WISC)

The WISC was published in 1949 and has been used extensively since that time. It was designed for testing children between the ages of five years and fifteen years of age. The WISC was standardized on a sample of 2,200 white American children who were selected as representative of the population in general.

The subtests of the WISC closely resemble those of the WAIS, but there are a few differences. A coding test is used in the WISC instead of the Digit Symbol, an optional Maze Test is included, and the Digit Span is optional. In the typical administration of the scale five verbal and five performance tests are given, but all twelve tests may be administered to a subject. Should an examiner wish to use fewer or more than ten tests, the scores would have to be prorated because the IQ tables are set up on the basis of the administration of ten tests. The verbal and performance tests of the WISC are as follows:

Verbal	*Performance*
Information	Picture Completion
Comprehension	Picture Arrangement
Arithmetic	Block Design
Similarities	Object Assembly
Vocabulary	Coding
Digit Span (Optional)	Mazes (Optional)

Wechsler (1949) excluded Digit Span and Mazes from the IQ tables because these two subtests produced relatively low correlations with other tests in the WISC. Another reason was that Mazes required a relatively long period of time for administration. An optional test might be given if the examiner had spoiled an item or if there were some other reason not to use the usual test, such as an examinee handicap. Fewer than ten tests might be given to save time and more than ten in order to gather more data. One should assume that shortening the scale may lower its validity and reliability.

Functions of the WISC Subtests

Glasser and Zimmerman (1967, pp. 39-102) have analyzed the subtests of the WISC in order to attempt to determine what each test measures. Table XI lists briefly the functions of each WISC subtest, but

TABLE XI
FUNCTIONS OF THE WISC SUBTESTS

Subtests	Function
Information	To determine how much general information the subject has abstracted from his surrounding environment.
Comprehension	To determine the level of the child's ability to use practical judgment in everyday social actions, the extent to which social acculturation has taken place, and the extent to which a maturing conscience or moral sense has developed.
Arithmetic	To measure the child's ability to utilize abstract concepts of number and numerical operations, which are measures of cognitive development.
Similarities	To determine the qualitative aspect of relationships which the subject has abstracted from his environment.
Vocabulary	To examine the subject's richness of ideas, his quality of language and abstract thinking.
Picture Completion	To measure capacity to identify visually familiar objects and to identify and isolate essential from non-essential characteristics.
Picture Arrangement	To measure perception, visual comprehension, planning involving sequential and causal events, and synthesis into intelligible wholes.
Block Design	To measure perceptions, analysis, synthesis, and reproduction of abstract designs.
Object Assembly	To measure perception, visual-motor coordination, and simple assembly skills.
Coding	To measure visual-motor dexterity and ability to absorb new material presented in an associative context.
Digit Span	To determine ability to attend, and immediate auditory recall.
Mazes	To measure planning and foresight, attention to instructions and visual-motor coordination.

From A. J. Glasser and Zimmerman: *Clinical Interpretation of the WISC*, 1967. Courtesy of Grune and Stratton. By permission.

the reader is encouraged to consult the book *Clinical Interpretation of the Wechsler Intelligence Scale for Children* for a more complete discussion of functions of the tests and clinical interpretation of the results of the WISC.

Wechsler Intelligence Scale for Children — Revised (WISC-R)

The WISC-R is a 1974 revision of the WISC. It has the same twelve tests as the 1949 WISC, and only ten of the tests are considered to be mandatory, in the interest of shortening administration time (Wechsler, 1974, p. 8). The IQs are calculated on the basis of the following subtests. (The numbers indicate the order of administration.)

Verbal	*Performance*
1. Information	2. Picture Completion
3. Similarities	4. Picture Arrangement
5. Arithmetic	6. Block Design
7. Vocabulary	8. Object Assembly
9. Comprehension	10. Coding (or Mazes)

Digit Span (Verbal) and Mazes (Performance) were not used in the construction of the IQ tables (Wechsler, 1974). They are supplementary tests that are used as substitutes if one of the regular tests cannot be administered for some valid reason or if a regular test was spoiled for some reason. A substitution may not be made just for convenience or because a child did not perform well on a regularly given subtest. All twelve tests may be administered, but if they are, Digit Span and Mazes are not to be used in calculating the IQs.

Wechsler Preschool and Primary Scale of Intelligence (WPPSI)

The WPPSI was published in 1967. It is similar to the WISC in organization and in content, and it was developed in order to provide a scale that could be used to measure the mental ability of children of preschool age (see Fig. 37). It can be used to test children whose ages range from 4 to 6.5 years. The WPPSI was standardized on a sample comprised of 100 boys and girls in each of six age groups from age 4 through age 6.5 (Wechsler, 1967, p. 13). There were 1,200 subjects in the sample that was stratified by age, sex, geographic location, race (white, nonwhite), urban-rural residence, and father's occupation.

The WPPSI has the following subtests, which are administered alternately (first a verbal, then a performance test).

Verbal	*Performance*
Information	Animal House
Vocabulary	(Animal House Retest)
Arithmetic	Picture Completion
Similarities	Mazes
Comprehension	Geometric Design
(Sentences)	Block Design

Figure 37. Administration of the *Wechsler Preschool and Primary Scale of Intelligence.* (Reproduced by permission of The Psychological Corporation.)

Reliability of the Wechsler Scales

How reliable are the Wechsler scales? The reliability coefficients shown in Table XII provide a partial answer to this question. The coefficients are those reported in the Wechsler manuals. The coefficients tend to be highest for the WAIS subtests and lowest for the

TABLE XII

RELIABILITY COEFFICIENTS FOR THE WECHSLER SCALES AND
SUBTESTS

Subtest or Scale	WAIS	WISC-R	WPPSI
Information	.91 to .92	.67 to .90	.77 to .84
Comprehension	.77 to .79	.69 to .87	.78 to .84
Similarities	.85 to .87	.74 to .87	.82 to .85
Arithmetic	.79 to .86	.69 to .81	.78 to .86
Vocabulary	.94 to .96	.70 to .92	.72 to .87
Digit Span	.66 to .71	.71 to .84	—
Sentences	—	—	.81 to .88
Picture Completion	.82 to .85	.68 to .85	.81 to .86
Picture Arrangement	.60 to .74	.69 to .78	—
Block Design	.82 to .86	.80 to .90	.76 to .88
Object Assembly	.65 to .71	.63 to .76	—
Coding	.92	.63 to .80	.62 to .84
Mazes	—	.62 to .82	.82 to .91
Geometric Design	—	—	.77 to .87
Verbal IQ	.96	.91 to .96	.93 to .95
Performance IQ	.93 to .94	.89 to .91	.91 to .95
Full Scale IQ	.97	.95 to .96	.96 to .97

NOTE: All coefficients are split-halves except for WISC-R Digit Span (Test-retest), WAIS Coding (Alternate-form), WISC-R Coding (Test-retest) and WPPSI Coding (Test-retest).

WPPSI subtests. The Full Scale IQ correlation coefficients are very high for all three instruments, indicating very satisfactory reliability for full-scale measures of intelligence.

Over the years many researchers have studied the test results of the Wechsler scales in order to check on the reliability of the scales when they have been used with various populations, and the findings are too numerous to report here. Suffice it to say that the data tend to support strongly the data presented in the Wechsler manuals.

Validity of the Wechsler Scales

A very great amount of research has been directed at the problem of evaluating the Wechsler scales with respect to validity. A short, general summary of some of the findings will be presented.

A source of evidence of content and construct validity for the WAIS is the set of correlation coefficients between subtest scores and Full Scale IQ. Wechsler (1958, p. 98) reports that these coefficients were found to range between .46 and .84 for seven age groups. The highest correlations were found for the verbal subtests of Information, Arithmetic, Similarities, and Vocabulary. Because all of the correlations between subtests and full-scale intelligence quotients are positive, one can assume that they all are measuring to some extent the same characteristic, supposedly a general mental factor.

Criterion-related validity for the WAIS may be inferred from the results of research in which WAIS scores have been correlated with various criteria. The results of several studies are given in Table XIII.

In looking at the correlations between WAIS scores (or other intelligence-test scores) and such criteria as grade-point averages, one should remember that school marks often are not highly reliable measures of achievement, so the reported correlations are probably lower than they should be. Also, school achievement is affected considerably by attitudes, motivation, and other variables. Should it be possible to hold these factors constant, researchers no doubt would report higher correlations between intelligence test scores and scholastic achievement.

With regard to the WISC, one can find evidence for content and construct validity in the correlations between subtest scores and Full Scale scores, as for the WAIS. The correlations are positive; they range from .44 to .94 for several age groups (Wechsler, 1974, pp. 36-46). The coefficients for the verbal tests tend to be higher than for the performance tests.

Criterion-related validity may be inferred from the results of several studies that show positive correlations between WISC or WISC-R scores and various criteria, such as other intelligence tests and achievement tests. The studies reported in the literature are too numerous even to list, but they tend to indicate a substantial positive correlation between WAIS scores and other criteria with which they should be expected to correlate positively. For both the Verbal Scale and the Full

TABLE XIII

CORRELATIONS BETWEEN WAIS SCORES AND VARIOUS CRITERIA

Researchers	Subjects	Criteria	Correlation V	P	FS
Wechsler (1958)	52 reformatory inmates	Stanford-Binet	.80	.69	.85
Brengelwann and Kenny (1961)	75 retardates	Leiter	.59	.75	
		Stanford-Binet	.79	.78	
McLeod and Rubin (1962)	81 subjects	Progressive Matrices	.67	.58	.68
Giannell and Freeburne (1963)	109 college students	Stanford-Binet			.897
		ACE Psychological			.882
		School Marks			.841
Olsen and Jordheim (1964)	109 college students	Grade-point average			.42
	120 college students	Grade-point average			.58
Conry and Plant (1965)	335 college students	Grade-point average	.64	.44	.62
	98 high school students	Rank in graduating class	.45	.23	.43
Knox, Grotelueschen, and Sjogren (1968)	55 adults	Achievement scores			.78

Scale the correlations between WISC scores and criteria appear to center around .70, but for the Performance Scale the correlations tend to center around .60.

The WPPSI subtests correlate positively with the Full Scale scores, as they do for the other Wechsler scales. The correlations reported in the manual range from .53 to .70, so there is some evidence of content and construct validity for the scale as a test of intelligence. Criterion-related validity may be inferred from the findings of several studies reported by researchers. The reported correlations between WPPSI scores and certain criteria vary from near zero to the upper .70s, and the Full Scale scores show a higher correlation with criteria such as scores from other mental-ability tests than do the Verbal or Performance scores.

Use of the Wechsler Scales

Judging from the relatively high positive correlations found between scores from the Stanford-Binet and Wechsler scales, these well-constructed instruments measure the same general mental ability (perhaps Spearman's "g"). Of course, the Wechsler scales provide three separate measures of IQ, namely, Verbal, Performance, and Full Scale, which may be an important advantage. The advantage is apparent when a subject has a verbal handicap, and thus cannot be tested satisfactorily with verbal items. It should not be assumed, however, that the Performance Scale is a completely satisfactory substitute for the Verbal Scale, the Full Scale, or the Stanford-Binet. The correlation coefficients simply are not high enough to permit them to be used interchangeably without question. Use of the Performance Scale, however, gives the examiner information about the examinee's ability that otherwise might be unavailable.

The Wechsler scales may be used to *classify* students with respect to general mental ability, should that be necessary. Wechsler (1974), for example, has classified WISC-R intelligence quotients according to IQ ranges, as seen in Table XIV. A score of 65, for example, would be in the mentally deficient range, while a score of 147 would be classified as very Superior.

The use of the subtests for diagnostic or clinical purposes rather than just for determining the level of general intellectual ability is a difficult task to say the least. In order to be able to use the subtests successfully for clinical purposes, one must have a thorough knowledge of the Wechsler scales, the related research (such as factorial studies), and a considerable amount of experience in the use of the scales.

In the diagnostic use of the Wechsler scales, the clinician considers the difference between Performance and Verbal IQs, the differences in subtest scaled scores, and the nature of responses to individual items. Significant differences between P and V scores or between certain subtest scores help the clinician formulate hypotheses about the sub-

An Introduction to Individual Appraisal

TABLE XIV

CLASSIFICATION OF WISC-R INTELLIGENCE QUOTIENTS

IQ	Percent Included	Classification
140 and above	2.3	Very superior
120-139	7.4	Superior
110-119	16.5	High average (bright)
98-109	49.4	Average
80-89	16.2	Low average (dull)
70-79	6.0	Borderline
69 and below	2.2	Mentally deficient

From the WISC-R Manual, p. 26. (Reproduced by permission of the Psychological Corporation.)

ject's behavior, personality, emotional status, or mental disorders. The test profile in Figure 38 illustrates how the scores might vary for a subject who was given the WISC-R.

The profile in Figure 38 shows each plotted scaled score and the three IQs: V, P, and Fs. Bands indicate the size of each standard error of measurement for the scaled scores. If the bands do not overlap for any two scaled scores, one may conclude that there probably is a difference in abilities or functions measured by the two subtests.

A brief analysis of just the profile in Figure 38 indicates that the subject's Performance IQ is considerably higher than the subject's Verbal IQ. This often occurs among persons who have a verbal handicap or language difficulty, but it may be found for other subjects also. Specific subtest strengths are evident for Vocabulary, Digit Span, Block Design, Object Assembly, and Coding, but there appears to be a weakness in Similarities, and perhaps in Arithmetic and Comprehension. The Full Scale IQ of 106 falls in the normal range, so this student would be capable of doing satisfactory school work. In the further analysis of the profile, a skilled examiner would make use of such information as the subject's behavior during the administration of the scale, subject's educational background, subject's cultural background, etc. Also, of course, the nature of responses to individual items might be significant. A great deal of caution should be used in formulating hypotheses about the subject because the Wechsler scales and other tests of intelligence are not infallible. When a subject has a very low score on a subtest, more than one hypothesis concerning the reason for the low score may be suggested. The first hypothesis to consider is that the subject really is deficient in whatever that subtest measures. Other hypotheses might involve the presence of stress, anxiety, a verbal or physical handicap, or some other condition. While Wechsler (1958), Lutey (1966), Glasser and Zimmerman (1967), and others believe that the Wechsler scales are useful as diagnostic tools in assessing such conditions as brain damage, anxiety states, or behavior patterns, other psychologists are skeptical.

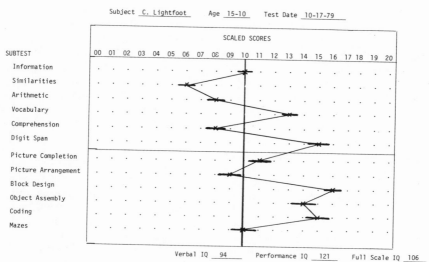

Figure 38. WISC-R profile.

Simensen and Sutherland (1974) conducted an extensive review of the literature pertaining to the diagnosis of brain damage through the use of the Wechsler scales. They concluded that because of the general disagreement and inconsistency among research findings, diagnosis of brain damage cannot be diagnosed on the basis of any pattern of scores.

Griffiths (1977) has found the child's performance on the WISC to be useful in diagnosing dyslexia. For example, when the child is asked to explain the story that the pictures tell, the examiner should note how the subject proceeds (right or left or in the middle). The examiner should also note whether the child inverts or reverses the blocks in Block Design. This may tell something about how letters, words, or numerals are being translated for that person by the brain. Thus, even without an elaborate system of pattern analysis, one may gain some useful diagnostic information from the Wechsler subtests.

Developmental Scales for Young Children

Assessing the mental ability of infants and very young children is a very difficult task, primarily because these subjects tend to have short attention spans, tend to become bored or tired easily, and tend to lack motivation for testing activities. Many young subjects will not respond well in the presence of a stranger, as the examiner is likely to be. For many years, however, determined efforts have been made to develop scales that would be useful in predicting the future mental development and performance of infants and children. The correlations reported in studies in which very young children were tested and then retested at a later age have tended to be below .50, and this means that early testing will yield dubious results. One reason for the low correlations is that the tests used with the very young child must be different from those used with older children and adults. With young subjects who have not yet developed verbal and language skills, it is necessary to rely upon sensori-motor tasks in order to do the testing. Such tasks may be tapping a somewhat different aspect of intelligence (or testing intelligence less well) than the tests designed for older persons.

Much of the early research that was done in the area of the mental growth and development of infants and young children was done at Yale University under the direction of Arnold Gesell. The *Gesell Developmental Schedules* provide tests at two levels. The *Infant Schedule* is used to test children between the ages of four and fifty-six weeks, and the *Preschool Schedule* is used with children aged from fifteen months to six years. According to Gesell and Amatruda (1947), the tests are useful in determining patterns of mental development in normal, subnormal, and superior children. They may also be used in the diagnosis of neurological impairment. The Schedules contain tests of motor behavior, adaptive behavior, language behavior, and personal-social behavior. The Schedules are systematic observations of behavior rather than tests in the usual sense, so the determination of validity and reliability is extremely difficult. With training and experience, however, examiners have demonstrated a high interrater reliability.

The *Merrill-Palmer Pre-School Scale*, the *Minnesota Pre-School Scale*, and the *Cattell Infant Intelligence Scale* also have been in use for several years, and have been very popular. The *Bayley Scales of Infant Development* and the *McCarthy Scales of Children's Abilities* are relatively recent instruments for the testing of young children.

The *Bayley Scales of Infant Development* (1969) were developed by Nancy Bayley as the culmination of forty years of work. The scales were standardized on a population of 1,262 children selected to reflect the proportion of children whose ages ranged from two months through thirty months in various subgroups (race, sex, geographic region, socioeconomic status and urban-rural residence). The thorough standardization has helped make the Bayley Scales a superior infant-testing instrument.

The scales are designed to provide a three-part evaluation of a child's mental development during the first 2.5 years of life. Supposedly, the three parts make unique contributions but also complement each other. The three parts of the Bayley Scale are the Mental Scale, the Motor Scale, and the Infant Behavior Record. Examples of items in the *Mental Scale* are responding to a bell, following a ring with the eyes, vocalizations, picking up cubes, etc. The items in the *Motor Scale* include lifting the head, efforts to sit, rolling over, standing, throwing a ball, etc. It takes about forty-five minutes to administer the scales (Figure 39).

The Bayley Scales provide a Mental Development Index and a Psychomotor Index. According to Bayley (1969, p. 4), "the primary value of the developmental indexes is that they provide the basis for establishing a child's current status, and thus the extent of any deviation from normal expectancy."

Split-half reliability coefficients for the Mental Scale range from .81 to .93, with a median of .88. Split-half coefficients for the Motor Scale range from .68 to .92, with a median of .84. Bayley attributes the lower coefficients found for the Motor Scale to the fact that there are only about half as many items in the Motor Scale. Validity is claimed for the instrument on the basis of an increase in performance with an increase in age. Bayley also reports correlations ranging from .47 to .57 between MDI scores and Stanford-Binet IQs.

The *McCarthy Scales of Children's Abilities* (MSCA) were developed by Dorothea McCarthy (1972). The MSCA is designed for use with children between the ages of 2.5 and 8.5, and it was standardized on 100

Figure 39. *Bayley Scales of Infant Development.* (Reproduced by permission of The Psychological Corporation.)

children at each of ten age levels, stratified according to age, sex, race, geographic area, urban-rural residence, and father's occupation.

The MSCA has six scales for measuring intellectual and motor development: Verbal, Perceptual-Performance, Quantitative, Memory, Motor, and General Cognitive. The *General-Cognitive Scale* is a composite of the Verbal, Quantitative, and Perceptual-Performance scales. The following behaviors are sampled by the subtests: Block Building, Puzzle-Solving, Pictorial Memory, Word Knowledge, Number Questions, Tapping Sequence, Verbal Memory, Right-Left Orientation, Leg Coordination, Arm Coordination, Imitative Action, Draw-a-Design, Draw-a-Child, Numerical Memory, Verbal Fluency, Counting and Sorting, Opposite Analogies, and Conceptual Grouping (Fig. 41).

The MSCA yields four kinds of scores: a cognitive index, scale indexes, mental age, and percentile ranks. The general cognitive index is a scaled score with a mean of 100 and a standard deviation of 16. The other individual indexes have a mean of 50 and standard deviation of 10.

McCarthy (1972) reports internal consistency coefficients, test-retest coefficients, and standard errors of measurement in the manual. The

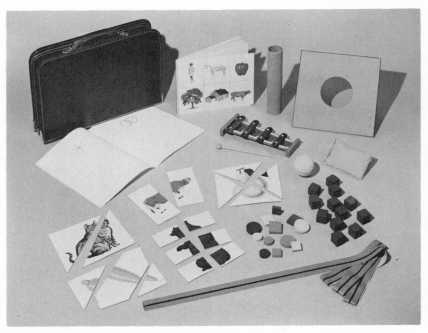

Figure 40. *McCarthy Scales of Children's Abilities.* (Reproduced by permission of The Psychological Corporation.)

reliability coefficients are generally in the upper .80s and lower .90s for the Verbal and General-Cognitive scales, and generally in the .70s and .80s for the other scales.

The manual also has validity data. Thirty-one children were tested with the MSCA and then tested four months later with the Metropolitan Achievement Tests. The correlations between Perceptual Performance scores and the MAT scores ranged from .40 to .51. For the Quantitative Scale, MAT correlations, the range was .38 to .51. The General Cognitive Scale scores also correlated at a low to moderate level (.34 to .54), but the Verbal, Memory, and Motor scale scores were poorly correlated with the MAT scores. A sample of thirty-five parochial school children was used for a concurrent validity study. In this study, MSCA scores were correlated with Stanford-Binet scores and WPPSI scores. The validity coefficients ranged from .02 for WPPSI Verbal scores versus MSCA Motor scores to .71 for WPPSI Full Scale scores versus MSCA General Cognitive scores. For the Stanford-Binet, the correlation coefficients ranged from .06 for S-B IQ versus MSCA Motor scores to .81 for S-B IQ versus MSCA General Cognitive scores.

In a study of kindergarten children ($N = 60$), Phillips et al. (1978) reported correlations of .74, .75, and .59 between the McCarthy GCI scale scores and WPPSI Full Scale, Verbal Scale, and Performance Scale scores respectively. They also reported a correlation of .71 between the McCarthy scale scores and *Columbia Mental Maturity Scale* scores.

Hynd et al. (1980) administered the MSCA and WISC-R to forty-four Native American primary-grade children and correlated subtest and scale scores for the two instruments. The GCI score correlated .83, .70, and .85 with Wechsler VSIQ, PSIQ, and FSIQ respectively.

GROUP MENTAL-ABILITY TESTS

Group-administered tests of mental ability have the advantages of permitting the testing of several persons at one time and requiring somewhat less time for administration than individual scales. In addition, a less skilled examiner can administer the group tests. Their major limitation is that they do not permit the close observation of the subject that is possible when an individual test or scale is administered.

The group tests of mental ability have been used extensively in schools and colleges since the days of the early group instruments that were developed by Arthur Otis and the Presseys. The group tests generally tap verbal and quantitative abilities, but some have items that assess other abilities also. The group tests in general are best suited for use with white, English-speaking subjects from middle or upper socioeconomic backgrounds. There are far too many of these group-administered tests to permit a discussion of all of them, and it should not be necessary to do so. Every school should have its test committee select the appropriate test or tests for that school. A few of the widely used instruments will be discussed briefly in order to give the reader an idea of the variations that occur among group mental-ability tests, and to emphasize the point that these instruments should be studied before they are selected for use.

Cognitive Abilities Test (CAT)

The CAT (Thorndike and Hagen, 1971) is published by Houghton Mifflin Company and is a successor to the *Lorge-Thorndike Intelligence Tests*. The *CAT* has ten levels, ranging from kindergarten to the twelfth grade, and is said to measure an individual's ability to use and manipulate abstract and symbolic relationships (Thorndike and Hagen, 1971, p. 3). The CAT has three batteries: Verbal, Quantitative, and Nonverbal. The *Verbal* battery is composed of four tests: Vocabulary, Sentence Completion, Verbal Classification, and Verbal Analogies. The subtests of the *Quantitative* Battery are Quantitative Relations, Number Series and Equation Relations, Number Series and Equation Building. The *Nonverbal* battery's three tests require no reading and are entitled Figure Analogies, Figure Classification, and Figure Synthesis.

The CAT was standardized on a population sample that consisted of approximately 20,000 students per grade, but the only variable that was used to stratify the sample was community size. The CAT manual does not describe the sample in specific terms, but it shows tables of proportions of subjects based upon geographic region and community size.

The manual provides percentiles, IQs, and stanines. There are separate scores for the Verbal, Quantitative, Nonverbal, and Total batteries.

The manual indicates that internal consistency reliability coefficients were found to range from .91 to .95 for a random sample taken from the standardization group.

Evidence of test validity of three types is cited by the test's authors. Content validity is assumed to have resulted through careful selection of items. Criterion-related validity was demonstrated by correlating CAT results with the results from the *Iowa Tests of Basic Skills* and the *Tests of Academic Progress*. The correlations between the three CAT batteries and the TAP ranged from .53 to .82, while the correlations between the CAT batteries and the ITBS ranged from .52 to .84. Additional evidence of validity is based upon test results for a sample of 554 students who were administered the CAT and *Stanford-Binet Intelligence Scale*. The reported correlations range from .72 to .78 for the Verbal Scale, .65 to .68 for the Quantitative Scale, and .60 to .65 for the Nonverbal Scale. The manual also has a discussion of the results of factor-analysis studies.

Henmon-Nelson Tests of Mental Ability

The *Henmon-Nelson Tests of Mental Ability,* 1973 Revision, authored by M. J. Nelson, T. A. Lamke, and J. L. French, are published by the Houghton Mifflin Company. The Primary Form is for kindergarten through grade 2 and contains eighty-six items. The Primary Form has the three subtests: Listening, Vocabulary, and Size and Number. Form I of the tests covers three grade levels: 3-6, 6-9, and 9-12, and each level has ninety items. Form I does not have subtests but does have item types that may be classified as Vocabulary, Sentence Completion, Opposites, General Information, Verbal Analogies, Verbal Classification, Verbal Inference, Number Series, Arithmetic Reasoning, and Figure Analogies. According to the authors, the tests are designed to "measure those aspects of mental ability which are important for success in school work."

The Primary Form was standardized on 5,000 children and Form I on approximately 48,000 students in regular school classes. The sample was stratified with respect to geographic area and community size.

The Henmon-Nelson provides deviation IQs with a mean of 100 and standard deviation of 16. Percentile ranks and stanines are also provided in the manual.

The *Examiner's Manual* shows odd-even reliability coefficients that range from .84 for Primary K to .96 for grade 6. The coefficients tend to center around .95. The manual contains reports of studies that provide evidence of criterion-related validity. In one study sixty children were administered the Primary Form and the *Metropolitan Achievement Test.* The correlation between the total score on Henmon-Nelson and the total score on the MAT was found to be .72. In another study involving grades 3, 6, and 9, scores for the Henmon-Nelson were correlated with scores for the *Lorge-Thorndike Intelligence Test,* the *Otis-Lennon Mental Ability Test,* and *Iowa Tests of Basic Skills.* The Henmon-Nelson versus Lorge-Thorndike correlations ranged from .78 to .83. The correlations between the Henmon-Nelson and Otis-Lennon ranged from .75 to .82. The Henmon-Nelson versus ITBS correlations varied between .60 and .86.

Short Form Test of Academic Aptitude

The SFTAA (Sullivan, Clark, and Tiegs, 1970) is a derivative of the popular *California Test of Mental Maturity* (CTMM). According to the authors, the SFTAA was designed to "assess the intellectual development attained by the student and to predict his potential rate of progress and level of success in school" (Examiner's Manual, p. 5). There are four subtests in the SFTAA (Vocabulary, Analogies, Sequences, and Memory), covering five levels for grades 1 through 12. Each level of the test has a language and nonlanguage section. The manual provides percentile ranks, standard scores, and stanines for the language section, nonlanguage section, and total test. Deviation IQs with a mean of 100 and standard deviation of 16 are also presented.

The SFTAA was standardized on a sample of 197,912 students in grades 1 to 12 in public and Catholic schools in 36 states. The test was standardized jointly with the *California Achievement Test,* 1970 Edition. The data pertaining to validity are too numerous to discuss here, and the reader is referred to the Technical Report for this information.

Other Multilevel Mental-Ability Tests

Several other multilevel tests of intellectual ability have been used extensively and deserve mention. As has been stated previously, anyone who intends to use a test should obtain a copy of it and its manual for thorough study prior to selection and use.

Analysis of Learning Potential (ALP)

This test, published by The Psychological Corporation (1970), has five levels for grades 1, 2-3, 4-6, 7-9, and 10-12. The test provides a score referred to as the Index of Learning Potential (ILP) and a General Composite Standard Score (GCSS). The test was designed to predict achievement in major areas of school work. It was standardized on a national sample of 150,000 students.

Otis-Lennon Mental-Ability Tests

This test, authored by A. S. Otis and R. T. Lennon, is published by The Psychological Corporation (1967). There are six levels of this instrument, ranging from Primary I to Advanced (K through 12). It is designed to measure verbal, numerical, and abstract reasoning abilities and to predict scholastic success. The test produces a single score that can be expressed as mental age, deviation IQ, percentile rank, and stanine. The test was standardized on approximately 200,000 students in 117 school systems in all fifty states. Sample items are shown in Figure 41.

Kuhlmann-Anderson Measure of Academic Potential

This test, authored by F. Kuhlmann and R. Anderson, is published by Personnel Press. It is the seventh edition of the Kuhlmann-Anderson Tests. There are eight levels that cover the kindergarten to grade 12 range. The test provides a Verbal, Quantitative, and Total score.

UTILIZATION OF TESTS OF MENTAL ABILITY

Tests that assess a student's vocabulary, the ability to understand verbal or quantitative relationships, the ability to deal with abstract concepts, etc., provide important information concerning the student's cognitive development. Teachers need this information in order to

Elementary I Level, Form J

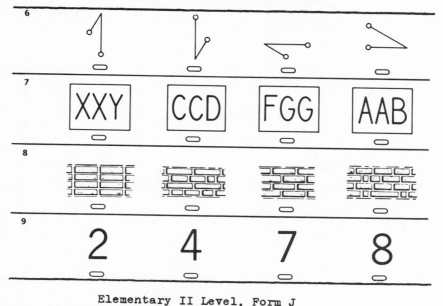

Elementary II Level, Form J

55. A is to Z as **first** is to –
  a second **b** alphabet **c** farthest **d** final **e** oldest

56. Which series contains a wrong number?
  f 1 3 5 7 9   **g** 2 4 6 8 10   **h** 2 5 8 11 14
  j 1 4 7 10 13   **k** 3 6 9 12 14

57. The drawings in the box go together in a certain way. Find the drawing that belongs where you see the question mark (?) in the box.

58. If the words below were arranged to make the *best* sentence, with which letter would the *last* word of the sentence begin?

  meanings us dictionaries word give
  f d   **g** g   **h** m   **j** u   **k** w

59. **Duck** is to **duckling** as **bear** is to – **F**
  a honey **b** cub **c** bearing **d** carry **e** polar

60.

Figure 41. Sample items from the *Otis Lennon Mental Ability Test.* (Reproduced from the Otis-Lennon Mental Ability Test. Copyright © 1967 by Harcourt Brace Jovanovich, Inc. Reproduced by special permission.)

plan lessons and activities that are suitable for each student and for a group as a whole. The scores from mental-ability tests help teachers, counselors, and school psychologists estimate learning capacities, determine readiness for certain activities (reading and arithmetic, for example), check on mental growth, and determine the effect of special education or training. The proper application of such information can lead to many important outcomes, such as improved self-concepts, greater satisfaction with school work, reduced frustration and boredom, greater academic achievement, and less disruptive behavior.

School counselors can use the data from mental-ability tests to help students acquire a better understanding of their learning potential, choose courses or programs wisely (when choices are available), plan for future education or careers, and make important decisions in their lives. For instance, a counselor can help the student who lacks superior mental ability realize that nuclear physics is not a realistic vocational choice, or help the gifted student see that an occupation that involves a low level of skill and much routine activity is not likely to be satisfying to that person. A counselor and student can make use of valid appraisal data in sorting out the promising vocational choices from the many alternatives. With respect to personal problems (such as those that involve feelings of inadequacy, hostility, aggression, etc.) it is axiomatic that they can be dealt with more effectively if the counselor has a good estimate of the client's intellectual capacity than if such information is lacking. Also, some counselors will select their approach to counseling on the basis of the client's level of mental ability, using certain techniques with the slow learner but not with the normal or gifted individual.

School psychologists would seldom write a psychological report intended for use by teachers, counselors, or administrators without an appraisal of the subject's level of mental ability. This information impacts so greatly on so many aspects of human behavior that it is indispensable.

Limitations of Mental Ability Tests

As useful as intelligence tests may be, they still have some serious limitations. One of the limitations of these instruments is that they sometimes are not adequately standardized on representative populations. Some of the standardization samples do not have a proper representation of subjects from various geographic areas and some do not include enough minority subjects. When the tests are standardized on children and youths in school only, the severely retarded, severely emotionally disturbed, and the dropouts will be excluded from the norm group. Lack of representativeness of the norm group can make the interpretation of data for members of the underrepresented group very difficult.

Another serious limitation is that the nature of the items, coupled with the time limits on some items, seems to arouse anxiety in some subjects to such an extent that they do not concentrate and respond as well as they might in a less stressful situation. It seems possible that the highly intelligent, confident subject has a special advantage over the anxious normal or subnormal subject on the timed intelligence test items because the former can work faster and also more efficiently than the latter, who may waste time on items that seem difficult. This possibility should be kept in mind when one utilizes the results of mental-ability tests.

GENERAL APTITUDE TESTS

Along with tests of general mental ability, counselors and school psychologists are likely to use *aptitude* tests of various types. An aptitude test, if valid, should measure potential for success in some school subject, course of study, occupation, or some other specific endeavor. Aptitude tests vary greatly with respect to design and purpose, and some are better suited for use in industry than for use in schools. In the sections that follow, only a few of the most widely used aptitude batteries will be discussed.

Primary Mental Abilities (PMA)

The PMA (Thurstone and Thurstone, 1965) is published by Science Research Associates. It was designed to measure five specific "primary mental abilities" and general mental ability. The five subtests that are used to sample the primary mental abilities are Verbal Meaning, Number Facility, Reasoning, Perceptual Speed, and Spatial Relationships. The PMA may be used at five different levels that cover the range of K through 12. Scores for the PMA are expressed as mental ages, percentile ranks, and IQs, but different scores are provided at the different levels. The PMA was standardized on 32,393 students enrolled in seventy-three schools. The standardization sample was stratified according to age, grade, and geographic region.

Test-retest reliability coefficients are reported in the manual. These coefficients vary considerably. The median reliability coefficients reported for the five tests and total score area follow: Verbal Meaning, .89; Number Facility, .81; Reasoning, .83; Perceptual Speed, .67; Spatial Relationships, .78; and Total, .91. In one validation study reported in the manual, correlations between the PMA total score and composite score on the *Iowa Tests of Basic Skills* ranged from .75 to .84.

Differential Aptitude Tests (DAT)

The DAT, developed by G. K. Bennett et al. (1974), is published by The Psychological Corporation. This battery, which takes approximately three hours to administer, consists of eight subtests. According to the authors of the DAT, the subtests are designed to measure the following abilities or aptitudes.

VERBAL REASONING: To understand, think, and reason with words — an ability needed in almost all school subjects but especially important in courses that require extensive reading or class discussion such as English, Social Studies, Science, and History. The ability to understand and use ideas expressed in words is important in jobs such as teacher, guidance counselor, social worker, reporter, editor, lawyer — and in jobs as diverse as life insurance salesman, policeman, bank teller, restaurant hostess, car rental clerk, and hospital attendant.

NUMERICAL ABILITY: To reason with numbers and solve mathematical problems — an ability related to the mastery of school subjects that require quantitative thinking such as business arithmetic, algebra, geometry, chemistry, and physics. Specific occupations require varying degrees of numerical ability — important in jobs such as economist, engineer, credit analyst, cost accountant, insurance underwriter, market research analyst, mathematician, and statistican — and needed in a variety of other jobs such as account executive, bank manager, broker, business manager, sales clerk, salesman, surveyor, and weather observer.

VR + NA (VERBAL PLUS NUMERICAL): An efficient indicator of general scholastic aptitude, the ability to learn from books and lectures and to master school subjects.

ABSTRACT REASONING: To think logically without words or numbers, to see and manipulate mentally the relationships among things, objects, patterns, diagrams, or designs — an ability useful in shop, drafting, and laboratory courses. Useful for computer programmers, systems analysts, and scientists. A special use of the Abstract Reasoning Test is the comparison of the score with that achieved on the Verbal Reasoning Test for students with foreign language backgrounds. The Abstract Reasoning score may be the better indicator of the foreign student's readiness to learn.

CLERICAL SPEED AND ACCURACY: The ability to compare and make simple letter and number symbols quickly and accurately — a perceptual-motor skill useful in business courses and in clerical tasks such as filing, coding, library cataloging, and stock room work. Needed for jobs such as bank teller, business manager, broker, cashier, clerk, cost accountant, salesman, stenographer, and typist.

MECHANICAL REASONING: To understand mechanical principles and devices and apply laws of everyday physics — to understand how appliances work and how tools are used. Courses in the physical sciences, technical studies, and manual training are easier for students who have mechanical reasoning ability. Useful in a wide variety of occupations such as auto mechanic, bulldozer operator, carpenter, drill press operator, longshoreman, photo-engraver, policeman, medical technologist, and engineer.

SPACE RELATIONS: To "think in three dimensions" or picture mentally the shape, size, and position of objects. An ability that is helpful in geometry, drafting, art, and design courses. Useful in jobs such as architect, bus driver, cabinet maker, die-maker, draftsman, dress designer, dental hygienist, geologist, nurse, and surveyor.

SPELLING: To recognize correct and incorrect spellings of common English words. The ability to spell correctly is needed for written reports in any school subject. Predicts success in typing and stenographic courses. Needed for jobs such as secretary, technical manual writer, editor — any job using writing skills.

LANGUAGE USAGE: Sensitivity to language structure, to recognize correct and incorrect word usage, grammar, and punctuation. An ability needed in English and other school subjects requiring class discussion and written reports. Command of language is needed in jobs such as copywriter, editor, lawyer, reporter, teacher, salesman — any job requiring written or oral communication.

The fifth edition (1974) of the DAT was standardized in 1972 on a sample of more than 64,000 students in thirty-three states and the District of Columbia.

The DAT provides scores for all eight of the subtests and for a measure of scholastic aptitude (sum of the VR and NA scores). Separate percentile norms are provided for males and females for fall and spring semesters. The DAT has two forms, S and T, that may be used for testing students in grades 8-12.

The authors of the DAT consider the instrument to be useful for educational and vocational planning, and they provide helpful explanations and suggestions in the pamphlet entitled *Your Aptitudes as Measured by the Differential Aptitude Tests*. This pamphlet discusses the meaning of the term aptitude, tells about the functions of the tests, discusses the application of DAT rest results, and gives some predictive-validity data. A section is devoted to the procedures for making a DAT profile.

The *DAT Career Planning Program Counselor's Manual* also has a useful test interpretation section. A sample DAT profile is shown in Figure 42.

The DAT manual presents a considerable amount of reliability and validity data. The reported reliability coefficients range from .87 to .94, except for Mechanical Reasoning for females (.70).

Some of the many predictive-validity coefficients for the correlation between the best predictors (VR, NA, and VR + NA) and school marks are as high as the .80s, but the median coefficients tend to be around .50. The best overall predictor for school marks is VR + NA. The reported coefficients for the correlation between the best DAT predic-

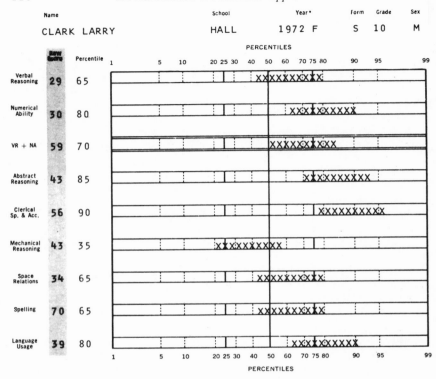

Figure 42. DAT profile. (Reproduced by permission of The Psychological Corporation.)

tors and standardized achievement test scores generally are in the .60s and .70s.

Academic Promise Test

The APT (G. K. Bennett et al., 1965) is also published by The Psychological Corporation and consists of four subtests: Verbal (V), Numerical (N), Abstract Reasoning (AR), and Language Usage (LU). This battery really amounts to a downward extension of the DAT. It takes about ninety minutes to administer the APT. The battery is used in grades 6-9.

This battery was standardized on a sample of more than 34,000 students in eighty-five school systems, in thirty-seven states. The manual shows the breakdown of the sample by geographic region and community size.

The APT yields scores given in terms of percentile ranks and stanines for boys and for girls. The scores may be plotted in a profile, such as Figure 16 in Chaper IV.

Alternate-form reliability coefficients are reported in the manual, and these generally are in the .80s and .90s. The APT Total-score reliabilities are .93 or .94 for each grade. A considerable amount of predictive validity data is presented in the manual, and these are too numerous to discuss. In general, the reported validity coefficients are for the relationships between the APT scores (AR, N, V, LU, AR + N, V + LU) and either school marks or achievement-test scores.

General Aptitude Test Battery

The *General Aptitude Test Battery* (GATB, 1962) is a well-known vocational aptitude battery that may be used to test high school seniors and adults. This battery is published by the U. S. Employment Service.

The GATB can be administered in approximately three hours when all of the twelve tests are given. Eight tests are paper-and-pencil tests and four are performance tests. The tests that make up the battery yield percentile ranks and standard scores for nine factors.

INTELLIGENCE (G): General learning ability; ability to understand instructions and underlying principles; ability to reason and make judgments. Measured by tests of three-dimensional space, vocabulary, and arithmetic reasoning.

VERBAL APTITUDE (V): Ability to understand meanings of words and to use them effectively; ability to comprehend language, to understand relationships between words, and to understand meanings of whole sentences and paragraphs. Measured by vocabulary tests.

NUMERICAL APTITUDE (N): Ability to perform arithmetic operations quickly and accurately. Measured by tests of computation and arithmetic reasoning.

SPATIAL APTITUDE (S): Ability to think visually of geometric forms and to comprehend the two-dimensional representation of three-dimensional objects; ability to recognize the relationships resulting from movements of objects in space. Measured by tests of three-dimensional space.

FORM PERCEPTION (P): Ability to perceive pertinent detail in objects or in pictorial or graphic material; ability to make visual comparisons and discriminations and see slight differences in shapes and shadings of figures and widths and lengths of lines. Measured by tool and form matching.

CLERICAL PERCEPTION (Q): Ability to perceive pertinent detail in verbal or tabular material; ability to observe differences in copy, proof-read words and numbers, and to avoid perceptual errors in arithmetic computation. Measured by tests of name comparison.

MOTOR COORDINATION (K): Ability to coordinate eyes and hands or fingers rapidly and accurately in making precise movements with speed. Ability to make a movement response accurately and swiftly. Measured by mark making.

USE OF APTITUDE TEST DATA

One would logically expect that aptitude tests would be very useful in predicting success or failure in academic work or in various occupations. Validity studies have shown that aptitude tests are useful, but much less so than one would expect. The reason for their limited validity is not necessarily in the design or construction of the instruments (for they generally are well designed and built) but in the fact that the degree of success in courses or occupations depends upon many factors, not just aptitude. Interest, maturation, past experience, values, and personality traits are some of the important factors related to human performance. Also, in some kinds of academic work or vocational work, certain combinations of aptitudes may be necessary for success. Then, too, success may be defined and measured in several different ways. A "successful" engineer may be considered successful because he has held his job for several years, or has earned a high income, or has received superior work ratings from a supervisor, or works for a big corporation. However, is the engineer who has a modest income, works for a small firm, receives no praise for his work, and has had several engineering jobs less successful? It is difficult to answer that question except on an individual-case basis.

Those who can use aptitude-test results most effectively know the tests well and know the various academic and vocational requirements well. Such persons are not likely to oversimplify the task of predicting success based upon aptitude-test data.

REFERENCES

Anastasi, Anne: *Psychological Testing*, 4th ed. New York, Macmillan, 1976.
Anastasiow, Nicholas: Educational relevance and Jensen's conclusions. *Phi Delta Kappan, 51:*32-35, 1969.
Balthazar, E. E. and Morrison, D. H.: The use of the Wechsler Intelligence Scales as diagnostic indicators of predominant left-right and indeterminate unilateral brain damage. *Journal of Clinical Psychology, 17:*161-165, 1961.
Bayley, Nancy: *The Bayley Scales of Infant Development*. New York, The Psychological Corporation, 1969.
Bennett, G. K. et al.: *Manual: Differential Aptitude Tests*. New York, The Psychological Corporation, 1974.
————: *Manual: The Academic Promise Tests*. New York, The Psychological Corporation, 1965.
Binet, Alfred: Le development de l'intelligence chez les enfants. *L'Annee Psychologique, 14:*1-90, 1908.
Brengelmann, C. and Kenny, J. T.: Comparison of Leiter, WAIS, and Stanford-Binet IQ in retardates. *Journal of Clinical Psychology, 17:*235-238, 1961.
Brody, E. B. and Brody, Nathan: *Intelligence: Nature, Determinants, and Consequences*. New York, Academic Press, 1976.

————: *The Seventh Mental Measurement Yearbook,* 2 vols. Highland Park, New Jersey, Gryphon Press, 1972.

Butcher, Harold J.: *Human Intelligence: Its Nature and Assessment,* 2nd ed. London, Methuen and Company, 1972.

Cattell, Psyche: *The Measurement of Infants and Young Children.* New York, The Psychological Corporation, 1947.

Cattell, Raymond B.: *Abilities: Their Structure, Growth, and Action.* New York, Houghton Mifflin Company, 1971.

————: Theory of fluid and crystallized intelligence: A critical experiment. *Journal of Educational Psychology, 54:*1-22, 1963.

———— and Cattell, H. K.: *Handbook for the Culture Fair Intelligence Test.* Champaign, Illinois, Institute for Personality and Ability Testing, 1959.

Conry, R. and Plant, W. T.: WAIS and group test predictions of an academic success criterion: High school and college. *Educational and Psychological Measurement, 25:*285-299, 1965.

Cronbach, L. J.: *Essentials of Psychological Testing.* 3rd ed. New York, Harper & Row, 1970.

Erlenmeyer-Kimling, L. and Jarvik, L. F.: Genetics and intelligence: Review. *Science, 142:*1477-1478, 1963.

Eysenck, H. J.: *The IQ Argument.* New York, The Library Press, 1971.

Fisher, Constance T.: Intelligence defined as effectiveness of approaches. *Journal of Counseling and Clinical Psychology, 33:*668-674, 1969.

Flavell, John J.: *The Developmental Psychology of Jean Piaget.* Princeton, New Jersey, Van Nostrand, 1963.

Freeman, Frank: *Mental Tests: Their History, Principles, and Applications.* Boston, Houghton Mifflin, 1962.

Fromm, Erika and Hartman, L. D.: *Intelligence: A Dynamic Approach.* Garden City, New York, Doubleday, 1955.

Gesell, A., Thompson, H., and Amatruda, C.: *The Psychology of Early Growth.* New York, Macmillan, 1938.

Gesell, Arnold and Amatruda, C. S.: *Developmental Diagnosis,* 2nd ed. New York, Hoeber, 1947.

Giannell, A. S. and Freeburne, C. M.: Comparative validity of the WAIS and Stanford-Binet with college freshmen. *Educational and Psychological Measurement, 23:*557-567, 1963.

Glasser, Alan J. and Zimmerman, I. L.: *Clinical Interpretation of the Wechsler Intelligence Scale for Children.* New York, Grune and Stratton, 1967.

Goddard, H. H.: A revision of the Binet scale. *The Training School Bulletin, 8:*56-62, 1911.

Goldfarb, W.: Infant rearing and problem behavior. *American Journal of Orthopsychiatry, 13:*249-265, 1943.

Goodenough, Florence L.: *Measurement of Intelligence by Drawings.* New York, World Book, 1926.

————: *Mental Testing: Its History, Principles, and Applications.* New York, Holt, 1949.

———— and Harris, D. B.: Studies in the psychology of children's drawings: II, 1928-1949. *Psychological Bulletin, 47:*369-433, 1950.

————, Maurer, R., and Van Wagenen, M.: *Minnesota Preschool Scales: Manual.* Minneapolis, Educational Test Bureau, 1940.

Griffiths, Anita N.: The WISC as a diagnostic remedial tool for dyslexia. *Academic Therapy, 12:*401-409, 1977.

Guertin, Wilson H. et al.: Research with the Wechsler Intelligence Scale for adults: 1960-65, *Psychological Bulletin, 66:*385-409, 1966.

Guilford, J. P.: *The Nature of Human Intelligence.* New York, McGraw-Hill, 1967.

Hewitt, P. and Massey, J. P.: *Clinical Clues From the WISC: Wechsler Intelligence Scale for Children with Special Sections on Testing Black and Spanish-Speaking Children.* Palo Alto, California, Consulting Psychologists Press, 1969.

Hynd, G. W. et al.: Concurrent validity of the McCarthy Scales of children's abilities with native American primary-grade children. *Measurement and Evaluation in Guidance, 13(1):*29-34, 1980.

Jensen, Arthur: How much can we boost IQ and scholastic achievement? *Harvard Educational Review, 39:*1-123, 1969.

Jones, H. Gwynne: The evaluation of the significance of differences between scaled scores of the WAIS: The perpetuation of a fallacy. *Journal of Consulting Psychology, 20:*319-320, 1956.

Kagan, J. et al.: Discussion: How much can we boost IQ and scholastic achievement? *Harvard Educational Review, 39:*273-356, 1969.

Kamin, L. J.: Jensen's last stand. *Psychology Today,* February, 1980, 117-123.

Kaufman, A. S. and Kaufman, N. L.: *Clinical Evaluation of Young Children with the McCarthy Scales.* New York, Grune and Stratton, 1977.

Kitzinger, Helen, and Blumberg, Eric: Supplementary guide to administering and scoring the WBIS. *Psychological Monograph, 65:*1-20, 1951.

Klineberg, O.: Negro-white differences in intelligence test performance. *American Psychologist, 18:*198-203, 1963.

Knox, Alan B., Grotelueschen A., and Sjogren, D.: Adult intelligence and learning ability. *Adult Education, 18:*188-196, 1968.

Lee, E. S.: Negro intelligence and selective migration: A Philadelphia test of the Klineberg hypotheses. *American Sociological Review, 16:*227-233, 1951.

Littell, W. M.: The Wechsler Intelligence Scale for children: Review of a decade of research. *Psychological Bulletin, 57:*132-156, 1960.

Lutey, Carol: *Individual Intelligence Testing: A Manual.* Greeley, Colorado, Executary, Inc., 1966.

———: *Individual Intelligence Testing: A Manual Supplement: Wechsler Preschool and Primary Scale of Intelligence (WPPSI).* Greeley, Colorado, Colorado State College Bookstore, 1967.

McCarthy, Dorothea: *Manual for the McCarthy Scales of Children's Abilities.* New York, The Psychological Corporation, 1972.

McCleod, Hugh N. and Rubin, Joseph: Correlation between Raven Progressive Matrices and the WAIS. *Journal of Consulting Psychology, 26:*190-191, 1962.

McNemar, Quinn: On WAIS difference scores. *Journal of Consulting Psychology, 21:*239-240, 1957.

———: *The Revision of the Stanford-Binet Scale: An Analysis of the Standardization Data.* Boston, Houghton Mifflin, 1942.

Nelson, M. J. et al.: *Examiner's Manual for the Henmon-Nelson Tests of Mental Ability.* Boston, Houghton Mifflin Company, 1973.

Olsen, Inger A. and Jordheim, Gerald D.: Use of WAIS in a student counseling center. *Personnel and Guidance Journal, 42:*500-507, 1964.

Piaget, Jean: The attainment of invariants and reversible operations in the development of thinking. *Social Research, 30:*283-299, 1963.

————: *The Psychology of Intelligence.* London, Routledge, 1950.

Quershi, M. Y.: The internal consistency of the WISC scores for ages 5 to 16. *Journal of Clinical Psychology, 24:*79-85, 1968.

Rapaport, D.: *Diagnostic Psychological Testing.* Chicago, Year Book Publishers, 1945.

Rappaport, Paul: Divided opinions on the split brain. *APA Monitor,* December, 1979, 9-10.

Raven, J. C.: *Guide to the Standard Progressive Matrices.* London, H. K. Lewis, 1960.

Rice, Berkeley: Brave new world of intelligence testing. *Psychology Today, 13:*27-41, 1979.

Robb, G., Bernardoni, L., and Johnson, R.: *Assessment of Individual Mental Ability.* New York, Harper and Row, 1972.

Salvia, John and Ysseldyke, J. F.: *Assessment in Special and Remedial Education.* Boston, Houghton Mifflin, 1978.

Samuda, R. J.: *Psychological Testing of American Minorities: Issues and Consequences.* New York, Harper and Row, 1975.

Sattler, J. B.: Analysis of functions of the 1960 Stanford-Binet Intelligence Scale, Form L-M. *Journal of Clinical Psychology, 21:*173-179, 1965.

Scarr, S. and Weinberg, R. A.: IQ performance of black children adopted by white families. *American Psychologist, 31:*726-739, 1977.

Shuey, Audrey M.: *The Testing of Negro Intelligence,* 2nd ed. New York, Social Service Press, 1966.

Simensen, R. J. and Sutherland, J.: Psychological assessment of brain damage. *Academic Therapy, 10:*69-81, 1974.

Skeels, H. M.: Effects of adoption of children from institutions. *Children, 12:*33-34, 1965.

Spearman, C.: *The Abilities of Man.* New York, Macmillan, 1927.

Speer, G. S.: The mental development of children of feebleminded and normal mothers. *Yearbook National Society for the Study of Education, 39* (Part II):309-314, 1940.

Sternberg, R. J.: The nature of human abilities. *American Psychologist, 34:*214-229, 1979.

Stoddard, George D.: *The Meaning of Intelligence.* New York, Macmillan, 1943.

Sullivan, E. T. et al.: *Examiner's Manual for the Short Form Test of Academic Aptitude.* Monterey, California, CTB/McGraw-Hill, 1970.

Super, Donald E. and Crites, John O.: *Appraising Vocational Fitness,* 2nd ed. New York, Harper and Row Publishers, 1962.

Terman, Lewis M.: Intelligence and its measurement: A symposium. *Journal of Educational Psychology, 12:*127-133, 1921.

———— and Merrill, Maud: *Measuring Intelligence.* Boston, Houghton Mifflin, 1916.

————: *Stanford-Binet Intelligence Scale Manual.* Boston, Houghton Mifflin, 1960.

————: *Stanford-Binet Intelligence Scale, 1972 Norms Edition.* Boston, Houghton Mifflin, 1972.

Thorndike, E. L. et al.: *The Measurement of Intelligence.* New York, Teachers College Press, 1927.

Thorndike, R. L. and Hagen, Elizabeth: *Examiner's Manual: Cognitive Abilities Test.* Boston, Houghton Mifflin, 1971.

————: *Measurement and Evaluation in Psychology and Education*, 4th ed. New York, Wiley, 1977.

Thurstone, L. L.: Primary mental abilities. *Psychometric Monograph*, No. 1, 1938.

———— and Thurstone, T. G.: *Primary Mental Abilities Test Manual*. Chicago, Science Research Associates, 1965.

Thurstone, T. G.: Primary mental abilities of children. *Educational and Psychological Measurement*, *1:*105-116, 1941.

Tryon, Warren, W.: The test-trait fallacy. *American Psychologist*, *34:*402-406, 1979.

United States Employment Service: *Guide to the Use of the General Aptitude Test Battery*. Washington, Government Printing Office, 1962.

Valett, R. E.: *Description of a Clinical Profile for the Stanford-Binet Intelligence Scale (L-M)*. Palo Alto, California, Consulting Psychologist Press, 1965.

Vernon, Philip E.: *Intelligence and Attainment Tests*. New York, Philosophical Library, 1960.

————: *The Structure of Human Abilities*. New York, Wiley, 1951.

Wadsworth, Barry: *Piaget's Theory of Cognitive Development*, 2nd ed. New York, Longman, 1979.

Wechsler, David: *The Measurement and Appraisal of Adult Intelligence*. Baltimore, Williams & Wilkins, 1958.

————: *The Measurement of Adult Intelligence*, 3rd ed. Baltimore, Williams & Wilkins, 1944.

————: *Wechsler Adult Intelligence Scale Manual*. New York, The Psychological Corporation, 1955.

————: *Wechsler Intelligence Scale for Children Manual*. New York, The Psychological Corporation, 1949.

————: *The Wechsler Intelligence Scale for Children-Revised Manual*. New York, The Psychological Corporation, 1967.

————: *Wechsler Preschool and Primary Scale of Intelligence Manual*. New York, The Psychological Corporation, 1967.

Wellman, B. L.: Iowa studies of the effects of schooling. *Yearbook of the National Society for the Study of Education*, *39* (Part II):377-399, 1940.

Wells, Donald and Pedrini, Duilio: Where to begin testing in the Stanford-Binet L-M. *Journal of Clinical Psychology*, *23:*182-183, 1967.

Wesman, Alexander G.: Intelligence testing. *American Psychologist*, *23:*267-274, 1968.

Wintsch, Susan: Twins research. *Indiana Alumni Magazine*, March 12-15, 1979.

Witelson, S. F.: Sex and the single hemisphere: Specialization of the right hemisphere for spatial processing. *Science*, *193:*425-427, 1976.

Yarrow, L. J.: Maternal deprivation: Toward an empirical and conceptual reevaluation. *Psychological Bulletin*, *58:*459-490, 1961.

Zimmerman, Irla, Woo-Sam, James, and Glasser, Alan: *Clinical Interpretation of the Wechsler Adult Intelligence Scale*, New York, Grune and Stratton, 1973.

Chapter 9

SOCIAL-EMOTIONAL APPRAISAL

$\mathbf{S}$OCIAL-EMOTIONAL APPRAISAL is the least academically oriented aspect of appraisal that is implemented in educational settings. Tests of mental ability, achievement, interests, and aptitude provide the standard types of measurement most frequently used in public school appraisal programs. By the time a student graduates from high school, scores on several mental ability tests, several achievement tests, one aptitude test, and one interest inventory will probably have accumulated on the cumulative record. Chances are, the student will have no social-emotional appraisal on file. Social-emotional appraisal devices usually are not administered to whole grade level populations at one time, as other forms of appraisal often are. Social-emotional appraisal is a more individualized form of appraisal, and a specific need for information available through this type of assessment must usually be stated to warrant investment in such an extended effort.

INDICATIONS FOR SOCIAL-EMOTIONAL APPRAISAL

Educators recognize that students bring their feelings and attitudes with them into the classroom, and that emotional factors cannot easily be separated out from the learning process; however, unless the student is having difficulty functioning in the academic setting, and intervention methods attempted have been singularly unsuccessful, emotional development will often be left to proceed on its own. Academic progress that falls below assessed academic abilities may be the first indication that emotional factors might be interfering with the learning process. If things are "upside down" at home, if social skills are not appropriate and peer relationships are disruptive, or if self-concept dips dangerously low, then academic performance may be the least of a student's concerns. A short attention span, withdrawing or acting-out behavior, failure to complete assignments, poor peer relationships, or poor attendance can be signals that some sort of emotional problem may be distracting the student from academic pursuits. Picking up on the signal often is the first step in appraising social-emotional development.

Social-emotional appraisal is more complex than other types of appraisal and usually requires a greater degree of interpretive skills. A student's affective or feeling states do not often come neatly packaged in a computer printout, and a list of traits does not reveal a great deal about what might be going on with a student without some analysis of the relevant data. Generally, a complex set of traits and indicators must be integrated into meaningful interrelationships if the collected information is to prove useful to those who work with the student. The objective of the appraisal is to help teachers, parents, counselors, administrators, and the student find more appropriate and successful ways for the student to cope and function effectively.

MISLEADING INDICATORS FOR SOCIAL-EMOTIONAL APPRAISAL

Nonemotional factors can produce emotional-type behaviors and symptoms. Before social-emotional appraisal is conducted, other possible sources or causes should be explored. Sometimes problems that seem to be emotional problems arise from physiological dysfunction that is undiagnosed or untreated. In this type of situation, treatment for the presumed emotional problem would not likely prove very successful; in fact, it may even aggravate the condition and arouse unwarranted concern over mental health. Diabetes or hypoglycemia may be interfering with metabolism; poor visual or auditory acuity may be affecting reading comprehension; or perhaps a kidney infection or malfunction may be responsible for those "accidents."

Physiological problems seem much more socially acceptable to parents and students than emotional ones. One mother actually seemed to prefer a brain tumor or lesion to emotional disturbance as a diagnosis. Even after consulting a neurologist who confirmed that the problems were emotionally based, the mother insisted on further tests, including a "brain wave test," "just to make sure." The suggestion that something might be wrong with one's emotional adjustment is sometimes a frightening and threatening diagnosis to consider, and an incorrect and uncorrected diagnosis carries with it some very negative aspects.

Problems can also arise when a teacher or parent overestimates a child's intellectual abilities. Mature verbal abilities and social skills may lead others to expect superior intellectual performance from a student with average abilities and thus generate fear of failure, tension, anxiety, and a frustrated desire to please. The quiet child who does not participate actively in discussion and does not score particularly well on tests may possess high abilities that are understimulated and may be manifesting symptoms of boredom more than lack of ability. An individual intellectual assessment can often clear up this type of misunderstanding.

The relationship between emotional problems and learning disabilities seems to increase the longer the learning disabilities go undiagnosed and untreated. By definition, the learning disabled child is of average or above-average intelligence; therefore, the child is very likely aware of the discrepancy between his performance and that of his classmates as well as the discrepancy between what his work looks like and what it is supposed to look like. Early detection and remediation of learning disabilities might be an effective preventive measure for future emotional disturbance. With the older child, who has passed the age for early detection, the combined intervention of academic and counseling levels can have more positive impact than working on either level exclusively. Appraisal of language/learning disabilities is discussed extensively in Chapter 10.

If maladjustment remains unexplained after the influence of nonemotional factors has been accounted for or remediated, emotional aspects may be involved in conjunction with (or to the exclusion of) physical, intellectual, or learning problems. The nature and extent of this involvement should be assessed directly through a social-emotional evaluation.

DATA COLLECTION (BACKGROUND INFORMATION)

The purpose of a social-emotional assessment is to provide concerned persons with answers to the questions "What is Johnny doing?" "Why is he doing it?" and "What is the best approach to dealing with the problem at hand?" The appraisal process involves collecting as much background and current information as is feasible. The data collected are interpreted from the position, "If I were this child, how would I be feeling; what needs are not being met; and what would I be trying to accomplish through my behavior?" Professional knowledge and skills are then used to define areas of concern and to suggest viable options for treatment of the problem.

The investigation begins with the collection of background information. Collection of data of this sort usually takes the form of an interview, questionnaire, or rating scale or some combination of the three. Descriptive information can be gathered from teachers, other school personnel, parents, and the student under consideration. Each of these sources has information about what has happened to the student in the immediate or remote past as well as what is happening currently, according to how each respondent remembers or perceives the history. Each source has opinions and attitudes that all affect how the student has been treated, is being treated, or is likely to be treated.

First-hand experience with adults significant to the student can provide a perspective to the social interactions that the child experiences regularly. Potentially destructive aspects or conditions in the student's environment may be illuminated, and the otherwise maladaptive behaviors of the student may thereby become considered as a normal reaction to adverse conditions.

The student's family can provide information concerning the family constellation and history, developmental milestones, medical history, and social experiences. School personnel can provide educational history, tests results, and a facet of social history. Family members and school personnel can contribute descriptions of what is going on as they perceive the situation and how the child is currently functioning. The age of the student will affect how much the student can contribute to this phase of the appraisal process, but self-reports are valuable contributions and should be included in the collection of pertinent background information.

Although much of the information collected is likely to be basic and factual, each perspective will be at least slightly unique. Probing these different perspectives will help prevent placement of undue emphasis upon a distorted perception. Some contradictions, either real or apparent, may be uncovered, as when a child is described as a "perfect angel" at home and simultaneously quite the opposite at school. Such contradictions will need to be resolved if an accurate understanding of the child and his problems is to be reached. Further investigation may be indicated, or information already available may need to be rearranged to bring about closure.

ASSESSMENT OF SOCIAL-EMOTIONAL INVOLVEMENT

In some cases a thorough and sensitive collection of background data may provide enough information to indicate appropriate intervention steps. If further appraisal is indicated, the background data can direct the investigator toward the most fruitful areas to explore. Such information can also be used to help select the most appropriate and valid appraisal instruments to use. Misleading information can be obtained by administering a test that is invalidated by the student's inability to respond through a particular channel. An intelligence quotient obtained from the Performance Scale of the *Wechsler Intelligence Scale for Children* will not likely be valid for the child with cerebral palsy. The projective drawings of a child who has poor motor skills might distort projections and invalidate hypotheses drawn from them.

Objectivity in Data Collection

In addition to possessing adequate diagnostic skills, the diagnostician should also utilize a high degree of objectivity. The diagnostician is not expected to become emotionally responsible for, or emotionally involved with, the student being appraised. The primary responsibility is to obtain an accurate assessment, and this is facilitated by objectivity. Parents and teachers have other responsibilities concerning the student that sometimes conflict with objectivity, and the diagnostician should be aware of the implications.

The teacher's responsibility is to teach. To teach implies arranging the setting and introducing information, concepts, and skills to be learned in such a way that the learning of the material or skills will be maximized. When the student fails to learn according to established criteria, the teacher usually seeks an explanation for the fact. When a child fails to learn, it is assumed that either the student or the teacher is primarily responsible. As the child experiences failure, so might the teacher, and each must account for the failure in some way.

Since failure seems to carry with it an emotional response, many explanations may take a form of rationalization. A teacher might label a child as "lazy," "boy-crazy," "immature," "brain damaged," or even emotionally disturbed. Since a child is viewed as functioning within a defined environment, and the parents are a significant part of that environment, the parents can also become a part of the explanation of failure. Such comments are made as "No wonder he's like he is. His parents just don't care about him. They're so busy with their own social lives that they don't give enough time and love to him." With another child, it might be said, "She's had five 'daddies' in the last year; no wonder she has a hard time concentrating on her studies with such instability at home." The spectrum of responsibility can also broaden to include last year's teacher who failed to teach the basic skills or building blocks necessary for success at the present level in a particular subject or grade. The family physician may even come in for some criticism for not prescribing medication for apparent hyperactivity.

Parents usually have even stronger emotional ties to the child than the teacher has. Most parents want their child to be successful. Failure on the child's part seems to reflect adversely on the quality of parenting. Many times such guilt is overemphasized and out of proportion, and parents seem particularly vulnerable to guilt feelings about their child's failure. They, like the teacher, may find others to share that burden. The mother may say to the father: "If your job didn't take you out of town so much, you could have been a better father, and we wouldn't have these problems now." The father might respond: "Well, if you didn't baby him so much, he'd know how to handle himself better." They might both criticize the teacher, saying, "That teacher just expects too much. After all, school isn't the most important thing in the world to a growing boy."

Every person involved with the child who has problems has some degree of failure to deal with, and by the time a child is referred for a social-emotional assessment, that sense of failure may have become rather acute. The counselor is often brought into the case to help solve the problem, and the counselor has the opportunity to enter with fresh perspective. In the early stages the counselor has usually had little or no previous history with the child and is less likely than others to become emotionally involved or entrapped by the student's behavior. The diagnostic responsibility of the counselors is to present as accurate an assessment as possible of what is going on with the child in the child's environment and to explore possibilities that might alleviate or ameliorate the problem. This involves no obligation to help or teach the child at this level of intervention. As diagnostician, the counselor does not risk failure with the child. The counselor neither expects nor requires the student to behave in certain ways, but accepts whatever behaviors the child presents and interprets them according to all available information.

Use of Projective Techniques for Appraisal

In exploring social and emotional constructs, more information is needed than can be provided through interviews, questionnaires, and rating scales. The assumption is made that the desired information is available, but not perhaps through direct exploration at a conscious level. The use of *projective techniques* can facilitate investigation at less conscious levels. These techniques can begin to illuminate the area that represents things about the student that neither the student nor others are aware of and yet are vitally affecting the student's functioning.

The postulated presence of subconscious and preconscious levels that impinge on behavior through symbolic processes directs the investigator to the use of projective techniques. With projective techniques, a neutral stimulus is presented to the subject and a response is elicited. Because little structure is provided by verbal instructions or other stimuli, the product is assumed to be a response projected from the needs, thoughts, feelings, or attitudes underlying behavior, and as such, arises from the internal states of the individual under consideration.

Sentence completion (or incomplete sentences) is a projective technique that was discussed in Chapter 5 along with other nontest devices, and thus will not be discussed further here.

The House-Tree-Person Technique (J. N. Buck; Western Psychological Services) is one of the techniques that require that the subject make a drawing of a person or object. The HTP drawing is evaluated on the basis of several features, such as quality, size, clothing, proportions of parts, etc. The authors of such devices believe that in making the drawings some subjects will reveal characteristics of their personalities, or evidence of neurosis or brain damage. When the HTP is administered, the subject is instructed to draw first a house, then a tree, and finally a person. Then the subject is asked to describe and explain the drawings (see Fig. 43).

The *Rorschach Inkblot Test* and the *Holtzman Inkblot Technique* are projective devices that use inkblots on cards as ambiguous stimuli. The subject is asked to tell what is seen on the card as each one is shown, in order to elicit associations. The associations are interpreted by a trained examiner who scores responses according to location, detail, form, color, movement, etc.

The *Thematic Apperception Test* (TAT) (H. A. Murray; The Psychological Corporation) was first published in 1935 and has been used extensively since that time as a projective technique. There are thirty

Figure 43. HTP drawings.

cards, each with a picture showing an ambiguous scene or situation. The subject is asked to tell a story about each picture, and the examiner interprets the story, paying special attention to the clues that may shed light on the subject's needs, conflicts, feelings, etc. There are several other apperception devices, such as the *Children's Apperception Test* (L. and S. Bellak; The Psychological Corporation), the *Blacky Pictures* (G. Blum; Psychodynamic Instruments), and the *Michigan Picture Test* (Science Research Associates). These techniques provide a minimum of structure and instruction, allowing as much freedom as possible for the interplay and expression of internal feelings states. From the information obtained through the student's responses, hypotheses are drawn that relate to underlying processes, values, needs, pressures, and goals. It is the manner in which the subject responds to stimuli and chooses to behave in a given situation that, when related to psychological constructs and the broad body of psychological knowledge, suggests to the skilled interpreter how the person likely thinks and feels.

Projective techniques provide observational data that can be compared with observations of others who engage in a similar activity at other times and places. In order to extract working hypotheses, one needs objective observation skills, thorough knowledge of psychological constructs, the ability to understand the underlying communications, and a great deal of human experience. The greater the availability of these attributes, the greater the probability that interpretation will be accurate and applicable. For information related to interpretations of data obtained from projective tests, one should consult appropriate books and journals.

Informal Projective Techniques

Aside from using skills and instruments that might be unfamiliar to the student, the counselor's behavior may be similar to that of other adults the student has encountered. Just like everybody else, the counselor asks the child questions, but the answer the student gives does not always command the center of the inquirer's attention. How the individual answers, as well as what answer is given, is significant to the counselor. What Susie says, or does not say, what she does or does not do, provide cues which suggest something about the child that might be developed into a working hypothesis concerning how the student functions.

Many kinds of responses are possible, but only one can be selected. How and why the student chooses to respond can reveal a great deal. Even a relatively straightforward question such as "What city is the capital of the nation?" can be answered in a variety of ways, and some of them may indicate projective aspects. If the response is as straightforward as the question, such as "Washington," little of psychological import may be gleaned from the word alone. Tone of voice or body language may be more significant, but the response itself is probably psychologically barren.

Other types of verbal responses can suggest something about the person and carry psychological implications. One child may answer the question this way: "Washington. I went to Washington once and saw the capitol. My brother pushed me down the steps and I hurt my knee. I got him back though. I made him spill his Coke all over his new pants, Mom got angry!" This type of response could suggest that the child is highly self-oriented and tends to respond to even relatively innocuous objective information on a personal level. Such a statement could also indicate signs of bids for attention, sympathy, and/or some passive-aggressive tendencies toward the brother, which could be explored further. On the other hand, the subject may be fabricating a story.

Any implication drawn should be drawn carefully and cautiously. The response "I don't know" may be a simple indication of a lack of knowledge. If the student frequently responds in that manner, it may indicate a person who takes very few risks or will not try anything unless guaranteed of success. If the student answers "I used to know that, but I forgot," or "I haven't learned that yet," or "I know that, but I just can't think of it right now," the underlying message might be "I feel inadequate right now because I can't answer your question, but it's not really my fault, so please don't think I'm dumb." Another student might answer the same question with a very elaborate answer. This student may be exceptionally bright and want to make sure the examiner knows it, or may feel inadequate or insecure and may be using intellectualization to cover those feelings and allay anxiety.

Nonverbal responses can also provide valuable clues to attitudes and feelings. A student who responds with silence, a tiny shrug of the shoulders, or staring out the window may be communicating fear of failure or rejection and may feel intimidated by adults or authority figures. Such a response could also be viewed as a manifest sign of withdrawal. Pushing back from the table, staring at the examiner, and folding arms over the chest can all be signs of negativism or hostility toward adults or authority figures, and may be viewed as manifest aggression. This kind of behavior is usually viewed more as acting out than withdrawal. Passive responses can indicate either withdrawal or aggression, but either way they tend to deny the responsibility of the student and put more responsibility on the examiner, if the examiner accepts it, and thereby shift anxiety away from the examinee.

Tone of voice may indicate a child who hedges bets by responding to a question in a questioning tone of voice and indirectly requesting confirmation for his answer, "Right?" This child may obtain that confirmation many more times than the examiner suspects. Volume, pitch, and emphasis may embelish or contradict the meaning conveyed by words alone. A simple question such as "What are you doing?" can take on a variety of meanings by emphasizing different words, speaking loudly or softly, by pitching the voice high (as with a whine) or low (as with a growl).

Discrepancies between verbal and nonverbal content point to the possible presence of conflicts within the individual. Approach-avoidance conflict concerning the diagnostician may be evidenced by verbal statements that are hostile in content but are countermanded by a more softened body posture. It could also be expressed by very polite and compliant statements with just a tinge of sarcasm around the edges. Sometimes it seems as though the student is saying, "If I can be as rude to you as I can and you still accept me, then maybe I can trust you." A touch of fear may creep through a facade of arrogance, or a twinge of sadness may reveal a hollow happiness.

As with other forms of assessment, the social-emotional assessment involves providing a stimulus, in the form of a picture, a question, or a setting in which to observe behavior. It entails observation of a response, keeping in mind that an individual cannot "not respond," that not to respond is a response, too. For the response to take on meaning, it must be compared with some criterion. A particular behavior could be compared with that of others with similar demographic make-up, or with other behaviors of the individual (or with one's own empathy). The result of this assessment is the formulation of hypotheses that can be useful in helping the individual to function more effectively. It points the direction to areas of change within the individual or the environment that will enhance the process of growth. If assessment is not carried through with action and change, however subtle the change might be, the usefulness and advisability of a social-emotional assessment is questionable, and perhaps time could be better spent in other ways.

Any information obtained can be used to formulate hypotheses about a person's social-emotional make-up and level of functioning. An individual intelligence test, in which the primary purpose is to measure intelligence, provides personality data as well. It provides the opportunity to observe responses to standardized tasks and compare them with defined norms and maturational levels. It takes a specific sampling of behavior from which emerge patterns, some of which are nomothetic, some ideographic.

An instrument such as the *Wechsler Intelligence Scale for Children* can often provide cues to *emotional* functioning as well as intellectual functioning. The student's responses can provide meaningful information about how that particular individual deals with frustration, success, failure, people, novel situations, and the self. In a broad sense, every response in a context carries with it some form and degree of feeling, some emotional involvement; therefore, any response can provide information and an understanding of the personality of the person observed. Observation is limited by the diagnostician, not necessarily the instrument itself. An examiner who has had fifteen years of experience in administering and interpreting the *Stanford-Binet Intelligence Scale* will likely find more of a projective nature than one who has had only one year's experience.

Affective or feeling responses can also be obtained from other appraisal instruments. The *Bender Visual Motor Gestalt Test* is a test of perceptual and motor functioning. It consists of nine figures, which are presented one at a time to be copied on a blank piece of paper. It is also useful in obtaining emotional indicators. Where the student places the first figure on the page, how the student arranges the designs on the page or pages, the quality of the drawings, the types of errors made, what the student says about the task, and the student's ability to comply with instructions all provide insights into self-perceptions and psychological constructs (see Figure 44).

When presented with the designs, some students will say "This is easy" and yet produce a relatively poor representation. Others will make numerous statements of disability ranging from "This is tricky" to "I can't draw." Seeming criticism of the task, the test, or the examiner can also be used to downplay one's anticipated failure. The student may project negativism through such statements as "What is this all for, anyway?" or "I had to do this for my teacher last week. Why do I have to do it again?"

Being taken out of class to sit in a small room with a stranger and answer questions may create some anxiety in the student. In dealing with feelings of discomfort the student may try flight instead of negativism or cooperation. The student may act out this uncomfortable

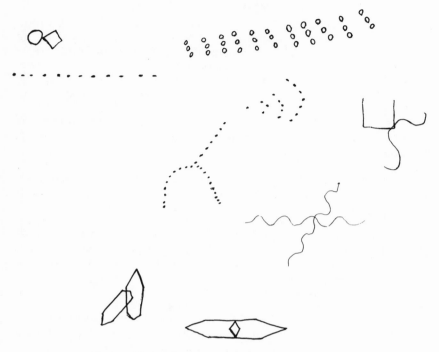

Figure 44. *Bender Visual Motor Gestalt* drawings.

feeling if the situation is perceived as sufficiently threatening to self-esteem or image. Many plausible and creative reasons for leaving the test setting can be devised by children. They have been known to say such things as "Am I going to miss recess (math, spelling)? I don't want to miss recess (math, spelling)," or "I forgot my pencil. I'll go back and get it."

The student may or may not ask questions at this point, and these questions, or the lack of them, are diagnostically significant. Oftentimes they contribute as much psychological insight into the student as the drawings themselves. If the child asks, "A house, any kind of house? Do you want me to draw *my* house? What kind of house do you mean? Can I draw my yard, too? Should I draw a chimney?," etc., a high need for structure or approval, dependency, or perhaps a low self-concept can be inferred, as well as possible anxiety in the presence of minimal cues. The needs of this student are probably quite different from those of the student who asks no questions, quickly tosses off a minimal product and acts totally disinterested in the activity.

Interpretation of Responses

Responses can be consistent across tasks or vary according to the task. If the child asks numerous questions concerning the family drawing but asks no questions about the drawing of the person, implications may apply to family relationships but not to self-image. A tree that manifests more pathology than a house postulates more concern with peer relationships than with family. In that sense, the student's responses may seem to be selective according to certain specific areas of conflict. It is the task of the counselor to tease out the patterns of healthy functioning from less healthy functioning. Particularly if levels of functioning vary in quality and quantity according to concern with self, social, or family relationships, such contexts should be included in the interpretation. Strong reliance should not be placed on one or even a few cues or indications. Major indications should be differentiated from minor ones and given more emphasis in evaluation.

The data obtained in social-emotional appraisal should be viewed as a symbolic representation of the complexities of the student's personality in which some aspects are more clearly visible than others. It is the task of the diagnostician to integrate complex bits of information into a meaningful and congruent whole that will accurately depict the complex social and emotional make-up of the individual under consideration.

More credence should be placed upon molar constructs than molecular ones. It is sometimes helpful to spread out all the drawings the student has produced, reflect on the student's behavioral style during testings, and ask a few questions. "What kind of feelings am I aware of in myself as I look at these drawings? What kind of mood or tone is depicted here? What messages come across the strongest? Which ones are only vaguely represented and perhaps being suppressed or repressed? What is missing and perhaps being denied? How would I likely be feeling if I were to create a drawing like this one?" Much valuable information can be obtained if the counselor serves as a catalyst and participates in the perspective of the student whose personality is being appraised.

A Double Mirror

When the counselor is projected into the appraisal process, two variables related to the diagnostic task are involved: (1) the ability of the counselor to perceive symbolic feelings empathically and (2) the counselor's own level of functioning, self-awareness, and insights into personal behavior. Because of the addition of these factors, interpreting projective data becomes, in part, a projective description of the examiner/interpreter.

If, for example, the counselor has not dealt with personal dimensions of sexuality and integrated these into the personality, it will be difficult for that counselor to assess accurately and objectively the sexual data represented in the protocol under consideration. If sexuality is a major interest or concern of the counselor, or if the sexual values and attitudes are strongly held, then sexual data may be misperceived. The only safeguard against this type of clinical error or overemphasis is an adequate awareness on the counselor's part of personal values, attitudes, understanding, and acceptance of the sexuality, or other constructs, of self and others. Failing that, adequate supervision and consultation become imperative. Maintaining contact with fellow professionals is a desirable and important aspect of professional growth and development. Similar risks exist for other dimensions or constructs such as Mother, Father, Authority, Personal Care, Socialization, Responsibility, Self-Concept, and Fantasy, as well as religious and economic values.

PERSONALITY INVENTORIES

Nonprojective techniques, such as personality inventories, add another dimension to social-emotional appraisal and tend to avoid possible distortions by the double mirror. Instead of observing how the student appears to function, one can use inventories to organize a variety of self-report statements into constructs that indicate the student's perception of self. The use of personality inventories tends to be quite limited in schools, probably because parents and school-board members are more reluctant to authorize the use of such instruments than they are to approve the use of the other appraisal devices. When they are used, they should be used only by well-qualified individuals.

The term *personality* generally refers to a combination or composite of a person's many characteristics, such as attitudes, interests, aptitudes, intelligence, and emotions that characterize that person's behavior. Used broadly, the term may include everything about a person, including physical traits and appearance. *Personality inventories*, however, only measure a portion of an individual's total personality. These devices should be referred to as inventories rather than tests because (1) unlike most tests, personality inventories do not have correct or incorrect answers and (2) personality inventories are supposed to determine how much a human quality (or qualities) exists, rather than level of aptitude, skill, or knowledge. Some personality inventories are designed to measure adjustment and some are designed to measure traits.

An example of structured standardized *adjustment* inventory is the *California Test of Personality*. This instrument was developed by W. W. Clark et al. and is published by CTB/McGraw-Hill. The CTP has five levels: Primary (for grades K-3), Elementary (grades 4-8), Intermediate (grades 7-10), Secondary (grades 9-college and adult). Section 1 of the CTP yields scores for Self-Reliance, Sense of Personal Worth, Sense of Personal Freedom, Feeling of Belonging, Freedom from Withdrawing Tendencies, Freedom from Nervous Symptoms, and Personal Adjustment. Section 2 provides scores for Social Standards, Social Skills, Freedom from Antisocial Tendencies, Family Relations, School Relations (Occupational Relations at adult level), Community Relations, and Social Adjustment. There is also a Total Adjustment score that is based on the Personal Adjustment and Social Adjustment scores.

Numerous reliability coefficients have been reported for the CTP, and they generally have been in the .80s, with the coefficients for the Total Adjustment score tending to be higher than for the part scores. Numerous validity studies have been conducted with widely varying results.

The *Minnesota Counseling Inventory,* published by the Psychological Corporation, and the *Bell Adjustment Inventory* (Stanford University Press) are other examples of adjustment inventories.

There are many standardized personality inventories that measure *traits* or *characteristics* rather than adjustment per se. Of course, one can infer adjustment or the lack of it from the trait scores acquired from a trait inventory, such as the *Sixteen Personality Factor Questionnaire* developed by R. B. Cattell (Institute for Personality and Ability Testing). The 16 PF is designed to measure sixteen personality factors that have been identified through factor analysis and is suitable for use with subjects who are sixteen years old or older.

The manual shows test-retest reliability coefficients ranging from .45 for source trait B (for one form in one study) to .93 for source trait H (in another study). Most of the reported test-retest reliability coefficients are in the .70s and .80s. The 16 PF is said to have construct validity as a result of careful item selection. Direct concept validities are shown in the manual. Table XV shows the primary source traits of the 16 PF.

The *Children's Personality Questionnaire* (CPQ), developed by R. B. Porter and R. B. Cattell and published by IPAT, is designed to measure fourteen primary personality traits that may be useful in predicting and evaluating emotional, social, and academic development. The CPQ has four forms for use with subjects in the 8-12 age range.

The *Edwards Personality Inventory* (A. L. Edwards; Science Research Associates), the *Omnibus Personality Inventory* (P. Heist et al.; The Psychological Corporation), and the *Minnesota Multiphasic Personality Inventory* (S. R. Hathaway and J. C. McKinley; The Psychological Corporation) are other examples of structured trait inventories that can be administered to school-age subjects.

In order to measure other important aspects of personality, certain special personality measuring devices may be used. For example, the *Tennessee Self Concept Scale* may be used to measure self-esteem. It is intended for use with subjects who are twelve years old or older and

TABLE XV

THE PRIMARY SOURCE TRAITS COVERED BY THE 16 PF TEST

Factor	Low Sten Score Description (1-3)	High Sten Score Description (8-10)
A	*Reserved,* detached, critical, cool, impersonal Sizothymia[a]	*Warmhearted,* outgoing, participating, interested in people, easy-going Affectothymia
B	*Less intelligent,* concrete-thinking, Lower scholastic mental capacity	*More intelligent,* abstract-thinking, bright Higher scholastic mental capacity
C	*Affected by feelings,* emotionally less stable, easily upset, changeable Lower ego strength	*Emotionally stable,* mature, faces reality, calm, patient Higher ego strength
E	*Humble,* mild, accommodating, easily led, conforming Submissiveness	*Assertive,* aggressive, authoritative, competitive, stubborn Dominance
F	*Sober,* prudent, serious, taciturn Desurgency	*Happy-go-lucky,* impulsively lively, enthusiastic, heedless Surgency
G	*Expedient,* disregards rules, feels few obligations Weaker superego strength	*Conscientious,* persevering, proper, moralistic, rule-bound Stronger superego strength
H	*Shy,* restrained, threat-sensitive, timid Threctia	*Venturesome,* socially bold, uninhibited, spontaneous Parmia
I	*Tough-minded,* self-reliant, realistic, no-nonsense Harria	*Tender-minded,* intuitive, unrealistic, sensitive Premsia
L	*Trusting,* adaptable, free of jealousy, easy to get on with Alaxia	*Suspicious,* self-opinionated, hard to fool, skeptical, questioning Protension
M	*Practical,* careful, conventional, regulated by external realities Praxernia	*Imaginative,* careless of practical matters, unconventional, absent-minded Autia
N	*Forthright,* natural, genuine, unpretentious Artlessness	*Shrewd,* calculating, socially alert, insightful Shrewdness
O	*Unperturbed,* self-assured, confident, secure, self-satisfied Untroubled adequacy	*Apprehensive,* self-reproaching, worrying, troubled Guilt proneness
Q1	*Conservative,* respecting established ideas, tolerant of traditional difficulties. Conservatism of temperament	*Experimenting,* liberal, analytical, likes innovation Radicalism
Q2	*Group oriented,* a "joiner" and sound follower Group adherence	*Self-sufficient,* prefers own decisions, resourceful Self-sufficiency
Q3	*Undisciplined self-conflict,* careless of protocol, follows own urges Low integration	*Controlled,* socially precise, following self-image, compulsive High self-concept control
Q4	*Relaxed,* tranquil, torpid, unfrustrated Low ergic tension	*Tense,* frustrated, driven, restless, overwrought High ergic tension

[a]Titles in roman type are the technical names for the factors and are explained more fully in the *Handbook*.

have at least a sixth-grade reading level. Several scores related to different aspects of self may be obtained with the TSCS.

The *Piers-Harris Children's Self Concept Scale* (E. V. Piers and D. B. Harris; McGraw-Hill) may be used with children in the elementary and secondary grades. According to the authors, ten factors related to self-concept are measured by the instrument.

The *IPAT Anxiety Scale — 1976 Revision* may be used to obtain a measure of anxiety. This scale, published by the Institute for Personality and Ability Testing, is a brief forty-item questionnaire designed for use with high school, college, and adult populations. For children in the fourth, fifth, and sixth grades, the *State-Trait Anxiety Inventory for Children* (C. D. Spielberger; Consulting Psychologists Press) may be used to measure anxiety.

Limitations of Personality-Assessment Devices

Those who make use of the data obtained from personality inventories or projective techniques should do so with the utmost caution, for these instruments have serious shortcomings. Among the most common criticisms of the instruments are the following:

1. Responses can be faked deliberately or without awareness.
2. The cultural background of the subject is not given sufficient consideration.
3. The evidence of predictive validity is often nonexistent or questionable.
4. The assumption that personality traits are stable and may be measured by paper-and-pencil instruments may not be valid.
5. The results obtained from such instruments are very difficult to interpret.

These general criticisms of personality-assessment devices do not apply equally to all such instruments, but it behooves school personnel to be mindful of the shortcomings in order to avert unsound judgments or decisions.

COMMUNICATION OF RESULTS

The time comes when the counselor has collected enough bits of information to begin to piece them together. Input has been received from parents, teachers, the student, and other appropriate persons and sources. Classroom observations have been made and tests have been given. Ample raw materials have been collected to begin constructing an evaluation. The counselor has understood the information available both cognitively and intuitively. Now the data must be integrated so that information concerning the student and the student's problem or situation can be communicated to those who need to know.

The counselor is responsible for communicating information obtained from the appraisal as accurately and as comprehensively as possible. If the recipient of the messages fails to understand, it may be that the person was not listening or perhaps was avoiding hearing what was undesirable to hear; but it may also be that the communication was couched in a "foreign" language, that of psychological jargon and technicality. Psychological terminology is still a foreign language to many people. For example, the meaning of the word "affect" and its derivatives *seems* to be commonly understood, but many classroom teachers as well as parents do not clearly perceive what those word forms mean, especially in a behavioral sense. It is easy to skip over a vaguely understood word, for it is a bother to use the dictionary, and perhaps embarrassing to ask someone to explain what seems to be obvious. Skipping over the meaning of such words introduces gaps in understanding. Overexplaining may risk the appearance of condescension, but it enhances the chances of achieving clear and accurate communication.

Clear communication begins with clarity from the speaker. If the counselor does not understand the concept to be communicated, the parent, student, or teacher will likely understand it even less. The recipient of a poorly communicated message may become confused or even decide that the information is useless or invalid.

Clarity is enhanced by the integration of data. A skilled counselor is in a position to integrate a wide variety of behaviors and perceive underlying meanings, goals, needs, fears, and inadequacies. The benefit of this position is realized by those who originally sought the appraisal. A recommendation that is understood and accepted is more likely to be followed than one which is not.

Integration of many bits of data can be facilitated by the use of categories. Affect can be categorized both temporally and situationally, through direct and indirect data. A student's intrapersonal, home and family, and social-environmental constructs can be compared and contrasted to form meaningful interpretations. Broad constructs can be used to explicate the present, assess the situation, and make recommendations for the future. If the construct can be described clearly enough, relevant examples can often be provided by the student, parent, or teacher, and this nearly always facilitates acceptance.

RESISTANCE TO INTERPRETATION

Even though recommendations may be made that are in the best interest of the student and are supported by appraisal data, resistance from the receivers of the recommendations may still be met. The teacher may have too many students to meet adequately this one student's needs, particularly if extra effort is required. The parent or student may resist recommendations for therapy or special-class placement because of a perceived stigma or denial that a problem or concern exists.

The resistance or denial can take several forms. The counselor may be confronted with such statements as "This doesn't tell me one thing I didn't already know." "All this is just a bunch of bunk. There's nothing wrong with this kid. He's just lazy, that's all. I'll see to it that he buckles down." Sometimes it is tempting to meet such resistance with an even stronger statement of the case, but this could lead to overstatement and then more difficulty. If someone did not want to hear something the first time around, saying it louder and longer sometimes makes it even more unpleasant and strengthens resistance instead of breaking it down.

Because the judgment of the counselor cannot be completely excluded from an appraisal (nor would that be necessarily desirable), it becomes unwise, if not unethical, to state almost any conclusion obtained from a social-emotional assessment categorically. Sometimes counselors make mistakes. Such *final-sounding* words as "is," "is not," "does," "does not," "always," and "never" are rarely appropriate in a report or evaluation. Instead, the use of such phrases and words as "appears to be," "seems to be," "it is likely (or unlikely) that," "sometimes," "often," "frequent(ly)," "rarely," and "occasional(ly)," keep the report within the realm of professional opinion and judgment rather than undisputed and undeniable psychological truths, which seem to be rare.

RECOMMENDATION AND FOLLOW-UP

Appraisal is a median process of psychological intervention. Its purpose is to define or clarify concerns that significant others have voiced about a particular student. On the basis of the complete appraisal, recommendations are made. Those who seek the assistance of the counselor's or psychologist's appraisal want to know not only what has been going on with the student, but also what can be done about it, if anything. If no behavior is to be changed in the student or his environment, the value of a social-emotional appraisal becomes significantly lowered.

Maximizing the effect of appraisal and rendering worthwhile the time and energy devoted to it entails a follow-up procedure. After the appraisal and communication of results and recommendations have been conducted, the progress (or lack of progress) of the student and others responsible for initiating specific change should be periodically checked. Contact with the student, the student's parents, and teachers is maintained to monitor and evaluate the impact of recommendations and adjust behavioral plans according to the feedback received.

REPORT OUTLINE

A thorough social-emotional appraisal would include (and discuss) background information relevant to the case, test results, appraisal of nontest data, and recommendations. The following outline is representative of a format for writing an appraisal report.

I. Reason for referral — includes who requested the appraisal, what behaviors in the student arouse concern, and questions/issues to be answered and explored

II. Background Information — includes what has happened to the student in the past, how the student has been dealt with, what problems the student has had, and how others perceive the individual

   A. Family History — includes identification of the immediate family members, demographic and social-economic data

   B. Developmental history — includes how the student has matured physiologically, developmental stages, and any problems the student might have had in early childhood

   C. Medical history — includes what the student has experienced medically, description of any illnesses, accidents, surgery, chronic conditions, general health, and use of medication

   D. Educational history — includes how the student has progressed educationally, participation in any special education programs, and identification of academic strengths and weaknesses

   E. Social-emotional history — includes how the student has developed socially, how the student gets along with others, behavior problems that might have been experienced, and mental health

III. Test Results — reports the results of tests, surveys, inventories, scales, and/or techniques administered to the student or observed

   A. Intellectual assessment — includes the student's present level of functioning, how the student goes about solving problems, what kind of thinking processes the student employs, learning style, how intellectual development may have been affected by nonintellective factors, and whether it appears that the student is using knowledge and skills effectively and appropriately

   B. Perceptual-motor assessment — includes how the student's perceptual and motor development have progressed, whether rate of growth is comparable to others of that age and grade, and to other areas of the student's development (such as physiological and intellectual) and whether perceptual-motor development may have been affected by neurological or non-neurological factors

   C. Social-emotional assessment — includes past, present, and possible future concerns of the student that may be related to intrapersonal, family and social-environmental concerns, the student's behavioral style, level of self-concept development, attitudes, and values

IV. Summary — includes significant background information and the student's overall level of functioning in intellectual, perceptual-motor, and social-emotional areas

V. Recommendations — includes a behavioral plan that outlines what directions or courses of treatment or interventions appear to be most appropriate to pursue, as indicated by the appraisal data.

REFERENCES

Anatasi, Anne: *Psychological Testing*, 4th ed. New York, Macmillan Company, 1976.

Bellak, Leopold: *The T.A.T., C.A.T., and S.A.T. in Clinical Use*, 3rd ed. New York, Grune and Stratton, 1975.

—— and Bellak, S. S.: *Senior Apperception Technique*. Larchmont, New York, The Psychological Corporation, 1974.

Bender, Lauretta: *A Visual Motor Gestalt Test and Its Clinical Use*. Research Monographs No. 3. New York, American Ortho-Psychiatric Association, 1938.

Berdie, Ralph and Layton, Wilburn: *Manual for the Minnesota Counseling Inventory*. New York, The Psychological Corporation, 1957.

Buck, John N.: *The House-Tree-Person Manual Supplement*. Los Angeles, Western Psychological Services, 1974.

Burns, Robert C. and Kaufman, S. Harvard: *Kinetic Family Drawings (K-F-D): An Introduction to Understanding Child Through Kinetic Drawings*. New York, Brunner/Mazel, 1972.

——: *Actions, Styles, and Symbols in Kinetic Family Drawings (K-F-D)*. New York, Brunner/Mazel, 1972.

Buros, Oscar K.: (Ed.) *The Seventh Mental Measurements Yearbook*. Volume 1. Highland Park, N.J., The Gryphon Press, 1972.

Chase, Clinton I.: *Measurement for Educational Evaluation*. Reading, Massachusetts, Addison-Wesley Publishing Co., 1974.

Clawson, Aileen: *The Bender Visual Motor Gestalt Test for Children*. Los Angeles, Western Psychological Services, 1962.

Cottle, William C.: "Interest and Personality Inventories," *Guidance Monograph Series, Series III: Testing*. Boston, Houghton Mifflin Co., 1968.

Cronbach, Lee J.: *Essentials of Psychological Testing*, 3rd ed. New York, Harper and Row Publishers, 1970.

DiLeo, Joseph H.: *Children's Drawings as Diagnostic Aids*. New York, Brunner/Mazel, 1973.

Fitts, William H.: *Manual for the Tennessee Self Concept Scale*. Nashville, Counselor Recordings and Tests, 1965.

Glasser, Alan J. and Zimmerman, Irla Lee: *Clinical Interpretation of the Wechsler Intelligence Scale for Children*. New York, Grune and Stratton, Inc., 1967.

Hammer, Emanuel F.: *The House-Tree-Person (H-T-P) Clinical Research Manual*. Los Angeles, Western Psychological Services, 1977.

Hewitt, Patricia S. and Massey, James O.: *Clinical Clues from the WISC Wechsler Intelligence Scale for Children*. Palo Alto, California, Consulting Psychologist Press, Inc., 1971.

Jolles, Isaac: *A Catalog for the Qualitative Interpretation of the House-Tree-Person (H-T-P)*. Los Angeles, Western Psychological Services, 1971.

Koppitz, Elizabeth M.: *The Bender Gestalt Test for Young Children.* New York, Grune and Stratton, Inc., 1964.

Manual for the 16 PF. Champaign, Illinois, Institute for Personality and Ability Testing, 1972.

Schildkrout, Mollie S., Shenker, I. Ronald, and Sonnenblick, Marsha. *Human Figure Drawings in Adolescence.* New York, Brunner/Mazel, Inc., 1972.

Wechsler, David: *Manual for the Wechsler Intelligence Scale for Children — Revised.* New York, The Psychological Corporation, 1974.

Chapter 10

APPRAISAL FOR PUPILS WITH LANGUAGE/LEARNING DISABILITIES

Steve is in the fourth grade. He is two years behind in reading, a year and a half behind in arithmetic, and cannot spell even simple words. His parents are concerned about his school failure. They blame it on the teachers. The fourth grade teacher says Steve is lazy and just isn't trying. How does Steve feel about all this? He just shrugs his shoulders and says, "I must be dumb. I can't seem to please anyone, so why even try?"

THIS DRAMA is enacted hundreds of times each year in our nation's schools. Upon careful diagnosis, it will be learned that Steve is not "dumb," he is not victimized by poor teaching, nor is he lazy. He has a learning disability, a true learning dysfunction, which will require special programming for him.

AN OVERVIEW OF LEARNING DISABILITIES

In pursuing the educational literature of the sixties and seventies, one is awed by the proliferation of information in the area of learning disabilities. During this short time span, educational journals cranked out articles on the subject, books were hurriedly written, and commercial materials hit the market with almost tornadic force. Parent groups with strong lobbying force were formed for the purpose of promoting legislation, college and universities created new courses, and schools began to prepare themselves for this group of pupils labeled as "learning disabled."

Trends have pervaded education throughout the decades, but seldom has one hit with such force as that of the field of learning disabilities. In fairness to researchers such as Goldstein, Strauss, Lehtinen, Cruickshank, as well as others, it must be acknowledged that research, though minimal, had begun before the sixties, but the great thrust of interest, research, and program implementation has come since that time. A look at the literature would tend to suggest that the impetus of the thrust of programming for learning disabilities at least partially coincided with the widespread implementation of individualized instruction.

Although educators have long been aware of the concept of indi-

208

vidualizing instruction for differentiated abilities of pupils, it was not until the early sixties that a serious, universal application of this principle was put into effect. Of course, when instructors became truly aware of differences, they began to focus on those children who were not learning for various reasons. Awareness of the field of learning disabilities was a very natural outgrowth of individualized instruction.

Definition

Much of the literature on learning disabilities centers around trying to define the term. Some scholars view it in a generic sense into which they would categorize any pupil who is not learning, regardless of the reasons. Into this generic category of learning disabled pupils would fall pupils who are failing to learn because of bilingual problems, disadvantaged children, emotionally disturbed children, pupils with sensory defects, those with physical handicaps that impede their learning, as well as the mentally retarded. Although these pupils have one commonality — difficulty in learning — their needs and natures are remarkably different. In each of these mentioned cases, assessment and remediation will take on different characteristics. Many of these will be discussed in Chapter 11.

On the other end of the spectrum of definitions of learning disability is the very restrictive one that equates learning disability with minimal brain dysfunction. It would appear that educators are treading on dangerous ground in getting into the medical aspects of the function of the brain. The diagnosing and labeling of a child as MBI (minimally brain injured) can be done only by a neurologist. Educators can deal with the behavioral manifestations that are, in most cases, learning disabilities. The term MBI has been around longer than the term LD (learning disabilities), but many educators object to it because the term is etiological in nature and does not appropriately describe the symptoms. The term does not help in the development of a sound therapeutic approach for remediation of the learning disabilities manifested.

In general, medical personnel might refer to students as MBI whereas an educator might prefer to diagnose them as LD. MBI suggests etiology, whereas LD suggests behavioral descriptions of children.

Most currently acceptable definitions of LD avoid the two extremes discussed above and accept a "middle-of-the-road" approach. The United States Office of Education has published this definition, which has been adopted by the Association for Children with Learning Disabilities:

> Children with special learning disabilities exhibit a disorder in one or more of the basic psychological processes involved in understanding or in using spoken or written languages. These may be manifested in disorders of listening, thinking, talking, reading, writing, spelling, or arithmetic. They include conditions which have been referred to as

perceptual handicaps, brain injury, minimal brain dysfunction, dyslexia, developmental aphasia, etc. They do not include learning problems which are due primarily to visual, hearing, or motor handicaps, to mental retardation, emotional disturbance, or to environmental disadvantage.

Many individuals have attempted to refine the definition. Each has come up with a little different idea, but almost all the definitions useful in assessment have these characteristics:

1. The key word in most definitions of LD is *discrepancy*. There exists a significantly wide gap in the pupil's capacity to learn and present performance.
2. The definitions may or may not deal with the subject of central nervous system dysfunction. It is difficult for educators to determine the etiology of the problem; therefore, most deal with symptoms and prescriptive programs of instruction.
3. The emphasis is on the basic disorders of the learning processes. It is tied directly to inabilities in the fields of reading, listening, thinking, talking, spelling, and arithmetic.
4. Most definitions exclude pupils whose primary problems are sensory or motor handicaps, mental retardation, emotional disturbance, and environmental deprivation. It is conceded that these pupils, too, have learning disabilities, but that they are secondary to the primary handicapping condition.

It is safe to say, then, that pupils with a true learning disability can be described in terms of their intactness. They have at least adequate vision and hearing; they have normal or above normal intelligence; they are intact emotionally; they are not markedly disadvantaged in environmental conditions or language development — and yet, they continue to have learning difficulties.

It is because of these pupils' intactness that they are so baffling to parents and to school personnel. A standard comment of parents of an LD child is ". . . but my other children are learning. Why can't Steve?"

Epidemiology

It is difficult to estimate the number of pupils who are truly learning disabled. First, it is difficult because of the disparity among the definitions. If one uses the broad, generic definition, as many as one-third of our school population may be identified as having some type of learning dysfunction. On the other hand, if the definition includes only those with a neurological report diagnosing MBI, the percentage may be quite small, as low as 1 to 2 percent.

Second, it is difficult to come up with a percentage because of the various uses made of epidemiological figures. Often, they are used by support groups to gain financial assistance and other resources, and have tended to become inflated. Conversely, a school system may tout a low percentage of pupils with learning problems to gain confidence with school boards and community patrons.

After a review of literature based on the commonalities of the definitions as discussed, it seems fair to place the percentage of pupils with true learning disabilities at between 7 and 12 percent of most school populations. This, of course, would vary somewhat from system to system.

Etiology

It should have been concluded from the discussion thus far that it is quite difficult to determine why children become victims of learning disabilities. The most common *causal* factor listed in the literature is a dysfunction of the central nervous system. Typically, this dates from events preceding or surrounding the birth process. This would include conditions such as diseases of the mother during pregnancy, prolonged absence of oxygen during or just after birth, premature or postmature birth, and many other abnormalities of the birth process.

Learning disabilities are many times attributed to maturational lag, either inherited or acquired. In this case, the child may enter kindergarten or first grade manifesting signs of immature behavior and inability to maintain a sustained attention span. During these important years, the foundation is being laid for all learning — reading, arithmetic, and writing. Because of the maturational lag, the child misses the fundamentals. Failure is overlaid with another year of failure until the pupil is completely learning disabled. The importance of early screening for intervention will be discussed later. Those who believe in maturational lag as a viable cause of learning disabilities will often console frustrated parents with the words, "Don't worry; they'll grow out of it." In some cases, they will. However, if they are missing vital, foundational information in the early grades, they are going to have a difficult time "catching up" even if they grow out of it.

Other causal factors may include unrealistic parental or teacher expectations, which in turn cause the pupil to develop a dislike for learning that impedes progress. Many times it becomes the rather uncomfortable job of the school personnel to help the parents internalize a more realistic view of their child's abilities. The student may be a child of average ability performing in an average manner, while the parents may prefer that their child perform at an above-average level.

In trying to determine an etiology, it is important to assess the student's self-concept, their perception of their place in the family, and their present educational setting. Any of these external factors could be contributing to the dysfunction in school.

In the area of learning disabilities, it is not so important to know *why* students are performing the way they are, but *what can be done about it.* This fact might be helpful to stress to parents who, out of frustration or even guilt, demand that school counselors or other school officials explain to them *why* Steve is not learning.

QUESTIONS TO BE ANSWERED BY DIFFERENTIAL DIAGNOSIS

The purpose of diagnosis and assessment is always to answer questions. What types of questions should be considered in a differential diagnosis of a child with suspected learning disabilities?

Does the Child Have a Learning Disability?

When Steve is sent to the school counselor or diagnostician with the simple explanation that "he is not learning," it is important to attempt to discover if he indeed does have a learning disability or if he has other types of problems. Solution strategies are quite different for learning disability students than for students who are suffering from emotional disturbance or some other exceptionality. The first step in determining if Steve has a learning disability is to check him for his intactness, as discussed earlier. Can he see with good acuity? Can he hear adequately in a classroom that may have a high noise level, such as an open-area classroom?

Talk to his present teacher and past teachers for signs of unusual, deviant types of emotional behavior in the classroom. If warranted, the school psychologist can check to determine if the child is actually emotionally disturbed, or if his behavioral problems are secondary to his learning disabilities.

It is important to assess his mental ability in an individual testing session, using his own language to determine if he has normal or above normal intelligence. An achievement test with age and grade norms should be given and compared with the scores on the intelligence test. Is there a discrepancy? Did he indeed perform significantly lower on areas of the achievement test than he should have, according to his capacity as measured by the individual intelligence test?

Learning disabilities should not be confused with the problems of slow learners. Slow learners are perhaps one of our most neglected groups in education. Their outward manifestations in the classroom may be very similar to those of the child with learning disabilities. The big difference is that slow learners are usually performing at or at least near their capacity. There is no large discrepancy between performance and capacity, as there is in a child with learning disabilities. Although slow learners should be of concern to school personnel, it is important not to confuse them with the learning disabled, for program implementation is quite different.

What characteristics are descriptive of the child with learning disabilities? The most exhaustive list of such characteristics was culled from over one hundred publications, compiled by Clements (1966), and are listed here in the order of frequency cited:

1. Hyperactivity
2. Perceptual-motor impairments
3. Emotional lability
4. General orientation defects
5. Disorders of attention (short attention span, distractibility)
6. Impulsivity
7. Disorders of memory and thinking
8. Specific learning disabilities in reading, arithmetic, writing, and spelling
9. Disorders of speech and hearing
10. Equivocal neurological signs and electroencephalographic irregularities.

The pupil who would possess all the above characteristics in the order listed is a statistical hypothetical model and does not exist in live data. However, most LD pupils exhibit several of these characteristics, separately or in combination with others.

Although these characteristics have been cited for all ages of school children, many educators feel that the junior and senior high school students with learning disabilities may begin to display a slightly different pattern of behavior. Either because of hormonal changes or environmental molding of behavior, older students may not have the same degree of hyperactivity as younger children. On the contrary, they may now be exhibiting signs of lethargy and listlessness. They may be suffering more acutely from problems in self-concept, brought on by the years of failure and emotional bruises. On the positive side, maturity may have lessened their problems in perceptual-motor skills in some cases.

What is the Present Achievement Level Of the Student?

Learning disabilities often do not show up until after the child starts to school. Children are most commonly referred to school specialists at about the third or fourth grade level. By this time in children's careers, they have begun to show the discrepancy between capacity and performance. It is most often manifested in reading failure. When the children in the third grade proudly carry their third grade basal readers home to read to Mom and Dad, and Steve brings home a thin primer reader, parents immediately begin to suspect that something is wrong. They, along with the already concerned teacher, seek avenues of help.

For these reasons, it is advisable for school systems to set up programs of preschool screening. Tests are available that can be given to preschool children to determine those who are high-risk for later learning disabilities. Intervention programs for these children can be begun immediately. In many cases, children will get the necessary help to enable them to perform adequately when they begin formal schooling.

The older children become before the learning disability is discovered, the poorer the chances for remediation. By the time pupils are in the upper elementary or junior and senior high grades, they become burdened under several years of failure. They usually have failed to learn to read adequately to perform in other subjects, nearly all of which are dependent on a certain level of reading attainment. In reviewing the literature and existing programs, one finds that there are some exemplary efforts being made with secondary students who are learning disabled. Many times they come to a maturity level at which they realize the importance of literacy skills as they relate to their sociability and employability skills. It is, then, if never before, that they have keen motivation to learn, despite their handicaps.

In assessing the child's present achievement, it is important to assess in every area of school performance. It is possible to have a learning disability in math and not in reading. It is possible to have isolated learning disabilities in areas such as spelling, handwriting, and directionality. In fact, it has been said by neurologists that no one is neurologically perfect. Everyone may have a learning disability in some area. Some have a poor sense of direction or misjudge distances, which makes it particularly difficult to drive in a city or even to engage in sports events. Some individuals are tone deaf; they are rendered completely incapable of singing or playing a musical instrument, especially for the enjoyment of others. Color blindness is a neurological imperfection that creates some minor problems in the lives of some individuals. Some people can not calculate well enough to keep a bank book balanced. All of these may be considered learning disabilities.

When the learning disability becomes incapacitating and debilitating, it becomes a problem to the child, parents, and school personnel. This is why reading and math are the two major learning disabilities on which attention is focused. The child who exhibits learning disabilities in one or two areas will or should show strengths in others. In assessment, it is of particular importance to find both the deficit areas and the areas of strengths, for the educational program will be based on both.

How Does the Student Learn?

In assessing learning disabled pupils, the question must be asked, "How have they learned what they *have* learned?" Obviously, they have been successful in learning some things, or they would not be functioning in a school setting, even though they may be operating in deficit areas. Information is processed through the five senses, with the visual and auditory channels operationally carrying most of the load in school learning. Most individuals have a preferred modality through which they process incoming information. For most, this preferred modality is visual. Remember the old adage, "A picture is worth a thousand words." There are a few auditory learners who prefer processing through listening. Pupils do not, however, often learn in modality isolation. They combine incoming information through both the eyes and ears, though one modality takes the lead, as it were. The kinesthetic (also referred to as tactile or haptic) is the modality of proprioception or feeling through the fingertips or other sensitive areas of the body. This method is often used with young children who have assessed deficits in both visual and auditory channels. The final two modalities — gustatory and olfactory — are not stressed in educational settings as much as the other three, though anyone who has been around a young child or baby realizes the great importance of these two modalities in learning.

In discussing the modalities in learning, we have now moved away from the concept of visual and auditory acuity — the ability to see and hear without impairment — and have moved into the area of visual and auditory discrimination. For example, Janet may have trouble in reading because she reverses words such as *was* and *saw*. When given a visual screening test, it was determined that she has perfect visual acuity. The problem is not one of visual acuity, but of visual discrimination. She may have a process deficit in the area of visual discrimination. Steve can not hear the difference between the spoken words *wind* and *when*. It has previously been determined that he does not have an auditory acuity problem. He can hear as well as anyone in the class. His problem is one of auditory discrimination; he has a process deficit in the area of auditory discrimination.

After determining pupils' preferred modality and their processing deficits, what follows? Again, educators disagree as to where to go from here. Many LD specialists believe strongly in the remediation of process deficits, particularly in young children. In this approach, Janet would get much repetitious practice in learning to discriminate visually. Steve likewise would get remediation in learning to hear differences in similar words. The majority of educators are now saying that pupils must be given instruction through their intact modalities. This would mean gearing reading instruction to how they learn best. If pupils have an auditory problem, a pure phonetics approach would be a poor method of reading instruction because of the high degree of auditory discrimination required for such a task. Conversely, it might be an excellent method for pupils who have a strong preference for the auditory modality.

Advocates of teaching through children's strong modalities feel that academic remediation is the quickest way to success, and that they should be taught "full-speed-ahead" however they learn best. These educators are wary that process deficits can be remediated, particularly if they are indeed a dysfunction of the central nervous system. This academic remediation through the preferred modality might mean that a science teacher will tape the textbook information for a child who learns best auditorially. The child who learns visually may need a variety of charts, maps, and graphs to be able to comprehend the teacher's lecture on social studies. These methods, like all individualized instruction, entail much extra work on the part of the teachers and other educational specialists, but they will reap rich dividends for the disabled learner. Success breeds success, and once the pupil has been successful at a learning task, the foundation will be laid for future successes in learning.

What Diagnostic Hypothesis Can Be Formulated?

Later in this chapter the various diagnostic instruments will be discussed, along with nontest assessment techniques. From this information must evolve a decision of tremendous import — the stating of a diagnostic hypothesis. It is fairly easy to test and record results; it is far more difficult to examine the information and come to a diagnostic hypothesis. In fact, this is a great fallacy in many testing and assessment programs — nothing happens. The test results are filed neatly into a cabinet and the next group of youngsters come in for the test battery.

For an LD pupil, the diagnostic hypothesis should include this information:

1. The amount of discrepancy between capacity and performance
2. Areas of strengths and weaknesses
3. Preferred modality for processing information
4. Programmatic prescription for remediation.

Because this is stated as a hypothesis and not factual information, observational and test data should be gathered periodically and the hypothesis tested against the data. At this point, it can be rejected in favor of an alternate hypothesis, or the present hypothesis retained, again temporarily, with periodic changes based on evaluation.

What is the Prognosis for the Learning-Disabled Student?

No sound educator will give to the public the answer to the question most frequently asked, "What is your 'cure' rate?" It is impossible to assess all the changes — educationally, emotionally, socially, and psychologically — brought about when a learning disabled child is accurately diagnosed and given proper education treatment. Research indicates that there are many successful programs that are bringing about rather dramatic results in the lives of learning disabled pupils. With increased refinement in assessment and therapeutic techniques, the future looks optimistic for these children. No one has all the answers; some pupils still are not learning, even with the best resources available. One fact can be accepted: the earlier diagnosis and therapeutic treatment are begun, the better the pupil's chances of overcoming or learning to compensate for the disability.

TYPES OF DIAGNOSTIC INFORMATION

Basically, the diagnosis of learning disabled pupils is divided into three categories: formal tests, informal tests, and nontest assessment. Formal tests hold many advantages in that they are usually easy to give with marked instructions for the examiner; they are standardized and normed as discussed in a previous chapter; they have reported validity and reliability. However, formal tests are often quite threatening to LD pupils who are already failing in school. The test may often resemble the school work they are asked to do day after day and at which they experience repeated failure. With an LD child, many times it becomes necessary to depend heavily on informal tests and nontest assessment to get a true diagnostic picture of the pupil.

Formal Tests

Sensory Acuity Tests

The first tests one would give to a suspected LD child would be those that determine if his problems in learning are due to visual or auditory acuity. If pupils cannot see or hear well, it is certain to affect their learning in school. The Snellen Eye Chart is used in many schools to determine visual acuity. While this is an accepted gross measure of acuity, a more accurate screening device is the *Keystone Visual Survey Test* using a telebinocular that yields fourteen subtests. On the basis of this more sophisticated test battery, which measures both near-point and far-point acuity, a referral may be made to an eye specialist if a need is indicated.

Most school systems have access to a pure-tone audiometer, which yields an audiogram indicative of the pupil's auditory acuity. Again, referral is made to an otologist if the initial screening test warrants it. Results from an audiometer are far more accurate than the gross measures of the watch-tick test or the whisper test still used in some schools.

If pupils appear to have a problem in either visual or auditory acuity, they are referred to medical authorities, and results are checked before proceeding with the remainder of the test battery. If the problem is sensory acuity, it can be cleared up through prescriptive treatment by medical personnel and presumably the cause of the problem in learning has been discovered. Most of the time it is not this simple. Yet this possibility can not be ruled out without the use of sensory checks.

Mental Tests

The mental test most frequently used to determine capacity for LD pupils is the *Wechsler Intelligence Scale for Children — Revised* (WISC-R). Since this test has been discussed at length in Chapter 8, it will be discussed here only as it relates to LD children. First, one would look at the total IQ score and the standard deviation to determine if pupils have normal or above intelligence. If they fall more than two standard deviations below the mean, they should be referred to special educators for more intensive testing for possible mental retardation. If they fall between one and two standard deviations from the mean, they could possibly be candidates for a class for slow learners. It should be remembered, however, that the scores could be depressed because of the learning disability. At this point, the examiner will begin to look at some other factors.

An obvious indicator of a possible learning disability is a significant difference between the Verbal IQ and the Performance IQ. A difference of fifteen points (one standard deviation) is usually considered the benchmark of significance, although many educators may suspect learning disabilities if the difference is as much as thirteen points. If pupils have a true learning disability in the area of language, the difference will favor the performance score. If they have a perceptual learning disability, the difference will be in favor of the verbal score. This information is only a gross measure and should be considered only in the light of other information gathered in the assessment.

Many diagnosticians and assessment personnel look for a pattern of distractibility by carefully examining the subtest scores of Arithmetic, Digit Span, and Coding to see if they are significantly lower than the others. Low scores in Arithmetic and Digit Span are strong indicators of process deficits in the auditory area. A low score in Coding might be indicative of a visual process deficit.

The WISC-R is often preferred by most LD specialists to the *Stanford-Binet* as the WISC-R leads the diagnostician into the area of prescription for learning remediation. A WISC-R profile of an assessed LD child is included in Figure 45 for examination.

From this profile, you will notice that the child's score falls within the normal range of intelligence, according to the Full Scale Score. Therefore, it can be concluded that any problems the pupil is having in learning should not be attributed to lack of capacity to learn. Look at the difference between the Verbal Score and Performance Score. It can be concluded that there is a significant difference in favor of the Performance score. This child's problems obviously are in the language area. Look at the subtests suggested for distractibility — Arithmetic, Digit Span, and Coding. Are they lower than the others? This child would appear to be distractible, according to this profile. It might be

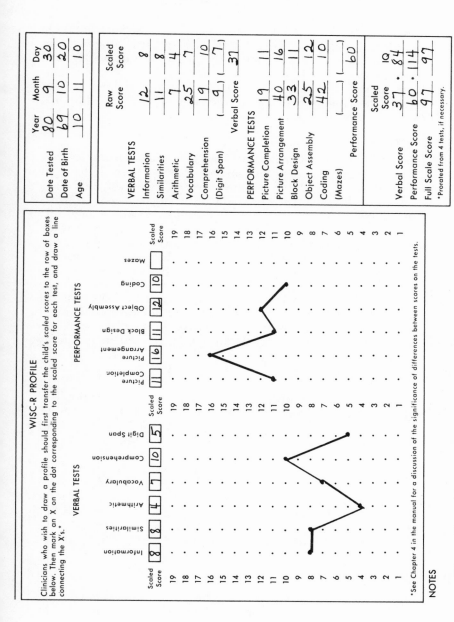

Figure 45. WISC-R Record Form. (Reproduced by permission of The Psychological Corporation.)

suspected that the student has trouble processing information when given orally.

The *McCarthy Scales of Children's Abilities,* also discussed in Chapter 8, is becoming a popular test for primary children. It is often used in states that prohibit the use of IQ tests. This test reports not an IQ but a GCI (General Cognitive Index), which has a mean of 100 and a standard deviation of fifteen, as do other major mental abilities tests. It yields much the same information as the WISC-R, but has additional measures of motor and memory factors.

Reading Tests

A good clinician can get much diagnostic information from having a child read orally and listening for patterns of errors to see if the child has any method of attack of unknown words. However, there are formal tests that should be used when the diagnostician needs information that can be quantified. Perhaps the most used reading diagnostic test is the *Gates-McKillop Reading Diagnostic Test,* which yields a variety of diagnostic information such as analysis of errors in oral reading, knowledge of words and word parts, auditory blending, and others.

A newer test is the *Woodcock Reading Mastery Test.* It has several advantages: it can be given in about twenty minutes; it spans the grade levels of K to 12, and it is less threatening than many more formal reading tests. It yields subtest scores of letter identification, word identification, word attack, word comprehension, and passage comprehension. It has alternate forms and is easily used in situations requiring pre- and posttest data.

Other Academic Skills Tests

One of the most frequently used achievement tests for LD pupils is the *Peabody Individual Achievement Test* (PIAT). This also is a rather quick, comprehensive, less threatening test that yields information in these areas: mathematics, reading recognition, reading comprehension, spelling, and general information.

Another popular achievement test is the *Wide Range Achievement Test* (WRAT), which examines the basic school subjects of reading (word recognition and pronunciation), spelling and arithmetic (computation). Three kinds of scores are reported in the results of the WRAT: grade equivalencies, percentiles, and standard scores, making it quite easy to determine the discrepancy between the IQ score and the achievement score.

Visual-Motor Tests

The *Bender Visual Motor Gestalt Test* is helpful in determining if the child has difficulty in visual-motor tasks. Although it has many uses in the hands of a trained clinician, the test is mainly used in the diagnosing of LD children to see if they have difficulty in motorically reproducing what they see. The design remains in view at all times. Memory is not a factor in this test. When pupils score low on the Bender, it is one indication that they may be having problems in academic work that requires visual-motor skills such as spelling, math, copying from the board or from a book.

For young children, the assessment might include the *Marianne Frostig Developmental Test of Visual Perception,* which yields five specific measures in the area of visual perception: (1) Eye-motor coordination, (2) Figure-ground discrimination, (3) Form constancy, (4) Position in space, and (5) Spatial relations. The norms are intended for preschool and first and second graders, but the test is used informally by many in diagnosing these types of problems in older children.

Auditory Discrimination Tests

For years clinicians have been using the *Wepman Test of Auditory Discrimination* to determine if the child has problems in the auditory area. The test is dependent upon the examiner's ability to pronounce the words correctly, and many times the dialectical differences of the examiner have been the variable in the child's low score. There are now other tests that are being used by speech pathologists and other communications specialists. One of the most frequently used ones at this time is the *Goldman-Fristoe-Woodcock Test of Auditory Discrimination,* which measures the pupil's ability to discriminate auditorily both in complete quiet and in noise. The latter of the two scores would probably be more indicative of the child's school performance since few would have a quiet classroom all day, every day. This test is on cassette tape and avoids the examiner area dialectal differences, which often is a disadvantage in the Wepman test.

Motor Tests

The previously mentioned *McCarthy Scales for Children's Abilities* has a good motor index that will give the examiner some idea of how the child is functioning motorically in relation to others of similar age groups. A test that is growing in acceptance among LD specialists is the *Test of Motor Impairment* by Stott. This test measures both fine and gross motor skills and is normed for various age levels.

Language Skills Tests

The *Illinois Test of Psycholinguistic Abilities* (ITPA) is often used to detect specific abilities and disabilities in the areas of language and communication. The test is based on Osgood's theoretical linguistic model and deals in areas of language functions in general, perceptual-motor tasks, memory, higher thought processes, and other abilities as well. The findings of this particular test can provide a basis for prescribing effective remedial educational programs. The *Detroit Tests of Learning Aptitudes* yields valuable information in determining the preferred learning modality of a child. An examination of selected subtests will be helpful in planning the child's program of remediation.

Preschool Screening Tests

It has been strongly stated previously that early screening for learning disabilities is necessary if the large percentage of our school population now suffering from the effects of learning disabilities is to be substantially reduced. Two tests that can be used effectively with preschoolers are *Meeting Street Screening Test* and *First Grade Screening Test*. It must be adamantly stressed that information from these tests cannot be used to label a child as learning disabled, but that it be used only for the purpose of identifying that pupil as a target for much enrichment in language development, readiness activities for reading and math, visual motor training, gross motor training, or any other areas in which there is an indication of a future problem. These two tests are designed to be administered to children in kindergarten. They identify cutoff scores for high-risk children for LD. These tests sample general information, body image, self-perception, perception of parental figures, visual-motor coordination, memory, and ability to follow directions.

Informal Instruments

Informal Reading Tests

Since many LD children do not respond to formal reading tests, which so painfully remind them of their failure in the school situation, it is desirable to try to tap the child's true reading abilities by administering informal reading tests. This is done in several ways, the most effective one being that of having the child read orally from a selected text. It is usually a good psychological practice to select a basal reader several grades below the pupil's actual grade placement, so that the child can experience success in the beginning of the test. The examiner will gradually select books of higher level until the child has reached the frustration level. The examiner will know when the child reaches the frustration level by the slowness of reading, the missing of a large percentage of the words, and outward nervous manifestations such as rapid breathing, hair twisting, etc. The level just below the frustration level is the level at which the child can best profit from instruction. At the instructional level, the student is able to pronounce from 80 to 90 percent of the words correctly.

While the examiner is having the child read orally, patterns of errors and for methods of word attack used by the child will emerge. This is valuable diagnostic information, which can lead directly into a prescription for the child.

Interest Inventories

When pupils are failing to learn in school, they often show an obvious dislike with the curriculum with which they are failing. Many times astute teachers can reach children by tapping their own particular field of interest. Many young people with learning disabilities in the field of reading have been motivated to read through paperbacks about motorcycles, space travel, or whatever "turns them on."

Through the use of inventories, teachers and counselors can determine the pupil's areas of interest. The inventory can be a printed one with questions posed by the examiner, or the inventory may be in the form of a conversation between student and teacher in which the teacher probes for any hint of interest.

One very reluctant nine-year-old boy was attending a reading clinic without much visible success. His one interest in life, according to his distraught clinician, was his father's dairy farm. One day in desperation, the clinician asked if she and her husband might spend a Saturday on the dairy farm. The child was delighted to have the couple as his special guests for the day. The next session in the clinic proved to be a turning point in the boy's success, for the clinician had gathered library books on dairy farming and taught the basic reading skills through material that was not only interesting to the child but non-threatening, as it was different from the regular basal readers in which he had experienced repeated failure.

Personality Assessment

Clinicians can administer informal personality assessments either through conversation with the child or through the use of such tests as the *School Apperception Method* (SAM) or *Children's Apperception Test* (CAT). In the SAM, for instance, children are shown pictures of children in various school situations. They are asked to respond to them freely, in an unstructured manner. Children with learning disabilities often reveal that they have poor self-concepts, that they feel inadequate for school tasks, and that they feel that others perceive them as incompetent. They will reveal these feelings about themselves through conversation by speaking in a debilitating manner about themselves, by resisting new situations for fear of new failure, or by inability to evaluate behavior in a realistic manner. Through these informal personality assessments, the examiner is able to get information about how pupils feel about their peers, and about their relationship to teachers, parents, and other significant authority figures in their lives.

Nontest Assessment

Perhaps one of the first theorems laid down in any test and measurements course is that assessment is more than testing. Almost any clinician can be trained to administer tests efficiently, but it takes years of experience for an examiner to become a truly competent diagnostician, combining all test data with other observations to come to the moment of making the diagnostic hypothesis.

Classroom Behavior Observations

Many times clinicians miss the most obvious and reliable source of information concerning the child's true behavioral patterns — the classroom teacher. Aware classroom teachers are in a position to observe children in almost every setting. Teachers see how pupils react to learning tasks; teachers intuitively know how pupils feel about themselves and how they react with others in the classroom and on the playground. Teachers are in a position to know something of the interpersonal relationships among parents and siblings from the pupils' informal conversations about themselves and their homes. They are observant of other signs of social and emotional problems. A wise clinician will make use of this information by questioning the teacher about the child and classroom performance.

Parents and Peer Ratings

Often it is helpful to have the parents of the suspected LD child in for an interview to determine how the child behaves in the home. When the parents realize that the examiner is trying to find the best possible solution strategies, they will usually cooperate in trying to arrive at the diagnostic hypothesis. The examiner will deftly ask questions that determine how the child is dealt with in the home with respect to behavioral problems, whether children are overprotected or allowed to take reasonable risks, whether they manipulate adults to their advantage, how they handle failure, how they are rewarded and punished for behaviors in the home, and if they exhibit any deviant behaviors. The parents should be questioned about pupils' relationships with siblings and peers. Do they have close friends, or are they avoided in games and activities in the neighborhood? Do they actively enter group situations or do they withdraw from group activities? Through this interview, the examiner will arrive at a possible decision about how the parents perceive their children and their relationships.

Although this information is usually derived from informal interviews, there are parent rating forms available that many schools and clinics use. They are usually constructed on a scale, which is numerically weighted. Parents are asked to fill them in individually, and the responses are compared by the clinician. While these rating scales are easy to administer and easy to codify for possible computer use, much more information can be gleaned by a professional clinician sitting down with the parents informally for about a thirty minute session. While the parents are available, it will be helpful to get a developmental history of the child regarding medical and educational history, motor development, and speech and language development.

Information from Cumulative Folders

If the child has been in school for any length of time, there is usually a wealth of information in the cumulative folder. This would include test results from other years, teacher anecdotal records, and health information. Absences from school may be significant. A comparison of how the child performed under various teaching styles may be important. A child may show a spurt of academic growth in the third grade and a significant drop in the fourth grade. A study of the comparisons may reveal something about how the child learns best, or conversely, why the child fails.

REFERENCES

Alnscow, Mel and Tweddle, David A.: *Preventing Classroom Failure, An Objective Approach.* New York, John Wiley and Sons, 1979.

Bannatyne, Alexander: *Language, Reading, and Learning Disabilities.* Springfield, Illinois, Charles C Thomas, Publisher, 1971.

Baren, Martin, Lieble, Robert, and Smith, Lendon: *Overcoming Learning Disabilities: A Team Approach.* Reston, Virginia, Reston Publishing Company, Inc., 1978.

Button, James E., Lovitt, Thomas C., and Rowland, Thomas D.: *Communications Research in Learning Disabilities and Mental Retardation.* Baltimore, Maryland, University Park Press, 1979.

Chaiken, William E. and Harper, Mary Joyce: *Mainstreaming the Learning Adolescent.* Springfield, Illinois, Charles C Thomas, Publisher, 1979.

Clements, Sam D.: *Minimal Brain Dysfunction in Children, Terminology and Identification,* Phase One of a Three-Phase Project, National Institute of Neurological Diseases and Blindness Monograph No. 3, Public Health Service Bulletin No. 1415, U. S. Department of Health, Education and Welfare, Washington, D. C., U. S. Government Printing Office, 1966.

Frierson, Edward D. and Barbe, Walter (Ed.): *Educating Children with Learning Disabilities.* New York, Appleton-Century-Crofts, 1967.

Hamill, Donald D. and Bartell, Nettie (Ed.): *Educational Perspectives in Learning Disabilities.* New York, John Wiley and Sons, Inc., 1971.

Johnson, Doris J. and Myklebust, Helmer R.: *Learning Disabilities, Educational Principles and Practices.* New York, Grune & Stratton, 1967.

Kirk, Samuel A.: *Educating Exceptional Children.* Boston, Houghton Mifflin Company, 1971.

Kozloff, Martin A.: *A Program for Families of Children with Learning Behavior Problems.* New York, John Wiley and Sons, 1979.

Lerner, Janet W.: *Children with Learning Disabilities.* Boston, Houghton Mifflin Company, 1971.

McCarthy, James J. and McCarthy, Joan F.: *Learning Disabilities.* Boston, Allyn and Bacon, Inc., 1969.

Myers, Patricia and Hamill, Donald D.: *Methods for Learning Disorders.* New York, John Wiley and Sons, Inc., 1969.

National Advisory Committee on Handicapped Children, *Special Education for Handicapped Children*, First Annual Report. Washington, D.C., Department of Health, Education, and Welfare, Office of Education, 1968.

Oettinger, Leon, Jr. (Ed.) and Majovski, Lawrence V. (Assoc. Ed.): *The Psychologist, the School, and the Child With MBD/LD*. New York, Grune & Stratton, Inc., 1978.

Smith, Robert M. (Ed.): *Teacher Diagnosis of Educational Difficulties*. Columbus, Ohio, Charles E. Merrill Publishing Co., 1969.

Tarnopol, Lester (Ed.): *Learning Disabilities: Introduction to Educational and Medical Management*. Springfield, Illinois, Charles C Thomas, Publisher, 1969.

Valett, Robert E.: *Programming Learning Disabilities*. Belmont, California, Fearon Publishers, 1969.

Chapter 11

ASSESSMENT FOR STUDENTS WITH EXCEPTIONALITIES

T HE HISTORY of education for children with exceptionalities includes little before 1799, when Jean Itard, a French physician
working with the deaf, began his therapy with the now-famous Wild
Boy of Aveyron in an attempt to remediate him. While Itard made little
progress with the boy, a movement was begun that was to bring us into
the 1980s with sophisticated measurement devices and legislation
assuring the rights of all exceptional children to an appropriate education.

Before Itard's work, society often viewed mental, physical, and emotional handicaps as divine punishment for human wrongdoing. Children with exceptionalities were often killed, or at best, left to fend for
themselves. Even in the nineteenth century, physical and mental handicaps would set a child apart from society. Programs for exceptional
children were first established in schools in the early 1900s. The term
"special education" began appearing in the literature around 1930.

Attitudes toward exceptional children began to change more rapidly
after World War II, when Americans began to claim the promises of
the four great freedoms, including the freedom from fear and want.
Some of the techniques developed to rehabilitate returning wounded
soldiers were extended to children with handicaps. With the returning
wounded soldiers also came a national awareness of children with
similar handicapping conditions such as blindness, impairments in
hearing, orthopedic handicaps, and emotional disturbance.

Programs for exceptional children expanded greatly during the
1960s, although efforts were fragmented. The philosophy of special
education included "special teachers" and "special classes." Labels
came into widespread use during this period as funding agencies
almost always funded according to categorical labels of an area of
exceptionality.

PUBLIC LAW 94-142

The 1970s brought great progress with new legislation, new national
commitment, and awareness. The single most important piece of legislation for exceptional children to date was passed in 1975 and is called
P.L. 94-142, *The Education for All Handicapped Children Act.* P.L. (Public
Law) 94 (passed by the 94th Congress) 142 (142nd law passed by the
94th Congress) guarantees free and appropriate education for all

handicapped children in the least restrictive environment. The law makes public education responsible for individuals age three to twenty-one and assures due process.

The federal definition of handicapped children in P.L. 94-142 is

> . . . mentally retarded, hard of hearing, deaf, speech impaired, visually handicapped, seriously emotionally disturbed, orthopedically impaired, or other health impaired children, or children with specific learning disabilities who by reason thereof require special education and related services.
>
> The term "children with specific learning disabilities" means those children who have a disorder in one or more of the basic psychological processes involved in understanding or in using language, spoken or written, which disorder may manifest itself in imperfect ability to listen, think, speak, read, write, spell, or do mathematical calculations. Such disorders include such conditions as perceptual handicaps, brain injury, minimal brain dysfunction, dyslexia, and developmental aphasia. Such term does not include children who have learning problems which are primarily the result of visual, hearing, or motor handicaps, or mental retardation, or emotional disturbance, or of environmental, cultural, or economic disadvantage. (20 U.S.C. 1402, as amended.)

The definitions appear to be nonspecific, varying in interpretation, thus allowing much latitude on the part of local agencies and personnel in deciding who should benefit from "special services."

In summary, the law requires that:

- handicapped persons be provided a *Free, Appropriate Public Education* and necessary support services
- handicapped students be educated in the *Least Restrictive Environment*
- *Nondiscriminating Evaluation Procedures* be established to attempt to remedy culturally or racially biased assessment and ensure appropriate classification and educational services
- *Due Process Procedures* be followed to provide safeguards for children and parents in educational assessment and planning
- *Individual Educational Programs* (IEPs) be developed to outline and meet the unique needs of each handicapped student.

Free Appropriate Education

WHAT IS A FREE, APPROPRIATE EDUCATION? This clause in the law means that education and related services will be provided to the handicapped person and to his/her parents or guardians at no cost to them. State, federal, and even private funding will subsidize the cost of education and related services. If a local education agency can not adequately meet the specific needs of a handicapped student in its district, it must provide transportation and costs to another center where resources are available.

If local school district personnel decide that a private school can best serve the handicapped child, the local district is responsible for all costs. However, if parents request private school or residential placement, even though the public school personnel feel that the handicapped child can be served in the public school setting, parents are responsible for costs incurred.

The word *appropriate* is not defined as such in the law, but its meaning is implied through the individual educational program (IEP) called for. Thus, if all persons involved agree to the IEP, that becomes the appropriate plan of education for the child.

Least Restrictive Environment

WHAT IS THE LEAST RESTRICTIVE ENVIRONMENT? Traditionally, handicapped students have been placed in special classrooms, special schools, residential or hospital settings. PL 94-142 uses the term least restrictive environment to indicate that the child will be placed in an *optimum* environment, whether this be the regular classroom, special classroom, or any other setting. With the least restrictive environment clause has come the concept of mainstreaming, although the term itself is not contained in the law.

Mainstreaming is an attempt to look for and create alternatives that will help general educators serve children with learning or adjustment problems, possibly in the regular classroom setting. The concept also involves uniting the skills of general education and special education so that all children may have equal opportunity.

The philosophy of mainstreaming would place a handicapped pupil in regular kindergarten or first grade with special education support. He/she should be removed to special classes or a special school only when the necessity to do so is shown and only for the periods required to prepare the pupil for return to regular class.

There are three factors involved in the philosophy of mainstreaming. The first is placement of students. In traditional special education classes, students are placed according to the categorical labels that have been assigned to them from psychometric evaluation. The concept of mainstreaming places students according to educational and social needs, emphasizing strengths as opposed to weaknesses.

The second factor is basic philosophy. Traditional special education calls for isolation while mainstreaming calls for integration into the main educational program of the school.

The third concept is that of diagnosis. Traditional special education makes diagnoses through formal testing and evaluation while the concept of mainstreaming calls for complete observation of skills, abilities, and interests.

It is important to remember that exceptional children are more *alike* than *different from* other children. All children learn and grow differently and at their own rate, depending upon their physical, mental, and emotional makeup and their own cultural and environmental experiences. Thus, all children need

- a rich, stimulating place in which to interact
- room to explore, discover, and organize information
- active involvement in the learning process; choices and practice in decision-making
- a feeling of being loved
- a feeling of security and respect and freedom from fear
- freedom to express feelings and be understood
- success
- play with other children
- challenges (Hennon, 1978, p. 7)

Underlying the philosophy of mainstreaming is the belief that most children can be best served in the regular classroom as opposed to isolating them with children of similar handicaps. The "least restrictive environment" clause, however, does imply that the needs of some severely handicapped children might best be met in a special class, special school, or residential or hospital setting. The law does *not* mandate that all handicapped children will be educated in the regular classroom.

While the term "mainstreaming" has caused no small amount of concern among special and regular educators, it is simply an attempt to place the special child in the best possible environment for his/her physical, social, intellectual, and emotional needs.

Nondiscriminatory Evaluation Procedures

WHAT ARE NONDISCRIMINATORY EVALUATION PROCEDURES? The law mandates that the assessment procedures used with the handicapped child must not be racially or culturally discriminatory. Specifically, there are two stipulations:

Such materials and procedures shall be provided in the child's native language or mode of communication. . . .
. . . no single procedure shall be the sole criterion for determining an appropriate education of a child.

Assessment must be carried out by qualified personnel, must be carefully planned for each child, and must come from several sources.

Due-Process Procedures

WHAT ARE DUE PROCESS PROCEDURES? Due process procedures assure fairness and appropriateness of decision-making concerning assessment and placement of each handicapped child. Each local school district will take steps necessary to attempt to ensure that one or both of the parents of the handicapped child are present at each meeting where decisions are made concerning the child. The local school personnel will take whatever steps are necessary to ensure that the parent understands the proceedings at a meeting, including arranging for an interpreter for parents who are deaf or whose native language is other than English.

Individual Educational Programs

WHAT ARE INDIVIDUAL EDUCATIONAL PROGRAMS? P.L. 94-142 mandates that each handicapped pupil have an individual educational program (IEP) on file. The IEP contains both long-range and short-range educational objectives. Individualized means that the IEP will address the specific needs of a single child, not an entire class. The law contains a specific definition describing the components of the IEP as follows:

> a written statement for each handicapped child developed in any meeting by a representative of the local education agency or an intermediate educational unit who shall be qualified to provide, or supervise the provision of, specially designed instruction to meet the unique needs of handicapped children, the teacher, the parents or guardian of such child, and whenever appropriate such child, which statement shall include (1) a statement of the present levels of educational performance of such child, (b) a statement of annual goals, including short term instructional objectives, (c) a statement of the specific educational anticipated duration of such services, and appropriate objective criteria and evaluation procedures and schedules for determining, on at least an annual basis, whether instructional objectives are being achieved. [Refer to Section 4 (a) (19) of the Act.]

The law requires that a minimum of four persons be involved in the development of the IEP. This would include the parents (or guardians), the teacher(s) of the child, a representative of the local educational agency, and whenever appropriate, the child. If an additional service person will be providing related services (i.e. speech therapy, physical therapy), it would be helpful for this person to be in on the planning. Finally, the P.L. 94-142 regulations require that a member of the assessment team or someone familiar with the procedures and the results of the assessment must participate in any IEP meetings conducted for handicapped children who have been evaluated for the first time.

The local education agency or school district has responsibilities concerning the IEP. Each local district must develop, or revise, whichever is appropriate, an IEP for every handicapped child at the beginning of the school year, and review and, if appropriate, revise its provisions periodically, but not less than annually. Each local district is responsible for initiating and conducting meetings for developing, reviewing, and revising a child's IEP.

The IEP is not an instruction plan but a management tool that is developed to assure that a child receiving special education services is appropriately served according to his/her learning needs, and that the special education designed is actually delivered and monitored.

If optimum assessment procedures have been followed, there will be an abundance of diagnostic data from which the school psychologist, consultants, teachers, and parents may construct the IEP. This will be complemented by the teachers' and parents' knowledge of the child's learning style and preferred modalities as well as other pertinent information.

In summary, P.L. 94-142 provides the most comprehensive plan to date for serving the exceptional child.

CATEGORIES OF EXCEPTIONALITY

Labeling continues to be a divisive issue among educators of special children. The practice of assigning labels to children of any age raises many problems such as mislabeling, stigmatizing, and the self-fulfilling prophecy. There are educators who feel that labels should be kept as far from the child as possible and that services needed should be the basis for classification. They would point out that some children may carry multiple labels because they have a combination of handicapping conditions.

While turmoil concerning labeling of children has continued to exist and is the topic of numerous journal articles, a recent survey (Barret and Brazil, 1979, p. 291) concluded that there is no current national movement away from traditional categories for the estimation, identification, and education of exceptional children in the United States. To the contrary, there appears to be an increase in the new categories.

Some educators believe that labels carry a negative connotation that results in lower teacher expectations, for both regular and special education teachers. Teachers may perceive a child described with a label as having more severe academic or behavioral problems and requiring more intensive special services than the same child without a label (Gillung and Rucker, 1977, p. 465).

There are parents and educators who would like to eliminate labels entirely. This appears to be an oversimplification of the problem. Labeling, if flexible and not regarded as an absolute truth, can be helpful in delivering services to children who otherwise would not meet local guidelines for special services. Categorization may be desirable for planning and implementing programs and systems of evaluation. There is no easy solution here. It would appear that labels will exist for several years to come and that extreme caution must be exercised in using them.

School personnel must become acquainted with the various categories of pupils served under the umbrella of special education, regardless of the existing philosophy concerning labels. Special education classes have traditionally included students categorized as:

Mentally Retarded
Learning Disabled (see Chapter 10)
Emotionally Disturbed
Orthopedically Handicapped
Deaf/Hearing Impaired
Blind/Visually Impaired
Speech Impaired
Gifted and Talented

It should be noted that the categories may vary slightly from state to state, with variations such as "disabled," "impaired," "disadvantaged," or "handicapped." One additional category included in special education is that of gifted and talented students. Although not disabled or impaired, their needs have not been traditionally met in the regular classroom. Many programs are attempting to meet the needs of this unique group of students through provisions in P.L. 94-142.

Mentally Retarded

A student who is mentally retarded is one who has been determined by certified personnel such as a psychologist, associate psychologist, or diagnostician to be functioning more than two standard deviations below the mean on individually administered scales of verbal ability, performance or nonverbal ability, and adaptive behavior. Instruments commonly used as assessment instruments for suspected mentally retarded students include the *Stanford-Binet*, the *Wechsler Intelligence Scales, McCarthy Scale of Children's Abilities*, and *Columbia Mental Maturity Scale*, among others.

The American Association on Mental Deficiency (AAMD) has gained wide acceptance with the following definition: "Mental retardation refers to substantially subaverage general intellectual functioning existing concurrently with deficits in adaptive behavior, and manifested during the developmental period."

Mental retardation is often divided into levels indicating the severity of the condition:

Mild (IQ approximately 52-68)
Moderate (IQ approximately 36-51)
Severe (IQ approximately 20-35)
Profound (IQ below 20)

Educators often use terms such as educable mentally retarded (EMR), trainable mentally retarded (TMR), and custodial, indicating the type of special educational assistance needed. According to AAMD, mild retardation is roughly equivalent to the educational term educable; moderate retardation includes those individuals who are likely to fall into the educational category of trainable; the severe group includes individuals sometimes called "custodial" or "life-support."

Approximately 2 percent of all children will meet the criteria for classification as mentally retarded. The majority of these will fall into the category of mild retardation and will, therefore, become a concern of the schools. The more profoundly and severely retarded children will be cared for in residential schools or hospitals.

The most common learning characteristics of the educable mentally retarded are the following:

• They tend to have difficulty with verbal concepts.
• They require more repetitive learning; they are less likely to learn spontaneously or incidentally.
• They tend to learn at a slower rate.
• They tend to be concrete thinkers, having difficulty with more abstract forms of learning.
• They have difficulty with transferring learning from one situation to another.
• They tend to have short-term memory problems.

It must be stated that these are general tendencies and characteristics and may not describe individual children who are mentally retarded. With careful teaching and instruction, many of these pupils can be taught to read, write, and do fundamental math, as well as many other aspects of typical school curriculum.

Emotionally Disturbed

A student who is emotionally disturbed or handicapped is one who demonstrates one or more of the following characteristics to a marked extent and over a period of time (chronic) and to a degree which adversely affects educational performance:

• an inability to learn that cannot be explained by intellectual, sensory, or health factors
• an inability to build or maintain satisfactory interpersonal relationships with peers and teachers
• inappropriate types of behavior or feelings under normal conditions
• a general, pervasive mood of unhappiness or depression; and
• a tendency to develop physical symptoms, pains, or fears associated with personal or school problems.

The report of individual assessment from the evaluating professional must specify (1) the type and severity of the emotional disturbance, (2) the functional implications of the disability for situations involving instruction, (3) the degree to which in-school and out-of-school behavior reflects symptoms consistent with the diagnosis, and (4) recommendations for behavioral management in the educational setting.

Rating scales and checklists are the most common type of assessment instruments used with children with suspected emotional disturbance. While assessment specialists may construct their own rating scales or observation instruments, there are a few commercially produced ones such as *Walker Problem Behavior Identification Checklist* published by Western Psychological Services, *Devereux Elementary School Behavior Rating Scale* published by the Devereux Foundation, and *Hahnemann High School Behavior Rating Scale* published by Hahnemann Medical College and Hospital, Philadelphia, Pennsylvania.

The most common complaints teachers have about emotionally disturbed students include acting out in the classroom, out-of-seat behavior, temper tantrums, swearing and verbal agressiveness, use of lewd gestures, refusing academic tasks, and hyperactivity. Disturbed classroom behavior includes excessive daydreaming, impulsivity, short attention span and inability to concentrate, inability to tolerate frustration, destructive with his own peers or school property, compulsively ritualistic in work or behavior, tends to be rigid in the manner in which he performs various tasks, resistant to changing to new activities, chronically fearful, apprehensive, or depressed.

All of the above characteristics may be seen in children who are quite normal in their behavior. The difference would be in frequency and duration, intensity, and persistency. Thus, an emotionally disturbed child could be described as exhibiting inappropriate behavior that is frequent, intense, and persistent.

The incidence figure on emotional disturbance is more difficult to determine than other types of handicapping conditions. Incidence in the school-age population will vary greatly, depending on the manner in which emotional disturbance is defined, and the methods used in screening and identification. Kirk (1972) reviewed various studies on the prevalence of emotional disturbance in the school age population and cites estimates from 2 percent to 22 percent. Probably the most widely accepted incidence figure for the purposes of establishing programs for the emotionally disturbed is 10 percent of school-age population. Not all of these children, of course, will need extensive special programming but all may profit from some form of program intervention for optimum learning.

Orthopedically Handicapped

The category of orthopedically handicapped includes crippled, other health impaired, and multiply handicapped persons. The crippled, other health impaired, and multiply handicapped population is composed of those individuals with physiological impairment and concomitant educationally related problems, requiring some modification of programs to meet their educational needs.

Conner and Cohen (1973) made the following statement concerning this population:

> There are developmental tasks ordinarily and commonly mastered in infancy, early childhood, adolescence, early adulthood, middle age, and later maturity. When the normal learning of these tasks is affected by a physical or health impairment or related disability, the individual regardless of age becomes part of the special population to be served. Limitations of physical dexterity, locomotion, and vitality produce a multiplicity of secondary functional deficits. Taken together, they in turn affect psychological as well as intellectual growth and performance. Lack of early social and educational experience and exposure, often accompanied by recurrent periods of hospitalization, combine to form possible perceptual and conceptual deficits. Personal rejection by peers, owing to the inability of the handicapped person to keep physical pace in the activities of daily living and also because of certain "embarrassing" physical problems associated with their condition, such as drooling or disfigurement or the need for special prophylactic equipment, like catheters, affect social adjustment as well as self-acceptance (pp. 8-9).

Children growing up with physical disabilities may have secondary emotional disabilities that will require special educational interventions. The instructional system planned for this type of handicapped child needs to be responsive to the multiple disabilities of the child and focused on individual educational objectives.

It is more difficult to list specific characteristics for the orthopedically handicapped group of children than for some of the other categories. Some common general health problems among this special group of children might include deviations in height and weight, skin problems, problems with posture and body mechanics, upper respiratory tract problems, general fatigue, restlessness, and irritability.

Approximately 1.5 percent of children have crippling conditions that are caused by disease, birth defects, or accidents (Hennon, p. 24). Some of these children will be able to mobilize themselves and attend regular classes with no special provisions. The more severe crippling conditions will require special locomotion facilities, architectural modifications in buildings, special seating arrangements, and modified learning strategies.

Assessment of these children often presents problems. Many times the child may use the same standardized test if given sufficient time and minor adaptations. Some may not be able to respond to performance items because they cannot manipulate the testing materials. Others may not be able to respond to the verbal items because of accompanying speech problems.

There are, however, several tests that are adaptable to the orthopedically handicapped child. Picture vocabulary tests and the *Progressive Matrices* allow the child to respond by pointing to pictures as does the *Columbia Mental Maturity Scale*.

The *Leiter International Performance Scale* and the *Porteus Maze Test* have been successfully used with children who cannot manipulate test material. The examiner removes material upon a signal from the student.

Observation on the part of parents, teachers, and other assessment personnel becomes extremely important in assessing the strengths and weaknesses of this particular population because of the limitations of standardized tests.

Deaf/Hearing Impaired

A student with a hearing impairment is one who has been determined to have a serious hearing loss even after corrective medical treatment and/or use of amplification. This determination is made by an otological examination performed by a licensed physician. The otological report specifies the type and severity of the hearing impairment. An audiological evaluation by a certified audiologist will also be conducted. This evaluation includes a description of the implications of the hearing loss for the student's hearing in a variety of circumstances with or without recommended amplification.

Auditory impairments affect about 1.5 percent of children. The severity of the hearing loss is measured in decibels. A child with a 60 decibel loss can hear loud conversation at about three feet and will exhibit a limited vocabulary and unwitting misunderstandings of conversations. A child with more than a 60 decibel hearing loss will be able to hear moderate voices at only a few inches from the ear or not at all (Hennon, p. 22).

Children who are hearing impaired usually exhibit behavioral symptoms in the classroom such as inattention, listlessness, frequent failure to respond to questions, and frequent requests to have words or statements repeated. They may have difficulty in group conversational situations as evidenced by frowning, straining forward when addressed, or generally failing to participate in group activities. They may look up suddenly with surprise, not knowing where a sound came from. Ear problems may include discharge from the ear, vertigo, ear noises such as ringing or buzzing, and tenderness about the ear.

Assessment of deaf or hearing impaired children again presents problems in using traditional tests in which the examiner asks questions in order to receive a response. Most of the tests that have been used with deaf children involve the adaptation of performance scales with instructions in sign language or pantomime. One scale standardized on deaf and hearing impaired children is the *Hiskey-Nebraska Test of Learning Aptitude* (NTLA).

Hiskey (1966) used 2,000 hearing impaired children in the restandardization of the original NTLA, and while subjects in several states were tested and some minority subjects were included, there is still a question concerning representativeness of the sample.

The NTLA has twelve subtests for testing persons between three and sixteen years of age. The subtests, which are administered with verbal instructions of hearing children and in pantomime with hearing-impaired children are as follows:

1. Bead Patterns (Ages 3-10)
2. Memory for Color (Ages 3-10)
3. Picture Identification (Ages 3-10)
4. Picture Association (Ages 3-10)
5. Paper Folding (Ages 3-10)
6. Visual Attention Span (All ages)
7. Block Patterns (All ages)
8. Completion of Drawings (All ages)
9. Memory for Digits (Ages 11 and older)
10. Puzzle Blocks (Ages 11 and older)
11. Picture Analogies (Ages 11 and older)
12. Spatial Reasoning (Ages 11 and older)

In the NTLA manual, Hiskey (1966) has reported reliability and validity data. The split-half coefficients range from .90 to .95 for different groups. Concurrent validity coefficients between the NTLA scores and scores for the *Stanford-Binet* and *WISC* are reported. A correlation of .86 was found between the NTLA and *Stanford-Binet* for a sample of ninety-nine hearing children, and a correlation of .78 was found for a similar comparison in a sample of fifty hearing children. Another study in which the NTLA scores were correlated with WISC scores for fifty-two hearing children produced a coefficient of .82. Hirshoren et al. (1977) have reported a correlation of .89 between WISC-R Performance scores and H-NTLA Learning Quotient scores (N = 59), which suggests that the scales measure similar abilities.

Blind/Visually Impaired

Probably more widespread screening exists for visual defects than any other handicapping conditions. The most commonly used device in schools is the Snellen Eye Chart, the familiar eye chart that hangs in the nurse's office of most schools. Many authorities feel that this chart is inefficient as a screening device and underrefers in many instances. That is, children with vision defects or potential defects may not be discerned by using the chart. For those who feel the Snellen is inadequate, instruments such as the *Keystone Visual Survey Tests,* the *Ortho-Rater, Professional Vision Tester,* and the *Titmus Biopter* are available. These are, of course, screening devices that signal the examiner to refer the child to an eye specialist for further testing.

The usual definition of legal blindness is that a person's visual acuity for distant vision does not exceed 20/200 in the better eye, with best correction; or the visual acuity is more than 20/200, but the widest diameter of his field of vision subtends an angle of no greater than 20 degrees. For educational purposes, a visually handicapped student may be defined as one who has been determined by a licensed eye specialist either to have no vision or to have a serious visual loss after correction.

The report of the individual assessment from the eye specialist should specify the type and severity of impairment. For students having residual vision, a functional vision evaluation performed by an educator of the visually handicapped or other specialist in functional low-vision assessment should be required. This report will include a description of the functional implications of the handicapping condition for the education process. Once an eye specialist has made a report on the child, an educator of the visually handicapped will be able to prescribe an educational plan based on the specific abilities of the child.

Common symptoms of visual handicaps are often manifested in the classroom before anyone is aware that the child has a visual problem. It is not unusual for the elementary teacher to discover a potential problem and call for screening measures for the child. These manifestations would include confusion of similar letters, holding materials at an unusual distance or angle, difficulty in copying from the chalkboard, poor eye-hand-coordination, failure to complete long reading assignments, and rubbing or brushing eyes frequently.

The National Society for the Prevention of Blindness (NSPB) reports that about one child in four of school age in the United States needs eye care; about 1 in 500 is partially sighted, including 42 percent of legally blind children and those with acuity after correction of better than 20/200 but less than 20/70 — the approximate acuity with correction at which it becomes possible for the person to read ordinary newsprint. Approximately one person in 2,000 is legally blind.

Children who are blind or partially sighted will present some unique problems in assessment. The examiner must use oral tests. If a school psychologist is in a position to test large numbers of visually impaired students, he/she may want to acquire special equipment, such as tests in Braille or on phonograph records.

The *Stanford-Binet* has been adapted for use with visually impaired children by Hayes. The verbal portions of the WISC-R and *McCarthy Scale of Children's Abilities* may be used. There is also an adaptation of the *Vineland Social Maturity Scale* for visually handicapped preschool children.

A number of special tests are available for testing the blind. One of these, the *Blind Learning Aptitude Test* (BLAT), is designed to be used with young children. Newland (1969) designed the BLAT to measure six kinds of intellectual behavior with a bas-relief format that uses dots and lines. It was standardized on a group of 961 blind students, and the sample was stratified on the basis of age, race, sex, geographic area, and socioeconomic status.

Newland (1969) has reported an internal-consistency coefficient of .93 for the BLAT as well as a test-retest coefficient of .87. For evidence of validity, Newland (1969, p. 10), states that (1) scores on the BLAT increase as chronological age increases; (2) the scores correlate well enough with the Hayes-Binet and WISC Verbal Scale to indicate comparable ability sampling, but low enough to suggest differences in the behavior samplings; and (3) the scores correlate well with educational achievement.

The *Haptic Intelligence Scale for Adult Blind* was developed by Shurrager and Shurrager (1964) for use with blind adults who are sixteen years old or older. The normative sample, which is composed of 700 blind and partially sighted persons between the ages of sixteen and sixty-four, is not truly representative of the blind population. The sample was, however, made up of several different age groups and had proportions of whites and nonwhites similar to the 1950 United States Census.

The subtests of the Haptic are *Digit Symbol, Object Assembly, Block Design, Object Completion, Pattern Board,* and *Bead Arithmetic.* These tests are modifications of the WAIS with changes made so that a tactile rather than visual mode can be used. For example, Digit Symbol has raised dots for numerals and Block Design has blocks with surfaces of smooth, rough, and half-rough, half-smooth texture (see Fig. 46).

Test reliability coefficients ranging from .70 for Object Assembly to .81 for Pattern Board have been reported by the test authors (Shurrager and Shurrager, 1964). A test-retest coefficient of .91 was also reported for a sample of 124 subjects. As for validity, the manual provides a table of correlations for Haptic subtests scores versus WAIS Verbal scores. The correlations reported range from .17 to .65, with most being between .30 and .50. The correlation of .65 is for the correlation of the Haptic Total score and WAIS Verbal score.

The *Leiter International Performance Scale* was constructed by Russel Leiter in 1929. It was revised several times, and in 1950 Grace Arthur published an adaptation of the Leiter scale (AALIPS).

The 1948 revision of the Leiter can be used for testing subjects between the ages of two and eighteen. The Arthur adaptation is suitable for ages two through twelve. Very little standardization information is provided in the Leiter manual.

The scale was designed to be a culture-free, nonverbal instrument for assessing general intelligence. It has been used with many different ethnic groups. The scale consists of a response frame and trays of response blocks. The 1948 revision has three trays and the AALIPS has two. When a test is administered, the examiner places a stimulus card

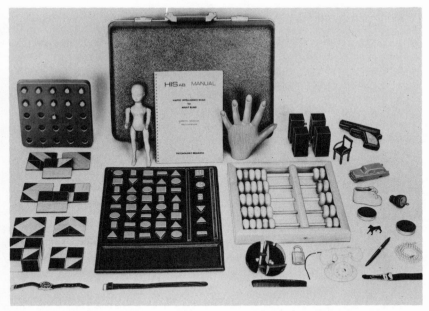

Figure 46. *Haptic Intelligence Scale.* (Reproduced by permission of Stoelting Company.)

on a response frame and pantomimes the directions. The subject responds by placing blocks in the response frame. The test items require matching forms, figures, or colors, in order to complete block designs, to classify objects, to complete number series, and to master similarities. The scale yields a mental age and ratio IQ.

Arnold (1951), Leiter (1959), and Sharp (1958) report reliability coefficients in the .90s for the 1948 Leiter. Several validity studies have been reported. The correlations between Leiter scores and Stanford-Binet scores generally have been in the .60s and .70s. Sharp (1957) reported correlations of .78, .80, and .83 between the Leiter and WISC Verbal, Performance, and Full Scale scores respectively. Alper (1958) reported Leiter-WISC correlations of .40 (V), .79 (P), and .77 (FS). The AALEPS manual gives correlation coefficients ranging from .56 to .93 for the comparison of AALIPS scores and Stanford-Binet scores.

Speech Impaired

A speech-impaired student is one who has been determined by a certified speech and hearing therapist to have a communication disorder, such as stuttering, impaired articulation, a language impairment, or a voice impairment. Articulation problems include substitutions of sound, omissions, and distortions of sounds. Stuttering problems include repetitions, hesitations, prolongations, and blocks. Language impairment includes developmental problems in language that may be due to auditory deficits or specific language disabilities. Voice problems include pitch, volume, and general quality of the voice. Other speech-related problems may be found among children who are hearing impaired or have organic difficulties, such as cleft palate and cerebral palsy.

Authorities disagree about both the definition of speech impairment and the incidence figure. The best incidence figures for school age children with speech impairments appear to fall between 3.5 and 5 percent of the population.

The report of the individual assessment from the specialist should specify the type and severity of the impairment and should include a description of the functional implications of the handicapping condition for the educational process.

Several behavioral manifestations of speech-impaired children will be exhibited in the classroom. These include distortion of sounds, talking "baby talk," making several efforts to speak (usually accompanied with jaw movement, eye blinks, or other movements) before vocalization occurs, appearing inattentive, and seldom participating in class or group discussions.

In assessing speech-impaired children, it may become necessary to omit portions of verbal tests or to extend the time period of response. With children who are severely handicapped, only the performance sections of tests such as *Stanford-Binet, WISC-R,* and *McCarthy Scale of Children's Ability* may be used. The *Callier-Azusa Scale* is a developmental scale designed to aid in assessment of multihandicapped children such as deaf-blind children.

Gifted and Talented

Gifted and talented children are considered the responsibility of special education programs in many school districts. They are "exceptional" children and thus would qualify for special program intervention. Interest in this special group of our school population has waxed and waned for the last half century. Lewis Terman began his famous studies of gifted children during the twenties. Recommendations were made for special education to satisfy the needs of gifted children, but programs undertaken in their behalf were generally few and inadequate before the 1950s.

About 1950, the movement to provide for gifted children was accelerated through the efforts of Terman, Paul Witty, and newly formed organizations such as the American Association for Gifted Children. Sputnik in 1957 changed our entire thinking on education, particularly the education of the gifted child. We began to search for the talented in math and science, as well as children who were gifted verbally, the traditional measure of giftedness.

Torrance of the University of Georgia began to publish widely in the area of creativity, developing tests to determine areas of creativity as well as giftedness in academic areas. In the literature, many terms describing gifted children may be found. Among them are genius, eminence, distinction, fame, creative ability, giftedness, gifted children, academically talented, or gifted and talented.

In 1972, the United States Office of Education developed a national definition of giftedness printed in *Education of the Gifted and Talented:*

> Gifted and talented children are those by virtue of outstanding abilities capable of high performance. These are children who require differentiated educational programs and/or services beyond those normally provided by the regular school program in order to realize their contribution to self and society.
>
> Children capable of high performance include those with demonstrated achievement and/or potential ability in any of the following areas; singly or in combination:
>
> 1. general intellectual ability
> 2. specific academic aptitude
> 3. creative or productive thinking
> 4. leadership ability
> 5. visual and performing arts
> 6. psychomotor ability
>
> It can be assumed that utilization of these criteria for identification of the gifted and talented will encompass a minimum of 3 to 5 percent of the school population.
>
> Evidence of gifted and talented abilities may be determined by a multiplicity of ways. These procedures should include objective measures and professional evaluation measures which are essential components of identification.
>
> Professionally qualified persons include such individuals as teachers, administrators, school psychologists, counselors, curriculum specialists, artists, musicians, and others with special training who are also qualified to appraise pupils' special competencies.

The Advisory Panel that formed this definition cautioned against the use of a definition that is too specific and does not allow for flexibility. In their report to the U.S. Commissioner of Education, they offer the following as an operational definition:

> Generally, the following evidence would indicate special intellectual gifts or talents:
>
> Consistently very superior scores on many appropriate standardized tests.
>
> Judgment of teachers, pupil personnel specialists, administrators, and supervisor familiar with the abilities and potentials of the individual.

Demonstration of advanced skills, imaginative insight, and intense interest and involvement.

Judgment of specialized teachers (including art and music), pupil personnel specialists, and experts in the arts who are qualified to evaluate the pupil's demonstrated and/or potential talent.

Most educators of the gifted believe that decisions about who should be included in a program for the gifted should be made by a committee and not a test scorer. This is based on the position that there is no single score or test dividing a gifted child from a nongifted child. A good resource for making those decisions is Gowan (1975).

SPECIAL CONSIDERATIONS IN ASSESSMENT FOR EXCEPTIONAL STUDENTS

Special Procedures

The examiner of special children must arrange testing conditions with special care. Sessions may have to be shortened to accommodate the short attention span of the handicapped child. The handicapping condition may preclude the student's being put into tiring conditions. Speeded tests, therefore, are usually inappropriate for most handicapped children.

The examiner should know something of the child's strengths, abilities, and disabilities before entering into the testing situation so as to have any special equipment that may be needed. It is extremely important for the examiner to build rapport with the child, encouraging, remaining patient, yet maintaining a firmness with the child. Some exceptional children have learned to use their handicaps to resist tasks. A tactful examiner will know how far to probe in searching for diagnostic information.

Criterion-Referenced Instruments Versus Standardized Tests

The degree and kind of handicap may determine whether a given child may be given a standardized test in its entirety. Many exceptional children may be administered traditional standardized norm-referenced tests without modification. It is difficult to determine, however, to what extent even a subtle handicap may affect the results. It will be obvious to the examiner that some standardized tests are out of the question for a particular handicapped student.

The chief mode of assessment of handicapped children continues to be traditional norm-referenced instruments. Many funding agencies encourage the use of norm-referenced instruments for reporting purposes. However, even in these tightly controlled projects, in-house assessment is at the discretion of the particular local district. Assessment experts who deal with exceptional children have always relied heavily on subjective reports, anecdotal records, and rating scales.

Criterion-referenced tests are emerging rapidly in the area of exceptional-children appraisal. While the norm-referenced or standardized tests are useful as a measure of child status relative to other children the same age, the criterion-referenced measures are *program* specific. They have the advantage of being tied directly to program objectives but, as such, lack the comparative interpretability of the standardized measure (MacTurk and Neisworth, 1978, p. 34). The criterion-referenced tests should aid greatly in the development of the individual educational program (IEP) previously discussed.

Assessment must be closely tied to intervention. The newly emerging criterion-referenced tests allow personnel to collect information as a routine part of the ongoing classroom activities and do not necessarily require the services of a trained psychologist to assess child progress.

As opposed to norm-referenced testing, which compares one child's performance to that of other children, criterion-referenced assessment sets a standard to which each child's performance is compared. Criterion-referenced measures are designed so that children's achievement is evaluated on clearly specified educational tasks. These measures represent a step toward systematic sequencing of learning tasks leading to proficiency in a given skill or behavioral area. Criterion-referenced tests appear to offer much promise in closing the gap between assessment and intervention.

Minority and Bilingual Students

The need for appropriate assessment instruments for minority and bilingual exceptional children appears critical. While the assessment of young children with potentially handicapping conditions may be difficult, it is especially difficult with bilingual handicapped children, because these children use two languages to varying degrees and few assessment instruments accommodate this (Mowder, 1979, p. 43). Many minority children may be misclassified as handicapped. PL 94-142 specified two conditions concerning the minority child. First, no single assessment instrument may be used as the sole criterion for placement; second, testing must be in the child's native language or mode of communication. This poses a number of problems because school assessment personnel are typically monolingual, and in addition, no tests have been developed that are totally nonbiased.

The presently used methods for assessing bilingual children for handicapping conditions falls into six categories according to Mowder (1979). These include (1) *Translating test instruments.* The mere translation of a test from English is a superficial adaptation and cannot be considered equivalent. (2) *Culture-fair tests.* Measurement experts feel the interest in developing culture-fair tests is declining as psychologists become increasingly aware that one test cannot be universally appropriate to individuals from all cultures, representing all languages. (3) *Behavior rating scales.* The usual resulting measures have too little generalizability. (4) *Regional Norms.* Once deficits are determined and differences documented, it may not make any difference until the educational system, curriculum, and instruction are modified to accommodate for the differences that the bilingual, culturally different child brings to school. (5) *Criterion-referenced measures.* Although this is a promising means of assessment, it is difficult to gain consensus on determining the objectives and the behavior criterion levels. (6) *Pluralistic assessment techniques.* This appears to be the most promising method of assessing the bilingual, multicultural child. It takes into account sociocultural factors, such as home and community.

Ecological-Environmental Assessment

Assessment experts are beginning to realize the need for a holistic-global approach to understanding the exceptional child. Even the newly emerging criterion-referenced tests will not be the total answer for assessing this special group of children.

The question might be asked, "What does the child need for an optimal environment?" This consideration would produce a more relevant individual educational plan (IEP) as required by PL 94-142. Children might be categorized, rather than by traditional labels, by services required to make up for environmental deficits. It can be assumed that a child from a deficient environment faces greater handicap than a child with an equal disability but a more enriched environment. Environmental appraisal should include the classroom, the general school environment, the community, and the home.

Thomas and Marshall (1977) state that the human ecology, or the interrelationship of man with his environment, involves a reciprocal association. An individual's actions affect his/her environment; conversely, changes in a person's habitats influence self-perceptions, behavior, and the situation. How well the child adapts depends on the following general component factors of programming: (a) the handicapping condition, (b) the family, (c) medical services, (d) training and educational services, and eventually, (e) the community as it relates singly to the individual, and the individual to the community. Thus, assessment and program implementation must take into consideration data-gathering from the child's environment, initial program recommendations, periodic reassessment, and program modification based on ongoing assessment of the child and child's environment.

This points out the need for nontest data as a major factor in making programmatic decisions for the exceptional child as well as for all pupils. Nontest data collecting techniques are discussed at length in Chapter 5.

Early Identification

Early identification of potentially handicapping conditions in young children may significantly reduce the impact of the deficits. Public Law

94-142 has given impetus to this goal of providing for the early identification and referral for treatment of children with potentially handicapping conditions before they become chronic and irreversible damage occurs.

While most medical and educational professionals accept the philosophical tenet of early identification, efforts toward such goals are fragmented. There are certainly obvious dangers involved. There is the possibility, for example, of misclassification or overidentification of very young children (Bersoff, 1977, p. 191).

Identification of special children may occur at any point from conception through birth, infancy, the preschool years, and the first years of formal schooling. The initial referral may come from any one of many professionals who come in contact with the child during the early years of development. These persons would include the obstetrician, the pediatrician, the pediatric nurse, the public health nurse, the dentist, the social worker, and the early childhood educator, as well as the parents or primary caregiver.

There may be roles the public schools can play to strengthen the early identification process. They must become advocates of early detection, organizing and coordinating communitywide developmental check-ups, training professionals, paraprofessionals, and community volunteers in awareness and identification techniques.

ADDITIONAL INSTRUMENTS COMMONLY USED WITH EXCEPTIONAL STUDENTS

There are basically four areas in which it is desirable to obtain results in assessing exceptional children. These areas include language skills, emotional and social development, intellectual abilities, and fine and gross motor skills.

Lanugage Skills

Normal language development of children may be affected by several handicapping conditions such as mental retardation, cerebral palsy, cleft palate, autism, visual and/or auditory impairment, speech impairment, and emotional and behavioral problems.

Several assessment instruments are commonly used to test language skills of exceptional children. These include *Detroit Tests of Learning Aptitude;* the verbal portions of *Wechsler Intelligence Scale for Children-Revised, Stanford-Binet,* and *McCarthy Scale of Children's Ability;* and the *Illinois Test of Psycholinguistic Ability* (ITPA).

The *Illinois Test of Psycholinguistic Abilities* (Kirk, McCarthy, and Kirk, 1968) is published by the University of Illinois Press. It was designed as a diagnostic test of language abilities for children, ages two through ten. It is based on Osgood's model (1957), isolating the language processes (i.e., decoding, association, encoding) and levels of organization (i.e., projective, integrational, and representation).

It is an objective psychometric device designed to assess language abilities systematically in order to facilitate intervention of deficiencies. Subtests include auditory reception, visual reception, auditory association, visual reception, auditory association, visual association, verbal expression, manual expression, grammatic closure, visual closure, auditory memory, visual memory, auditory closure, and sound blending.

The ITPA has been widely used in assessing language strengths and deficits of exceptional children and has influenced the development of subsequent instruments. Remedial programs have been developed and correlated with it.

This test is administered individually and requires special training for its use. Caution should be used in generalizing results from the ITPA subtests to exceptional children since the test was normed almost exclusively with middle-class, average-achieving white students. Even with its shortcomings, it can yield valuable information concerning language development of exceptional children, information necessary for the formulation of the individual educational program (IEP) required by PL 94-142.

Emotional and Social Development

Developmental lags in emotional and social development may occur in exceptional children either as a primary or a secondary cause. The emotional and/or social deficit may be so severe as to handicap the child in other developmental aspects such as language or motor skills. This would be a primary cause. On the other hand, a handicapping condition such as blindness, orthopedic handicaps, or a severe speech problem may lead to difficulties in emotional and social development.

The assessment of exceptional children should include a component for evaluating emotional and social development. This is often done by checklists of behavior, using either formal or informal tests. Such instruments might include *Walker Problem Behavior Checklist* (1970) published by Western Psychological Services, *Adaptive Behavior Scales* (1974) published by the American Association on Mental Deficiency, and *Vineland Social Maturity Scale* (1965), published by the American Guidance Services, Inc.

Edgar A. Doll, author of the *Vineland Social Maturity Scale*, has been a leading advocate of the necessity for assessing social and emotional competence in making decisions concerning exceptional children. The norming of the test was done in Vineland, New Jersey, using a small number of adults and children.

The *Vineland* scale assesses progress toward social maturity, competence, and independence in subjects from birth to adulthood. The test includes 117 items of habitual social activity, which range from infant behaviors such as a baby's laugh to behavior expected by mature adults. The items are arranged in increasing difficulty and represent progressive instruction in self-help, self-direction, locomotion, communication, and social relations. Scoring is similar to the *Stanford-Binet* procedure, with basal and ceiling ages established in each area. Total scores may be converted to social ages or social quotients.

Answers to the questions are elicited by the examiner from the parent or primary caretaker of the child. The examiner will need practice and experience in mastering the interview techniques, learning to recognize the possible biases of the informant.

Test-retest reliabilities and item validation studies are reported, though the samples are small. Despite its weaknesses and limitations, the *Vineland* is a valuable instrument in the hands of a trained examiner.

Intellectual Abilities

In assessing exceptional children for later intervention, it is necessary to know something of the strengths the child possesses in knowing, perceiving, and recognizing. To what extent can he/she reason and solve problems?

The child's handicapping condition may depress intellectual development. The deaf/hearing impaired or blind/visually impaired child may experience a developmental lag because of lack of sensory input. The emotionally disturbed child may have limiting experiences leading to problems in cognitive development.

The most common instruments used in assessing intellectual abilities of exceptional children are the *Wechsler Intelligence Scale for Children-Revised,* the *Stanford-Binet,* and *McCarthy Scale of Children's Abilities.* Each of these is individually administered, which is desirable in assessing exceptional children.

The *McCarthy Scale of Children's Abilities* (MSCA) was published in 1972 by the Psychological Corporation. It yields a General Cognitive Index (GCI) with a mean of 100 and a standard deviation of 15. Because it does not yield an IQ per se, it is acceptable in some local districts and states that have restrictions against using an IQ score.

It assesses strengths and weaknesses of children 2.5 to 8.5 years of age. The MSCA is comprised of eighteen separate tests grouped into six scales — verbal, perceptual-performance, quantitative, general cognitive, memory, and motor (see Chapter 8).

The instrument yields valuable information to the evaluator as the profile of scores is examined. The MSCA was standardized on a stratified sample of 1,032 cases. Good reliability and validity data are reported. This test appears to hold promise in the area of assessment of exceptional children.

Subjects with certain difficulties or handicaps must be tested with special tests or scales in order to obtain a useful measure of mental ability. Many of these instruments are of the nonverbal type.

Tests that use sets of pictures in the testing of individuals are especially useful for those persons who have language or speech difficulties or disorders. Three of these tests will be discussed briefly in order to acquaint the reader with this kind of instrument.

The *Peabody Picture Vocabulary Test* (PPVT) is designed "to provide an estimate of a subject's verbal intelligence through measuring his hearing vocabulary" (Dunn, 1965, p. 25). It was standardized on 4,012 subjects whose ages ranged from 2.5 to 18. Because all these subjects lived in or near Nashville, Tennessee, and were white, there is a serious limitation with respect to formulation of the norm group. Another serious limitation is that it measures just verbal ability and only through the use of vocabulary items.

The PPVT utilizes 150 plates that are arranged by ascending order of difficulty by age level. Each plate has four pictures on it. The examiner reads a stimulus word and the subject points to the picture that best represents the word (Fig. 47). This untimed test can be administered in about fifteen minutes. Because no verbal response is required, the PPVT is suitable for testing those subjects who have speech impairments, reading problems, cerebral palsy, or who are withdrawn or mentally deficient.

Figure 47. Administration of the *Peabody Picture Vocabulary Test*. (By permission of American Guidance Service, Inc.)

Dunn (1965) reports reliability and validity data in the PPVT manual. Alternate-form reliabilities range from .67 to .84 for the standardization sample. Four studies of test-retest reliability have yielded coefficients ranging from .54 to .88. In order to achieve content validity, Dunn used *Webster's New Collegiate Dictionary* to find words that could be represented by a picture or drawing. Words were selected in such a way as to avoid some kind of bias related to the response or decoy items (Dunn, 1965, p. 32). Dunn reports various studies that relate to the validity of the test. PPVT-*Stanford-Binet* IQ correlations range from .43 to .92, while PPVT-WISC full scale IQ correlations range between .30 and .84. Thus, both reliability and validity coefficients are much more variable (and generally lower) than for the *Stanford-Binet* and *Wechsler* scales.

The *Pictorial Test of Intelligence* was developed by French (1964) to test normal and handicapped children between ages three and eight. The PTI was standardized on a sample of 1,830 children whose ages ranged from three years to eight years. The sample was selected to be representative of the United States population.

The scale consists of 137 response cards and 54 stimulus cards. Each response card has four drawings from which the subject must choose the correct drawing. The cards are used for the following subtests:

1. *Picture Vocabulary*. This subtest measures verbal comprehension. The child must respond to a word spoken by the examiner by selecting the drawing or the response card that best represents the meaning of the stimulus word.
2. *Form Discrimination*. The test measures the ability to match forms and differentiate between shapes. The child must match a drawing on the stimulus card with one of four on the response card.
3. *Information and Comprehension*. This subtest measures knowledge and general understanding. The child's responses reflect verbal comprehension, alertness to environment and opportunities. Twenty-four response cards are used to get twenty-nine answers.
4. *Similarities*. The test is designed to measure ability to generalize. The child must indicate which of four drawings on a card does not belong with the others. Twenty-two cards are used.
5. *Size and Number*. This is a test that measures quantitative ability through the sampling of perception and recognition of size, number symbol recognition and comprehension, ability to count, and ability to solve problems. The subtest has thirty-one items and utilizes eight stimulus cards and nineteen response cards.
6. *Immediate Recall*. The test measures ability to retain momentary perceptions of size, space, and form relationships. The examiner shows a stimulus card for five seconds, removes it, and asks the subject to select the same design from a response card. Nineteen stimulus and response cards are used.

The drawings are arranged on the response cards in such a way that an examiner can observe the subject's eye movements, and thus the child may answer with a "looking response." A pointing or verbal response is also acceptable, of course. The test generally will require an administration time of about forty-five minutes.

French (1964) has reported KR 20 reliabilities ranging from .87 for three-year-olds to .93 for six-year-olds. Test-retest reliabilities ranging from .69 to .96 have also been reported.

Content validity has been assumed on the basis of item selection and test development. Construct validity is inferred from data showing increasing scores with age. Criterion-related validity studies are reported in the PTI manual, and the correlations range from .53 to .82, with many in the .70s.

The *Columbia Mental Maturity Scale* (Burgmeister and Blum, 1972) is another widely used pictorial test that is suitable for testing the orthopedically handicapped subject. It was standardized on a sample of 2,600 children stratified on the basis of race, sex, parental occupation, and geographic region.

The CMMS is designed to assess general reasoning ability, through the use of ninety-two figural and pictorial items that are arranged in eight levels. It may be used to test children between the ages of 3.5 years and 9 years, 11 months. Each item consists of a series of from three to five drawings printed on a card. The child is required to look at all the drawings on the card, select the one that is different from the others, and indicate by pointing to it. The scale can be administered in about twenty minutes.

The manual shows split-half and test-retest reliabilities. The split-half coefficients range from .85 to .91, while the test-retest coefficients range from .84 to .86.

Fine and Gross Motor Skills

Since many exceptional children may have some deficiencies in language skills, tests using nonspeech responses become important in assessment. Emotionally disturbed or frightened children can sometimes be motivated to cooperate on performance-type tests. Skills of children from different ethnic backgrounds as well as speech-impaired children can often be tapped with these tests.

For educational intervention, it is imperative to evaluate the exceptional child's skills in fine and gross areas. Tests commonly used are the *Beery-Buktenica Developmental Test of Visual-Motor Integration* (1967) published by Follet Educational Corporation, *Bender Motor Gestalt Test for Children* (1962) published by the American Orthopsychiatric Association, *Frostig Developmental Test of Visual Perception* (1961) published by Consulting Psychologists Press, and *Bruininks-Oseretsky Test of Motor Proficiency* (1977) published by American Guidance Services, Inc.

The *Bender Visual Motor Gestalt Test for Children* is comprised of nine designs (see Fig. 45) which the child copies under specified conditions. It is scored for accurateness of detail in reproduction.

It was developed in 1938 by Lauretta Bender and has been widely used as an assessment instrument of children's perceptual and motor abilities as well as other purposes. It has, for example, been used as a determinant of school readiness as well as possible emotional disturbance. Some researchers think it holds promise as an index of intellectual achievement.

In 1963, Koppitz developed an objective scoring system for the *Bender* that is now generally used in assessment batteries in schools and clinics. The Koppitz's scoring system yields a score based on an assessment of shape, rotation, integration, and perseveration in the nine drawings. Other scoring systems have been developed, but all lack substantial population norms.

Public Law 94-142 has given a new urgency to awareness, early identification, and assessment of exceptional children. While good basic evaluative techniques can be transferred to this special population, the clinician should be aware of characteristics of the various groups of exceptionalities as well as particular tests that are commonly used.

Only through precise assessment can the individual educational program (IEP) be relevant to the specific needs of a special child.

REFERENCES

Alper, A. E.: A comparison of the WISC and the Arthur Adaptation of the Leiter International Performance Scale with mental defectives. *American Journal of Mental Deficiency, 63:*312-316, 1958.

Anderson, Luleen S., Griffin, Carol Lee, and Hunt, Barbara M.: Screening children for kindergarten; process and promise. *Elementary School Guidance and Counseling, 13:*93-98, 1978.

Arnold, S. F.: A technique for measuring mental ability of the general palsied. *Psychological Service Center Journal, 3:*171-178, 1951.

Bersoff, Donald N.: Law, education, and psychology. *Journal of School Psychology, 15:*191-199, 1977.

Brewer, Garry D. and Kakalik, James S.: *Handicapped Children — Strategies for Improving Services.* New York, McGraw-Hill Book Company, 1979.

Burgmeister, B. B. and Blum, L. H.: *Columbia Mental Maturity Scale,* 3rd ed. New York, The Psychological Corporation, 1972.

Chinn, Philip C.: The exceptional minority child: Issues and some answers. *Exceptional Children, 45:*532-536, 1979.

Cohen, Shirley, Semmes, Marilyn, and Guralnick, Michael J.: Public Law 94-142 and the education of preschool handicapped children. *Exceptional Children, 45:*279-284, 1979.

Conner, Frances D. and Cohen, Michael (Eds.): *Leadership Preparation for Education of Crippled and Other Health Impaired Multiply Handicapped Populations.* New York, Teachers College, Columbia University, 1973.

Cross, Lee and Goin, Kennith W.: *Identifying Handicapped Children: A Guide to Casefinding, Screening, Diagnosis, Assessment and Evaluation.* New York, Walker and Company, 1977.

Dinnage, Rosemary: *The Handicapped Child.* London, The National Bureau for Cooperation in Child Care, 1970.

Dunn, Lloyd M.: *Peabody Picture Vocabulary Test Manual.* Circle Pines, Minnesota, American Guidance Service, 1965.

Education of the Gifted and Talented. Report to Congress by the U. S. Commissioner of Education and background papers submitted to the U. S. Office of Education, Washington, D. C.: U. S. Government Printing Office, 1972.

Evans, DeEtte Britt; *Screening Guide for Exceptionalities.* Moravia, New York, Chronicle Guidance Publications, Inc., 1979.

Fallen, Nancy H. with McGovern, Jill E.: *Young Children with Special Needs.* Columbus, Ohio, Charles E. Merrill Publishing Company, 1978.

Forness, Steven R.: Behavioristic orientation to categorical labels. *Journal of School Psychology, 14:*90-95, 1976.

————: Implications of recent trends in educational labeling. *Journal of Learning Disabilities, 7:*445-449, 1974.

French, J. L.: *Manual: Pictorial Test of Intelligence.* Boston, Houghton Mifflin, 1964.

Gallagher, James J. and Bradley, Robert H.: Early identification of developmental difficulties. *Yearbook of the National Society for the Study of Education,* Part II. Chicago, University of Chicago Press, 1972.

Garrett, John E. and Brazil, N.: Categories used for identification and education of exceptional children. *Exceptional Children, 45:*291-292, 1979.

Gillung, Tom B. and Rucker, Chauncy N.: Labels and teacher expectations. *Exceptional Children, 43:*464-465, 1977.

Gowan, John Curtis: How to identify students for a gifted child program. *The Gifted Child Quarterly, 3:*260-263, 1975.

Hennon, Malinda A.: *Identifying Handicapped Children for Child Development Programs.* Atlanta, Humanics Press, 1977.

Hirshoren, Alfred et al.: The WISC-R and Hiskey-Nebraska Test with deaf children. *American Annals of the Deaf, 122:*392-394, 1977.

Hiskey, M. S.: *Hiskey-Nebraska Test of Learning Manual.* Lincoln, Nebraska, Union College Press, 1966.

Lathey, Jonathan: Assessing classroom environments and prioritizing goals for the severely retarded. *Exceptional Children, 45:*190-195, 1978.

Leiter, R. G.: *Examiner Manual for the Leiter International Performance Scale.* Chicago, Stoelting, 1969.

————: Caucasian norms for the Leiter International Performance Scale 1949. *Psychological Service Center Journal, 1:*136-138, 1949.

————: *General Instructions for the Leiter International Performance Scale.* Chicago, Stoelting, 1969.

————: Part I of the manual for the 1948 revision of the Leiter International Performance Scale. *Psychological Service Center Journal, 2:*1-72, 1959.

MacTurk, Robert and Neisworth, John T.: Norm-referenced and criterion-based measures with preschoolers. *Exceptional Children, 45:*34-39, 1978.

Magliocca, Larry A., Rinaldi, Robert T., Drew, John L., and Kunzelmann, Harold P.: Early identification of handicapped children through a frequency sampling technique. *Exceptional Children, 45:*415-420, 1977.

McDaniels, G.: Successful programs for young handicapped children. *Educational Horizons, 56:*26-33, 1977.

McNamara, Joan and McNamara, Bernard: *The Special Child Handbook.* New York, Hawthorn Books, Inc., 1977.

Meier, J.: *Screening and Assessment of Young Children at Developmental Risk,* DHEW Publication No. 73-90. Washington, D.C., President's Committee on Mental Retardation, 1973.

Mowder, Barbara A.: Assessing the bilingual handicapped student. *Psychology in Schools, 16:*43-50, 1979.

Newland, T. E.: *Manual for the Blind Learning Aptitude Test: Experimental Education.* Urbana, Illinois, T. Ernest Newland, 1969.

Prehm, Herbert J. and McDonald, James E.: The yet to be served — a perspective. *Exceptional Children, 45:*502-507, 1979.

Sharp, H. C.: A comparison of slow learner's scores on three individual intelligence scales. *Journal of Clinical Psychology, 13:*372-374, 1957.

————: A note on the reliability of the Leiter International Performance Scale 1948 revision. *Journal of Consulting Psychology, 22:*320, 1958.

Shurrager, H. C. and Shurrager, P. S.: *Haptic Intelligence Scale for the Adult Blind.* Chicago, Psychology Research, 1964.

Stoneman, Zolinda and Gibson, Sara: Situation influences on assessment performance. *Exceptional Children, 45:*166-169, 1978.

Thomas, Ellidee D. and Marshall, Melody J.: Clinical evaluation and coordination of services: An ecological model. *Exceptional Children, 44:*16-22, 1977.

Torrance, E. Paul: *Gifted Children in the Classroom.* New York, Macmillan, 1965.

Chapter 12

APPRAISAL FOR MINORITY STUDENTS

Imagine that you have just moved to a country called Blatka. You enroll Ted, your school-aged child, in the fourth grade with his age mates where he begins to learn the basics of the language.

One day a test examiner takes Ted into a strange room and begins to give him an intelligence test using the Blatkan language. This test is heavily laden with Blatkan culture and normed on a Blatkan population.

Two weeks later, the examiner calls you in to say that, because your child has scored two standard deviations below the mean, he is considered mentally retarded and will be so placed in accordance with the results of this test.

W HILE THE ABOVE is an imaginary situation, it is a reality that minority children are being tested and labeled in public schools. It is a fact that blacks and children with Spanish surnames are being "overlabeled" as mentally retarded, and that Anglo children are "underlabeled" (Mercer, 1977).

The appraisal of minority and culturally different children is one of the most burning issues in psychometrics today. As ethnic groups have organized and become militant in seeking recognition and status, a movement for fairness in examinations and school placement has heightened. The last two decades indicate a marked increase in research in assessing minority groups and a demand for examining the norming procedures on major standardized tests.

Traditional intelligence tests are said to be unfair to some minority group children in the sense that such children have fewer test-taking skills, are less motivated to take tests, may tend to have less rapport with the examiner, are less responsive to speed pressures, and are more willing to settle for lower levels of achievement (Clarizio, 1978, p. 107) than majority subjects.

Who are these minority children? The literature reports a diversity in defining and describing characteristics of these children. In 1971, The Council for Exceptional Children (CEC) Delegate Assembly provided the following definition:

A minority group is any group which because of racial or ethnic origin constitutes a distinctive and recognizable minority in our society. Pres-

256

ent examples of minority groups would include Blacks or Afro-Americans, American Indians, Mexican Americans, Puerto Ricans, and Oriental (Asian) Americans (CEC Handbook, 1978, p. 87).

Many of these minority children will have cultural differences that will distinguish them from other children to the extent that they require modifications both in appraisal and in instructional techniques. Other minority children may have become so acculturated and assimilated into the dominant culture that they could hardly be considered culturally different (Chinn, 1978, p. 107).

One question, for example, on a widely used intelligence test asks, "What is the thing to do when you cut your finger?" The intended response is that the child would seek some type of first aid, including a bandage or antiseptic. The item writer has assumed that all children have had training in first aid and have access to a well-equipped medicine cabinet at home. Some would ask if this is a fair assumption for children from culturally different backgrounds. Some children might answer, "Suck your finger until it stops bleeding," because of past successful experience when no other help was available. According to the test manual, this is an incorrect answer with no points awarded to the score, which will eventually yield a purported intelligence quotient.

Thus, tests are thought by some to be both unfair and invalid because they emphasize verbal intelligence, an ability that is more readily developed in middle-class environments than in lower-class surroundings. Since general information, arithmetic skills, and vocabulary — common areas tapped by intelligence tests — are affected by experience, content of this nature is often regarded as biased against children from culturally different backgrounds (Clarizio, 1978, p. 107).

It is impossible to cite incidence figures for minority children in public schools because of the wide variations in defining these children. It is somewhat less difficult to note the number of children who speak a language other than English as their primary language. The Bureau of the Census (1976) reports that over 8.8 percent of the population of persons who are four-years-old and older identify a language other than English as their primary language. This is a substantial number of children for whom appropriate appraisal and curricular intervention must be planned.

HISTORICAL ANTECEDENTS

The first major American intelligence test, the *Stanford-Binet Intelligence Scale,* was introduced by Lewis M. Terman in 1916. It was formulated to be used to test soldiers in World War I; after the war, the use of this and other like tests spread rapidly. A testing movement had begun that would bring the nation into the 1980s using millions of copies of standardized tests of academic ability and achievement in a given year. Noted one prominent psychologist (Holtzman, 1971), it is a rare individual indeed, especially among children and young adults in the United States, who has not taken a standardized mental-ability test — a test that probably has played a significant role in determining that person's place in society.

The 1916 *Stanford-Binet* maintained its dominance in the testing world for twenty years, until the 1937 revision. This revision retained the majority of the old test items but was extended downward to the two-year-old level and upward to the twenty-two-year-old level. As had the original revision, this version also omitted the use of black children in preparing its normalization data (Guthrie, 1976).

Terman, who served a term as president of the prestigious American Psychological Association (APA), originally standardized his test on a sample of 1,000 children and 400 adults — all white. However, he called for special education classes for black and brown children: "Children of this group should be segregated in special classes and be given instruction which is concrete and practical. They can not master abstractions" (1916, p. 92).

It is surprising that throughout this period of intelligence testing, few attempts were made to censure the tests or even to voice skepticism; Terman's views soared as words of great wisdom for aspiring neophyte psychologists. The mental testers, with the sanction of school officials, were given free rein to test any school-age children. Parental consent was unthought of during this period (Guthrie, 1976).

During these early years, few, if any, blacks or other minorities were represented among the psychologists and psychometrists who were writing and making observations of intelligence testing and the minority child. One early effort was that of Dr. Horace Mann Bond, professor at Langston University, who called for active participation against what he called: ". . . insidious propaganda . . . which seeks to demonstrate that the Negro is intellectually and physically incapable of assuming the dignities, rights and duties which evolve upon him as a member of modern society" (1924, p. 61).

In an article in 1927, Bond called the testing of black children a major indoor sport of white psychologists. To prove his case, he set up a testing program using black children from professional and middle-class homes. Using efforts to gain "fullest rapport" with these children, his results were surprising even to him: 63 percent made scores above 106; 47 percent equaled or exceeded IQs of 122; 26 percent made scores over 130. Bond concluded that these exceptional children "were not out of the ordinary . . . the same sort of a group could be selected in any Negro community, provided the same sociocultural background of the subjects existed." Bond's findings were a benchmark in pointing out the importance of the race of the examiner relative to that of the subject, of the rapport between examiner and subject, and social-class variables (Guthrie, 1976).

Besides the early efforts in intelligence testing, minority groups were given personality tests that placed stigmas on them. Guthrie (1976), in his history, reported that widespread personality stereotyping had categorized the Black American as easygoing and happy, the Mexican-American as hot-blooded and excitable, and the native American as stolid and savage. All American minority groups were generally classified as lazy.

Although there were researchers and practitioners who vociferously reacted to the stigmatization brought about as a result of the widespread testing of intelligence and personality, the testing movement continued to have wide public acceptance during the period from World War I until about 1955. At that time, widespread controversy began concerning the use of standardized tests for use in decision-making involving minority children. Laosa (1977), in reviewing the literature of the last two decades, found these principal criticisms of standardized assessment practices:

1. Standardized tests are biased and unfair to persons from cultural and socioeconomic minorities since most tests reflect largely white, middleclass values and attitudes, and they do not reflect the experiences and the linguistic, cognitive, and other cultural styles and values of minority group persons.
2. Standardized measurement procedures have fostered undemocratic attitudes by their use to form homogeneous classroom groups which severely limit educational, vocational, economic, and other societal opportunities.
3. Sometimes assessments are conducted incompetently by persons who do not understand the culture and language of minority group children and who thus are unable to elicit a level of performance which accurately reflects the child's underlying competence.
4. Testing practices foster expectations that may be damaging by contributing to their self-fulfilling prophecy which ensures low-level achievement for persons who score low on tests.
5. Standardized measurements rigidly shape school curricula and restrict educational change.
6. Norm-referenced measures are not useful for instructional purposes.
7. The limited scope of many standardized tests causes them to appraise only a part of the changes in children that schools should be interested in producing.
8. Standardized testing practices foster a view of human beings as having only innate and fixed abilities and characteristics.
9. Certain uses of tests represent an invasion of privacy.

JUDICIAL INFLUENCE

In looking over the historical antecedents to assessment of the minority child and the resulting judicial influence, one should begin with the landmark case of *Brown vs. Board of Education,* the 1954 Supreme Court decision. This decision was to bring in a new era, signaling the civil rights movement to call for voting rights, equal job opportunities, and equal access to public accommodations.

Schools were forced to consider the legality of educational practices that affected racial balance and the allocation of resources. Oakland and Matuszek (1977) have summarized litigation as it applies to assessment practices:

> Assessment practices have entered into the litigation process in at least three ways. Perhaps the majority of civil rights cases reviewed by federal courts affecting education have utilized test data to document the effects of alleged discriminatory practices. In these cases test data are entered as reliable and valid evidence. Another group of cases, however, directly challenges the use of certain psychological tests and assessment practices with minority group children as being discriminatory. For example, the legality of classifying children, of assigning them to special education classes or low-ability groups or excluding them from certain educational programs has been considered. A third set of cases considers the appropriateness of curricula to advance minority students' language, academic, social, and vocational development. While testing is not directly an issue raised by the plaintiffs or defendants, it becomes an issue in the resolution of cases (p. 38).

In the case of *Hobson vs. Hanson* (1967), the presiding judge concurred with the plaintiffs, who had argued that black and disadvantaged children were unfairly placed in lower academic tracks based on results of standardized tests. The courts ruled that the tracking system should be abolished and that this form of segregation was unlawful.

In 1968, plaintiffs for eleven Mexican-American children filed a complaint, *Arreola vs. Santa Ana Board of Education,* seeking an injunction against placement of minorities in special education classes without due process and parental involvement. This case was eventually settled out of court, but it set a precedent for similar litigation.

In 1971, a major class action suit, *Larry P. vs. Riles,* was filed on behalf of several black children in California who were allegedly placed in classes for mentally retarded wrongfully as a result of testing procedures that failed to recognize their unfamiliarity with white, middle-class culture and that ignored their language aptitudes and experiences. The court ordered that the school district not assign black students to the classes for mentally retarded by relying primarily on the results of IQ tests such as *WISC-R* and *Stanford-Binet.*

In 1974, in the case of *Lau vs. Nichols,* plaintiffs charged that the San Francisco schools had failed to provide special language instruction to a group of Chinese-speaking children. The U.S. Supreme Court ruled that California requires that a student attend school and insists on mastery of English as a requirement for graduation. "Under these state-imposed standards there is no equality of treatment merely by providing students with the same facilities, textbooks, teachers, and curriculum; for students who do not understand English are effectively foreclosed from any meaningful education." This ruling led to the development of a task force to set forth procedures to insure the proper use of assessment techniques with bilingual or non-English-speaking children.

During the seventies, several groups such as the National Education Association Task Force and the Association of Black Psychologists called for a moratorium on all standardized testing. Their positions basically stated that tests should not be used in any way that would lead to labeling and classifying of students. Several states and community school districts also passed legislation declaring moratoriums on standardized testing. Several other groups felt that the moratoriums were a step backward in assessment. Donald Ross Green (1973) presented those against the moratorium in stating:

> Perhaps there are places where ability tests are being so substantially misused and misinterpreted that a moratorium is in order. However, the justification of such a step assumes a level of stupidity and ignorance on the part of school teachers and school administrators that is hard to believe. Most of the people in our public schools are intelligent and fair minded people; those who are not will hurt children with or without tests (p. 53).

Assessment practices for minority children have been strongly influenced by legislation. The above-mentioned cases are simply representative of the last three decades of judicial influences that have affected the testing of minority and disadvantaged children. One of the most significant pieces of legislation in this century, P.L. 94-142, will be discussed later in this chapter.

CURRENT ISSUES

Several issues in the appraisal for minority students are currently being examined by professionals as well as parents and members of lay organizations.

Developing Examiner Sensitivity and Training

In assessing minority and disadvantaged children, the examiner must be unprejudiced, empathic, and objective. These characteristics, however, are not sufficient to obtain maximum results. The examiner should be well acquainted with the culture and verbal patterns of the child being tested. This type of sensitivity cannot be obtained by reading the literature; it almost necessitates a prolonged contact with the minority group being tested (Robb, Bernardoni, and Johnson, 1972).

Some would even argue that *only* a minority examiner can effectively assess and teach children of that particular minority group. The fallacy here is that mediocre and poor examiners would exist among the minorities as well as the nonminorities. Most assessment professionals feel that this is a highly questionable staffing practice. This would simply be another form of segregation with all its disadvantages. Also, it is highly unlikely that any teacher or examiner can become completely knowledgeable with respect to characteristics and needs of children of all minority groups (Chinn, 1979). Ideally, all examiners should possess specialized skills in language fluency, cultural awareness, and knowledge of the background of the children they assess. In reality, there are insufficient numbers of psychologists and assessment professionals who possess these skills.

Researchers have looked at the examiner's race and its effect on intelligence test performance. A few researchers have found that differences in racial membership do affect examiner/examinee relations. However, the greater research evidence indicates that this is usually not the case with regard to the performance of black or white participants on either individual or group administered intelligence tests (Clarizio, 1978).

The key factor, then, becomes the degree of sensitivity with which the examiner approaches the task of assessing the child who is culturally different.

> Sensitivity is one of the most desirable qualities in teachers of minority children. Sensitivity can be viewed in terms of responding, appreciating, and allowing differentness. Sensitivity suggests an open mind that is receptive to the cultural contributions each child in the class can offer. Sensitivity can develop through learning from the children, from numerous publications of cultural diversity, and by the individual's receptiveness to experiences in cultural diversity available in the community (Chinn, 1979, p. 535).

A few guidelines for developing this sensitivity include the following:

1. Learn everything you can about the history, culture, and language patterns in the predominant group(s) in your community. Be an active learner and take advantage of every situation to further your knowledge of these groups.
2. Observe the children both in the school, the community, and, when possible, their home through visitations.
3. Value each child and his/her uniqueness. Allow the children latitude to be themselves. Let the children know that you value cultural diversity.
4. Use action and words that will build the child's self-esteem and feelings of adequacy.
5. Begin each assessment or teaching period with an activity in which the children can experience success before moving into more difficult areas.

In summary, examiner sensitivity to the specific needs of culturally different children appears to override concerns such as examiner's race, culture, and language.

Public Law 94-142

Earlier in this chapter, legislation that has affected the assessment of minority children was discussed. Perhaps the most significant piece of legislation in regard to minority children of the past few decases has been Public Law 94-142 (1975), discussed in Chapter 11. While earlier laws had made provisions that testing and evaluation materials were to be selected and administered so as not to be racially or culturally discriminatory, P.L. 94-142 went a step further. It stated that no single assessment instrument may be used as a single criterion for placement in an educational setting and that testing must be in the child's native language or mode of communication.

This law further restricts federal funds to state or local education agencies that fail to employ nondiscriminatory testing and evaluation procedures. It stipulates that school authorities must fully inform the parents or guardian in the parents' or guardians' *native language,* unless it clearly is not feasible to do so. Parents and guardians in turn have the right to present complaints with respect to any matter relating to the identification, evaluation, or educational placement of the child.

Related Factors Such as Nutrition, Self-Concept, Motivation, Anxiety, and Language Skills

There appears to be an increasing amount of research relating nutrition to the acquisition of such skills as reading and computation. Many professional organizations, such as International Reading Association and others, have formed committees to study the effects of nutrition on learning. While there is a proliferation of research studies, particularly in the past two decades, on this topic, there are few conclusions. While researchers have generally found correlation between poor nutrition and lack of school achievement, it is difficult to partial out the effects of nutrition alone. Poor nutrition is so interrelated with other factors related to disadvantaged groups that it is difficult to single it out for research purposes. Most assessment professionals would agree, however, that children who are chronically hungry cannot give their best efforts in an appraisal situation and will, more than likely, score lower on tests than they would under optimal conditions.

Much has also been written about the correlation between poor self-concept and lowered mental ability among the disadvantaged and culturally different. One of the major difficulties in finding conclusive statements in this research is the wide variation in definitions of the term *self-concept.* It appears to be used interchangeably with the terms self-image, self-esteem, and self-perception, among others. Self-concept is generally thought to be the composite picture that people hold of themselves. This would include attitudes, thoughts, and beliefs. Children do not come into the world with a fixed self-concept, but form these attitudes, thoughts, and beliefs concerning themselves during the first few years of life. Many child psychologists and other professionals feel that the years between the ages of three to seven are the most crucial.

Children from minority homes often lack the environmental stimulation that leads to formation of healthy self-concepts. They may live in overcrowded conditions where parents must give their major efforts to solving such problems as unemployment, lack of financial security, and desertion by family members. Problems are compounded with these minority children face racial or ethnic discrimination in the neighborhood and in the schools. It is no wonder that children from such conditions come into appraisal situations apathetic and fearful, causing lowered performance on tests.

Traditional tests in appraisal are said to be unfair to minority group youth in the sense that such children have fewer test-taking skills, are less motivated to take tests, may have less rapport with the examiner, are less responsive to speed pressures, and are more willing to settle for lower levels of achievement (Clarizio, 1978). Middle-class children have more opportunity through preschool activities to internalize the motive to achieve than do children from disadvantaged or culturally different homes; thus, they come to school with a higher motivation to do well on tests.

Test anxiety is present in almost all testing situations, no matter how much preparation individuals may have had prior to coming to the situation. Performance on tests appears to be affected by how well individuals can withstand the accompanying pressure. Children from disadvantaged and minority backgrounds as a group experience higher test anxiety than do middle-class children. Test anxiety is heightened by fear of the examiner, fear of failure, fear of being punished for incorrect responses, and loss of status and esteem. The examiner must be aware of how stress is affecting the student he/she is assessing and take every measure possible to reduce the test anxiety and stress in order to obtain a more valid score.

According to Thorndike and Hagen (1977), environments that provide a less than adequate background for coping with tasks that intelligence tests present are characterized by some or all of the following:

1. A home language other than standard English — either a foreign language or a nonstandard dialect.
2. Home values that place little emphasis on book learning and getting ahead in school.
3. Home, social, and economic pressures that make it difficult for parents to provide a stable and supportive environment for the child.

4. Parents who have not learned how to function as teachers for their young children.
5. A shortage of the material possessions and lack of the economic stability that provides toys, books, and games as well as relaxed and comfortable living conditions.
6. A sense of separation and alienation from the dominant culture.

The examiner must be aware of the dominant language, nutritional factors, self-concept, motivation, and anxiety of the minority child in an attempt to come to valid decisions based on assessment techniques.

ALTERNATIVES TO TRADITIONAL TESTING

Although P.L. 94-142 states that the child must be tested in his primary mode of communication or native language, the law is left open to interpretation concerning the type of tests that should be given to the disadvantaged and minority child. While some assessment professionals would favor using standardized instruments that have been translated, most favor the use of alternatives to the traditional intelligence and achievement tests that are so heavily laden with verbal factors. Some of these alternatives will be discussed.

Culture-Fair Tests

With the growing dissatisfaction with traditional standardized tests came the culture-free and culture-fair testing movements. The culture-free test was an attempt to "strip the individual of his cultural veneer in order to reveal and expose his true and inherent abilities" (Samuda, 1975).

It soon became apparent that it was impossible to develop such a test and the emphasis shifted to the development of "culture-fair" tests. These tests attempt to minimize culturally specific details such as language, reading, and speed that affect test content and test-taking behaviors (Laosa, 1976). Researchers made an effort to select only those experiences, knowledge, and skills common to all cultures. The tests, then, are generally composed of nonverbal tasks requiring no verbal response on the part of the test-taker. Directions are given orally or in pantomime, and materials consist of pictures of commonly known objects, drawings, and diagrams.

Examples of culture-fair tests include the *Leiter International Performance Scale, Cattell's Culture-Fair Intelligence Tests,* and *Raven's Progressive Matrices.* While many researchers and practitioners are reporting satisfactory results using these tests with the culturally different and disadvantaged children, Oakland and Matuszek (1976) feel that the interest in culture-fair tests is on the decline. They report that psychologists are becoming more aware that one test cannot be universally appropriate to all individuals from diverse cultures.

Subjective Measures

Nontest assessment such as the use of behavior rating scales, observation, and anecdotal records are suggested as an alternative to formal standardized assessment. Most of these techniques are discussed elsewhere in this book, but they are especially important tools to the sensitive professional desiring to gain more information about the minority child. Cautions should be added at this point. Because the measures are subjective in nature, their validity is questionable. Many critics of the standardized tests feel that the use of subjective measures will benefit minority children; it must be pointed out that the same elements in standardized tests that may prove debilitating to these children might also be present in subjective measures. The importance of a well-trained, sensitive examiner again becomes the crucial point here.

Pluralistic Model of Assessment

Mercer and Lewis (1976) proposed the pluralistic model of assessment called SOMPA *(System of Multicultural Pluralistic Assessment)*. SOMPA draws from three assessment models — the medical model, the social system model, and the pluralistic mode. The underlying philosophy is that each model will provide a different and important perspective of the child's competencies. The medical model examines perceptual-motor development and health conditions that may influence classroom learning.

The social system model assesses the child's ability to adapt in family, school, and community roles. The pluralistic model measures critical aspects of the child's sociocultural background and yields a predictive source for learning potential.

The SOMPA appears to hold promise for the assessment of children from minority backgrounds. It has demonstrated effectiveness in identifying truly handicapped minority children and has been equally effective in keeping a large number of minority children from improper placement in special education classes.

Measures of the Environment

Environmental factors appear to influence greatly the school achievement of children of minority groups. In assessing the strengths and weaknesses of such children, it is important to develop an assessment procedure that will take into account environmental factors, including the classroom, the general school environment, the community, and the home. This idea of evaluating the environment certainly is not new; appraisal professionals have been attempting to measure it for years. However, there still appears to be no valid instrument to measure these determinants. Evaluation of the environment becomes a subjective evaluation on the part of the observer. This fact should not diminish efforts to obtain as much information as possible from the environment of the child.

In assessing the environment, and how conducive it is for later school achievement, particularly the home, the following questions might serve as a beginning point.

1. What language is used in the home?
2. What opportunities are provided for vocabulary development?
3. What language models does the child have in the home?
4. What opportunities are provided for learning?
5. Are books and newspapers available in the home or elsewhere?
6. Is the child provided with assistance in the facilitation of learning?
7. Is there a reward system for the child in intellectual development?

Criterion-Referenced Tests

A natural alternative to the traditional standardized tests are the newly emerging criterion-referenced tests, discussed in Chapters 3 and 11. They are also referred to as "objective based" tests because they attempt to measure the extent to which an individual has reached an objective or a standard. Behavioral objectives state the task against which student performance is measured. The tests are used to determine if a given student has reached a predetermined level of performance on a given skill or task. Although objective-based tests have been around for decades, the entire issue of criterion-referenced tests is both current and controversial. The idea of criterion-referenced tests is to compare an individual student with a standard rather than with another student.

Criterion-referenced tests appear to hold promise for the minority students in that they will be assessed in terms of strengths and weaknesses and not compared to other students. Inherent in the assumption that criterion-referenced tests hold promise is the fact that the tests are valid and reliable, but this assumption cannot be made in many cases. Criterion-referenced tests are often constructed by local school personnel who have little experience in test construction. The development of a good criterion-referenced test requires careful attention to certain essential questions, such as (1) Who determines the objectives? (2) Who sets the behavioral criterion levels? (3) Do test items accurately reflect the behavioral criteria? (4) What constitutes a sufficient sample of criterion levels? (5) Do the test scores obtained describe an individual's response pattern (Bohem, 1973, p. 120)?

Even with all its obvious weaknesses, however, the criterion-referenced test could hold some promising directions for assessing the minority child.

Emphasis on a Diagnostic-Prescriptive Model

Assessment of the minority child, as with any child, should always have as its goal an appropriate program of intervention to provide the child with optimum opportunity for achievement. Too often, files of diagnostic information are accumulated for a given child, and the child never seems to benefit from that information. Assessment must, therefore, be fused with intervention to be effective. This means that diagnosis must be continuous, and diagnosis must be interrelated with intervention. Diagnosis must reveal strengths upon which intervention can be built. The diagnostic-prescriptive model assumes that direct relationships exist between diagnosis and prescription or intervention and that each component strengthens and sheds light upon the other.

SELECTED INSTRUMENTS

Culture-Fair Tests

One of the most commonly used tests that purports to be culturally fair is the *Progressive Matrices Test* developed by Raven in 1938 with subsequent later versions. The test is composed of sixty designs, called matrices, each of which has a part missing. The subject is required to select the missing piece from among several alternatives. The text can be administered individually or in groups. The test is primarily nonverbal, instructions are kept to a minimum, and there are no time limits. For these reasons, it is considered to be appropriate to use with children from minority groups to obtain a "g" factor. The test yields a percentile score and not an IQ, although several researchers have found a relatively high correlation between scores on the *Progressive Matrices* and the full-scale WISC score.

The *Leiter International Performance Scale* (see Chapter 11) is another commonly used culture-fair test. This test also is untimed and conducted with a minimum of instructions. It may be given in pantomime to children who do not have facility with the language. A card containing pictures is shown on a frame. The child solves the problems presented on the frame by inserting wooden blocks into the proper place. The tasks include matching forms, pictures, shapes, and colors. Each problem begins with an easy task and becomes progressively more difficult. This test mainly assesses a child's ability to organize perceptions and discriminate among them. The test yields an MA and a ratio IQ. Many critics feel that the norms are questionable and that the test is not entirely culture-free since it tests such skills as the ability to tell time.

One of the first attempts to construct an intelligence test that was culturally free was the *Cattell Culture-Fair Intelligence Test,* published in 1944. A later revision in the 1950s was entitled *Culture-Fair Intelligence Test.*

The *Culture-Fair Intelligence Test,* published by the Institute for Personality and Ability Testing, was developed by R. B. Cattell and K. S. Cattell in order to measure learning potential without the influence of verbal fluency, cultural climate, and educational level. This nonverbal instrument consists of three scales: Scale 1 (for children aged 4-8 years and for adult retardates); Scale 2 (for subjects aged 8-14 years and for adults of average intelligence); and Scale 3 (for college students or others of high intelligence). Each scale has four subtests for measuring a person's ability to understand relationships among various items, such as designs or figures. The four *Culture-Fair* subtests are referred to as Series, Classification, Matrices, and Conditions. Scale 1 has additional subtests that sample cultural information and verbal comprehension. Scale 1 requires individual administration of some of the subtests. The reported reliability coefficients tend to be lower than for the verbal tests previously discussed. As for validity, the Cattells believe that they have demonstrated construct validity, and they have reported moderate positive correlations with other tests of mental ability. Sample items are shown in Figure 48.

Kidd (1962) has voiced a common criticism of this and other like tests: "a truly culture-free test appears to be an impossibility because even methods of manipulation of material objects are culturally determined."

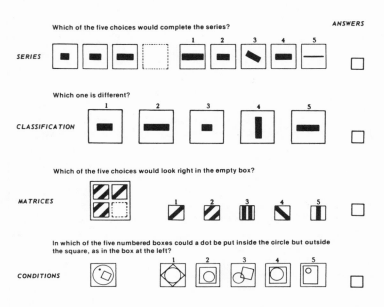

Figure 48. Sample items from the *Culture Fair Intelligence Test.*

Bilingual Tests

Many standardized tests have been translated into other languages in an attempt to assess more accurately the child whose primary language is not English. This method has numerous disadvantages. Merely translating a test into another language does not remove the cultural biases inherent in the test. Also, any translation would have limited usage because of numerous dialectical differences within the language. Also, children may not read fluently in the language in which they speak predominantly. Translating existing standardized tests has left much to be desired in the movement to accommodate the culturally different child.

In working with children who speak two or more languages, it often becomes necessary to assess the children to determine their dominant language — the language in which they are best able to learn. An example of such a test, and there are dozens of them, is the *Pictorial Test of Bilingualism and Language Dominance* (1975) by Nelson, Fellner, and Norell, published by South Texas Testing Service in Corpus Christi, Texas. The test is designed to provide an objective measure of a child's language development in English and Spanish and has additional procedures to determine the favored or predominant language.

A complete annotated bibliography of language dominance measures may be found in the appendix of Oakland's book (1977) on assessment of minority children.

Tests for Gifted Minority Students

Just as minority children are often misclassified as children with learning disabilities or mental retardation because of the difficulties encountered in appraisal due to language differences, so minority children may be overlooked for classes for gifted and talented. In recent years, much attention has been given to both assessment and programming for the gifted and talented child. This emphasis has waxed and waned through the years, but the gifted children appear to be back in the limelight.

It is particularly important for school personnel to be committed to identifying and providing curricular needs for the minority gifted and talented child. Torrance has suggested using instruments that appear to lack cultural bias in assessing this group of children. He has suggested the *Torrance Tests of Creative Thinking* and *Taylor and Ellison's Alpha Biographical Inventory.*

Torrance also suggested nontest appraisal for use in identifying the minority gifted child. He has developed a list of eighteen creative behaviors, which are sets of characteristics he feels are beneficial in identifying strengths and giftedness among culturally different students. He further has suggested that teachers and appraisal personnel attempt to develop a sensitivity that will aid them in observing, with a high degree of awareness, giftedness among the disadvantaged and culturally different.

SUMMARY

Controversy has always surrounded the appraisal of strengths and weaknesses of children. The controversy is compounded when these children are from a culturally different or minority background. The last three decades have been fraught with charges, countercharges, and litigation regarding the appraisal of minority children. Recent legislation has attempted to insure that children are tested in their own language and that more than one measurement criterion be used in determining placement for these children.

Alternatives to traditional norm-referenced testing for the minority children have included culture-fair tests, subjective measures, pluralistic assessment models, criterion-referenced tests, and emphasis on descriptive and prescriptive appraisal. Perhaps the most critical element in the appraisal of minority children is a well-trained sensitive examiner who is able to use nontest assessment to determine the curricular needs of this particular group of children.

REFERENCES

Bohem, A. E.: Criterion-referenced assessment for the teacher. *Teachers College Record, 75:*117-126, 1973.

Bond, Horace Mann: Intelligence tests and propaganda. *The Crisis, 28:*61, 1924.

Chinn, Philip C.: The exceptional minority child; issues and some answers. *Exceptional Children, 7:*532-536, 1979.

Clarizio, Harvey: Nonbiased assessment of minority group children. *Measurement and Evaluation in Guidance, 11:*106-113, 1978.

Council for Exceptional Children: *CEC Handbook.* Reston, Virginia, The Council for Exceptional Children, February, 1978.

Green, Donald Ross: Experts answer your questions on testing. *The Instructor,* 1973.

Guthrie, Robert B.: *Even the Rat Was White, A Historical View of Psychology.* New York, Harper and Row, Publishers, 1976.

Holtzman, W. H.: The changing world of mental measurement and its social significance. *American Psychologist, 26:*546-553, 1971.

Kidd, A. H.: The culture-fair aspects of Cattell's test of g: Culture free. *Journal of Genetic Psychology, 101:*343-362, 1962.

Laosa, Luis M.: Nonbiased assessment of children's abilities: Historical antecedents and current issues. *Psychological and Educational Assessment of Minority Children.* New York, Bruner, Mazel Publishers, 1977.

Mercer, Jane: *System of Multicultural Pluralistic Assessment, Conceptual, and Technical Manual.* Project IMPART, 1977.

Mercer, Jane and Lewis, J. F.: A system of multicultural pluralistic assessments (SOMPA). *With Bias Toward None.* Lexington, Kentucky, Coordinating Office of Regional Resource Centers, 1976.

Mowder, Barbara A.: Assessing the bilingual handicapped child. *Psychology in Schools, 16:*43-50, 1979.

Oakland, Thomas (Ed.): *Psychological and Educational Assessment of Minority Children.* New York, Bruner Publishers, 1977.

Oakland, Thomas and Matuszek, Paula: Using tests in nondiscriminatory assessment. *Psychological and Educational Assessment of Minority Children.* New York, Bruner, Mazel Publishers, 1977.

Robb, George P., Bernardoni, L. D., and Johnson, Ray W.: *Assessment of Individual Mental Ability.* New York, Harper and Row, 1972.

Samuda, Ronald J.: *Psychological Testing of American Minorities: Issues and Consequences.* New York, Dodd, Mead, 1975.

Terman, Lewis: *The Measurement of Intelligence.* Boston, Houghton Mifflin, 1916.

Thorndike, R. and Hagen, E.: *Measurement and Evaluation in Psychology and Education,* 4th ed. New York, Wiley and Sons, 1977.

Torrance, E. Paul: *Discovery and Nurturance of Giftedness in the Culturally Different.* Reston, Virginia, The Council for Exceptional Children, 1977.

Chapter 13

SYNTHESIZING AND UTILIZING APPRAISAL DATA

THROUGHOUT THE CHAPTERS of this book, the collection of every possible kind of data has been discussed. Through the use of appraisal instruments as well as the collection of nontest data, it is possible to accumulate enough information on a given student to write a complete biography. A look in the files of almost any school office will reveal the proliferation of data available on students in their cumulative folders, which follow them from kindergarten through high school graduation.

Most school districts have prescribed periods of survey and diagnostic testing throughout the school year, including achievement tests, interest inventories, personality scales, aptitude tests, visual and auditory screening instruments, readiness tests for various content areas, and even periods in which teachers are asked to write anecdotal comments regarding social and emotional growth of each student.

While the last decade has brought a refinement in the collection of appraisal data, there appears to be a widespread weakness in the synthesis and utilization of these various data. With more sophisticated methods of appraisal and the high level of training of appraisal experts, efforts may be fragmented. For example, it is possible that several individuals may be responsible for collecting the different segments of appraisal data. The school nurse may conduct the visual and auditory screening tests; the school psychologist may administer the aptitude and personality tests; subject-area teachers may be responsible for giving the achievement tests. It is possible that all this information may end up in the student's folder in bits and pieces, lacking synthesis and thus lacking utilization in making decisions concerning students' instructional programs and career goals. The appraisal personnel must work in concert toward the goals of synthesizing and utilizing all data collected to the benefit of the students, parents, and the school program.

GENERALLY ACCEPTED PRINCIPLES

In synthesizing and utilizing appraisal data, there are several principles that are generally accepted by teachers, counselors, and other appraisal professionals.

273

Appraisal Is Continuous

While there may be intensive periods of appraisal in a given school, the appraisal process really never ends. The process is cyclical in nature, followed by the establishing of objectives and teaching strategies. Appraisal continues throughout the establishment of objectives and teaching strategies. As more information is gleaned, objectives may change slightly, which in turn will alter the teaching strategies.

There are two schools of thought concerning how much appraisal data should be obtained before objectives are written and teaching strategies begun. Many believe that as much information as possible should be gathered on a given student before intervention or remediation is begun. After a period of appraising aptitude, achievement, physical abilities, and social and emotional background, school personnel will then take this information, synthesize it, write objectives or an individual educational plan (IEP), and then begin the educational program. Those who adhere to this school of thought believe that much information is necessary before decisions that affect the student's future are made.

Others believe that intensive appraisal may intimidate the student and magnify his weaknesses, thus lowering self-concept. Many students, especially those who are burdened by several years of academic failure, become test resistant. They enter into a testing situation with extreme anxiety, which may alter the test results. Professionals who exercise this caution may favor limiting the period of appraisal. They may favor the use of nontest appraisal techniques (see Chapter 5) in a nonthreatening situation to obtain enough information to begin intervention strategies. The strategies would provide for early success for the student and would become increasingly more difficult. In the meantime, appraisal would occur periodically as the student builds self-confidence.

Regardless of whether appraisal is intensive in the beginning or obtained in increments, it should be continuous throughout the school year. The plan of obtaining appraisal information should be flexible enough to take into account the changing nature of the students, their home environment, and programmatic decisions at school. The maturation process of students throughout the year mandates a continuous appraisal of their progress or lack of achievement in certain areas.

Appraisal Is Integrated with Programming

The goal of all appraisal efforts should be the improvement of decision making concerning students' educational and career goals. Appraisal is never an end in itself. While it is time-consuming, it saves time in the long run by helping school personnel to avoid trial and error methods of instruction and guidance. It helps to avoid unnecessary instruction and practices.

How much appraisal data should be collected? Only enough to make sound decisions and to verify those decisions. There is a tendency to obtain far more information than can possibly be used. This information may be stored in pupils' cumulative folders, never to be seen again. Each school district should develop a philosophy of appraisal. The philosophy should attempt to answer such questions as Who should be tested? For what purposes? How will data be utilized? Who will profit from the data collected? The most important part of the philosophy will pertain to the utilization of the data.

In some school districts, different personnel are assigned the tasks of obtaining the appraisal data and utilizing the data. There is a danger in this practice in that much of the information may not be used in making programmatic decisions. For example, an educational diagnostician who is responsible only for collecting appraisal information may have a tendency to obtain such a profusion of data that much of the information will go unused. On the other hand, the personnel responsible for writing educational objectives and teaching strategies may have missed much nontest assessment and observation by not being involved in the obtaining of appraisal data. There are some advantages to having the personnel who are responsible for obtaining the appraisal data write, or at least assist in writing, the educational plans. However the task is accomplished, there is a need for much cooperation among school personnel in moving from appraisal to actual instruction and classroom strategies. Appraisal that is not integrated with programming is an abominable waste of time, money, and effort.

Appraisal Is Personalized

While it may be economically sound, from both time and money points of view, to give every student the same battery of tests, the practice is educationally unsound. Each student brings to school different needs, backgrounds, and goals. For this reason, it becomes necessary to personalize the battery of tests to obtain information that will benefit the student. In planning a school appraisal program, it may be feasible to include a core of tests every student will take. For example, the achievement and aptitude tests may be necessary for all students. The test battery will vary as individual needs are considered. If a child has a suspected visual problem, special tests of visual acuity and perception should be given as a part of his battery. If initial appraisal data indicate a possible auditory problem, tests of auditory acuity and perception should become a part of the battery. If there are suspected problems in motivation, perhaps an interest inventory should be added.

Highly specialized tests are available for most types of exceptionality (see Chapter 11). The astute appraisal expert will carefully plan the test battery of each student, personalizing it to meet the individual needs of that student.

Appraisal that is personalized can be very beneficial in assisting personnel in making decisions for programming and for guidance purposes. Appraisal that is personalized may lead to referrals to the school nurse, to a pediatrician, an eye or ear specialist, a neurologist, the school psychologist, or other professionals, who will in turn assist in sound decision making.

Appraisal Leads to Diagnostic Hypotheses

Regardless of personal or district philosophies concerning appraisal, there comes a time when formal appraisal must cease and the existing data must be acted upon. It becomes necessary to take the collected information and synthesize it. The bits and pieces of diagnostic information must be melded into a meaningful whole in order that programmatic or guidance decisions may be made. This process can be initiated with the formation of a *diagnostic hypothesis*.

A diagnostic hypothesis is an assumption or theory concerning a given student's compilation of information. This assumption or theory allows the appraisal personnel to seek specific intervention or remediation programming for the child. Since hypotheses are unproven, appraisal continues during the implementation phase of instruction in an attempt to evaluate the efficacy of the hypotheses. After a period of time and evaluation, the diagnostic hypotheses may be retained as valid, or they may prove untenable and rejected in favor of new hypotheses.

In approaching a diagnostic hypothesis, it is necessary to take all existing data and carefully examine them for areas in which bits and pieces begin to reinforce each other. Conversely, the examiner must look for contradicting bits of information. At this point of examining data, it may become necessary to give a few additional tests in an attempt to account for discrepancies or contradictions. The examiner should be cautioned here, however, to realize that there will always exist these contradicting bits of data. This is due, in part, to varying testing conditions, variations in students' attitudes toward test-taking from one period of time to the next, and the variable validity and reliability of the specific tests.

The synthesized data will begin to yield student strengths and weaknesses as they are analyzed. Every student tested, no matter how handicapped or how retarded in achievement, will have strengths, and these strengths should be identified early. Although Johnny may have a history of failure, he will have some accomplishments. It becomes necessary to look at these accomplishments and ask "How has he learned what he *has* learned?" After a base of strengths has been identified, the weaknesses may be enumerated from the data.

The formulation and utilization of a diagnostic hypothesis is necessary to move from the state of data collection to data utilization. The hypothesis will be retained, altered, or rejected as programming is begun and new appraisal data accrued.

USES OF APPRAISAL DATA

Appraisal data may be used in a variety of ways. The collection of data is not an end in itself; it is a means to the end of sound decision making. This decision making relates to the students' instructional programs, guidance, counseling, and planning for the future.

Assisting in Making Programmatic Decisions

As previously mentioned, one of the most common uses of data is assisting school personnel in making programmatic decisions concerning students. In Chapter 11, the IEP (individualized educational plan) was discussed. This plan must be on file for every student enrolled in special education. The plan includes the educational objectives and teaching/learning strategies that will best suit the child's specific needs. The plan can be written only after a period of intensive appraisal to determine the student's strengths and weaknesses. By studying appraisal data, it is possible to develop strategies that may help the students come closer to the goal of reaching their potentials.

Besides assisting individual students, school personnel can use appraisal data as a base for total curriculum change when it is necessary. For example, if the students of an entire district score poorly on mathematics tests, the curriculum committee may decide on the basis of this fact and other supporting data to increase the emphasis on the reading and solution of math problems. All programmatic decisions should be based on substantial and significant data gained through the appraisal process.

Evaluating Teaching Strategies

Besides using data to make programmatic decisions concerning groups and individuals, appraisal data can and should be used to help in the evaluation of teaching strategies. As new techniques are tried, an appropriate plan of evaluation should be built in for determining the efficacy of such strategies and programs. New strategies may be field-tested with small groups, using preappraisal and postappraisal data before implementing the strategies on a district-wide basis.

Reporting to Students and Parents

A major responsibility of school personnel concerns marking and reporting practices. In most school situations, marks must be assigned and reported to the students and to their parents.

According to Remmers, Gage, and Rummel (1960), the specific purposes of marking systems are to provide a basis for the following:

1. information for parents on pupil status or progress
2. promotion and graduation
3. motivation of school work
4. guidance of learning
5. guidance of educational and vocational planning
6. guidance of personal development
7. honors
8. participation in many school activities
9. reports and recommendations to future employers
10. data for curriculum studies
11. reports to a school the pupil may attend later.

In the use of any system of preparing reports for purposes listed above, appraisal data will be utilized.

In reporting to students and parents, there are certain principles that must be followed. Lien (1967) lists seven such principles (which were covered to some extent in Chapter 4):

1. Make sure that both you and the person to whom you are interpreting the test results have a clear, immediate goal in mind that will serve as a reason for the interpretation. This goal might be the possible assignment of a student to a special class or a recommendation for promotion or retention.
2. Avoid the use of specific scores whenever possible. Since raw scores are of little value in interpretation, it becomes necessary for the parent or student to have a point of reference. This might be grade or age equivalents, percentile ranks, or stanines.
3. Never discuss the implication of scores in terms of absolute answers. The teacher or counselor should constantly remind himself that all scores are subject to error and no single score is precise enough to make projections in absolute terms.
4. Try to concentrate on increasing understanding rather than posing as an expert. This is a time for building mutual understanding. The use of technical terms and educational jargon may be a detriment to the establishing of this rapport.
5. Remember, understanding and acceptance are not synonymous terms. The teacher or counselor, after interpreting the data, should allow the student or parent time to question and express any doubts. Both parents and students should be encouraged to express their true feelings in the conference.
6. Never compare one student with another particular student. Remember that test results are confidential between the school and the parent. Stress the idea of uniqueness and individuality, rather than comparing one student with another.
7. After the tests have been interpreted, discussion between the school personnel and the student and/or parents should be continued.

Follow-up activities should be planned. Just as appraisal is continuous, so should be the dialogue between the school and the home.

EXAMPLES OF DATA SYNTHESIS

Two examples of data synthesis will be presented in order to show how data may be synthesized for use by school personnel. The first example involves an elementary school male who was referred to appraisal personnel because of suspected learning disabilities. The second case involves a young woman, high school age, who has been referred to the school counselor for a vocational-choice problem. The two cases differ in format because of the purpose of the study and the availability of the data pertaining to the individual being studied.

Case One

Name: Bobby Jones
Age: Eleven years, three months

STATEMENT OF THE PROBLEM

Bobby's mother, Mrs. Jones, reported that Bobby has had learning difficulties that manifested themselves particularly in the area of reading. She stated that she has been aware of this difficulty in school since the latter part of his first grade year. He was seen in April of this year by his school counselor, who suggested that Bobby have an in-depth appraisal.

FAMILY AND ENVIRONMENT

Bobby lives with both natural parents, two older brothers, thirteen and twelve, and a sister who is seven. Both parents completed the eleventh grade. The father is a farmer and the mother is a housewife. The three sons actively participate in the running of the farm, rotating chores. According to Mrs. Jones, Bobby enjoys farm life and hopes to have his own farm some day. The relationship among family members is reported as "good." Mrs. Jones indicated that Bobby is closest to his oldest brother, but she described much interaction among all the children.

PERINATAL HISTORY

The mother reported a normal pregnancy and delivery with Bobby.

MEDICAL HISTORY

Bobby has had mumps, measles, and chicken pox, but without complications. According to Mrs. Jones, when Bobby was six years old, a bone disorder was discovered by an orthopedic surgeon. Bobby was confined to crutches for two years, but since his parents were unable to restrict Bobby completely from using his leg, surgery (a bone graft in the femur bone) was performed. Mrs. Jones reported Bobby's having surgery in May of 1979. He was in a body cast from May to July of that year, then was confined to crutches until the following September. She reported that the femur bone is still in a healing or ossification process.

EDUCATIONAL HISTORY

Bobby attended preschool for one year at age six. He entered first grade at age seven, and he was retained in first grade. After repeating this year, he was promoted to second grade. According to the mother, he became very unhappy and refused to attempt any second grade work. The mother reported that after eight weeks, Bobby had made no progress in school work or in his attitude toward school. She stated that when he was questioned by teachers and the principal, he said that he "belonged in third grade with the third graders" who were his own age. The decision was made to let him "try third grade for six weeks," and although the work seemed difficult for Bobby, his teachers felt it would do more damage to place him back in second grade, so he was allowed to remain in third grade.

The mother said that when Bobby was eight years old he was tutored for a year in a phonics reading program. The family purchased records to work on the phonics, but Mrs. Jones said the records helped very little, if any, in strengthening his phonological skills. The mother is very pleased with the present school program; she said that the curriculum is flexible, and each student is allowed to progress at his own level in areas of math and reading. She indicated his best subject is math, and his weakest area is reading.

SOCIAL AND EMOTIONAL DEVELOPMENT

The mother described Bobby as having many friends. She said he is an active part of the family unit and appears to enjoy every aspect of their home life. She indicated that he is protective of his younger sister and that he seeks older boys his brothers' ages for friends.

MOTOR DEVELOPMENT

The mother reported that Bobby crawled at eight months, walked and began self-feeding at eleven months. She said that his motor development was very good, in spite of the leg surgery and long periods of confinement. According to Mrs. Jones, Bobby has always been active, even climbing trees and riding a bicycle when he was in a cast. He now plays PeeWee football.

SPEECH AND LANGUAGE DEVELOPMENT

The mother described Bobby's speech development as "normal," saying that he had no particular difficulties with word or sound production. She said that he began using conversational speech at twenty months, and that his speech developed at much the same ages as that of her other children.

She reported that Bobby is effective in communicating verbally. His test performance in any academic area is greatly enhanced when he is given an oral test; usually a written test presents such a problem to him that he scarcely gets it read in the allotted testing time.

TEST RESULTS

Sensory Acuity:

> *Keystone Visual Survey Test* — within normal limits on all fourteen subtests
>
> *Pure-tone Audiometer* — indicated that bilateral hearing sensitivity was within normal limits

Mental Ability Test:

Wechsler Intelligence Scale for Children-Revised

Verbal Tests		Performance Tests	
Information	8	Picture Completion	11
Similarities	8	Picture Arrangement	16
Arithmetic	4	Block Design	11
Vocabulary	7	Object Assembly	12
Comprehension	10	Coding	10
(Digit Span)	(7)		
Verbal Score	84	Performance Score	114

Full Scale Score 97

Performance Tests:

Wide Range Achievement Test

Reading	1.9 (grade)	76 (standard)	5 (percentile)
Spelling	2.2	78	7
Arithmetic	4.2	96	39

Informal Reading Test: Bobby is reading approximately two years below his present grade placement. His apparent strengths are initial letter sounds, blending initial letter sounds, auditory blending, and cooperative behavior. His apparent weaknesses are reversals, comprehensive, sight vocabulary, and oral reading.

Visual Motor Test: The *Bender Gestalt* revealed a developmental age of approximately 10.10, which is within normal limits.

Social Test: The *School Apperception Method* was given to Bobby. On this test, he exhibited anxiety about his poor reading skills in school.

SUMMARY

Bobby is an eleven-year-old boy of average intellectual abilities. Therefore, any problems he is currently having in school should not be due to intellectual factors. He has the capacity to be performing on grade level. He is performing almost two years below his present grade placement in reading and is showing some difficulty in the area of spelling. He does not show a learning disability in mathematics.

During the testing situation, he demonstrated deficiencies in ability to concentrate on a given verbal task, a possible auditory channel deficiency, and an anxiety in test situations. He shows no problems in visual or auditory acuity according to the screening devices. The discrepancy of thirty points between the verbal and performance scores on the WISC-R is usually indicative of a specific learning disability in the area of language.

RECOMMENDATIONS

A. To the School:
    1. Bobby would probably profit from as much individual instruction as is possible. He should understand at all times what is expected of him. Directions should be stated simply and clearly.
    2. Because of his distractibility, he should be put into a highly structured environment where there is a reduction of extraneous auditory and visual stimuli.
    3. Oral or informal testing would be of greater value and more appropriate, because of his feelings of anxiety and his poor reading ability, than regular testing.
    4. Enrichment activities should be made available to him in all areas of the stated strengths and weaknesses.
    5. Positive reinforcement should be given whenever possible to encourage and motivate him.
    6. Reading instruction should be given visually as much as possible. Because of Bobby's auditory deficiency, it will be difficult for him to learn to read using a pure phonetic approach.
B. To the Parents:
    1. Bobby should be given as much encouragement as possible for his achievements at home and school.
    2. He should be encouraged to discuss activities that interest him, as he needs much practice in verbal communication.
    3. Provision should be made to find games in which the entire family may participate in order to improve his vocabulary development.
    4. Recreational reading for Bobby would be a strength builder. Comic books, cartoons in magazines, and easy-read books would all improve his oral reading as well as build up his desire to read.

Case Two

Name: Mary Ann Smith
Age: Seventeen years, ten months

STATEMENT OF THE PROBLEM

Mary Ann, a high school student who is nearing completion of her senior year, has sought the help of a school counselor in making a decision about a vocational choice. She has listed three choices of occupations, but wonders whether any of the three is a realistic choice that she will eventually find satisfying. The three choices are (1) Engineer, (2) Secretary, and (3) Insurance Agent. Analysis and integration of the appraisal data available may reveal whether any or all of the initial occupational choices are appropriate for Mary Ann. The analysis will begin with interests, even though they are not the best predictors of success. Interests mainly provide a convenient starting point in the process of examining appraisal data.

INTEREST

Mary Ann's Kuder scores (Vocational Form C), in Table XVI, suggest very strong interest on the Persuasive scale and strong interest on the Social Service scale. Low interests are indicated for the Artistic, Mechanical, and Musical scales. The combination of high interest on the Persuasive and Social Service scales, according to the manual, suggests the following occupations for consideration:

1. High School Teacher of Social Studies
2. Personnel and Employment Manager
3. Vocational Counselor
4. Employment and Personnel Relations Worker
5. Personnel Clerk; Personnel Worker (not manager)
6. Telephone Operator
7. Insurance Salesman
8. Stocks and Bonds Salesman

In considering Kuder scores, one must be mindful of the fact that Kuder C does not permit a person's profile to indicate all high or low interest on all scales. If some scale scores are high, others will have to be low. This is not true of the Strong-Campbell and other interest inventories. Thus, one must be careful in interpreting Kuder scores, for areas of high interest or low interest may not be indicated when they should be.

The *Strong-Campbell Interest Inventory* data are also shown in Table XVI. Mary Ann's special scale score of 20 for Academic Orientation is very low and indicates that the subject has little interest in academic pursuits. At this point one would wonder whether she would be satis-

TABLE XVI
INTEREST INVENTORY RESULTS

Kuder Interest Inventory Data

Scale	PR	Result
Outdoor	44	
Mechanical	25	Low Score
Computational	66	
Scientific	47	
Persuasive	95	Very High Score
Artistic	12	Very Low Score
Literary	55	
Musical	4	Very Low Score
Social Service	84	High Score
Clerical	45	

Strong-Campbell Interest Inventory Data
Occupational Themes

Theme	Score	Results
Realistic	27	Very Low Score
Investigative	34	Low Score
Artistic	32	Very Low Score
Social	49	Average Score
Enterprising	44	Average Score
Conventional	48	Average Score

Special Scales
Academic Orientation 20
Introversion — Extroversion 44

Basic Interest Scales

Theme	Scale	Score	Results
R	Agriculture	36	Low
R	Nature	24	Very Low
R	Adventure	38	Low
R	Military Activity	41	Low
R	Mechanical	30	Very Low
I	Science	33	Very Low
I	Mathematics	37	Low
I	Medical Science	46	Average
I	Medical Service	38	Low
A	Music	36	Low
A	Art	34	Very Low
A	Writing	33	Very Low
S	Teaching	40	Low
S	Social Service	49	Average
S	Athletics	55	Average
S	Domestic Arts	34	Very Low
S	Religious Activities	50	Average
E	Public Speaking	51	Average
E	Law/Politics	45	Average
E	Merchandising	40	Low
E	Sales	48	Average
E	Business Mgmt.	46	Average
C	Office Practices	48	Average

Occupational Scales

Very Dissimilar	Dissimilar	Average	Similar	Very Similar
Occup. Therapist	Rad. Tech.	Instrum. Assembl.	Beautician	(None)
Engineer	Medical Tech.	Army Officer		
Chemist	Pharmacist	Phys. Ed. Teacher		
Dietician	Dentist	Dental Hygienist		
Computer Prog.	Phys. Therapist	Math/Sci. Teacher		
Physicist	Mathematician	Optometrist		
Art Teacher	Veterinarian	College Prof.		
Int. Decorator	Physician	Speech Pathol.		
Librarian	Psychologist	Advert. Exec.		
Dir. of Christian		Artist		
Ed		Musician		
Home Ec.		Entertainer		
Teacher		Lang. Teacher		
		Reporter		
		YWCA Staff		
		Elem. Teacher		
		Recreation Leader		
		Guidance Couns.		
		Flight Attend.		
		Life Ins. Agent		
		Lawyer		
		Buyer		
		Banker		
		Credit Mgr.		
		Secretary		
		Dental Assist.		

fied with college work, and yet she has had good marks in school. The Introversion-Extroversion score of 44 indicates that Mary Ann probably is comfortable in social settings. Average scores are shown for three General Occupation Themes: Social, Enterprising, and Conventional. There are no high theme scores, but there is a very low Realistic Theme score, which may mean that Mary Ann tends to dislike outdoor, technical, and mechanical activities. The Kuder profile seems to corroborate this. There are no significantly high Basic Interest Scale scores, but there are several very low scores: Nature, Mechanical, Science, Art, Writing, and Domestic Arts, for example. These scores are in general agreement with the Kuder scale scores.

Turning to the Occupational Scales, one can see that Mary Ann's profile shows interests that are *similar* to one occupation: Beautician. Very dissimilar interests are apparent for Occupational Therapist, Engineer, Chemist, Dietician, Computer Programmer, Physicist, Art Teacher, Interior Decorator, Librarian, Director of Christian Education, and Home Economics Teacher.

Aptitudes

Mental ability and aptitude test scores are presented next in this analysis (Table XVII). The DAT results indicate that Mary Ann has

TABLE XVII
ACADEMIC APTITUDE AND ACHIEVEMENT DATA

Aptitude Data

Test	Percentile Rank
DAT Battery (Junior Year)	
Verbal Reasoning	55
Numerical Ability	70
VR + NA	60
Abstract Reasoning	35
Clerical Sp. and Acc.	99
Mechanical Reasoning	45
Space Relations	50
Spelling	90
Language Usage	75
SFTAA (Grade 11-5)	Language: 40 Non-Language: 58 Total: 48
PSAT/NMSQT (Junior Year)	Verbal: 44 Math: 70 Selection Index for College Bound: 23

Achievement Data
School Marks

Grade 9		Grade 10		Grade 11	
Drama	B	Typing	A B B	Gen. Office	A A A
Algebra	C C C	Spanish	B B B	Algebra	B C B
English	B B B	Geometry	B C B	History	B C B
Spanish	B B B	Phys. Science	B C B	English	B B B
Health	B B	English	B B A	Biology	B B A

California Achievement Test Results
(Grade 10-5)

Test	Percentile Rank
Reading Vocabulary	72
Reading Comprehension	56
Total Reading	64
Spelling	81
Language Mechanics	91
Language Expression	90
Total Language	92
Math Computations	84
Math Concepts and Applications	82
Total Mathematics	84
Total Battery	83
Reference Skills	94

above-average scores for Verbal Reasoning, Numerical Ability, and VR + NA; high scores for Spelling and Language Usage; and an exceptionally high score for Clerical Speed and Accuracy. Her Abstract Reasoning and Mechanical Reasoning scores are somewhat low.

Mary Ann's performance on the *Short Form Test of Academic Aptitude* (Table XVII) is generally below her performance on the DAT when Language, Non-Language, and Total scores are compared with DAT scores for Verbal Reasoning, Numerical Ability, and VR + NA. Even when one considers the fact that the SFTAA and DAT are two different instruments, and that they should not be expected to yield identical scores, there still is more discrepancy than should be expected for these particular subtests. The PSAT/NMSQT Verbal score (44) is considerably below the DAT Verbal Ability score (55), but the Math score (70) agrees perfectly with the NA score (70). Mary Ann's Selection Index score of 23 is quite low, suggesting low potential for college work. Her college-work potential looks much better, however, when her record of academic achievement (Table XVII) is considered.

ACHIEVEMENT

In general, this student has a good academic record when grades and achievement tests scores are considered (Table XVIII). Her science and mathematics marks are lower than her marks in Spanish, typing, and general office courses, but her overall marks do not indicate any serious difficulty with school work. The results for the *California Achievement Tests* also indicate a high level of academic achievement. Her reading scores, while low when compared with the other scores, are somewhat above average. Her Total Language score (92) is definitely higher than her Total Mathematics score (84), but both are well above average. Her Reference Skill score of 94 is very high.

DATA ANALYSIS

Considering the data presented, has Mary Ann apparently made realistic vocational choices? Each choice will be examined with this question in mind.

Mary Ann's first choice of a vocation is Engineering. Neither the Kuder scores nor the Strong-Campbell scores indicate that she would find satisfaction in this kind of occupation. In fact, the Strong-Campbell results indicate dissimilar interests for engineering. Her DAT profile also does not provide much support for engineering. While her numerical aptitude score is above average for her norm group, it is not especially high. Furthermore, other aptitudes that are associated with success in engineering, such as abstract reasoning and mechanical reasoning, are low. The space relations and verbal aptitude areas are only average. Furthermore, her academic aptitude test results tend to be low or near average except for the mathematics score on the PSAT/NMSQT (PR = 70). Mary Ann's past achievement in mathematics, an important subject-matter area for engineers, does not strongly support engineering as an occupational choice. Her mathematics scores for the *California Achievement Tests* are high, but her marks in algebra and geometry are Bs and Cs. The overall pattern of data suggests that engineering is not a realistic choice for this student.

Mary Ann's second choice of an occupation is Secretary. While the Kuder and Strong-Campbell profiles indicate only average interest in clerical work, her school marks for typing and general office classes are mostly As. The marks tend to show interest in the clerical work field, as well as ability. Her *California Achievement Tests* results for spelling, language, and reference skills are high, suggesting a high degree of knowledge that relates closely to secretarial work. Looking at the aptitude data, one can see that the percentile ranks for Clerical Speed and Accuracy, Spelling, and Language Usage range from high to extremely high, so her potential for success as a secretary appears to be high. The SFTAA and PSAT/NMSQT data appear to indicate sufficient academic potential for course work in a clerical-studies program. Mary Ann's second occupational choice is well supported by the test data.

Mary Ann's third occupational choice is Insurance Agent. From the standpoint of interest, the Kuder results indicate that she would probably be satisfied with the kind of work done by an insurance salesperson, because she has high scores for both the Persuasive and Social Service scales. The Strong-Campbell profile indicates only average interest for Life Insurance Agent. Mary Ann's school marks in the general office course, in mathematics, and in English appear to indicate sufficient ability for the work of an insurance salesperson. For this occupation, the important scores from the *California Achievement Tests* are Total Reading, PR = 64; Total Language, PR = 92; Total Math, PR = 84; and Reference Skills, PR = 94. Turning to the DAT for evidence of relevant aptitudes, one can see that the Spelling, Language Usage, and Clerical aptitude scores are high to very high. Also, there appears to be sufficient aptitude in the Verbal Reasoning and Numerical Ability areas for success in insurance selling. While the SFTAA indicates only minimal academic aptitude, the PSAT/NMSQT mathematics score is well above average, and there appears to be enough learning potential to acquire the knowledge and special skills that the insurance agent must have. It appears that the third occupational choice deserves serious consideration.

Additional Considerations

The foregoing analysis of the test data for Mary Ann constitutes an important step in the process of helping her make an occupational choice. In this case three tentative choices were made and each was examined with respect to the test data available. In similar cases the student may not have any tentative choices, and thus the counselor and student must "start from scratch" and decide what occupational areas to explore. Of course, when all tentative choices are unrealistic there has to be a kind of starting-over process. The counselor and student could go back to basic interests and proceed to examine and integrate the data for achievement and aptitudes. In Mary Ann's case other occupations that seem worthy of exploration are beautician, dental assistant, flight attendant, reporter, salesperson, school counselor, and YWCA staff member (or a similar occupation).

Another important point to keep in mind is that other information, such as other test scores and nontest data, can be added for a more complete integration of data and a better understanding of the student. One should readily think of data concerning attitudes, values, experiences, and personality traits as related information. Parent attitudes, family financial resources, student goals and aspirations, and student motivation for school work should also be considered.

Of course, one should always assume that there is a possibility that the available data are not valid and exercise a high degree of caution throughout the whole process of data analysis. Finally, when test scores and related data are analyzed and synthesized, the student should receive adequate counseling. That is to say, there should be ample opportunity for the student to interact with the counselor, to engage in further exploration of self and occupations, and finally to make a decision. The counselor's role should be that of an interested, informed facilitator whose main concern is that the student will have a real opportunity to arrive at a sound decision. It is not the counselor's responsibility to decide what the student should do; rather, the counselor should assume the responsibility of helping the client examine the alternatives and, hopefully, choose the best one.

Appraisal information is useful only as it is synthesized and utilized in decision making concerning the students and school programs. The collection of appraisal data is not an end in itself but a means of attempting to maximize opportunities of helping each student meet his or her potential, while in school and in the future. Appraisal is continuous. As school personnel work with individual students, they gain increasing understanding of the students' backgrounds, strengths, and weaknesses and continuously modify programmatic decisions in light of new appraisal information.

REFERENCES

Aiken, Lewis R.: *Psychological Testing and Assessment,* 3rd ed. Boston, Allyn and Bacon, Inc., 1976.

Hedges, William D.: *Evaluation in the Elementary School.* New York, Holt, Rinehart, and Winston, Inc., 1969.

Lien, Arnold J.: *Measurement and Evaluation of Learning.* Dubuque, Iowa, William C. Brown Company, Publishers, 1971.

Remmers, H. H., Gage, N. L., and Rummel, J. Francis: *A Practical Introduction to Measurement and Evaluation.* New York, Harper and Brothers Publishers, 1960.

Sax, Gilbert: *Principles of Educational and Psychological Measurement and Evaluation,* 2nd ed. Belmont, California, Wadsworth Publishing Company, 1980.

Chapter 14

ISSUES AND ETHICS

EVER SINCE the rapid growth of educational and psychological measurement in the 1920s and 1930s, there has been a considerable amount of public concern connected with the use of appraisal instruments, especially those that are designed to assess mental ability or personality traits. This concern is related to the instruments, the persons who use them and the use made of the data generated by them. While there is evidence of strong support for the use of appraisal devices (schools and agencies continue to use them on a large scale), there is also evidence of strong opposition to their use; and this may be found in articles, speeches, legislative hearings, and books (see chapter references). The criticisms relate chiefly to standardized tests, but to some extent they apply to all appraisal tools and techniques. The principal concerns or issues may be categorized as follows: Invasion of Privacy, Fairness to Minorities, and Use of Appraisal Data. Each of these areas of concern will be discussed separately, but to some extent they overlap and are interrelated.

INVASION OF PRIVACY

Many people are deeply concerned about having test results and other such data recorded in cumulative records that may be examined, lawfully or illegally, by others. While "invasion of privacy" is a concern that is generally aimed at standardized personality and intelligence tests, Cronbach (1970, pp. 509-510) maintains that any test is an invasion of privacy for the subject who does not wish to reveal himself. Cronbach's criteria for determining whether testing is justified are (1) the individual's consent to the administration of the particular inventory and (2) the need for the information. School administrators and other personnel generally are sincere in taking the position that they have a need to test students in order to provide appropriate guidance or instruction for them.

The codes of ethics of various professional organizations recognize the right to privacy. For example, Principle 5b in *Ethical Standards of Psychologists* (1979, p. 4) states:

> Information obtained in clinical or consulting relationships or evaluative data concerning children, students, employees and others are discussed only for professional purposes and only with persons clearly concerned with the case. Written and oral reports should present only data germane to the purposes of the evaluation and every effort should be made to avoid undue invasion of privacy.

In *Ethical Standards* (American Personnel and Guidance Association, 1974), there are statements that relate to privacy rights. Section B-5 states:

Records of the counseling relationship including interview notes, test data, correspondence, tape recordings, and other documents are to be considered professional information for use in counseling, and they are not part of the public or official records of the institution or agency in which the counselor is employed. Revelation to others of counseling material should occur only upon the express consent of the counselee.

In Section C-1 of *Ethical Standards* there is another statement that pertains indirectly to privacy:

It is the member's responsibility to provide adequate orientation or information to the examinee(s) prior to and following the test administration so that the results of testing may be placed in proper perspective with other relevant factors.

In Section C-7 and Section C-8, the right to privacy is mentioned indirectly:

The purpose of testing and the explicit use of the results should be made known to the examinee prior to testing. The counselor has a responsibility to ensure that instrument limitations are not exceeded and that periodic review and/or retesting are made to prevent counselee stereotyping.

The examinee's welfare and explicit prior understanding should be the criteria for determining the recipients of the test results. The member is obligated to see that adequate interpretation accompanies any release of individual or group test data. The interpretation of test data should be related to the examinee's particular concerns.

Certainly the users of tests and inventories should be fully aware of the need to honor the examinee's right to privacy. As Aiken (1979, pp. 286-287) states:

Whenever a test is administered, it is important to make the purposes of the test clear to every examinee, explaining what will be done with the scores. Examinees should also be informed of their rights to privacy. They should understand that they can refuse to answer questions which they consider improper, and that questions concerning private matters will be asked for sound reasons rather than merely to take advantage of a person or to satisfy the examiner's idle curiosity. Young children may not understand the ethical concerns of the tester, but an examiner has an ever greater obligation to be cautious when testing children, they are too often and too easily exploited.

Following the administration of a test, the examinee is entitled to a clear explanation of the results, or when the children are quite young, the parents are entitled to useful test information. If tests are administered and no opportunity is provided for an explanation of the results, the testing may be regarded as "snooping" and strongly rejected

(Yamamoto, 1966). It must be emphasized, however, that not all confidential information should be made available to the public. The indiscriminate release of raw data or test results that many persons cannot comprehend can have unfortunate consequences because of misunderstanding or misconceptions. If the opportunity for a meaningful discussion of appraisal results is provided by competent school personnel, the examinee and/or parents can be assisted, and the concern regarding invasion of privacy may be alleviated.

FAIRNESS TO MINORITIES

Do standardized tests and inventories discriminate against the members of minority groups? Are the instruments unfair? These are two important questions that are asked by many test critics.

Test and inventories do discriminate with respect to individuals and with respect to groups. That is to say, individual examinees get difference scores, and groups get different mean scores. If the DAT battery yields a VR percentile rank of 90 and NA percentile rank of 40 for Ken Kramer, the instrument has made a distinction between two aptitudes, one being high and one low. If, on the same battery, Ron Ronson had scores of 50 and 85 for VR and NA respectively, the instrument would have "discriminated" in another way; that is, by indicating that Ron has less verbal aptitude but greater numerical aptitude than Ken. The DAT might also indicate that the seniors at East High School score significantly higher on the VR test (on the average) than do the students of West High School. Such discriminations can be used to improve instruction and guidance, as indicated in earlier chapters. *Unfair* discriminations, of course, should be deplored. An example of this would be to disregard a student's language handicap and use a verbal aptitude score to deny the student an opportunity to reach a worthy goal, such as a scholarship.

Many educators and psychologists have expressed the belief that intelligence tests are culturally biased against such minority groups as blacks, Mexican Americans, American Indians, and poor whites. Some authorities (Jensen, 1976, 1979, Ornstein, 1976), however, disagree with the contention that there is significant cultural bias in such tests. As Ornstein (1976, p. 404) views the matter, "the fact that disadvantaged students do poorly on the IQ tests does not mean that the tests are unfair or biased. The tests reflect the unfairness of social and environmental conditions, and the conditions (like the test) are fairly valid for predicting school success."

Minority students tend to have fewer test-taking skills, are less motivated to take tests, have less rapport with examiners, are less concerned about speed of performance and are less motivated to achieve than majority subjects, so minority students often have test scores that are lower than they ought to be. This is not to imply that all minority students score below other students. In fact, there is a considerable amount of overlap of scores when minority students are compared with the white majority on aptitude, intelligence, and achievement tests, with many minority subjects having scores that exceed the mean score for the majority subjects. Some minority students appear not to have any cultural or language handicaps and perform well on mental-ability and achievement tests. For the others, however, school personnel should guard against the possibility of cultural bias and unfair discrimination. One important way to prevent unfair discrimination is to use several criteria when making important decisions that involve test scores. Such criteria as school marks, teachers ratings, achievement test scores, work samples, oral interviews, and a "culture-fair" test (which is also not equally valid for individuals and must be used cautiously and judiciously) can be used to judge an intelligence test score as reasonably accurate or as probably inaccurate.

USE OF TESTS AND INVENTORIES

While any appraisal instruments or techniques *can* be used effectively to enhance the growth and development of children and youths, these tools can also be *misused*. This point has been rather well stressed already in relation to the *privacy* and *fairness* issues. There also are other concerns that merit consideration.

Some critics of the use of tests fear that the reporting of data obtained from the tests on which some minorities tend to score low will reinforce the notion that those minorities are inferior to the white majority. This certainly is an understandable concern that should be foremost in the mind of test users who should strive to prevent the stigmatization of any group because of test scores. School personnel should always exercise the utmost care in communication (oral and written) with students, parents, the media, and the public with respect to the various aspects of testing and the meaning of the results. Good communication and sensitivity should go a long way toward the prevention of *group labeling*.

Another unfortunate labeling that may occur as a result of test scores is *individual* labeling. As a result of a low test score a child may be labeled as dumb, stupid, or dense. Not only is such a stigma deleterious to the child's self-concept, but sometimes a child will accept the label and perform accordingly. It is as though there is a power of suggestion that goes with the label. Also, there is a danger that teachers and parents may accept the label and act less positively toward the child than they should, perhaps even rejecting the individual, knowingly or otherwise. A child or youth who is labeled "genius," "brain," or "egghead" may also be victimized. In this instance the person may develop a "superiority complex" that will make the development of social relationships difficult. Or, the individual may attempt to hide any evidence of intellectual superiority through mediocre achievement, faked indifference to school activities, or even misbehavior. It should be emphasized, however, that not all students succumb to labeling. There are those who will succeed in spite of it, and some may even relish it. Still, this is a practice that has little to recommend it and ought to be avoided.

Some critics of *mental-ability* tests believe strongly that commonly used instruments lack sufficient validity for placing students in special classes or for predicting achievement. They believe that too many errors are being made in placement and in vocational counseling. The opponents of tests have stated that some of the tests deny opportunity to persons who have special important talents (Brim, 1965). These critics feel that such human qualities as altruism, creativity, foresight, and judgment are not adequately assessed by the present paper-and-pencil instruments, and that too much importance is placed on a single score for general mental ability.

Critics of *standardized achievement* tests have expressed the viewpoint that these tests exert too great an influence on school programs. Specifically, there is a concern that those persons who develop the tests also determine the curriculum for the school that uses the tests and that, in effect, the tests make decisions for school personnel. Critics may believe that the tests group children, determine their futures, support their goals, restrict creativity, help them become dishonest and undermine the foundations of education. As Rudman (1977, p. 181) says, however, tests do none of these things:

> Teachers, parents, and others who come in contact with children do these things. Tests yield data when responded to by children. Teachers and administrators translate the data into information. We use this information as we draw upon our own experiences to help us decide which alternatives to consider and which alternative to select.

Standardized achievement tests also have been criticized on the grounds that they (1) prevent individualized instruction; (2) place too little emphasis upon critical thinking or inquiry skills; (3) do not measure or reflect valuing skills; (4) are not valid for local school use; (5) force teachers to teach to a national standard; and (6) kill the creative urges in children and teachers. Rudman (1977) maintains that while some of the critics are responsible, and some of their criticisms have some basis in fact, other critics are insufficiently knowledgeable to speak on such an important subject as standardized testing. Rudman's comments concerning these criticisms are deserving of serious attention by all who are genuinely concerned about the use of standardized tests in schools.

ETHICAL STANDARDS

Some references have already been made to the codes of ethics that may be referred to by test users. *The Ethical Standards of Psychologists* (1979) has eight principles of professional conduct that relate directly or indirectly to the use of appraisal data, especially Principle 8 (Utilization of Assessment Techniques). While these principles are specifically written for psychologists, they can serve as a useful reference for school personnel other than psychologists.

The *APGA Policy Statement: Responsibilities of Users of Standardized Tests* provides test users with very useful guidelines for the broad field of tests and measurements.

The American Personnel and Guidance Association also has published the previously mentioned *Ethical Standards* (1974) that have the following sections:

1. Section A: General
2. Section B: Counselor-Counselee Relationship
3. Section C: Measurement and Evaluation
4. Section D: Research and Publication
5. Section E: Consulting and Private Practice
6. Section F: Personnel Administration

Because it relates directly to the appraisal process, Section C is presented:

Section C*

Measurement and Evaluation

The primary purpose of educational and psychological testing is to provide descriptive measures that are objective and interpretable in either comparative or absolute terms. The member must recognize the need to interpret the statements that follow as applying to the whole range of appraisal techniques including test and nontest data. Test results constitute only one of a variety of pertinent sources of information for personnel, guidance, and counseling decisions.

1. It is the member's responsibility to provide adequate orientation or information to the examinee(s) prior to and following the test administration so that the results of testing may be placed in proper perspective with other relevant factors. In so doing, the member must recognize the effects of socioeconomic, ethnic, and cultural factors on test scores. It is the member's professional responsibility to use additional unvalidated information cautiously in modifying interpretation of the test results.

2. In selecting tests for use in a given situation or with a particular counselee, the member must consider carefully the specific validity,

---

* Copyright 1974 American Personnel and Guidance Association. Reprinted with permission.

reliability, and appropriateness of the test(s). "General" validity, reliability, and the like may be questioned legally as well as ethically when tests are used for vocational and educational selection, placement, or counseling.

3. When making any statements to the public about tests and testing, the member is expected to give accurate information and to avoid false claims or misconceptions. Special efforts are often required to avoid unwarranted connotations of such terms as IQ and grade equivalent scores.

4. Different tests demand different levels of competence for administration, scoring, and interpretation. Members have a responsibility to recognize the limits of their competence and to perform only those functions for which they are prepared.

5. Tests should be administered under the same conditions that were established in their standardization. When tests are not administered under standard conditions or when unusual behavior or irregularities occur during the testing session, those conditions should be noted and the results designated as invalid or of questionable validity. Unsupervised or inadequately supervised test-taking, such as the use of tests through the mails, is considered unethical. On the other hand, the use of instruments that are so designed or standardized to be self-administered and self-scored, such as interest inventories, is to be encouraged.

6. The meaningfulness of test results used in personnel, guidance, and counseling functions generally depends on the examinee's unfamiliarity with the specific items on the test. Any prior coaching or dissemination of the test materials can invalidate test results. Therefore, test security is one of the professional obligations of the member. Conditions that produce most favorable test results should be made known to the examinee.

7. The purpose of testing and the explicit use of the results should be made known to the examinee prior to testing. The counselor has a responsibility to ensure that instrument limitations are not exceeded and that periodic review and/or retesting are made to prevent counselee stereotyping.

8. The examinee's welfare and explicit prior understanding should be the criteria for determining the recipients of the test results. The member is obligated to see that adequate interpretation accompanies any release of individual or group test data. The interpretation of test data should be related to the examinee's particular concerns.

9. The member is expected to be cautious when interpreting the results of research instruments possessing insufficient technical data. The specific purposes for the use of such instruments must be stated explicitly to examinees.

10. The member must proceed with extreme caution when attempting to evaluate and interpret the performance of minority group members or other persons who are not represented in the norm group on which the instrument was standardized.

11. The member is obligated to guard against the appropriation, reproduction, or modifications of published tests or parts thereof

without the express permission and adequate recognition of the original author or publisher.

12. Regarding the preparation, publication, and distribution of tests, reference should be made to:

   a. *Standards for Educational and Psychological Tests and Manuals,* revised edition, 1973, published by the American Psychological Association on behalf of itself, the American Educational Research Association, and the National Council on Measurement in Education.

   b. "The Responsible Use of Tests: A Position Paper of AMEG, APGA, and NCME," published in *Measurement and Evaluation in Guidance* Vol. 5, No. 2, July 1972, pp. 385-388.

Effective use of the various appraisal instruments and techniques by school personnel depends to a great extent upon how closely such individuals adhere to the principles stated in the professional codes of ethics. The ethical standards are available, and they cover all important aspects of appraisal, but they must be taken seriously and followed consistently in order to have a significant positive influence on the use of appraisal data in schools.

REFERENCES

Aiken, Lewis: *Psychological Testing and Assessment,* 2nd ed. Boston, Allyn and Bacon, 1976.

American Personnel and Guidance Association: *APGA Policy Statement: Responsibilities of Users of Standardized Tests.* APGA Press, Washington, D.C., 1980.

American Personnel and Guidance Association: *Ethical Standards.* APGA Press, Washington, D.C., 1974.

American Psychological Association: *Ethical Standards of Psychologists.* Washington, D.C., 1979.

Black, Hillel: *They Shall Not Pass.* New York, Morrow, 1963.

Brim, O. G., Jr.: American attitudes toward intelligence tests. *American Psychologists, 20:*125-130, 1965.

Clarizio, Harvey: Nonbiased assessment of minority group children: *Measurement and Evaluation in Guidance, 11:*106-113, 1978.

Corey, Gerald, Schneider, Marianne, and Callanan, Patrick: *Professional and Ethical Issues in Counseling and Psychotherapy.* Monterey, California, Brooks/Cole, 1979.

Coughlan, E. K.: Nader hits standardized tests. *The Chronicle of Higher Education,* September 13, 1976.

Cronbach, Lee J.: *Essentials of Psychological Testing,* 3rd ed. New York, Harper and Row, 1970.

Green, R. L., Griffore, R. J., and Simmons, C.: A restatement of the IQ/culture issue. *Phi Delta Kappan, 57:*674-676, 1976.

Gross, Martin: *The Brain Watchers.* New York, Random House, 1962.

Herndon, Terry: The case is a poor one. *Phi Delta Kappan, 57:*689, 1976.

Hoffman, Banesh: *The Tyranny of Testing.* New York, Crowell-Collier-Macmillan, 1962.

Houts, P. L.: Behind the call for test reform and abolition of the IQ. *Phi Delta Kappan, 57:*669-672, 1976.

Jensen, A. R.: *Bias in Mental Testing.* New York, Free Press, 1980.

————: IQ tests are not culturally biased for blacks and whites. *Phi Delta Kappan, 57:*676, 1976.

McKenzie, Gary R.: Testing: Proceed with caution. *Elementary School Journal, 76:*226-271, 1976.

Nettler, Gwynn: Test burning in Texas. *American Psychologist, 14:*682-683, 1959.

Ornstein, Allan: IQ tests and the culture issue. *Phi Delta Kappan, 57:*403-404, 1976.

Robb, G., Bernardoni, L. and Johnson, R.: *Assessment of Individual Mental Ability.* New York, Harper and Row, 1972.

Rudman, H. C.: The standardized test flap. *Phi Deltan Kappan, 59:*179-185, 1977.

Samuda, R. J.: *Psychological Testing of American Minorities: Issues and Consequences.* New York, Dodd, Mead, 1975.

Yamamoto, Kaoru: Psychological Testing: Invasion of Privacy? *Educational Leadership, 23:*5, 1966.

ORDINATES AND PROPORTIONS OF AREA BETWEEN THE MEAN AND GIVEN STANDARD SCORES

z	*Area*	*Ordinate*	z	*Area*	*Ordinate*
00	.0000	.3989	.30	.1179	.3814
.01	.0040	.3989	.31	.1217	.3802
.02	.0080	.3989	.32	.1255	.3790
.03	.0120	.3988	.33	.1293	.3778
.04	.0160	.3986	.34	.1331	.3765
.05	.0199	.3984	.35	.1368	.3752
.06	.0239	.3982	.36	.1406	.3739
.07	.0279	.3980	.37	.1443	.3725
.08	.0319	.3977	.38	.1480	.3712
.09	.0359	.3973	.39	.1517	.3697
.10	.0398	.3970	.40	.1554	.3683
.11	.0438	.3965	.41	.1591	.3668
.12	.0478	.3961	.42	.1628	.3653
.13	.0517	.3956	.43	.1664	.3637
.14	.0557	.3951	.44	.1700	.3621
.15	.0596	.3945	.45	.1736	.3605
.16	.0636	.3939	.46	.1772	.3589
.17	.0675	.3932	47	.1808	.3572
.18	.0714	.3925	.48	.1844	.3555
.19	.0753	.3918	.49	.1879	.3538
.20	.0793	.3910	.50	.1915	.3521
.21	.0832	.3902	.51	.1950	.3503
.22	.0871	.3894	.52	.1985	.3485
.23	.0910	.3885	.53	.2019	.3467
.24	.0948	.3876	.54	.2054	.3448
.25	.0987	.3867	.55	.2088	.3429
.26	.1026	.3857	.56	.2123	.3410
.27	.1064	.3847	.57	.2157	.3391
.28	.1103	.3836	.58	.2190	.3372
.29	.1141	.3825	.59	.2224	.3352

z	Area	Ordinate	z	Area	Ordinate
.60	.2257	.3332	1.00	.3413	.2420
.61	.2291	.3312	1.01	.3438	.2396
.62	.2324	.3292	1.02	.3461	.2371
.63	.2357	.3271	1.03	.3485	.2347
.64	.2389	.3251	1.04	.3508	.2323
.65	.2422	.3230	1.05	.3531	.2299
.66	.2454	.3209	1.06	.3554	.2275
.67	.2486	.3187	1.07	.3577	.2251
.68	.2517	.3166	1.08	.3599	.2227
.69	.2549	.3144	1.09	.3621	.2203
.70	.2580	.3123	1.10	.3643	.2179
.71	.2611	.3101	1.11	.3665	.2155
.72	.2642	.3079	1.12	.3686	.2131
.73	.2673	.3056	1.13	.3708	.2107
.74	.2703	.3034	1.14	.3729	.2083
.75	.2734	.3011	1.15	.3749	.2059
.76	.2764	.2989	1.16	.3770	.2036
.77	.2794	.2966	1.17	.3790	.2012
.78	.2823	.2943	1.18	.3810	.1989
.79	.2852	.2920	1.19	.3830	.1965
.80	.2881	.2897	1.20	.3849	.1942
.81	.2910	.2874	1.21	.3869	.1919
.82	.2939	.2850	1.22	.3888	.1895
.83	.2967	.2827	1.23	.3907	.1872
.84	.2995	.2803	1.24	.3925	.1849
.85	.3023	.2780	1.25	.3944	.1826
.86	.3051	.2756	1.26	.3962	.1804
.87	.3078	.2732	1.27	.3980	.1781
.88	.3106	.2709	1.28	.3997	.1758
.89	.3133	.2685	1.29	.4015	.1736
.90	.3159	.2661	1.30	.4032	.1714
.91	.3186	.2637	1.31	.4049	.1691
.92	.3212	.2613	1.32	.4066	.1669
.93	.3238	.2589	1.33	.4082	.1647
.94	.3264	.2565	1.34	.4099	.1626
.95	.3289	.2541	1.35	.4115	.1604
.96	.3315	.2516	1.36	.4131	.1582
.97	.3340	.2492	1.37	.4147	.1561
.98	.3365	.2468	1.38	.4162	.1539
.99	.3389	.2444	1.39	.4177	.1518

z	*Area*	*Ordinate*	z	*Area*	*Ordinate*
1.40	.4192	.1497	1.80	.4641	.0790
1.41	.4207	.1476	1.81	.4649	.0775
1.42	.4222	.1456	1.82	.4656	.0761
1.43	.4236	.1435	1.83	.4664	.0748
1.44	.4251	.1415	1.84	.4671	.0734
1.45	.4265	.1394	1.85	.4678	.0721
1.46	.4279	.1374	1.86	.4686	.0707
1.47	.4292	.1354	1.87	.4693	.0694
1.48	.4306	.1334	1.88	.4699	.0681
1.49	.4319	.1315	1.89	.4706	.0669
1.50	.4332	.1295	1.90	.4713	.0656
1.51	.4345	.1276	1.91	.4719	.0644
1.52	.4357	.1257	1.92	.4726	.0632
1.53	.4370	.1238	1.93	.4732	.0620
1.54	.4382	.1219	1.94	.4738	.0608
1.55	.4394	.1200	1.95	.4744	.0596
1.56	.4406	.1182	1.96	.4750	.0584
1.57	.4418	.1163	1.97	.4756	.0573
1.58	.4429	.1145	1.98	.4761	.0562
1.59	.4441	.1127	1.99	.4767	.0551
1.60	.4452	.1109	2.00	.4772	.0540
1.61	.4463	.1092	2.01	.4778	.0529
1.62	.4474	.1074	2.02	.4783	.0519
1.63	.4484	.1057	2.03	.4788	.0508
1.64	.4495	.1040	2.04	.4793	.0498
1.65	.4505	.1023	2.05	.4798	.0488
1.66	.4515	.1006	2.06	.4803	.0478
1.67	.4525	.0989	2.07	.4808	.0468
1.68	.4535	.0973	2.08	.4812	.0459
1.69	.4545	.0957	2.09	.4817	.0449
1.70	.4554	.0940	2.10	.4821	.0440
1.71	.4564	.0925	2.11	.4826	.0431
1.72	.4573	.0909	2.12	.4830	.0422
1.73	.4582	.0893	2.13	.4834	.0413
1.74	.4591	.0878	2.14	.4838	.0404
1.75	.4599	.0863	2.15	.4842	.0395
1.76	.4608	.0848	2.16	.4846	.0387
1.77	.4616	.0833	2.17	.4850	.0379
1.78	.4625	.0818	2.18	.4854	.0371
1.79	.4633	.0804	2.19	.4857	.0363

z	Area	Ordinate	z	Area	Ordinate
2.20	.4861	.0355	2.60	.4953	.0136
2.21	.4864	.0347	2.61	.4955	.0132
2.22	.4868	.0339	2.62	.4956	.0129
2.23	.4871	.0332	2.63	.4957	.0126
2.24	.4875	.0325	2.64	.4959	.0122
2.25	.4878	.0317	2.65	.4960	.0119
2.26	.4881	.0310	2.66	.4961	.0116
2.27	.4884	.0303	2.67	.4962	.0113
2.28	.4887	.0297	2.68	.4963	.0110
2.29	.4890	.0290	2.69	.4964	.0107
2.30	.4893	.0283	2.70	.4965	.0104
2.31	.4896	.0277	2.71	.4966	.0101
2.32	.4898	.0270	2.72	.4967	.0099
2.33	.4901	.0264	2.73	.4968	.0096
2.34	.4904	.0258	2.74	.4969	.0093
2.35	.4906	.0252	2.75	.4970	.0091
2.36	.4909	.0246	2.76	.4971	.0088
2.37	.4911	.0241	2.77	.4972	.0086
2.38	.4913	.0235	2.78	.4973	.0084
2.39	.4916	.0229	2.79	.4974	.0081
2.40	.4918	.0224	2.80	.4974	.0079
2.41	.4920	.0219	2.81	.4975	.0077
2.42	.4922	.0213	2.82	.4976	.0075
2.43	.4925	.0208	2.83	.4977	.0073
2.44	.4927	.0203	2.84	.4977	.0071
2.45	.4929	.0198	2.85	.4978	.0069
2.46	.4931	.0194	2.86	.4979	.0067
2.47	.4932	.0189	2.87	.4979	.0065
2.48	.4934	.0184	2.88	.4980	.0063
2.49	.4936	.0180	2.89	.4981	.0061
2.50	.4938	.0175	2.90	.4981	.0060
2.51	.4940	.0171	2.91	.4982	.0058
2.52	.4941	.0167	2.92	.4982	.0056
2.53	.4943	.0163	2.93	.4983	.0055
2.54	.4945	.0158	2.94	.4984	.0053
2.55	.4946	.0154	2.95	.4984	.0051
2.56	.4948	.0151	2.96	.4985	.0050
2.57	.4949	.0147	2.97	.4985	.0048
2.58	.4951	.0143	2.98	.4986	.0047
2.59	.4952	.0139	2.99	.4986	.0046
			3.00	.4987	.0044

A GLOSSARY OF MEASUREMENT TERMS*

BLYTHE C. MITCHELL, *Consultant, Test Department*

This glossary of terms used in educational and psychological measurement is primarily for persons with limited training in measurement, rather than for the specialist. The terms defined are the more common or basic ones such as occur in test manuals and educational journals. In the definitions, certain technicalities and niceties of usage have been sacrificed for the sake of brevity and, it is hoped, clarity.

The definitions are based on the usage of the various terms as given in the current textbooks in educational and psychological measurement and statistics, and in certain specialized dictionaries. Where there is not complete uniformity among writers in the measurement field with respect to the meaning of a term, either these variations are noted or the definition offered is the one that the writer judges to represent the "best" usage.

---

academic aptitude. The combination of native and acquired abilities that are needed for school learning; likelihood of success in mastering academic work, as estimated from measures of the necessary abilities. (Also called *scholastic aptitude, school learning ability, academic potential*)

achievement test. A test that measures the extent to which a person has "achieved" something, acquired certain information, or mastered certain skills — usually as a result of planned instruction or training.

age norms. Originally, values representing typical or average performance for persons of various *age* groups; most current usage refers to sets of complete score interpretive data for appropriate successive age groups. Such norms are generally used in the interpretation of mental ability test scores.

alternate-form reliability. The closeness of correspondence,

---

* From *Test Service Notebook 13*. By permission of Harcourt Brace Jovanovich, Inc.

or correlation, between results on alternate (i.e., equivalent or parallel) forms of a test; thus, a measure of the extent to which the two forms are consistent or reliable in measuring whatever they do measure. The time interval between the two testings must be relatively short so that the examinees themselves are unchanged in the ability being measured. See RELIABILITY, RELIABILITY COEFFICIENT.

anecdotal record. A written description of an incident in an individual's behavior that is reported objectively and is considered significant for the understanding of the individual.

aptitude. A combination of abilities and other characteristics, whether native or acquired, that are indicative of an individual's ability to learn or to develop proficiency in some particular area if appropriate education or training is provided. Aptitude tests include those of general academic ability (commonly called mental ability or intelligence tests); those of special abilities, such as verbal, numerical, mechanical, or musical; tests assessing "readiness" for learning; and prognostic tests, which measure both ability and previous learning, and are used to predict future performance — usually in a specific field, such as foreign language, shorthand, or nursing.

Some would define "aptitude" in a more comprehensive sense. Thus, "musical aptitude" would refer to the combination not only of physical and mental characteristics but also of motivational factors, interest, and conceivably other characteristics, which are conducive to acquiring proficiency in the musical field.

arithmetic mean. A kind of average usually referred to as the *mean*. It is obtained by dividing the sum of a set of scores by their number.

average. A general term applied to the various measures of central tendency. The three most widely used averages are the arithmetic mean (mean), the median, and the mode. When the term "average" is used without designation as to type, the most likely assumption is that it is the *arithmetic mean*.

battery. A group of several tests standardized on the same sample population so that results on the several tests are comparable. (Sometimes loosely applied to any group of tests administered together, even though not standardized on the same subjects.) The most common test batteries are those of school achievement, which include subtests in the separate learning areas.

bivariate chart (bivariate distribution). A diagram in which a tally mark is made to show the scores of one individual on *two variables.* The intersection of lines determined by the horizontal and vertical scales form cells in which the tallies are placed. Such a plot provides frequencies for the two distributions, and portrays the relation between the two variables as a basis for computation of the product-moment correlation coefficient.

ceiling. The upper limit of ability that can be measured by a test. When an individual makes a score which is at or near the highest possible score, it is said that the test has too low a "ceiling" for him; he should be given a higher level of the test.

central tendency. A measure of central tendency provides a single most typical score as representative of a group of scores; the "trend" of a group of measures as indicated by some type of average, usually the *mean* or the *median.*

coefficient of correlation. A measure of the degree of relationship or "going-togetherness" between two sets of measures for the same group of individuals. The correlation coefficient most frequently used in test development and educational research is that known as the Pearson or *product-moment r.* Unless otherwise specified, "correlation" usually refers to this coefficient, but *rank, biserial, tetrachoric,* and other methods are used in special situations. Correlation coefficients range from .00, denoting a complete absence of relationship, to +1.00, and to −1.00, indicating perfect positive or perfect negative correspondence, respectively. See CORRELATION.

composite score. A score which combines several scores, usually by addition; often different weights are applied to the contributing scores to increase or decrease their importance in the composite. Most commonly, such scores are used for *predictive* purposes and the several weights are derived through multiple regression procedures.

concurrent validity. See VALIDITY (2).

construct validity. See VALIDITY (3).

content validity. See VALIDITY (1).

correction for guessing (correction for chance). A reduction in score for wrong answers, sometimes applied in scoring true-false or multiple-choice questions. Such scoring formulas $(R - W$ for tests with 2-option response, $R - \frac{1}{2}W$ for 3 options, $R - \frac{1}{3}W$ for 4, etc.) are intended to discourage guessing and to yield more accurate rankings of examinees in terms of their true knowledge. They are used much less today than in the early days of testing.

correlation. Relationship or "going-togetherness" between two sets of scores or measures; tendency of one score to vary concomitantly with the other, as the tendency of students of high IQ to be above average in reading ability. The existence of a strong relationship — i.e., a high correlation — between two variables does not necessarily indicate that one has any causal influence on the other. See COEFFICIENT OF CORRELATION.

criterion. A standard by which a test may be judged or evaluated; a set of scores, ratings, etc., that a test is designed to measure, to predict, or to correlate with. See VALIDITY.

criterion-referenced (content-referenced) test. Terms often used to describe tests designed to provide information on the specific knowledge or skills possessed by a student. Such tests usually cover relatively small units of content and are closely related to instruction. Their scores have meaning in terms of *what* the student knows or can do, rather than in their relation to the scores made by some external reference group.

criterion-related validity. See VALIDITY (2).

culture-fair test. So-called culture-fair tests attempt to provide an equal opportunity for success by persons of all cultures and life experiences. Their content must therefore be limited to that which is equally common to all cultures, or to material that is entirely unfamiliar and novel for all persons whatever their cultural background. See CULTURE-FREE TEST.

culture-free test. A test that is free of the impact of all cultural experiences; therefore, a measure reflecting only hereditary abilities. Since culture permeates all of man's environmental contacts, the construction of such a test would seem to be an impossibility. Cultural "bias" is not eliminated by the use of non-language or so-called performance tests, although it may be reduced in some instances. In terms of most of the purposes for which tests are used, the validity (value) of a "culture-free" test is questioned; a test designed to be equally applicable to all cultures may be of little or no practical value in any.

curricular validity. See VALIDITY (2).

decile. Any one of the nine points (scores) that divide a distribution into ten parts, each containing one-tenth of all the scores or cases; every tenth percentile. The first decile is the 10th percentile, the eighth decile the 80th percentile, etc.

deviation. The amount by which a score differs from some reference value, such as the mean, the norm, or the score on some other test.

deviation IQ (DIQ). An age-based index oi general mental ability. It is based upon the difference or deviation between a person's score and the typical or average score for persons of his chronological age. Deviation IQs from most current scholastic aptitude measures are standard scores with a mean of 100 and a standard deviation of 16 for each defined age group.

diagnostic test. A test used to "diagnose" or analyze; that is, to locate an individual's specific areas of weakness or strength, to determine the nature of his weaknesses or deficiencies, and, wherever possible, to suggest their cause. Such a test yields measures of the components or subparts of some larger body of information or skill. Diagnostic achievement tests are most commonly prepared for the skill subjects.

difficulty value. An index which indicates the percent of some specified group, such as students of a given age or grade, who answer a test item correctly.

discriminating power. The ability of a test item to differentiate between persons possessing much or little of some trait.

discrimination index. An index which indicates the *discriminating power* of a test item. The most commonly used index is derived from the number passing the item in the highest 27 percent of the group (on total score) and the number passing in the lowest 27 percent.

distractor. Any incorrect choice (option) in a test item.

distribution (frequency distribution). A tabulation of the scores (or other attributes) of a group of individuals to show the number (frequency) of each score, or of those within the range of each interval.

equivalent form. Any of two or more forms of a test that are closely parallel with respect to the nature of the content and the number and difficulty of the items included, and that will yield very similar average scores and measures of variability for a given group. (Also referred to as *alternate, comparable,* or *parallel* form.)

error of measurement. See STANDARD ERROR OF MEASUREMENT.

expectancy table ("expected" achievement). A term with two common usages, related but with some difference:

(1) A table or other. device for showing the relation between scores on a predictive test and some related outcome. The outcome, or criterion status, for individuals at each level of predictive score may be expressed as (a) an average on the outcome variable, (b) the percent of cases at successive levels, or (c) the probability of reaching given performance levels. Such tables are commonly used in making predictions of educational or job success.

(2) A table or chart providing for an interpretation of a student's obtained score on an achievement test with the score which would be "expected" for those at his grade level and with his level of scholastic aptitude. Such "expectancies" are based upon actual data from administration of the specified achievement and scholastic aptitude tests to the same student population. The term "anticipated" is also used to denote achievement as differentiated by level of "intellectual status."

extrapolation. In general, any process of estimating values of a variable beyond the range of available data. As applied to test norms, the process of extending a norm line into grade or age levels not tested in the standardization program, in order to permit interpretation of extreme scores. Since this extension is usually done graphically, considerable judgment is involved. Extrapolated values are thus to some extent arbitrary; for this and other reasons, they have limited meaning.

f. A symbol denoting the *frequency* of a given score or of the scores within an interval grouping.

face validity. See VALIDITY (1).

factor. In mental measurement, a hypothetical trait, ability, or component of ability that underlies and influences performance on two or more tests and hence causes scores on the tests to be correlated. The term "factor" strictly refers to a theoretical variable, derived by a process of *factor analysis* from a table of intercorrelations among tests. However, it is also used to denote the psychological interpretation given to the variable—i.e., the mental trait assumed to be represented by the variable, as verbal ability, numerical ability, etc.

factor analysis. Any of several methods of analyzing the intercorrelations among a set of variables such as test scores. Factor analysis attempts to account for the interrelationships in terms of some underlying "factors," preferably fewer in number than the original variables, and it reveals how much of the variation in each of the original measures arises from, or is associated with, each of the hypothetical factors. Factor analysis has contributed to an understanding of the organization or components of intelligence, aptitudes, and personality; and it has pointed the way to the development of "purer" tests of the several components.

forced-choice item. Broadly, any multiple-choice item in which the examinee is *required* to select one or more of the given choices. The term is most often used to denote a special type of multiple-choice item employed in personality tests in which the options are (1) of equal "preference value," i.e., chosen equally often by a typical group, and are (2) such that one of the options discriminates between persons high and low on the factor that this option measures, while the other options measure other factors. Thus, in the *Gordon Personal Profile,* each of four options represents one of the four personality traits measured by the *Profile,* and the examinee must select both the option which describes him *most* and the one which describes him *least.*

frequency distribution. See DISTRIBUTION.

g. Denotes *general* intellectual ability; one dimensional measure of "mind," as described by the British psychologist Spearman. A test of *"g"* serves as a general-purpose test of mental ability.

grade equivalent (GE). The grade level for which a given score is the real or estimated average. Grade-equivalent interpretation, most appropriate for elementary level achievement tests, expresses obtained scores in terms of *grade* and *month* *of grade,* assuming a 10-month school year (e.g., 5.7). Since such tests are usually standardized at only one (or two) point(s) within each grade, grade equivalents between points for which there are data-based scores must be "estimated" by *interpolation.* See EXTRAPOLATION, INTERPOLATION.

grade norms. Norms based upon the performance of pupils of given grade placement. See GRADE EQUIVALENT, NORMS, PER-CENTILE RANK, STANINE.

group test. A test that may be administered to a number of individuals at the same time by one examiner.

individual test. A test that can be administered to only one person at a time, because of the nature of the test and/or the maturity level of the examinees.

intelligence quotient (IQ). Originally, an index of brightness expressed as the ratio of a person's mental age to his chronological age, MA/CA, multiplied by 100 to eliminate the decimal. (More precisely — and particularly for adult ages, at which mental growth is assumed to have ceased — the ratio of mental age to the mental age normal for chronological age.) This quotient IQ has been gradually replaced by the deviation IQ concept.

It is sometimes desired to give additional meaning to IQs by the use of verbal descriptions for the ranges in which they fall. Since the IQ scale is a continuous one, there can be no inflexible line of demarcation between such successive category labels as very superior, superior, above average, average, below average, etc.; any verbal classification system is therefore an arbitrary one. There appears to be, however, rather common use of the term *average* or *normal* to describe IQs from 90-109 inclusive.

An IQ is more definitely "interpreted" by noting the normal percent of IQs within a range which includes the IQ, and/or

[intelligence quotient (IQ), continued.]

by indicating its percentile rank or stanine in the total national norming sample. Column 2 of Table 1 shows the normal distribution of IQs for M = 100 and S.D. = 16, showing percentages within successive 10-point intervals. (For IQs whose S.D. is greater than 16, the percentages for the extreme IQ ranges will be larger, and those for IQs near the mean will be smaller, than those shown in the table.) Table 1 indicates that 47 percent, approximately one-half of "all" persons, have IQs in the 20-point range of 90 through 109; an IQ of 140 or above would be considered as extremely high, since fewer than one percent (0.6) of the total population reach this level, and fewer than one percent have IQs below 60. From the cumulative percents given in Column 3, it is noted that 3.1 percent have IQs below 70, usually considered the mentally retarded category. This column may be used to indicate the percentile rank (PR) of certain IQs. Thus an IQ of 119 has a PR of 89, since 89.4 percent of IQs are 119 or below; an IQ of 79 has a PR of 10.6, or 11. See DEVIATION IQ, MENTAL AGE.

Table 1. Normal Distribution of IQs with Mean of 100 and Standard Deviation of 16

(1) IQ Range	(2) Percent of Persons	(3) Cumulative Percent
140 and above	0.6	100.6
130-139	2.5	99.4
120-129	7.5	96.9
110-119	16.0	89.4
100-109	23.4 ⎫ 46.8	73.4
90- 99	23.4 ⎭	50.0
80- 89	16.0	26.6
70- 79	7.5	10.6
60- 69	2.5·	3.1
Below 60	0.6	0.6
Total	100.0	

internal consistency. Degree of relationship among the items of a test; consistency in content sampling. See SPLIT-HALF RELIABILITY.

interpolation. In general, any process of estimating intermediate values between two known points. As applied to test norms, it refers to the procedure used in assigning interpretive values (e.g., grade equivalents) to scores between the successive average scores actually obtained in the standardization process. Also, in reading norm tables it is necessary at times to interpolate to obtain a norm value for a score between two scores given in the table; e.g., in the table shown here, a percentile rank of 83 (from 81 + ⅓ of 6) would be assigned, by *interpolation,* to a score of

Score	Percentile Rank
51	97
48	87
45	81

46; a score of 50 would correspond to a percentile rank of 94 (obtained as 87 + ⅔ of 10).

inventory. A questionnaire or check list, usually in the form of a self-report, designed to elicit non-intellective information about an individual. Not tests in the usual sense, inventories are most often concerned with personality traits, interests, attitudes, problems, motivation, etc. See PERSONALITY TEST.

inventory test. An achievement test that attempts to cover rather thoroughly some relatively small unit of specific instruction or training. An inventory test, as the name suggests, is in the nature of a "stock-taking" of an individual's knowledge or skill, and is often administered prior to instruction.

item. A single question or exercise in a test.

item analysis. The process of evaluating single test items in respect to certain characteristics. It usually involves determining the difficulty value and the discriminating power of the item, and often its correlation with some external criterion.

Kuder-Richardson formula(s). Formulas for estimating the reliability of a test that are based on *inter-item consistency* and require only a single administration of the test. The one most used, formula 20, requires information based on the number of items in the test, the standard deviation of the total score, and the proportion of examinees passing each item. The Kuder-Richardson formulas are not appropriate for use with speeded tests.

mastery test. A test designed to determine whether a pupil has mastered a given unit of instruction or a single knowledge or skill; a test giving information on *what* a pupil knows, rather than on how his performance relates to that of some norm-reference group. Such tests are used in computer-assisted instruction, where their results are referred to as content- or criterion-referenced information.

mean (M). See ARITHMETIC MEAN.

median (Md). The middle score in a distribution or set of ranked scores; the point (score) that divides the group into two equal parts; the 50th percentile. Half of the scores are below the median and half above it, except when the median itself is one of the obtained scores.

mental age (MA). The age for which a given score on a mental ability test is average or normal. If the average score made by an unselected group of children 6 years, 10 months of age is 55, then a child making a score of 55 is said to have a mental age of 6–10. Since the mental age unit shrinks with increasing (chronological) age, MAs do not have a uniform interpretation throughout all ages. They are therefore most appropriately used at the early age levels where mental growth is relatively rapid.

modal-age norms. Achievement test norms that are based on the performance of pupils of normal age for their respective grades. Norms derived from such age restricted groups are free from the distorting influence of the scores of underage and overage pupils.

mode. The score or value that occurs most frequently in a distribution.

multiple-choice item. A test item in which the examinee's task is to choose the correct or best answer from several given answers or options.

N. The symbol commonly used to represent the number of cases in a group.

non-language test. See NON-VERBAL TEST.

non-verbal test. A test that does not require the use of words in the item or in the response to it. (Oral directions may be included in the formulation of the task.) A test cannot, however, be classified as non-verbal simply because it does not require reading on the part of the examinee. The use of non-verbal tasks cannot completely eliminate the effect of culture.

norm line. A smooth curve drawn to best fit (1) the plotted mean or median scores of successive age or grade groups, or (2) the successive percentile points for a single group.

normal distribution. A distribution of scores or measures that in graphic form has a distinctive bell-shaped appearance. Figures 1 and 2 show graphs of such a distribution, known as a *normal, normal probability,* or *Gaussian* curve. (Difference in shape is due to the different variability of the two distributions.) In such a normal distribution, scores or measures are distributed symmetrically about the mean, with as many cases up to various distances above the mean as down to equal distances below it. Cases are concentrated near the mean and decrease in frequency, according to a precise mathematical equation, the farther one departs from the mean. *Mean* and *median* are identical. The assumption that mental and psychological characteristics are distributed normally has been very useful in test development work.

norms. Statistics that supply a frame of reference by which meaning may be given to obtained test scores. Norms are based upon the actual performance of pupils of various grades or ages in the standardization group for the test. Since they represent average or typical performance, they should not be regarded as standards or as universally desirable levels of attainment. The most common types of norms are deviation IQ, percentile rank, grade equivalent, and stanine. Reference groups are usually those of specified age or grade.

objective test. A test made up of items for which correct responses may be set up in advance; scores are unaffected by the opinion or judgment of the scorer. Objective keys provide for scoring by clerks or by machine. Such a test is contrasted with a "subjective" test, such as the usual essay examination, to which different persons may assign different scores, ratings, or grades.

omnibus test. A test (1) in which items measuring a variety of mental operations are all combined into a single sequence rather than being grouped together by type of operation, and (2) from which only a single score is derived, rather than separate scores for each operation or function. Omnibus tests make for simplicity of administration, since one set of directions and one overall time limit usually suffice. The Elementary, Intermediate, and Advanced tests in the *Otis-Lennon Mental Ability Test* series are omnibus-type tests, as contrasted with the *Kuhlmann-Anderson Measure of Academic Potential,* in which the items measuring similar operations occur together, each with its own set of directions. In a *spiral-omnibus* test, the easiest items of each type are presented first, followed by the same succession of item types at a higher difficulty level, and so on in a rising spiral.

percentile (P). A point (score) in a distribution at or below which fall the percent of cases indicated by the percentile. Thus a score coinciding with the 35th percentile (P_{35}) is regarded as equaling or surpassing that of 35 percent of the persons in the group, and such that 65 percent of the performances exceed this score. "Percentile" has nothing to do with the percent of correct answers an examinee makes on a test.

percentile band. An interpretation of a test score which takes account of the measurement error that is involved. The range of such bands, most useful in portraying significant differences in battery profiles, is usually from one standard error of measurement below the obtained score to one standard error of measurement above it.

percentile rank (PR). The expression of an obtained test score in terms of its position within a group of 100 scores; the percentile rank of a score is the percent of scores equal to or lower than the given score in its own or in some external reference group.

performance test. A test involving some motor or manual response on the examinee's part, generally a manipulation of concrete equipment or materials. Usually *not* a paper-and-pencil test.

(1) A "performance" test of mental ability is one in which the role of language is excluded or minimized, and ability is assessed by what the examinee *does* rather than by what he says (or writes). Mazes, form boards, picture completion, and other types of items may be used. Examples include certain *Stanford-Binet* tasks, the Performance Scale of *Wechsler Intelligence Scale for Children, Arthur Point Scale of Performance Tests, Raven's Progressive Matrices.*

(2) "Performance" tests include measures of mechanical or manipulative ability where the task itself coincides with the objective of the measurement, as in the *Bennett Hand-Tool Dexterity Test.*

(3) The term "performance" is also used to denote a test that is actually a *work-sample;* in this sense it may include paper-and-pencil tests, as, for example, a test in bookkeeping, in shorthand, or in proofreading, where no materials other than paper and pencil may be required, and where the test response is identical with the behavior about which information is desired. *SRA Typing Skills* is such a test.

The use of the term "performance" to describe a type of test is not very precise and there are certain "gray areas." Perhaps one should think of "performance" tests as those on which the obtained differences among individuals may *not* be ascribed to differences in ability to use verbal symbols.

personality test. A test intended to measure one or more of the non-intellective aspects of an individual's mental or psychological make-up; an instrument designed to obtain information on the affective characteristics of an individual—emotional, motivational, attitudinal, etc. — as distinguished from his abilities. Personality tests include (1) the so-called *personality* and *adjustment inventories* (e.g., *Bernreuter Personality Inventory, Bell Adjustment Inventory, Edwards Personal Preference Schedule*) which seek to measure a person's status

[personality test, continued.]
on such traits as dominance, sociability, introversion, etc., by means of self-descriptive responses to a series of questions; (2) *rating scales* which call for rating, by one's self or another, the extent to which a subject possesses certain traits; and (3) *opinion or attitude inventories* (e.g., *Allport-Vernon-Lindzey Study of Values, Minnesota Teacher Attitude Inventory*). Some writers also classify interest, problem, and belief inventories as personality tests (e.g., *Kuder Preference Record, Mooney Problem Check List*). See PROJECTIVE TECHNIQUE.

power test. A test intended to measure level of performance unaffected by speed of response; hence one in which there is either no time limit or a very generous one. Items are usually arranged in order of increasing difficulty.

practice effect. The influence of previous experience with a test on a later administration of the same or a similar test; usually an increased familiarity with the directions, kinds of questions, etc. Practice effect is greatest when the interval between testings is short, when the content of the two tests is identical or very similar, and when the initial test-taking represents a relatively novel experience for the subjects.

predictive validity. See VALIDITY (2).

product-moment coefficient (r). Also known as the Pearson r. See COEFFICIENT OF CORRELATION.

profile. A graphic representation of the results on several tests, for either an individual or a group, when the results have been expressed in some uniform or comparable terms (standard scores, percentile ranks, grade equivalents, etc.). The profile method of presentation permits identification of areas of strength or weakness.

prognosis (prognostic) test. A test used to predict future success in a specific subject or field, as the *Pimsleur Language Aptitude Battery*.

projective technique (projective method). A method of personality study in which the subject responds as he chooses to a series of ambiguous stimuli such as ink blots, pictures, unfinished sentences, etc. It is assumed that under this free-response condition the subject "projects" manifestations of personality characteristics and organization that can, by suitable methods, be scored and interpreted to yield a description of his basic personality structure. The *Rorschach* (ink blot) *Technique,* the *Murray Thematic Apperception Test* and the *Machover Draw-a-Person Test* are commonly used projective methods.

quartile. One of three points that divide the cases in a distribution into four equal groups. The lower quartile (Q_1), or 25th percentile, sets off the lowest fourth of the group; the middle quartile (Q_2) is the same as the 50th percentile, or median, and divides the second fourth of cases from the third; and the third quartile (Q_3), or 75th percentile, sets off the top fourth.

r. See COEFFICIENT OF CORRELATION.

random sample. A sample of the members of some total population drawn in such a way that every member of the population has an equal chance of being included — that is, in a way· that precludes the operation of bias or "selection." The purpose in using a sample free of bias is, of course, the requirement that the cases used be representative of the total population if findings for the sample are to be generalized to that population. In a *stratified* random sample, the drawing of cases is controlled in such a way that those chosen are "representative" also of specified subgroups of the total population. See REPRESENTATIVE SAMPLE.

range. For some specified group, the difference between the highest and the lowest obtained score on a test; thus a very rough measure of spread or variability, since it is based upon only two extreme scores. Range is also used in reference to the possible spread of measurement a test provides, which in most instances is the number of items in the test.

raw score. The first quantitative result obtained in scoring a test. Usually the number of right answers, number right minus some fraction of number wrong, time required for performance, number of errors, or similar direct, unconverted, uninterpreted measure.

readiness test. A test that measures the extent to which an individual has achieved a degree of maturity or acquired certain skills or information needed for successfully undertaking some new learning activity. Thus a *reading readiness* test indicates whether a child has reached a developmental stage where he may profitably begin formal reading instruction. *Readiness* tests are classified as *prognostic* tests.

recall item. A type of item that requires the examinee to supply the correct answer from his own memory or recollection, as contrasted with a *recognition item,* in which he need only identify the correct answer.

Columbus discovered America in the year _____

is a *recall* (or *completion*) item. See RECOGNITION ITEM.

recognition item. An item which requires the examinee to recognize or select the correct answer from among two or more given answers (options).

Columbus discovered America in
   (a) *1425*   (b) *1492*   (c) *1520*   (d) *1546*
is a *recognition* item.

regression effect. Tendency of a predicted score to be nearer to the mean of its distribution than the score from which it is predicted is to its mean. Because of the effects of regression, students making extremely high or extremely low scores on a test tend to make less extreme scores, i.e., closer to the mean, on a second administration of the same test or on some predicted measure.

reliability. The extent to which a test is consistent in measuring whatever it does measure; dependability, stability, trustworthiness, relative freedom from errors of measurement. Reliability is usually expressed by some form of *reliability coefficient* or by the *standard error of measurement* derived from it.

reliability coefficient. The coefficient of correlation between two forms of a test, between scores on two administrations of the same test, or between halves of a test, properly corrected.

The three measure somewhat different aspects of reliability, but all are properly spoken of as reliability coefficients. See ALTERNATE-FORM RELIABILITY, SPLIT-HALF RELIABILITY COEFFICIENT, TEST-RETEST RELIABILITY COEFFICIENT, KUDER-RICHARDSON FORMULA(S).

representative sample. A sample that corresponds to or matches the population of which it is a sample with respect to characteristics important for the purposes under investigation. In an achievement test norm sample, such significant aspects might be the proportion of cases of each sex, from various types of schools, different geographical areas, the several socioeconomic levels, etc.

scholastic aptitude. See ACADEMIC APTITUDE.

skewed distribution. A distribution that departs from symmetry or balance around the mean, i.e., from normality. Scores pile up at one end and trail off at the other.

Spearman-Brown formula. A formula giving the relationship between the reliability of a test and its length. The formula permits estimation of the reliability of a test lengthened or shortened by any multiple, from the known reliability of a given test. Its most common application is the estimation of reliability of an entire test from the correlation between its two halves. See SPLIT-HALF RELIABILITY COEFFICIENT.

split-half reliability coefficient. A coefficient of reliability obtained by correlating scores on one half of a test with scores on the other half, and applying the Spearman-Brown formula to adjust for the doubled length of the total test. Generally, but not necessarily, the two halves consist of the odd-numbered and the even-numbered items. Split-half reliability coefficients are sometimes referred to as measures of the *internal consistency* of a test; they involve content sampling only, not stability over time. This type of reliability coefficient is inappropriate for tests in which speed is an important component.

standard deviation (S.D.). A measure of the variability or dispersion of a distribution of scores. The more the scores cluster around the mean, the smaller the standard deviation. For a normal distribution, approximately two thirds (68.3 percent) of the scores are within the range from one S.D. below the mean to one S.D. above the mean. Computation of the S.D. is based upon the square of the deviation of each score from the mean. The S.D. is sometimes called "sigma" and is represented by the symbol σ. (See Figure 1.)

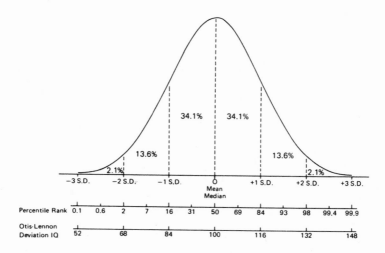

Figure 1. Normal curve, showing relations among standard deviation distance from mean, area (percentage of cases) between these points, percentile rank, and IQ from tests with an S.D. of 16.

standard error (S.E.). A statistic providing an estimate of the possible magnitude of "error" present in some obtained measure, whether (1) an *individual* score or (2) some *group* measure, as a mean or a correlation coefficient.

(1) standard error of measurement (S.E. Meas.): As applied to a single obtained score, the amount by which the score may differ from the hypothetical true score due to errors of measurement. The larger the S.E. Meas., the less reliable the score. The S.E. Meas. is an amount such that in about two-thirds of the cases the obtained score would not differ by more than one S.E. Meas. from the true score. (Theoretically, then, it can be said that the chances are 2:1 that the actual score is within a band extending from *true score minus 1 S.E. Meas.* to *true score plus 1 S.E. Meas.;* but since the true score can never be known, actual practice must reverse the true-obtained relation for an interpretation.) Other probabilities are noted under (2) below. See TRUE SCORE.

(2) standard error: When applied to group averages, standard deviations, correlation coefficients, etc., the S.E. provides an estimate of the "error" which may be involved. The

group's size and the S.D. are the factors on which these standard errors are based. The same probability interpretation as for S.E. Meas. is made for the S.E.s of group measures, i.e., 2:1 (2 out of 3) for the 1 S.E. range, 19:1 (95 out of 100) for a 2 S.E. range, 99:1 (99 out of 100) for a 2.6 S.E. range.

standard score. A general term referring to any of a variety of "transformed" scores, in terms of which raw scores may be expressed for reasons of convenience, comparability, ease of interpretation, etc. The simplest type of standard score, known as a z-score, is an expression of the *deviation* of a score from the mean score of the group *in relation to* the standard deviation of the scores of the group. Thus:

$$\text{standard score } (Z) = \frac{\text{raw score } (X) - \text{mean } (M)}{\text{standard deviation (S.D.)}}$$

Adjustments may be made in this ratio so that a system of standard scores having any desired mean and standard deviation may be set up. The use of such standard scores does not affect the relative standing of the individuals in the group or change the shape of the original distribution. T-scores have a M of 50 and an S.D. of 10. Deviation IQs are standard scores with a M of 100 and some chosen S.D., most often 16; thus a raw score that is 1 S.D. above the M of its distribution would convert to a standard score (deviation IQ) of $100 + 16 = 116$. (See Figure 1.)

Standard scores are useful in expressing the raw scores of two forms of a test in comparable terms in instances where tryouts have shown that the two forms are not identical in difficulty; also, successive levels of a test may be linked to form a continuous standard-score scale, making across-battery comparisons possible.

standardized test (standard test). A test designed to provide a systematic sample of individual performance, administered according to prescribed directions, scored in conformance with definite rules, and interpreted in reference to certain normative information. Some would further restrict the usage of the term "standardized" to those tests for which the items have been chosen on the basis of experimental evaluation, and for which data on reliability and validity are provided. Others would add "commercially published" and/or "for general use."

stanine. One of the steps in a nine-point scale of standard scores. The stanine (short for *standard-nine*) scale has values from 1 to 9, with a mean of 5 and a standard deviation of 2. Each stanine (except 1 and 9) is ½ S.D. in width, with the middle (average) stanine of 5 extending from ¼ S.D. below to ¼ S.D. above the mean. (See Figure 2.)

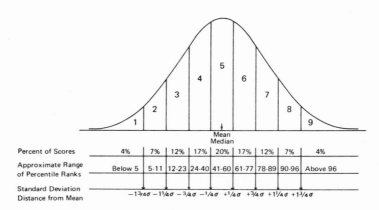

Percent of Scores	4%	7%	12%	17%	20%	17%	12%	7%	4%
Approximate Range of Percentile Ranks	Below 5	5-11	12-23	24-40	41-60	61-77	78-89	90-96	Above 96
Standard Deviation Distance from Mean		$-1\frac{3}{4}\sigma$	$-1\frac{1}{4}\sigma$	$-\frac{3}{4}\sigma$	$-\frac{1}{4}\sigma$	$+\frac{1}{4}\sigma$	$+\frac{3}{4}\sigma$	$+1\frac{1}{4}\sigma$	$+1\frac{3}{4}\sigma$

Figure 2. Stanines and the normal curve. Each stanine (except 1 and 9) is one half S.D. in width.

survey test. A test that measures general achievement in a given area, usually with the connotation that the test is intended to assess group status, rather than to yield precise measures of individual performance.

t. A critical ratio expressing the relationship of some measure (mean, correlation coefficient, difference, etc.) to its standard error. The size of this ratio is an indication of the significance of the measure. If *t* is as large as 1.96, significance at the .05 level is indicated; if as large as 2.58, at the .01 level. These levels indicate 95 or 99 chances out of 100, respectively.

taxonomy. An embodiment of the principles of classification; a survey, usually in outline form, such as a presentation of the objectives of education.

test-retest reliability coefficient. A type of reliability coefficient obtained by administering the same test a second time, after a short interval, and correlating the two sets of scores. "Same test" was originally understood to mean identical content, i.e., the same form; currently, however, the term "test-retest" is also used to describe the administration of different forms of the same test, in which case this reliability coefficient becomes the same as the alternate-form coefficient. In either case (1) fluctuations over time and in testing situation, and (2) any effect of the first test upon the second are involved. When the time interval between the two testings is considerable, as several months, a test-retest reliability coefficient reflects not only the consistency of measurement provided by the test, but also the stability of the examinee trait being measured.

true score. A score entirely free of error; hence, a hypothetical value that can never be obtained by testing, which always involves some measurement error. A "true" score may be thought of as the average score from an infinite number of measurements from the same or exactly equivalent tests, assuming no practice effect or change in the examinee during the testings. The standard deviation of this infinite number of "samplings" is known as the *standard error of measurement.*

validity. The extent to which a test does the job for which it is used. This definition is more satisfactory than the traditional "extent to which a test measures what it is supposed to measure," since the validity of a test is always specific to the purposes for which the test is used. The term validity, then, has different connotations for various types of tests and, thus, a different kind of validity evidence is appropriate for each.

(1) content, curricular validity. For achievement tests, validity is the extent to which the *content* of the test represents a balanced and adequate sampling of the outcomes (knowledge, skills, etc.) of the course or instructional program it is intended to cover. It is best evidenced by a comparison of the test content with courses of study, instructional materials, and statements of educational goals; and often by analysis of the processes required in making correct responses to the items. *Face validity,* referring to an observation of what a test appears to measure, is a non-technical type of evidence; apparent relevancy is, however, quite desirable.

(2) criterion-related validity. The extent to which scores on the test are in agreement with *(concurrent validity)* or predict *(predictive validity)* some given criterion measure. Predictive validity refers to the accuracy with which an aptitude, prognostic, or readiness test indicates future learning success in some area, as evidenced by correlations between scores on the test and future criterion measures of such success (e.g., the

relation of score on an academic aptitude test administered in high school to grade point average over four years of college). In concurrent validity, no significant time interval elapses between administration of the test being validated and of the criterion measure. Such validity might be evidenced by *concurrent* measures of academic ability and of achievement, by the relation of a new test to one generally accepted as or known to be valid, or by the correlation between scores on a test and criteria measures which are valid but are less objective and more time-consuming to obtain than a test score would be.

(3) construct validity. The extent to which a test measures some relatively abstract psychological trait or construct; applicable in evaluating the validity of tests that have been constructed on the basis of an analysis (often factor analysis) of the nature of the trait and its manifestations. Tests of personality, verbal ability, mechanical aptitude, critical thinking, etc., are validated in terms of their construct and the relation of their scores to pertinent external data.

variability. The spread or dispersion of test scores, best indicated by their standard deviation.

variance. For a distribution, the average of the squared deviations from the mean; thus the square of the standard deviation.

INDEX